W9-BGE-778

Centre for Learning Alternatives
3400 Westwood Drive
Prince George, BC
V2N 1S1

Echoes 11

Fiction, Media, and Non-Fiction

Francine Artichuk

Graham Foster

Janeen Werner-King

Diana Knight

Liz Orme

Kevin Reed

Peter Weeks

OXFORD
UNIVERSITY PRESS

OXFORD
UNIVERSITY PRESS

70 Wynford Drive, Don Mills, Ontario M3C 1J9
oup.com/ca

Oxford University Press is a department of the University of Oxford.

It furthers the University"s objective of excellence in research, scholarship, and
education by publishing worldwide in

Oxford   New York
Auckland   Bangkok   Buenos Aires   Cape Town   Chennai
Dar es Salaam   Delhi   Hong Kong   Istanbul   Karachi   Kolkata
Kuala Lumpur   Madrid   Melbourne   Mexico City   Mumbai   Nairobi
São Paulo   Shanghai   Singapore   Taipei   Tokyo   Toronto

and an associated company in Berlin

Oxford is a registered trade mark of Oxford University Press
in the UK and in certain other contries

Published in Canada
By Oxford University Press

Copyright © Oxford University Press Canada 2001

The moral rights of the author have been asserted

Database right Oxford University Press (maker)

First published 2001

All rights reserved. No part of this publication may be reproduced,
stored in a retrieval system, or transmitted, in any form or by any means,
without the prior permission in writing of Oxford University Press,
or as expressly permitted by law, or under terms agreed with the appropriate
reprographics rights organization. Enquiries concerning reproduction
outside the scope of the above should be sent to the Rights Department,
Oxford University Press, at the address above.

You must not circulate this book in any other binding or cover
and you must impose this same condition on any acquirer.

National Library of Canada Cataloguing in Publication Data

Main entry under title:
Echoes 11: fiction, media, and non-fiction

ISBN 0-19-541630-9 (bound).—ISBN 0-19-541710-0 (pbk.)

1. Readers (Secondary). 2. English language—Rhetoric. I. Artichuk, Francine.
PE1121.E29 2001   808'.0427   C2001-902005-8

Printed and bound in Canada
This book is printed on permanent (acid-free) paper ∞.

3 4 — 04 03 02

Cover and text design: Brett Miller
Cover art and unit opening illustrations: Josée Masse

Contents (by genre)

Unit 2 Drama   127

Stage Plays

Unit 3 Short Fiction   189

Unit 6 Non-Fiction   **411**

Contents (by theme)

Humans and Nature

Media Echo:
Landscapes and Images   522

Journeys and Adventure

Poetry Echo:
Journeys

Passions

Drama Echo:
Romance and Reality

Essays Echo:
The Thrill of the Crowd

Exploring Cultural Identity

Politics and Human Rights

Life's Learning

Recovering the Past

Personal and Social Relationships

Humour and Satire

Introduction

Echoes is a multi-genre anthology featuring a wide range of quality selections designed to engage student interest. The anthology is organized into seven key genres. The genres represented are diverse, reflecting a broad definition of "text." The texts included range from poems, short stories, dramas, and essays to film scripts, radio plays, fine art, photo essays, informational texts, posters, and advertisements. While the anthology is organized by genre, a detailed table of contents by theme also allows students and teachers the flexibility to approach their study by the themes of their choice.

Each selection in the anthology begins with a clear set of Learning Goals presented in student-accessible language, so that students are immediately aware of some key focus points for their study. Following each selection is a short author biography and a set of Responding activities organized into those related to Meaning, Form and Style, and Creative Extension. These activities offer a variety of reading, writing, listening, speaking, viewing, and representing opportunities. Students both analyze texts closely and develop their own creative responses.

Echo Sections

One of the most unique features of the anthology is the "Echo" sections. Each unit includes at least one, if not two Echoes. Each Echo focuses on a timeless or universal question. The Echo sections include a core selection from the genre (a poem in the Poetry unit; an essay in the Essays unit), along with a number of related texts from different genres, media, and often time periods. Students have the opportunity to make connections among texts, to compare different forms and styles, and to examine the universal question from a number of different perspectives. Students practise key critical thinking and analytical skills, recognize and assess various points of view, and explore how various forms and styles affect meaning.

Each Echo section includes the following elements:

- a title which identifies the key theme of the section
- a provocative question to stimulate and focus student thinking
- a paragraph summarizing the overall issues raised by the different selections
- learning goals related to the whole section
- a core selection from the genre followed by a full set of responding activities organized under the headings of meaning, form and style, and creative extension
- related selections from different genres, media, and often time periods including such varied texts as fine art, photographs, film scripts, poems, informational texts, songs, interviews, essays, and posters
- connecting questions after each Echo piece that allow students to analyze it and relate it to the central theme of the Echo and the core piece
- "Reflecting on the Echo" activities that allow students to reflect on the Echo theme after studying the selections, make connections among the pieces, and develop their own creative responses. These activities are designed to appeal to different learning styles and multiple intelligences.

We hope you enjoy your journey through this anthology and the *Echoes* program.

Poetry

Margaret Atwood on poetry:

For me it has a lot to do with the rediscovery of language or concentration on the word. If you're writing a novel, you're concentrating on much larger units—not that you don't pay attention to your sentences et cetera, but the potency of the individual word tends to be more spread out. You're really concentrating on starting something on page 30 that you finish on page 250. The wavelengths are a lot longer, the pattern much larger. Poetry is a very concentrated form, and therefore the explosiveness of each word becomes much greater.

Poetry

♪ Pablo Neruda

Learning Goals

- identify the poet's purpose
- examine changes in the narrator's character
- analyze imagery and paradox
- create an original poem or visual representation

And it was at that age . . . Poetry arrived
in search of me. I don't know, I don't know where
it came from, from winter or a river.
I don't know how or when,
no, they were not voices, they were not words, or silence,
but from a street I was summoned,
from the branches of night,
abruptly from the others,
among violent fires
or returning alone,
there I was without a face
and it touched me.

I did not know what to say, my mouth
had no way
with names,
my eyes were blind, and something started in my soul,
fever or forgotten wings,
and I made my own way,
deciphering
that fire,
and I wrote the first faint line,
faint, without substance, pure
nonsense,
pure wisdom
of someone who knows nothing,

and suddenly I saw
the heavens
unfastened
and open,
planets,
palpitating plantations,
shadow perforated,
riddled
with arrows, fire and flowers,
the winding night, the universe.

And I, infinitesimal being,
drunk with the great starry
void,
likeness, image of
mystery,
felt myself a pure part
of the abyss,
I wheeled with the stars,
my heart broke loose on the wind.

Translation: Alastair Reid

∽ Pablo Neruda is the pen name of Neftali Ricardo Reyes y Basualto. Neruda first published his poems under pseudonyms because his father, a railway worker, objected to his son becoming a poet. At the age of 16, Neruda first used the pen name by which he later became internationally known. A poet and diplomat, he served as ambassador and consul to many countries for his native Chile. In 1971, he was awarded the Nobel Prize for Literature. *(Born Chile 1904; died 1973)*

(Responding Activities p. 14)

Did I Miss Anything?

❦ Tom Wayman

Learning Goals

- analyze how the form of a poem conveys meaning
- examine how breaking grammar rules creates particular effects
- analyze verbal irony
- create a storyboard and ironic poem

*Question frequently asked by
students after missing a class*

Nothing. When we realized you weren't there
we sat with our hands folded on our desks
in silence, for the full two hours

    Everything. I gave an exam worth
    40 per cent of the grade for this term
    and assigned some reading due today
    on which I'm about to hand out a quiz
    worth 50 per cent

Nothing. None of the content of this course
has value or meaning
Take as many days off as you like:
any activities we undertake as a class
I assure you will not matter either to you or me
and are without purpose

    Everything. A few minutes after we began last time
    a shaft of light descended and an angel
    or other heavenly being appeared
    and revealed to us what each woman or man must do
    to attain divine wisdom in this life and
    the hereafter
    This is the last time the class will meet
    before we disperse to bring this good news to all people on earth

Nothing. When you are not present
how could something significant occur?

Everything. Contained in this classroom
is a microcosm of human existence
assembled for you to query and examine and ponder
This is not the only place such an opportunity has been gathered
but it was one place

And you weren't here.

Tom Wayman is a poet, editor, and teacher. His poems often focus on the workplace, work experiences, and the importance of work in our daily lives. Born in Ontario, he now lives and works in Vancouver. Tom Wayman won the A. J. M. Smith Prize for distinguished achievement in Canadian poetry in 1976. *Waiting for Wayman* (1973) was his first collection. His major volume of selected poems is *Did I Miss Anything?: Selected Poems* (1993). *(Born Hawkesbury, Ontario 1945)*

(Responding Activities pp. 14–15)

1958

ᛋ Gwendolyn MacEwen

Learning Goals

- explore theme in a poem
- explain effects of poetic techniques such as irony, point of view, allusions, and repetition
- write an essay or create an advertising brochure

was a fabulous year
when you parked in the lot at the lakeshore
next to the Palais Royale
and necked for hours in those souped up cars,
you
savages of the Fifties, your terrible perfect
bodies
looped around the gearshift, the wheel, along the
dashboard, and the smell, the smell
of his black leather jacket, and the smell,
the smell
of the lake and the fish and the United States –

O,
those guys spoke in crazy cryptic monosyllables, and
those girls said nothing and were mean and cracked gum
and looked you up and down like you were *nowhere*,
them in their
black batwing sweaters and skirts with slits
and little black low-heeled shoes and smoking
Black Cat corktips because the package
looked mysterious, and
some girls wore crinolines and socks
folded over at least three times
and Peter Pan collars with plastic roses
holding them together —

Someone was always the Queen of the School and
she taught you how to use a lipstick *brush*, not
a messy old tube; she
was Xenobia, she
was Cat Woman, she
was so tough she made you faint, who went
like you
to Western Technical High School where
the boys learned shop and the girls
sewed shaky seams in dresses they would never wear,
where
everyone had ducktails and smelled of Vitalis
and you cracked your gum, cracked your gum
and died inside
and looked the whole world up and down.

Gwendolyn MacEwen published her first poem in *The Canadian Forum* at the age of 17. She is the author of over 20 books in various genres, including two novels, two short-story collections, and three children's books. She won Governor General's Awards for *The Shadow-Maker* in 1969 and *Afterworlds*, which was published in the year of her death and contains the poem "1958." (Born Toronto, Ontario 1941; died 1987)

(Responding Activities p. 16)

Letter to Sir John A. Macdonald

♂ Marilyn Dumont

Learning Goals

- examine the meaning and use of stereotypes
- analyze irony and satire
- create original poems based on a model
- present a dramatic reading

Dear John: I'm still here and halfbreed,
after all these years
you're dead, funny thing,
that railway you wanted so badly,
there was talk a year ago
of shutting it down
and part of it was shut down,
the dayliner at least,
'from sea to shining sea,'
and you know, John,
after all that shuffling us around to suit the settlers,
we're still here and Métis.

We're still here
after Meech Lake and
one no-good-for-nothin-Indian[1]
holdin-up-the-train,
stalling the 'Cabin syllables /Nouns of settlement,
/. . . steel syntax [and] /The long sentence of its exploitation'[2]
and John, that goddamned railroad never made this a great nation,
cause the railway shut down and this country is still quarrelling over unity,
and Riel is dead[3]
but he just keeps coming back
in all the Bill Wilsons yet to speak out of turn or favour

---

[1] a reference to Manitoba MLA Elijah Harper who stalled the Meech Lake Accord in the Manitoba Parliament because it did not recognize the distinct status of Aboriginal peoples in Canada

[2] a quote from the poem by F. R. Scott, "Laurentian Shield"

[3] Louis Riel was the Métis leader who was hanged for his role in the North-West Rebellion in 1885.

because you know as well as I
that we were railroaded
by some steel tracks that didn't last
and some settlers who wouldn't settle
and it's funny we're still here and callin ourselves halfbreed.

Marilyn Dumont is a teacher and writer. Before writing and teaching full-time, she worked in video production. Her poetry and prose have appeared in several literary journals and anthologies. She published "Letter to Sir John A. Macdonald" in *A Really Good Brown Girl* (1996) and won the Gerald Lampert Memorial Award in 1997. (*Born Alberta 1955*)

(Responding Activities pp. 16–17)

Reach Out and Touch

ᔑ Maxine Tynes

Learning Goals

- write a theme statement
- analyze tone and mood
- create and present a dramatic monologue
- write a narrative based on a poem

baby girl, baby boy behind me on the bus
reach out
and touch the curly electric of my hair
your fingers dipped in the
brown skin magic of my neck
to see if it comes off
your mama
slapping hands away
hush-up of your questions
and wondering out loud why it doesn't come off.
I turn and smile for you,
but you're already lost
in the silence and the fear that motherlove wraps you in.
I should have sat beside you
snugged up my big warm self up close
held you while your mama juggled parcels.
then you would know it's o.k.

ᔑ   Maxine Tynes, a poet of Africadian descent, writes dramatic poetry about social and personal issues. Her first book, *Borrowed Beauty* (1987), which includes the poem "Reach Out and Touch," won the Milton Acorn People's Poet of Canada Award. Two later volumes, *Woman Talking Woman* (1990) and *The Door of My Heart* (1993), include both poems and stories. (*Born Dartmouth, Nova Scotia 1949*)

(Responding Activities pp. 17–18)

Experience

ॐ Dorothy Livesay

Learning Goals

• speculate about
  meaning using
  cues in a poem

• analyze the
  character of a
  narrator

• interpret the use
  of symbols

• write from
  different points
  of view

• create a parody

"For your own good" they said,
And they gave me bread
Bitter and hard to swallow.
My head felt tired after it,
My heart felt hollow.

So I went away on my own road
Tasting all fruits, all breads:
And if some were bitter, others were sweet—
So I learned
How the heart is fed.

ॐ   Dorothy Livesay is particularly admired for her love poems and her poems on political issues. Born in Winnipeg, she moved in 1920 to Toronto where she became involved in socialism and women's rights. When she was 18, she published *Green Pitcher* (1928), her first poetry collection. Her political concerns were expressed in collections such as *Day and Night* (1944), winner of a Governor General's Award. *(Born Winnipeg, Manitoba 1909; died 1996)*

(Responding Activities pp. 18–19)

Common Magic

❧ Bronwen Wallace

Learning Goals

- interpret the title of a poem
- closely examine a poet's use of language and poetic devices
- analyze a poem's thesis
- research and develop a photo or art essay

Your best friend falls in love
and her brain turns to water.
You can watch her lips move,
making the customary sounds,
but you can see they're merely
words, flimsy as bubbles rising
from some golden sea where she
swims sleek and exotic as a mermaid.

It's always like that.
You stop for lunch in a crowded
restaurant and the waitress floats
toward you. You can tell she doesn't care
whether you have the baked or french-fried
and you wonder if your voice comes
in bubbles too.

It's not just women either. Or love
for that matter. The old man
across from you on the bus holds
a young child on his knee; he is singing
to her and his voice is a small boy
turning somersaults in the green
country of his blood.
It's only when the driver calls his stop
that he emerges into this puzzle
of brick and tiny hedges. Only then
you notice his shaking hands, his need
of the child to guide him home.

All over the city
you move in your own seasons
through the seasons of others: old women, faces

clawed by weather you can't feel
clack dry tongues at passersby
while adolescents seethe
in their glassy atmospheres of anger.

In parks, the children
are alien life-forms, rooted
in the galaxies they've grown through
to get here. Their games weave
the interface and their laughter
tickles that part of your brain where smells
are hidden and the nuzzling textures of things.

It's a wonder that anything gets done
at all: a mechanic flails
at the muffler of your car
through whatever storm he's trapped inside
and the mailman stares at numbers
from the haze of a distant summer.

Yet somehow letters arrive and buses
remember their routes. Banks balance.
Mangoes ripen on the supermarket shelves.
Everyone manages. You gulp the thin air
of this planet as if it were the only
one you knew. Even the earth you're
standing on seems solid enough.
It's always the chance word, unthinking
gesture that unlocks the face before you.
Reveals the intricate countries
deep within the eyes. The hidden
lives, like sudden miracles,
that breathe there.

(Responding Activities p. 19)

Poet and essayist Bronwen Wallace was born in Kingston and educated at Queen's University. Her political activism led her to work with auto workers, to co-found a women's bookstore, and to work in a battered women's shelter. She was also a creative writing teacher at Queen's University. *Marrying in the Family* (1980) was her first volume of poetry. Her other publications include the book of stories *People You'd Trust Your Life To* (1990). Wallace also wrote essays and created two films. *(Born Kingston, Ontario 1945; died 1989)*

RESPONDING ACTIVITIES

Poetry – Pablo Neruda

Meaning

1. Who is the speaker in this poem? Justify your answer.

2. How does the character of the speaker change from the beginning of the poem to the end? Note specific evidence in each stanza of how the character describes himself.

Form and Style

3. a) What kinds of images are used most often after the line, "and suddenly I saw" in stanza two? Cite specific examples.
   b) How does this imagery contribute to our understanding of the speaker's thoughts and feelings when he first encounters poetry?

4. A *paradox* is a contradictory statement that when examined carefully, actually is true. Explain how the speaker's first lines of poetry could be "pure nonsense, / pure wisdom."

Creative Extension

5. Create a visual representation of Neruda's poem including a number of the poem's images. Use the layout, colour, and style in your art to convey the poet's ideas and feelings.

6. Make point-form notes about an activity such as a sport, music, or art that you or someone you know enjoys doing. What images might you use to describe the freedom, wonder, and sense of purpose that the activity gives you or another person? Using your notes, write a poem about the discovery of this activity. Write in the first-person point of view and use Neruda's poem as a model.

Did I Miss Anything? – Tom Wayman

Meaning

1. a) Every stanza in this poem starts with a one-word sentence fragment (e.g., "Nothing") rather than a complete sentence (e.g., "You missed nothing."). Why is a sentence fragment more effective?
   b) Except for a period after each sentence fragment, this poem uses very little punctuation. Capital letters and line breaks indicate the end of a thought, but there is no punctuation at the end of sentences, particularly sentences at the end of stanzas. What effect does this use of punctuation have on the meaning of the poem?

2. a) For each stanza, paraphrase what the teacher actually says (the *text*). Then write what he or she really means but does not say (the *subtext*). This difference between the text and subtext creates the verbal *irony* and humour in this poem.

Stanza #	Literal paraphrase of the text	The ironic subtext—what is really meant
1	We couldn't do anything when you weren't here, so we just sat at our desks and did nothing.	Do you really think you're so important the whole world stops and twiddles its thumbs when you're not here?

    b) Review your chart. Why does the teacher deliberately use verbal irony? In what other situations might someone rely on verbal irony? Why?

Form and Style

3. Why are some stanzas in this poem indented while others are not? Explain why the poet chose this pattern. What literary techniques are used in the stanzas that are not indented, and in the stanzas that are indented?

4. What kinds of images are used repeatedly in stanzas one, two, and three? What images are used in stanzas four and six? What is the significance of this change in the type of imagery?

Creative Extension

5. Adapt one stanza of this poem to a storyboard for a short animated video. Use between five to ten frames. Use a variety of camera shots and angles, choose music to set the mood, and incorporate sound effects. Then write a memo to your teacher explaining the choices you made to create particular effects. Point out one or two challenges you encountered and the strategies you used to meet them.

6. In an ironic poem, the speaker is aware of a double meaning, but the listener is not. Understatement and overstatement (hyperbole) are often used to create irony. Write an ironic poem using understatement and overstatement, and indent the stanzas to show the contrast visually.

Your poem could be a response to one of the following questions:
- How are you doing? (Asked by someone after you have been hurt physically or emotionally)
- Are we there yet? (Asked repeatedly by children when travelling)
- Do you understand? (Asked when someone obviously does not, such as a traveller in a country where he or she does not speak the language)
- Your own question with the approval of your teacher.

1958 – Gwendolyn MacEwen

Meaning

1. This poem recreates the environment of a high school in the late 1950s, but the experience described is a lot like that in high schools today. What aspects of the experience are not bound by time? Record your response in your journal. Refer to the text and to contemporary situations in high schools to complete your comparison.

2. a) Explain the *irony* of the beginning, "1958 / was a fabulous year."
    b) Xenobia, the name in the last stanza, comes from the root *Xeno*, meaning "stranger" or "guest." What is the significance of this name when applied to the character referred to as "the Queen of the School"?
    c) Find the *oxymoron* in stanza one and explain its meaning.

Form and Style

3. Why does the author use the second-person pronoun "you" instead of the first-person pronoun "I"? What is the poet asking the reader to do by using the pronoun "you"?

4. The poet repeats some phrases, but changes a few of the words slightly each time. Identify the repetition. Explain how the meaning of the lines changes as they are repeated. How do the repeated lines build to a climax?

Creative Extension

5. An *allusion* is a reference to a person, place, event, or other work that contributes to the meaning a writer wants to convey. Research the allusions to Cat Woman and Peter Pan collars. Write an essay explaining how these allusions enhance the portraits of the girls in the poem. Consider the ideas of conformity and stereotype, and the popular culture of the 1950s.

6. Create an advertising brochure for three styles of clothing described in the poem. Use a variety of sources to research clothing styles that were popular in the 1950s. Design one outfit suitable for the girl who was "mean and cracked gum," one for the girls who wore crinolines and socks, and one for the boys described in the poem.

    Use the layout, colour, and style in your sketches, printouts, or clip art to convey the poet's ideas and feelings about the characters who wear these styles.

    Include a paragraph of advertising, or copywriting, to sell each of these product lines.

Letter to Sir John A. Macdonald – Marilyn Dumont

Meaning

1. a) What stereotypical words and phrases does Marilyn Dumont use to describe the Métis people? Carefully examine the context in each case and decide why the poet uses these terms and phrases.

b) Which phrase containing stereotypical terms is repeated in the poem? How does the phrase change? What are the effects of this change on its meaning?

2. List at least three examples of *irony* from the poem. For each example, explain why the word or phrase is ironic.

Form and Style

3. A *pun* is a play on words. The words can be similar in sound (homonyms), but differ in meaning, or it may be a play on different meanings of one word (such as grave, meaning serious or a place where someone is buried). Quote at least three puns from the poem, explain the double meanings, and explain how this technique contributes to the satire.

4. In a *dramatic monologue*, a speaker reveals his or her innermost thoughts and feelings to an implied listener. What attitudes and feelings of the narrator are revealed in this monologue? Support your answer with evidence from the poem.

Creative Extension

5. A poem written in the form of a letter in a familiar, conversational style is called an *epistle*. Write an epistle using plain language and include personal details, questions, and suggestions. Use a graphic organizer to collect your thoughts before you begin writing. Your epistle may be in verse, or in a more conventional letter format, but should deal with an issue you feel strongly about. For example:
   - Why don't you love me?
   - Canadian heroes are unsung.
   - Nature is antagonistic to humankind.

6. Make a plan to write a poem imitating the style and techniques used by Marilyn Dumont. Create a point-form list of poetic techniques used in each stanza and write a brief remark about the effect that you will try to achieve by using each technique with your poem. Then, write a poem either from the point of view of the ghost of Sir John A. Macdonald or of the current prime minister, and write a poetic apology to the Métis people. Present a dramatic reading of your poem.

Reach Out and Touch – Maxine Tynes

Meaning

1. How does each woman on the bus react to the young child's actions? Why?

2. Write a theme statement expressing your interpretation of the main idea in this poem. Support your statement with specific references to the text.

Form and Style

3. Describe the *tone* and *mood* of this poem. Provide examples of specific techniques Maxine Tynes uses to convey this mood and tone.

4. Explain the *irony* that surrounds the "motherlove" in this poem.

5. Imagine you were on the bus, sitting across the aisle from the mother and child. How would you have "read" the situation? Write and present a dramatic monologue revealing your perceptions and reactions. Record your monologue on audio or videotape. Use the techniques of effective oral presentation including pitch, pace, volume, gestures, and facial expressions.

6. In your own words, describe how the child felt and how the child's feelings change during the ride on the bus. Write a short first-person narrative to express the child's experience.

Experience – Dorothy Livesay

Meaning

1. Who are "they" in the lines: "'For your own good' they said, / And they gave me bread"? Support your answer with specific reasons.

2. The speaker talks about how her heart feels in stanzas one and two. She does not tell us how her head feels in stanza two. How do you think her head feels? Why?

Form and Style

3. a) What do the foods (the bitter bread, and the bitter and sweet fruits and breads) symbolize? Why is the bread in stanza one "hard to swallow"?
    b) What does the speaker's heart represent? Why does it feel empty in stanza one, but full in stanza two? Why is the bitter bread not as hard to swallow in stanza two?

4. In the context of stanza one, what does the title, "Experience," mean? In the context of stanza two, what does the title mean? Describe the narrator of the poem and speculate why she would choose to experience the bitter and the sweet.

Creative Extension

5. Write two letters, one from the narrator's parents to the narrator, and the other from the narrator to her parents. In the first, explain why you want the narrator to have certain experiences. In the second, explain why you need to choose your own experiences. Design your letters on computer if possible, and choose different layouts and type styles to reflect the different "voice" you adopt.

6. Write a parody of this poem called "Inexperience." A *parody* is an imitation that aims to ridicule or satirize. Since you will be making fun of inexperience, your tone will be very different from that in Dorothy Livesay's poem.
    *   Use a sustained metaphor that takes on symbolic meaning (do not use Livesay's extended metaphor of feeding, and the variety of tastes).
    *   Make sure each stanza defines the title "Inexperience," and that stanza two has a much more important definition. Don't state the definition directly, but let the symbolic meanings and your extended metaphor show the reader what inexperience is.

- In stanza one, present the effect of the inexperience on the speaker's heart and head.
- In stanza two, present another effect of the second kind of inexperience. End the stanza with a statement of what you learned that ties into the metaphor.
- Present a dramatic reading of your poem.

Common Magic – Bronwen Wallace

Meaning

1. The title of this poem is an *oxymoron*. Based on your reading of the poem, explain how magic can be common. How can a contradiction like this be true?

2. Each of the first three stanzas is a character sketch of someone who is transformed by "common magic." Describe the characters and identify the common magic that transforms each of them.

Form and Style

3. What literary device is used in the lines, "All over the city / you move in your own seasons / through the seasons of others"? How does this device help the poet make suggestions about society?

4. a) Why does Wallace describe the children as "alien life-forms" in stanza five? What does this metaphor imply about children? About adults? Is the metaphor appropriate? Why or why not?

   b) Another line states that the children's games "weave the interface." Between what? What else in this stanza creates an "interface"? How?

Creative Extension

5. The poem ends with the lines:

   > It's always the chance word, unthinking
   > gesture that unlocks the face before you.
   > Reveals the intricate countries
   > deep within the eyes. The hidden
   > lives, like sudden miracles,
   > that breathe there.

   These lines can be considered the poem's *thesis* or controlling idea. Paraphrase the poem's conclusion in your journal and write on the following questions. Do the examples in the poem make this conclusion logical? Why or why not? Do you agree with the poet's conclusion? Explain your views.

6. Create a photo or art essay on the theme of "common magic." Research appropriate visuals in various sources including magazines, the Internet, books, and newspapers. Make your selections carefully to express your interpretation of the theme. Your concluding visual should be a strong one summarizing your main idea. Include titles or captions as appropriate. In your journal, keep a running commentary explaining how you conduct your research and make your selections.

Memories Have Tongue

✂ Afua Cooper

Learning Goals

• analyze character development

• examine use of dialect

• develop and write a proposal

• create a storyboard and video

My granny say she have a bad memory when I ask her to tell
me some of her life
say she can't remember much but
she did remember the 1910 storm and how dem house blow down
an dey had to go live with her granny down bottom house
Say she have a bad memory, but she remember
that when her husband died, both of them were thirty,
she had three little children, one in her womb,
one in her arms, one at her frocktail. She remember when
they bury him how the earth buss up under her foot
and her heart bruk inside
that when the baby born she had no milk
her breasts refused to yield.
She remember how she wanted her daughter to grow up and be
a postmistress but the daughter died at an early age
she point to the croton-covered grave at the bottom of the
yard. Say her memory bad, but she remember
1938
Frome
the riot
Busta
Manley[1]
but what she memba most of all is that a pregnant woman,
one of the protesters, was shot an' killed by soldiers.
Say she old now her brains gathering water

---

[1] reference to the workers strike in Jamaica in 1938. One of the centres of the strike was Frome Estate in Westmoreland. Norman Manley and Alexander Bustamante were labour leaders and later became leaders of the country.

but she remember
that she liked dancing as a young woman
and yellow was her favourite colour. She remember
too that it was her husband's father who asked
for her hand. The Parents sat in the hall and discussed
the matter. Her father finally concluded that her man was
an honourable person and so gave his consent.
Her memory bad but she remember
on her wedding day how some of her relatives
nearly eat off all the food. It was all right, though, she
said, I was too nervous to eat anyway.

Afua Cooper was born in Jamaica, but has made Toronto her home since 1980. A poet and academic, she is the author of many poetry collections. Her book *Memories Have Tongue* was named first runner-up for the Casa de las Americas prize in 1992. She has recorded some of her poetry on an album entitled *Womantalk*. (*Born Jamaica*)

(Responding Activities p. 32)

An African Elegy

Ben Okri

Learning Goals

• interpret a poet's
  choice of words

• analyze an elegy

• apply effective
  research
  techniques

• write a report and
  persuasive essay

We are the miracles that God made
To taste the bitter fruit of Time.
We are precious.
And one day our suffering
Will turn into the wonders of the earth.

There are things that burn me now
Which turn golden when I am happy.
Do you see the mystery of our pain?
That we bear poverty
And are able to sing and dream sweet things

And that we never curse the air when it is warm
Or the fruit when it tastes so good
Or the lights that bounce gently on the waters?
We bless things even in our pain.
We bless them in silence.

That is why our music is so sweet.
It makes the air remember.
There are secret miracles at work
That only Time will bring forth.
I too have heard the dead singing.

And they tell me that
This life is good
They tell me to live it gently
With fire, and always with hope.
There is wonder here

And there is surprise
In everything the unseen moves.
The ocean is full of songs.
The sky is not an enemy.
Destiny is our friend.

Nigerian writer Ben Okri was educated in Lagos, Nigeria and at the University of Essex in England. His partly autobiographical novels, *Flowers and Shadows* (1980) and *The Landscapes Within* (1981), and two collections of short stories, *Incidents at the Shrine* (1986) and *Stars of the New Curfew* (1988), established his international reputation. *The Famished Road* (1991) won the prestigious Booker Prize. "An African Elegy" appeared in the collection *An African Elegy* (1992). (*Born Lagos, Nigeria 1959*)

(*Responding Activities pp. 32–33*)

'Callum' *in memory of a novice miner*

❧ Milton Acorn

Learning Goals

• examine
  characterization
  in a poem

• analyze rhythm
  and its effects

• apply effective
  research
  techniques

• create a report,
  song, multimedia
  presentation, or
  journal entry

He had hair like mustard-weed;
shoulders like a scoop;
eyes like a lake you see the rocks on bottom;
and his voice swung a loop
with music in what it said
that tangled inside your head.

'Callum' was his name
— pronounced as if he'd sign it on the sun.
From 'The Island' he came:
don't know which one.

We dropped to work in our cage,
hearts somewhere behind on a parachute.
That pusher was cute
— saw him a guy who'd count doing right important,
put him at a hard job beside a well
. . . a hundred and forty feet,
and he fell.

Look anywhere:
at buildings bumping on clouds,
at spider-grill bridges:
you'll see no plaque or stone for men killed there:
    but on the late shift
the drill I'm bucking bangs his name in code
. . .'Callum';
tho where 'The Island' is I'll never know.

Milton Acorn was a strong advocate of Canadian nationalism and the rights of working people. Many of his poems draw on images of everyday life, particularly from his native Prince Edward Island. When his poetry collection *I've Tasted My Blood* failed to win the Governor General's Award in 1969, a group of Toronto poets created a poetry award for Acorn and named him "the people's poet." One of his later collections, *The Island Means Minago* (1975), won the Governor General's Award. *(Born Charlottetown, Prince Edward Island 1923; died 1986)*

(Responding Activities pp. 33–34)

I Grew Up

⟋ Lenore Keeshig-Tobias

Learning Goals

- examine a narrator's perspective
- analyze effects of a refrain
- write a poem based on a model
- research and report on other works by an author

i grew up on the reserve
thinking it was the most
beautiful place in the world

i grew up thinking
"i'm never going
to leave this place"

i was a child
a child who would
lie under trees

watching the wind's rhythms
sway leafy boughs
back and forth

and rocking me as
i snuggled in the grass
like a bug basking in the sun

i grew up on the reserve
thinking it was the most
beautiful place in the world

i grew up thinking
"i'm never going
to leave this place"

i was a child
a child who ran
wild rhythms

through the fields
the streams
the bush

eating berries
cupping cool water
to my wild stained mouth

and hiding in the
treetops with
my friends

we used to laugh at teachers
and tourists who referred to
our bush as "forest" or "woods"

"forests" or "woods"
were places of
fairytale text

were places where people,
especially children, got lost
where wild beasts roamed

our bush was where we played
and where the rabbits squirrels
foxes deer and the bear lived

i grew up thinking
"i'm never going
to leave this place"

i grew up on the reserve
thinking it was the most
beautiful place in the world

Lenore Keeshig-Tobias is a member of the Chippewa of Nawash First Nation on the Bruce Peninsula in Ontario. Often delicate and humorous, her poems draw on realities of Aboriginal life and
the mythological symbols of her people. Her poetry has appeared in numerous journals
and anthologies. "I Grew Up" first appeared in *Canadian Women's Studies, 1983*. She has also written two bilingual (English/Ojibway) children's books. *(Born Wiarton, Ontario 1950)*

(Responding Activities p. 34)

Siren Song

✺ Margaret Atwood

Learning Goals

- interpret explicit and implicit messages in a poem
- analyze tone
- examine how allusions contribute to understanding
- apply effective research and essay writing skills

This is the one song everyone
would like to learn: the song
that is irresistible:

the song that forces men
to leap overboard in squadrons
even though they see the beached skulls

the song nobody knows
because anyone who has heard it
is dead, and the others can't remember.

Shall I tell you the secret
and if I do, will you get me
out of this bird suit?

I don't enjoy it here
squatting on this island
looking picturesque and mythical

with these two feathery maniacs,
I don't enjoy singing
this trio, fatal and valuable.

I will tell the secret to you,
to you, only to you.
Come closer. This song

is a cry for help: Help me!
Only you, only you can,
you are unique

at last. Alas
it is a boring song
but it works every time.

Margaret Atwood is one of Canada's most prominent contemporary writers. A poet, novelist, short-story writer, and literary critic, she first attracted attention with her poetry in collections such as *The Circle Game* (1966) and *The Journals of Susanna Moodie* (1970). Both volumes won Governor General's Awards. Her many novels include *The Handmaid's Tale* (1986), *Alias Grace* (1996), and *The Blind Assassin* (2000). Her work has been translated into over 30 languages and she has been awarded several Canadian and international awards including the Giller Prize and the Booker Prize. (*Born Ottawa, Ontario 1939*)

(*Responding Activities p. 35*)

Go to the Ant

Irving Layton

Learning Goals

• interpret theme
• compare tone,
  point of view, and
  imagery in two
  poems
• present a
  dramatic reading
• present a musical
  interpretation

I'm watching an ant
push an object
five times its weight & size,
some white dead thing
it holds onto for dear life
— such determination
— such tenaciousness
and won't drop for an instant

Fate in the form
of my foot
could smear it
and all its sober virtues
on the stony rubble
my shadow falls on
and I half-raise my foot
to bring it down

But instead finally
hop across
black ant and object
wondering as I do
whether that natural creature
was telling me something
I was too old to learn
or perhaps didn't care to know

Irving Layton was born in Romania. His family immigrated to Canada in 1913 and settled in Montreal. His confident and sometimes hyperbolic voice winds through his many poetry collections, including *A Red Carpet for the Sun* (1959), winner of a Governor General's Award, and *For My Brother Jesus* (1976), where "Go to the Ant" appears. His work has been published internationally. (Born Romania 1912)

(Responding Activities pp. 35–36)

Weakness

Alden Nowlan

Learning Goals

• examine narrative purpose in a poem

• analyze how form affects meaning

• retell a poem in a different genre and from a different point of view

• write an editorial or letter to the editor

Old mare whose eyes
are like cracked marbles,
drools blood in her mash,
shivers in her jute blanket.

My father hates weakness worse than hail;
in the morning
    without haste
he will shoot her in the ear, once,
shovel her under in the north pasture.

Tonight
    leaving the stables
he stands his lantern on an over-turned water pail,
turns,
    cursing her for a bad bargain,
and spreads his coat
carefully over her sick shoulders.

Alden Nowlan's first collection of poetry, *The Rose and the Puritan* (1958), consisted of the short, anecdotal lyrics that would become his trademark. He received a Governor General's Award for *Bread, Wine and Salt* (1967). "Weakness" was published in *An Exchange of Gifts* (1985). In later years, he turned to other genres of writing including autobiography, short stories, and plays. (*Born Windsor, Nova Scotia 1933; died 1983*)

(Responding Activities p. 36)

RESPONDING ACTIVITIES

Contemporary Lyric Poems (pages 20–31)

Memories Have Tongue – Afua Cooper

Meaning

1. a) The grandmother in this poem repeatedly says she has a bad memory. Does she? How do you know? Why do you think she says she has a bad memory?
   b) In your own words, summarize the seven events that the grandmother remembers.

2. a) Consider the order in which the grandmother tells her memories. What does the order reveal about her feelings toward these memories?
   b) What similarities can you find in the details the grandmother remembers about the different events? What do these common details reveal about her feelings and attitudes?

Form and Style

3. *Dialect* is a form of speech used in a particular area or region. Quote words and phrases that represent the dialect used in this poem. Why do you think Afua Cooper uses dialect, colloquial speech, and idiom as she has the narrator present the grandmother's memories? What point might she be making about the language of poetry?

4. What stylistic devices does Afua Cooper use to create the character of the grandmother? Use a graphic organizer to identify the traits of the grandmother in this poem, and to record the details from the poem that suggest she has those traits.

Creative Extension

5. Working in small groups, develop and write a proposal to create a short documentary video based on this poem. Follow the form and style of a formal proposal. Be persuasive and professional.

6. Working in small groups, create a storyboard for a short documentary film based on this poem. Use Cooper's poem as the basis for the dialogue and narration, but feel free to adapt it if you choose to change the point of view from which the story is told. Include music and sound effects, as well as varied camera shots, movements, and angles to suggest the character of the grandmother and her feelings about her various memories. Shoot at least a segment of the video using role players if possible.

An African Elegy – Ben Okri

Meaning

1. a) Imagine the poet had left the word "African" out of the title. Read the poem again. How would this change in title affect your interpretation of the poem?
   b) Explain the meaning of the three short sentences that conclude the poem. Why does Okri put these last points in separate, short sentences?

2. Examine the pronouns used in this poem.
   a) Who are the people referred to as "we"?
   b) Who is the "you" in the poem?
   c) Who are the people referred to as "they" in the second last stanza?

Form and Style

3. Make a note of all the references to miracles and the inexplicable throughout the poem. What is the significance of these references? Why are time and fate often mentioned together with miracles?

4. a) An *elegy* is a lament for the loss of a particular person that ends in a consolation. It can also be a meditation on the mortality of human beings and the things they value. What features of each of these definitions does Okri use in "An African Elegy"? Support your answer with references to the poem.
   b) Why is the poem's title ironic?

Creative Extension

5. Conduct research into the life, work, and accomplishments of Ben Okri. Write a report about the poet and refer to at least one other poem by him in your writing. Use the reference to his poetry to support your findings about the particular concerns he addresses in his writing and his accomplishments.

6. Ben Okri comments on human destiny in this poem. Write a persuasive essay in which you argue for or against the importance and reality of destiny. In other words, do you think that you personally have a destiny? Does your community? Does the human race?

'Callum' – Milton Acorn

Meaning

1. Who is the narrator in this poem and how was he associated with Callum? Justify your answer.

2. Do you think Callum's death was avoidable or unavoidable? Support your position.

Form and Style

3. a) What similes and metaphors does the poet use to describe Callum? What impression do they create of this character?
   b) Why does the poet use single quotation marks in 'Callum' and 'The Island'?

4. a) The narrator describes Callum's voice in a stanza that has a musicality of its own. Describe the *rhythm* of the last three lines in the first stanza.
   b) Note three specific examples of how the poet uses line length to evoke sounds and meanings. What effects do these techniques have on you as the reader?

Creative Extension

5. Research mining disasters in Canada and prepare a short report, multimedia presentation, or original song about one of particular interest or importance.

6. Milton Acorn's poetry often speaks for the labourers in Canada. One Canadian reporter called him a "troubadour of the working class." Poet Al Purdy wrote about him: "the Acorn-tree always walked on its roots, and always into sunlight. It lifts the heart."

    Write a journal entry from Milton Acorn's point of view. Explain why you want to speak for the working class people of Canada. Describe your hopes and dreams, your ideals and beliefs, and your poetry. Research Web sites about Milton Acorn for background on the poet and his writing to prepare for this assignment.

I Grew Up – Lenore Keeshig-Tobias

Meaning

1. What kind of relationship did the narrator have with nature as she grew up? Refer to specific images from the poem to support your answer.

2. Near the end of the poem, the narrator contrasts what others refer to as the "forests" or "woods" to what she and her community call "the bush."
    a) What images does the narrator use to describe the fairytale "forests" or "woods"? What mood or feeling do these images create? How?
    b) What fairy tales could the poet be referring to when she says that forests or woods were fairytale places "where . . . children, got lost / where wild beasts roamed"?
    c) In contrast, how does the narrator describe "the bush"? What mood or feeling is created by this description? How do the images create these feelings?
    d) Explain the effect of this contrast. How would you interpret the poet's meaning?

Form and Style

3. What is the effect of the refrain:

    > i grew up on the reserve
    > thinking it was the most
    > beautiful place in the world
    >
    > i grew up thinking
    > "i'm never going
    > to leave this place"?

4. Why do you think the poet reverses the order of the stanzas in the refrain at the end of the poem? Support your answer.

Creative Extension

5. Write a poem describing a place where you grew up using "I Grew Up" as a model.

6. Research and read other poems by Lenore Keeshig-Tobias such as "A Healing Time." Write an essay analyzing at least two poems and explaining what you learn about her culture from her work.

Siren Song – Margaret Atwood

Meaning

1. a) Who is the speaker in this poem? To whom is she speaking? Support your opinion.
   b) What is the song that is irresistible?

2. The speaker lures the reader into the poem with the promise of revealing a secret? What do you think the secret is? Support your interpretation with evidence from the poem.

Form and Style

3. a) What is the speaker's attitude toward the Sirens? Note specific words, phrases, or images in your answer.
   b) What is the speaker's attitude toward the reader? Support your answer with evidence from the poem.
   c) Based on this analysis of *tone* in the poem, how would you define the speaker's personality?

4. a) Why does the Siren say her song "is a boring song"?
   b) What does she imply when she says her song "works every time"?
   c) Explain the *irony* of this ending.

Creative Extension

5. Some readers might describe the tone of Margaret Atwood's poem as light and comic. Others may describe it as sarcastic or even a little sinister. Write a short persuasive essay stating your opinion. Support your argument with specific references to the poem.

6. Research the mythological Sirens. How does Atwood use this allusion to comment on what writers do? Present your findings in a short oral report or essay.

Go to the Ant – Irving Layton

Meaning

1. a) What makes the narrator decide not to crush the ant? What details in the poem lead you to this conclusion?
   b) In your view, what was the message the ant gave to the narrator that he was "too old to learn or perhaps didn't care to know"? Discuss your interpretation with others in a small group and explain your view.

2. What are the "sober virtues" of the ant? Support your answer with evidence from the poem. Why does Layton call these qualities "sober virtues"?

Form and Style

3. a) The pronoun "it" is used ambiguously in stanza two. Provide at least two possible meanings given the context.

b) What qualities of fate does Layton emphasize in the metaphor that compares fate to the narrator's foot?

4. Using a graphic organizer, compare tone, point of view, and imagery in Layton's poem with those in Tagore's poem "An Ordinary Person" on page 74. Based on your findings, summarize each author's message and attitude about "ordinary" people and creatures, and the lessons they have for us.

Creative Extension

5. Present a dramatic reading of Layton's poem. Use pitch, pace, volume, gestures, and facial expression to reinforce the attitudes and feelings of the narrator toward the ant. Use sustained eye contact to emphasize the key lines of the poem and to suggest why the narrator changes his mind about killing the ant.

6. Find and record instrumental theme music for each stanza of the poem. Use the music to reveal the narrator's changing attitudes toward the ant. In a journal entry, identify the speaker's attitude in each stanza and explain how the music you have selected reinforces those attitudes.

Weakness – Alden Nowlan

Meaning

1. In small groups, discuss how the title of this poem relates to its content. Make notes describing the various "weaknesses" portrayed in the poem. Why is the father's weakness a surprise? Share your ideas with other groups.

2. What does the speaker mean by "cursing her for a bad bargain"? Explain your answer in a few sentences.

Form and Style

3. This poem is in three stanzas. Explain the narrative purpose of each stanza. In other words, how does each stanza develop the story?

4. How does the form of the third verse differ from the first? What is the effect of this change on the reader and his or her interpretation of the meaning?

Creative Extension

5. Retell the story in the poem from the point of view of the son. Tell it as a children's story and include illustrations if you can. If possible, present the story in a hand-bound book complete with a cover and well-thought-out page layouts.

6. Nowlan's poem suggests that while the horse served a practical purpose for the farmer, he also felt an emotional connection to it. Today, the majority of people live in cities and towns. Some people argue that many of us have lost a sense of connection and interdependence with animals. We buy our food at the supermarket without a thought to where it originally came from. Write an editorial or a letter to the editor of a major newspaper expressing your point of view on this issue.

January Morning/Downtown Vancouver

❧ Earle Birney

Learning Goals

- interpret meaning by creating images and sub-titles
- analyze sound and rhythm
- examine the visual impact of metaphors
- create an original descriptive poem and editorial cartoon

Dawn comes grey as a gull's wing

Between groaning foghorns
the first freighter's basso profundo[1]
demands admission at the Lion's Gate

Trucks wake the dead alleys
downtown becomes hands on wheels
toes roaring motors
fingers triggering horns tempers

Heels quicken on pavements
soles shuffle at reds
jaws yawn then fix in waiting dreaming
come alive with green with buses
fall into rhythm with words gum cigarettes
Heads infinite in variety
absorb into buildings
mesh with repetition with keys
desks counters wheels receivers

The streets wait outside
chained to their hydrants
humming with wires tires talk
buildings' faces look down—
the glassy young expressionless
the old weathered into compassion
necklaced with concrete heraldry
or wearing bustles of wooden pillars
classical grimy   they hold up nothing

---

[1] deep bass sound. A basso profundo is a bass singer with an especially deep range of voice.

Whatever their characters they weep now
as rain twines through chipped granite
snakes down great panes
to patter on awnings cartops
and a sudden carnival of umbrellas bobbing

Rain stops   almost
Beyond the farthest ski-slope
a cyclops eye through cloud-crack
kindles the hats of hotels
glorifies antennae   the webs of bridges
bronzes the inlet
disappears

(The Park is dark wintergreen and drip
that stealthily mounts again to drizzle
chilling the fern and cedar
fir and salal and last year's grass
postponing the flowers
locked in the frosted earth)

the first hours are passing when money
is made   contacts reputations
bargains promises mistakes
trains phonecalls women men
made and unmade as the rain
rivers again
over meadows of glass
drips from the noses
of statues and under the cloud
cloaking the mountains
invisibly deepens to snow

Noon whistles over the millyards
Umbrellas tumble from doorways
bosoms are flattened by raincoats
Eating begins with drinking
juices martinis flattery
Celery is chewed   arguments briefings burgers
In the lanes pigeons patrol the backs of cafes
glaucous gulls are mewing over the harbour ships

The morning is gone

Earle Birney is one of Canada's most renowned poets. From 1946 to 1965, he was a professor of English at the University of British Columbia where he introduced Canada's first creative writing department. His first collection of playful and experimental poems, *David* (1942), won a Governor General's Award, as did his second collection, *Now is Time* (1945). *(Born Calgary, Alberta 1904; died 1995)*

(Responding Activities p. 49)

Kindly Unhitch That Star, Buddy

✺ Ogden Nash

Learning Goals

- compare personal ideas and values with those in a text
- paraphrase a text
- examine how language contributes to satire
- adapt a poem to a comic strip
- research and write a profile

I hardly suppose I know anybody who wouldn't rather be a success than a
    failure,
Just as I suppose every piece of crabgrass in the garden would much
    rather be an azalea,
And in celestial circles all the run-of-the-mill angels would rather be
    archangels or at least cherubim and seraphim,
And in the legal world all the little process-servers hope to grow up into
    great big bailiffim and sheriffim.
Indeed, everybody wants to be a wow,
But not everybody knows exactly how.
Some people think they will eventually bear diamonds instead of rhinestones,
Only by everlasting keeping their noses to their ghrinestones,
And other people think they will be able to put in more time at Palm
    Beach and the Ritz
By not paying too much attention to attendance at the office but rather
    in being brilliant by starts and fits.
Some people after a full day's work sit up all night getting a college
    education by correspondence,
While others seem to think they'll get just as far by devoting their evenings
    to the study of the difference in temperament between brunettance
    and blondance.
In short, the world is filled with people trying to achieve success,
And half of them think they'll get it by saying No and half of them by
    saying Yes,

And if all the ones who say No said Yes, and vice versa, such is the fate of
humanity that ninety-nine percent of them still wouldn't be any better
off than they were before,
Which perhaps is just as well because if everybody was a success nobody
could be contemptuous of anybody else and everybody would start in
all over again trying to be a bigger success than everybody else so they
would have somebody to be contemptuous of and so on forevermore,
Because when people start hitching their wagons to a star,
That's the way they are.

The humorous verse of American poet Ogden Nash shows him a master of irony, adept at
questioning American life and values. His books include *Cricket of Cavador* (1925) and *Good
Intentions* (1942). "Kindly Unhitch That Star, Buddy" is from *A Penny Saved is Impossible* (1981).
(Born Rye, New York 1902; died 1971)

(*Responding Activities p. 50*)

I Lost My Talk

ᑫ Rita Joe

Learning Goals

- interpret the character and message of the speaker

- examine use of pronouns, parallelism, and metaphor

- create a visual representation

- research a poet's career and create a Web site

I lost my talk
The talk you took away.
When I was a little girl
At Shubenacadie school.

You snatched it away:
I speak like you
I think like you
I create like you
The scrambled ballad, about my word.

Two ways I talk
Both ways I say,
Your way is more powerful.

So gently I offer my hand and ask,
Let me find my talk
So I can teach you about me.

ᑫ   Rita Joe's poems often deal with the time she spent at the Indian Residential School in Shubenacadie, Nova Scotia, but also reflect a positive outlook on life and on the revival of her Mi'kmaq culture. Her first book of poems, *Poems of Rita Joe*, was published in 1978. "I Lost My Talk" was published in *Song of Eskasoni: More Poems of Rita Joe* (1988). Rita Joe received the Order of Canada in 1990. She continues to publish poetry and other work, and is active in education. *(Born Whycocomogh, Nova Scotia 1932)*

(Responding Activities pp. 50–51)

A Speech at the Lost-and-Found

ᔒ Wislawa Szymborska

Learning Goals

- examine aspects of fantasy and reality
- explain irony
- write a comparison-contrast essay
- write and present a short speech

I lost a few goddesses while moving south to north,
and also some gods while moving east to west.
I let several stars go out for good, they can't be traced.
An island or two sank on me, they're lost at sea.
I'm not even sure exactly where I left my claws,
who's got my fur coat, who's living in my shell.
My siblings died the day I left for dry land
and only one small bone recalls that anniversary in me.
I've shed my skin, squandered vertebrae and legs,
taken leave of my senses time and again.
I've long since closed my third eye to all that,
washed my fins of it and shrugged my branches.

Gone, lost, scattered to the four winds. It still surprises me
how little now remains, one first person sing., temporarily
declined in human form, just now making such a fuss
about a blue umbrella left yesterday on the bus.

ᔒ   Since 1931, Wislawa Szymborska has been living in Krakow, Poland. She has published 16 collections of poetry and her poems have been translated into many languages. She was the Goethe Prize winner (1991) and Herder Prize winner (1995). In 1996 she received the Polish PEN Club prize and the Nobel Prize for Literature. "A Speech at the Lost-and-Found" appears in her *Collected Poems* (1996). *(Born Western Poland 1923)*

(Responding Activities pp. 51–52)

In Exile *for Rebeca*

Barbara Kingsolver

Learning Goals

- analyze imagery and its impact
- understand empathy of a narrator
- rewrite a poem from a different point of view
- research allusions and present findings

These mountains I love
are knuckles
of a fist
that holds your dreams to the ground

while a ghost-woman boards the city buses
you knew, lifts her eyes to another horizon,
living the life you planned.

A thousand lives like hers move
through Santiago, invisible as a decade without days.
Their colours bled out through the last
open doors of Chile
while Victor Jara[1] curled his soul in his fist
and threw it to a cold star
and Allende[2] died.

In the streets near your home
a ghost-woman moves
through walls that were not yet built,
through trees that have grown surprisingly
in fourteen years.

---

[1] Victor Jara was a Chilean musician who was made a political prisoner and was executed in 1973.

[2] Allende – a reference to Salvador Allende who was president of Chile from 1970–73 and achieved the presidency through a free election. His socialist beliefs made him a target of the military and he was overthrown by a military coup in 1973.

To know you
is to learn to resist the beauty
of the single red rose in a glass.
It could belong on my table
were it not for roots and leaves,
the possibility of fruit,
the stem
that is only cut once.

Barbara Kingsolver's fiction and poetry are rich with the language and imagery of her native Kentucky. Best-selling works of fiction include *The Bean Trees* (1988) and *The Poisonwood Bible* (1998). Kingsolver published a collection of poetry, *Another America: Otra America* in 1992. This collection contains "In Exile." (*Born Kentucky 1955*)

(*Responding Activities p. 52*)

A Consecration

Tom Dawe

Learning Goals

• share inter-
  pretations of
  meaning

• examine effects of
  changes in form
  by adding stanza
  breaks

• write a personal
  memoir

• free-write around
  an image from
  a poem

Luke remembered
their last days on the island
gathering what was
to be taken as young gulls swayed
above the sun-grazed swell
and a lingering mist
ghosted in the garden gleam.
And he remembered
the clergyman telling them
to burn all the boards
from the dismantled church
because such wood was consecrated.
But next day Luke's brother came
in the big white skiff
and took the wood away
to build a house.
And as the months passed
Luke was uneasy
about the anointed wood
until that morning
when he heard the meek cry
of his brother's firstborn
within the sanctuary
of the new walls
as dawn stroked window glass
and kettle mist ascended
to the sturdy beams.

(Responding Activities p. 53)

Tom Dawe's poems have been published widely in journals, anthologies, and magazines around the world. His collections include *In Hardy Country*, *Hemlock Cove*, and *After*. The poem "A Consecration" is from *Island Spell: Poems by Tom Dawe* (1981). *(Born Conception Bay, Newfoundland)*

Digging

Seamus Heaney

Learning Goals

- analyze an author's use of simile
- understand context (time, place, etc.)
- recognize effective use of flashbacks
- create a visual representation and write a personal essay

Between my finger and my thumb
The squat pen rests; snug as a gun.

Under my window, a clean rasping sound
When the spade sinks into gravelly ground.
My father, digging. I look down

Till his straining rump among the flowerbeds
Bends low, comes up twenty years away
Stooping in rhythm through potato drills
Where he was digging.

The coarse boot nestled on the lug, the shaft
Against the inside knee was levered firmly.
He rooted out tall tops, buried the bright edge deep
To scatter new potatoes that we need picked
Loving their cool hardness in our hands.

By God, the old man could handle a spade.
Just like his old man.

My grandfather cut more turf in a day
Than any other man on Toner's bog.
Once I carried him milk in a bottle
Corked sloppily with paper. He straightened up
To drink it, then fell to right away

Nicking and slicing neatly, heaving sods
Over his shoulder, going down and down
For the good turf. Digging.

The cold smell of potato mould, the squelch and slap
Of soggy peat, the curt cuts of an edge
Through living roots awaken in my head.
But I've no spade to follow men like them.

Between my finger and my thumb
The squat pen rests.
I'll dig with it.

Irish poet Seamus Heaney worked as an English teacher and lecturer before being appointed professor of poetry at Oxford in 1989. Economic in his use of language, *Death of a Naturalist* (1966) reveals his preoccupation with environmental themes. "Digging" is from this collection. He won the Nobel Prize for Literature in 1995. (*Born Northern Ireland 1939*)

(*Responding Activities pp. 53–54*)

RESPONDING ACTIVITIES
Contemporary Lyric Poems (pages 37–48)

January Morning/Downtown Vancouver – Earle Birney

Meaning

1. List the numbers 1 through 11 along the margin of a notebook page. Beside each number, which represents a corresponding verse from the poem, write a one-word subtitle to describe the essential idea in each stanza.

2. Retell this poem as an illustrated mini-book or storyboard with no words.

Form and Style

3. Earle Birney has been described as a poetic artist of sound and rhythm. List and explain at least five *onomatopoeic* words or phrases (their sound reflects their meaning) he uses to convey the sounds and rhythms of this downtown Vancouver morning.

4. Note and describe three particularly vivid metaphors from the poem that helped you visualize clearly the scene described by Birney.

Creative Extension

5. a) Write a poem or descriptive piece about a morning you remember. Pay particular attention to sensory details (sights, sounds, etc.) and use a variety of literary devices (metaphors, onomatopoeic words, etc.) to create the scene. Choose one of the following topics or use one of your own.
   - a getting-ready-for-school morning
   - Monday morning at the bus stop
   - Saturday morning at the mall
   - the morning of a special celebration
   - a morning rehearsal or sports practice

   b) Revise your writing, paying attention to your theme or controlling idea. Accent and organize the main ideas to reveal your controlling idea. As you revise, make connections among your ideas with helpful transitions that bring the details together.

6. Imagine this poem is to be published in a major newspaper or magazine. You are asked to create an editorial cartoon or illustration that will appear with the poem. Consider carefully what aspect of the poem you will illustrate and what message you want your illustration to convey. Then decide on the content and focus. Remember to keep it clear and simple; you want your audience to get the message immediately.

Kindly Unhitch That Star, Buddy – Ogden Nash

Meaning

1. According to Nash, what does success do to an individual? Do you agree? Why or why not?

2. Nash opens with a list of the hopes for success of people in general, plants, heavenly beings, and workers in the legal world. Then he adds two pairs of contrasts. Use the following chart headers to paraphrase how the various groups define success and think they will achieve it.

Some people define success as:	And think they will achieve success by:	Whereas others define success as:	And think they will achieve it by:

Form and Style

3. Nash coins several words. He does this in part to maintain the rhyme scheme, but also to create a tone that pokes fun at humanity's pursuit of success in its various forms. Identify four words Nash coins and explain how they create a ridiculing tone.

4. A key metaphor is that of hitching a wagon to a star. What associations does Nash want the reader to make with the wagon and with the star? How does this metaphor enhance his satire?

Creative Extension

5. Adapt this poem to a comic strip. Use the pictures to enhance the hyperbole (exaggeration) and understatement in the poem.

6. Research Nash's life and accomplishments. Use a variety of print and non-print sources. Then write a biographical profile of the poet including references to his major works. If possible, write your profile on computer and e-mail it to your classmates. Include hyperlinks to Web sites and other useful electronic information sources. Be sure to document your sources accurately.

I Lost My Talk – Rita Joe

Meaning

1. What do you learn about the speaker of the poem from each stanza?

2. Where in the poem do the speaker's feelings change? What indicates the change?

Form and Style

3. State three observations about the style of this poem and describe the effects. Consider diction, syntax, rhythm, imagery, etc.

4. a) Examine stanza two. What is the effect of Rita Joe's frequent use of the pronouns "I" and "you" in this stanza? What technique does she use in structuring these lines?
    b) Explain the metaphor in the last line of the stanza.

Creative Extension

5. Create a visual representation of "I Lost My Talk" that reflects the culture and captures the changing emotions of the speaker. Include images from the poem and use the layout, colour, and style in your art to convey the changes in tone. Design a one- to two-page written analysis of your visual. Explain how you used various techniques to develop the theme and tone.

6. Research Rita Joe's career and accomplishments and read more of her poetry. Use the information you discover to create a Web site that other students can use as an introduction and guide to her work. Provide a written analysis of the audience you were targeting and how you used language, layout, colour, symbols, and font to suit your audience. Describe the strengths of your work, the challenges you faced, and the strategies you used to overcome those challenges. Explain what you would change or do differently if you were to do a similar project in the future.

A Speech at the Lost-and-Found – Wislawa Szymborska

Meaning

1. What unusual details in the first two sentences capture the reader's attention? What questions do the unusual details raise?

2. List the items the narrator has lost and explain the significance of the losses.

Form and Style

3. What aspects of this poem are based on fantasy? What aspects are based on reality? How does the combination of fantasy and reality reveal the narrator's identity?

4. In the second stanza, we realize that the narrator is a human being. Explain the *irony* of the ending.

Creative Extension

5. Write and present your own "speech at the lost-and-found." Think of a time when an object you lost made you reflect on some aspect of your past or present circumstances. The object can be something important to you or trivial. The tone of your speech can be light and humorous or serious. Record your speech on audiotape. Use pitch, pace, and volume to emphasize your major ideas and emotions.

6. Write an essay comparing and contrasting Szymborska's use of reality and fantasy with Tagore's use of the ordinary and extraordinary in "An Ordinary Person," page 74. Consider these questions:
    *   What is each author's purpose or theme?
    *   What is each author's attitude toward "ordinary" people and events?
    *   How does each author use fantasy, diction, and imagery to develop his or her theme?
    *   How can the same techniques be used for different purposes?

In Exile – Barbara Kingsolver

Meaning

1. a) List all images that suggest violence in this poem. What impact do these images have on you as the reader?
    b) The term "ghost-woman" is used twice in this poem. Who is the ghost-woman in each case? What evidence supports your interpretation? What does calling this person a "ghost-woman" imply?

2. Explain the opening image of the poem: "These mountains I love / are knuckles / of a fist / that holds your dreams to the ground."

Form and Style

3. Why does the narrator use a metaphor to compare the exiled person to a rose? Justify your answer with specific references to the poem.

4. What words and phrases indicate the narrator empathizes with the exiled person? Why is the narrator's understanding important?

Creative Extension

5. Rewrite the poem from the viewpoint of the woman who lives in exile. What images would she use to describe her situation now and in the past? Use the imagery to connect her reasons for having to leave her country to some of her feelings about her new country. Or, use the imagery to create a sense of the culture she left and the culture in which she now lives. Conclude with a metaphor that explains how she feels living in the gap between two cultures. Present a dramatic reading of your poem.

6. Research the *allusions* to Allende and Victor Jara. Select the most important details you discover and explain how they contribute to your understanding of the poem. Be sure to document your sources accurately. Prepare a multimedia presentation that incorporates the most important details you discovered and explains how they contributed to your understanding of the poem.

A Consecration – Tom Dawe

Meaning

1. What is troubling Luke, and how does he reveal a sense of conscience? What event puts Luke's mind at ease? Why do these events change the way Luke feels? Discuss your interpretations in small groups and then share your views with the class.

2. Define the term "consecration." What is the consecration described in this poem?

Form and Style

3. How does Tom Dawe achieve unity of form and content in this poem?

4. Dawe does not break this poem into stanzas. Why? Indicate stanza breaks where you think they would work to enhance the meaning. Write a brief explanation for your decisions.

Creative Extension

5. Write a brief personal memoir about a time that you felt "guilty by association" or uneasy about breaking a sacred trust.

6. On a piece of paper or using a word-processing program, free-write about mist. Write without stopping and without considering word choice, spelling, or grammar. Identify the lines in Dawe's poem where mist is described. Free-write for at least five minutes more about each of these lines from the poem.

   Read over your free-writing and select the sections you like best. Combine them into one file or piece of writing. Revise your creative writing, this time paying attention to word choice, spelling, grammar, and correct Canadian style, until you have a single, coherent piece of writing.

Digging – Seamus Heaney

Meaning

1. a) How does the narrator "dig" with a pen? For what do you think he is digging? Support your interpretations with evidence from the poem.
   b) In the lines, "Between my finger and my thumb / The squat pen rests; snug as a gun," what quality or qualities does the poet suggest a pen shares with a gun?
   c) There are no other references to weapons in the poem. Does the simile belong in the poem? Why or why not? If you were to change the simile, to what would you compare the pen? Why?

2. a) In what country do you think the poem takes place? Refer to details and vocabulary from the poem to support your answer.

b) Three generations are presented in Heaney's poem. How is the narrator different from his father and grandfather? How is he similar to them? Support your interpretations.

Form and Style

3. How does Heaney appeal to the reader's senses throughout the poem? Cite specific words and phrases that reflect what the narrator sees, hears, and smells. Why does Heaney use this technique?

4. Quote the line where the first flashback begins. What sparks this flashback? Where does the second flashback begin? What prompts it? What purpose does each flashback serve?

Creative Extension

5. Create a visual representation of Heaney's poem. Include images from the poem and use the layout, style, and colour in your art to convey Heaney's attitudes about similarities and differences across the generations. Attach a one- or two-page analysis of your visual explaining how you used various techniques to reinforce Heaney's tone and ideas.

6. Write a personal essay about the influence of families on children. Consider your own experience, the experiences of the narrator in "Digging," and the experiences of individuals that you have encountered in another text (poem, article, story, or film). How do families influence their children and what are the limitations of their influence?

Human Conflict and Struggle

How does conflict and struggle affect the human spirit?

Struggle and conflict have been part of human life for centuries. How have they affected the human spirit? What conflicts have people witnessed in the last century? What actions might help to break cycles of conflict and violence? In this Echo section, through poems, a painting, a film excerpt, and modern song lyrics, artists explore some of the ways people have reacted to conflicts at various periods in human history.

Learning Goals

- examine a theme from different perspectives
- explore how different forms, techniques, language, and styles express meaning
- compare ideas, tone, mood, and techniques in different genres

In Goya's greatest scenes we seem to see

Lawrence Ferlinghetti

This poem by American writer Lawrence Ferlinghetti was inspired by the painting shown on page 57—The Colossus by Spanish artist Francisco Goya. The painting led Ferlinghetti to reflect on human struggle through the centuries.

In Goya's greatest scenes we seem to see
                              the people of the world
          exactly at the moment when
                they first attained the title of
                              'suffering humanity'
        They writhe upon the page
                        in a veritable rage
                              of adversity

Heaped up
　　groaning with babies and bayonets
　　　　　　under cement skies
　　in an abstract landscape of blasted trees
　　　bent statues bats wings and beaks
　　　　slippery gibbets
　　cadavers and carnivorous cocks
　　and all the final hollering monsters
　　　in the
　　　　'imagination of disaster'
　　they are so bloody real
　　　　　　it is as if they really still existed

And they do
　　　Only the landscape is changed
They still are ranged along the roads
　　plagued by legionaires
　　　　　false windmills and demented roosters

They are the same people
　　　　　only further from home
　　on freeways fifty lanes wide
　　　on a concrete continent
　　　　　spaced with bland billboards
　　　illustrating imbecile illusions of happiness
The scene shows fewer tumbrils
　　　　but more maimed citizens
　　　　　　in painted cars
　　and they have strange license plates
　　and engines
　　　that devour America

⁊ Lawrence Ferlinghetti was a leading figure in the Beat movement of the 1950s. His experimental poems can be light and satirical in tone, but they often focus on major social issues
or American political policy. His first book of poetry was *Pictures from the Gone World* (1955).
Others include *A Coney Island of the Mind* (1958) where "In Goya's greatest scenes" appears.
(*Born New York 1919*)

The Colossus
Francisco Goya

♌   The Spanish painter and engraver Francisco Goya painted portraits of kings but also terrifying images of war, gods, and monsters. His etchings include *The Disasters of War*, depicting scenes from the French invasion of Spain in 1810. Among his last works are the "black paintings" with horrific images such as *Saturn Devouring One of His Sons* (1822). *(Born Spain 1746; died 1828)*

RESPONDING

Meaning

1. Ferlinghetti describes Goya's painting "The Colossus" in the first stanza. What main idea does Ferlinghetti see in the painting? What details does he add? What does he leave out? Why do you think he takes this poetic licence? Support your opinion with reference to the poem's second stanza.

2. What comparison does Ferlinghetti make in the poem? What contrasts does he note? What is the purpose of his comparison and contrast?

Form and Style

3. Ferlinghetti uses some very unusual language and images in his descriptions. Cite three lines from the poem that contain unusual images. Define any unfamiliar words and then explain why you think the poet chose these images.

4. Describe the layout of this poem and the impression it gives you on the page. How does the way the poem looks on the page connect to Goya's painting? What do the line lengths reveal about the way people respond to adversity?

Creative Extension

5. Ferlinghetti makes the transition from his reflection on Goya's painting to the violence done in the modern world with an *allusion*—a reference to a work by another author. The lines, the people "still are ranged along the roads / plagued by legionaires / false windmills and demented roosters" come from the 1605 novel *Don Quixote* by Miguel de Cervantes. A man reading about the chivalry of knights decides to go on a quest to correct the wrongs of his own world. In one of his adventures, he sees a windmill as a threatening giant and engages one in a jousting match. His lance gets caught in the sail, lifts him and his horse off the ground, and both have a painful fall.

    In a short piece of writing, comment on why you think Ferlinghetti uses this allusion. What might Ferlinghetti be saying about dealing with adversity?

6. Find a well-known painting from the past that captures your attention and imagination. The painting does not have to deal with violence and war. In a poem or paragraph, describe the painting vividly so that the reader can recreate the scene in his or her imagination. Choose words and images to reflect the tone and mood of the painting. In the last stanzas of the poem or the last lines of your paragraph, compare the painting to a modern scene. Comment on similarities and differences between the two scenes.

The Baker

Heather Cadsby

In this contemporary poem, Canadian poet Heather Cadsby expresses an individual's emotional response when she realizes her baker is a survivor of the Holocaust. The Holocaust, in which over 6 million Jewish people were put to death in Nazi Germany, is one of the most horrific events of the twentieth century.

I would buy anything from you
last week's bread
cakes I'm allergic to
something I've never tried before.
It's that blue code on your arm
four numbers I can't decipher.
They are fixed veins.

Ovens belch and sweat
and you mold, bake
and remember
other barely brown loaves.
Your face is stamped
with kick-shod feet
and the reek of screams.
None of that grows stale.

Yet now here
as you push and jab
sweet dough
I see no revenge.
My gentile money
arms me with bagels
stuffs me with tears.

Heather Cadsby received a BA from McMaster University in Hamilton, Ontario, in 1961 and a Permanent Elementary School Teacher's Certificate in 1964. She published "The Baker" in *Traditions* in 1981 and *Decoys* with Mosaic Press in 1988. She has also published widely in anthologies and worked in the Writers in the Schools program. (Born Belleville, Ontario 1939)

Connecting

1. Why does the narrator say, "I would buy anything from you / last week's bread / cakes I'm allergic to . . ."?

2. Each stanza in this poem contains at least one powerful image. Identify these images. Explain their meaning and their impact on you as the reader.

3. a) How does the narrator respond to her experience at the end of the poem? How has the baker responded to his experience? How do these responses suggest that people can deal with conflicts and injustices?

    b) How does the tone and conclusion of this poem compare with those of Ferlinghetti's poem?

Hiroshima Exit

✑ *Joy Kogawa*

In this poem, Canadian writer Joy Kogawa presents a look back at the bombing of Hiroshima by Americans during World War II. She suggests her hope for a way to break the cycle of conflict and blame.

In round round rooms of our wanderings
Victims and victimizers in circular flight
Fact pursuing fact
Warning leaflets still dip down
On soil heavy with flames,
Black rain, footsteps, witnessings—

The Atomic Bomb Memorial Building:
A curiosity shop filled with
Remnants of clothing, radiation sickness,
Fleshless faces, tourists muttering
"Well, they started it."
Words jingle down
"They didn't think about us in Pearl Harbor"
They? Us?
I tiptoe round the curiosity shop
Seeking my target
Precision becomes essential
Quick. Quick. Before he's out of range

Spell the name
America?
Hiroshima?
Air raid warnings wail bleakly
Hiroshima
Morning.
I step outside
And close softly the door
Believing, believing
That outside this store
Is another door

A Canadian of Japanese descent, Joy Kogawa and her family, along with many other Canadians of Japanese descent in British Columbia, were interned and relocated during World War II. Currently living in Toronto, she has published collections of poetry, including *A Choice of Dreams* (1974) with "Hiroshima Exit" and *Woman in the Woods* (1985). She is known best for her novel *Obasan* (1981). *(Born Vancouver, British Columbia 1935)*

Connecting

1. What words in the first stanza suggest a circle or cycle? Why do you think the poet uses these words? Explain your answers.

2. What does the narrator do to break the cycle of conflict in this poem? Quote from the poem to support your answer.

3. After considering the works of Goya, Ferlinghetti, Cadsby, and Kogawa, which artist would you say is most hopeful that cycles of conflict can be broken? Which is the least hopeful? Where would you place the others on the scale? Explain your reasons.

The War and Beyond 1939-1959

The following script depicts the opening scenes from a documentary film describing the outbreak of World War II and its effect on Japanese Canadians.

Voice Over:
In September, 1939, Victoria artist Emily Carr wrote these words:
"It is war, . . . after days in which the whole world has hung in an unnatural, horrible suspense, while the radio has hummed first with hope and then with despair. . . . war halts everything, suspends all ordinary activities."

//Queen on Lion's Gate Bridge//

Voice Over:
Immediately before the war, BC was starting to shake off the Depression. The Lion's Gate Bridge, a symbol of British Columbia's entry into the age of modern transportation, was completed in the Spring of 1939. The King and Queen came to Vancouver to dedicate the new landmark. War broke out soon after. British Columbians once again dedicated themselves—and in many cases their lives—to saving the British Empire. Once again, they signed up to fight in Europe.

Then, on December 7, 1941, the war came suddenly much closer.

//bombs, Pearl Harbor// up on planes//

Voice Over:
The Japanese bombed Pearl Harbor. That pushed the Americans into World War Two. But Pearl Harbor also had an electrifying effect on BC's West Coast. Japanese fishermen lived and worked all along the coast. Surely they were all spies! Decades of racism quickly found expression in blind paranoia.

Barman:
If you talk to individuals who were young people during the Second World War, I mean they will still talk with very real and genuine emotion about the fear of the Japanese. There were reports of Japanese bombings, or attacks on lighthouses on the coast. There were great fears of the Japanese coming across from Japan.

//shots of propaganda comic books//

Joy Kogawa:
The comic books, and the strange appearance of these creatures with bright yellow skin and big wide teeth . . . and somehow I am associated with this horror. It's too strange to think about. And frightening.

//stills of Kogawa as a young girl//

Voice Over:
Joy Kogawa was 4 years old when the war started. Born in Vancouver, living in this house in the Marpole District.

Joy Kogawa:
And I learned very early, very young, that there was nastiness, strangeness, and unkindness out there. I learned it in the buses, in the streetcars, in the stores, and on the streets. I learned that very early. And I also learned that there was protection from that. The family protected you from that.

Voice Over:
But the family couldn't protect Kogawa—or any other Japanese Canadian —from what came next . . . what has been described as one of the worst official crimes in Canada's history.

Kogawa:
There were about 21 000 of us along the coast. And the whole lot of us that were along the coast were sent out.

//stills of RCMP confiscating Japanese property; RCMP interrogations; living quarters at the PNE; a Japanese man leaving the PNE with his baby boy//

Voice Over:
All Japanese Canadians living on the West Coast—new immigrants as well as Canadian-born—were rounded up. Hastings Park became a huge, make-shift detention centre. The RCMP seized and sold off Japanese fishboats, homes, cars, and businesses. Tore out their roots on the coast to ensure they'd never return.

All Japanese were sent away—inland—to internment camps like Green-wood, New Denver, Slocan. It was a jarring dislocation.

Joy Kogawa's father, an Anglican priest, took this footage himself . . . It shows the internment camp the family was sent to in Slocan City.

Kogawa:
What I'm told is that when we got into the shack that was to be our home with its newspaper walls, I'm told that I sat in the corner and wept, when I was told we had to stay there.

But for me, the hugest trauma was when we left Slocan and couldn't come home. I always wanted to come home. I spent my entire life dreaming about going home, and that meant to me back to Vancouver, back to our house, back to my room, and back to Stanley Park and the music in the amphitheatre in Stanley Park, and Woodwards, and Christmas, and the city. That was home. That's what I dreamed of and it never ever came back.

Barman:
It's not until 1949 that Japanese are allowed to go back to the coast which was where almost all of them lived before the war. A great number of people were led to believe that they had no real choice but to go back to Japan and a considerable number of people did go back to Japan who'd been in BC.

Voice Over:
Those who didn't go back to Japan were forced to settle east of the Rockies —away from the coast.

Kogawa:
In the second removal, the dream of coming home was lost. But people were sent to wherever in Canada they were acceptable as labourers. And in our case, we went to the . . . sugar beet fields of Alberta . . . And it was grim. It was grim. I think that was the thing, the place that broke my Mom. And ya. My Mom had been such an elegant woman who loved her finery and her teasets and she kind of lost it. Because of the hardship of it all.

Connecting

1. What are the effects of stereotyping and scapegoating on individuals? Refer to specific details from the script to support your answers.

2. What broke Joy Kogawa's mother's spirit? What crushed Kogawa's spirit?

3. a) This script combines words and images. Choose one example of this combination that made the strongest impression on you and explain why.
    b) Why is telling a story of suffering through paintings, films, or words important for individuals, for the community, and for humanity?

 # The Sound of a Gun

♪ *Chris de Burgh*

In this contemporary song, British artist Chris de Burgh presents a modern world in which violence is used as a way to resolve conflict. The lyrics and music work together to create a powerful and moving effect.

> I have seen the diamond stylus,
> Cut a groove from north to south,
> Heard them calling from the islands for a better day,

One by one they tell their story,
One by one it's just the same,
"They've taken our leaders,
And all their believers are paralyzed,
And now we can't turn back—somebody is watching you!
Don't turn round—yesterday's gone!
And even the children are waking at midnight in tears,
Didn't anyone hear? Mother, mother, mother . . ."

Hush child go to sleep, it's only the sound of a gun,
Hush child go to sleep, it's only the sound of a gun;

Looking out my bedroom window,
I remember early days,
When the shot that wounded millions took our breath away,
But now the shadow of a gunman,
With his balaclava eyes, is making the news,
Calling out the warnings on the telephone,
"You're in the line of fire—wish there was another way!
Line of fire—anything goes,"
And who is the winner, and what will the minister say,
At the end of the day? Never, never, never, never!

Hush child go to sleep, it's only the sound of a gun,
Hush child go to sleep, it's only the sound of a gun;

This is bella soma[1], this is bella soma . . .
Mother, mother, mother . . .

Hush child go to sleep, it's only the sound of a gun,
Hush child go to sleep, it's only the sound of a gun,

Hush child go to sleep, it's only the sound of a gun,
Hush child do not weep,
It's only the sound of a world on the run,
You're hearing the sound of a gun.

---

[1] Soma is a plant whose juices can be used to make an intoxicating liquor; in the novel *Brave New World* by Aldous Huxley, soma is the drug the state distributes to people to keep them happy and acquiescent.

ECHO

Chris de Burgh was born in Argentina where his father worked for the British government. After travelling widely, the family settled in Ireland. His real success came when he released his number one hit "Lady In Red" in 1986. The song "The Sound of a Gun" is from his *Man on the Line* (1984) album. *(Born Argentina 1948)*

Connecting

1. a) Explain the irony of the mother's response in the refrain of this song: "Hush child go to sleep, it's only the sound of a gun." What does her response tell us about the society in which she and her child live?

   b) What other lines in the poem reinforce this view of the mother and child's society?

2. What events might the song be referring to in the lines: "I remember early days, / When the shot that wounded millions took our breath away"? What is the significance of the fact that the shooting affected millions of people and took their breath away?

3. What might the bella soma in the song correspond to in Ferlinghetti's poem, "In Goya's greatest scenes"? What other correspondences can you see between the song and the poem? Explain your answers. How are the purposes of these two writers similar? Different?

REFLECTING ON THE ECHO

1. Write a journal entry on the selection in this Echo section that presents conflict to you in the most meaningful way. Explain what thoughts and feelings the selection evokes for you. What lines, sentences, or visual images did you find most effective? How do you see the text addressing concerns in today's world? Exchange your journal entries with other students and reply verbally or in writing to each other. Using e-mail would be a useful way to carry out this dialogue.

2. Select another work (poem, story, painting, poster, etc.) that you have read, heard, or seen for this Echo section. Write an interpretation of the work, explain why you would include it in the Echo, and comment on how it presents yet another perspective on the question of how conflict affects the human spirit.

3. Create a storyboard for a public service commercial about stopping violence. Use lines from the print texts or images from the visuals in this Echo. Present the commercial to the class.

Sonnet 55

❧ William Shakespeare

Learning Goals

- use paraphrasing to understand meaning
- examine use of irony
- write an original sonnet
- write a comparison-contrast essay

Not marble nor the gilded monuments
Of princes shall outlive this powerful rime,
But you shall shine more bright in these contents
Than unswept stone, besmeared with sluttish time.
When wasteful war shall statues overturn,
And broils root out the work of masonry,
Nor Mars his sword nor war's quick fire shall burn
The living record of your memory.
'Gainst death and all oblivious enmity
Shall you pace forth; your praise shall still find room
Even in the eyes of all posterity
That wear this world out to the ending doom.
    So, till the judgment that yourself arise,
    You live in this, and dwell in lovers' eyes.

❧ An unrivalled dramatist and poet in his time, William Shakespeare is still considered England's greatest playwright. In addition to comedies such as *Much Ado About Nothing* and tragedies such as *Romeo and Juliet*, he wrote 154 sonnets. Many dealt with themes of love, fate, and the ravages of time. The sonnets were first printed in 1609. (*Born England 1564; died 1616*)

(*Responding Activities p. 77*)

The Good Morrow

ꙮ John Donne

Learning Goals

- identify a speaker's attitude
- examine use of pronouns
- analyze an extended metaphor
- write from a different point of view
- present a dramatic reading

I wonder, by my troth, what thou and I
Did, till we loved? Were we not weaned till then?
But sucked on country pleasures, childishly?
Or snorted we in the seven sleepers' den?[1]
'Twas so; but this, all pleasures fancies be.
If ever any beauty I did see,
Which I desired, and got, 'twas but a dream of thee.

And now good-morrow to our waking souls,
Which watch not one another out of fear;
For love, all love of other sights controls,
And makes one little room an everywhere.
Let sea-discoverers to new worlds have gone,
Let maps to others, worlds on world have shown,
Let us possess one world, each hath one, and is one.

My face in thine eye, thine in mine appears,
And true plain hearts do in the faces rest;
Where can we find two better hemispheres,
Without sharp North, without declining West?
Whatever dies was not mixed equally;
If our two loves be one, or, thou and I
Love so alike that none do slacken, none can die.

(Responding Activities pp. 77–78)

ꙮ   John Donne was one of the Metaphysical poets of the seventeenth century. These poets were known for their ingenuity and wit—particularly in their use of unconventional imagery. Donne's passionate, colloquial, and sometimes abrupt tone distinguished his poems from those of the Elizabethan poets before him. His work consists of love poems, religious poems, verse satires, and sermons. Poems such as "The Good Morrow," "The Canonization," and "The Bait" were published in the 1590s. *(Born London, England c. 1572; died 1631)*

---

[1] a reference to seven Christian youths who were persecuted under the Roman empire and sealed in a cave where they slept for nearly two centuries. When they awoke, Christianity had been established as a world religion.

The World Is Too Much With Us

✑ William Wordsworth

Learning Goals

- apply strategies to define unfamiliar vocabulary
- write a theme statement
- compare language, imagery, and theme to another poem
- write a comparison-contrast essay and original poem

The world is too much with us: late and soon,
Getting and spending, we lay waste our powers:
Little we see in Nature that is ours;
We have given our hearts away, a sordid boon![1]
This sea that bares her bosom to the moon;
The winds that will be howling at all hours,
And are up-gathered now like sleeping flowers;
For this, for everything, we are out of tune;
It moves us not.—Great God! I'd rather be
A pagan suckled in a creed outworn.[2]
So might I, standing on this pleasant lea,[3]
Have glimpses that would make me less forlorn;
Have sight of Proteus rising from the sea;
Or hear old Triton blow his wreath'd horn.[4]

(Responding Activities pp. 78–79)

✑   William Wordsworth was one of the leading Romantic poets of the late eighteenth century. To Wordsworth, poetry was a way to express personal thoughts and feelings spontaneously and sincerely. The Romantic poets emphasized emotional directness, personal experience, and freedom of imagination. In 1797, Wordsworth collaborated with poet Samuel Taylor Coleridge on the collection *Lyrical Ballads*. "The World is Too Much With Us" was written between 1802 and 1804. *(Born England 1770; died 1850)*

---

[1] boon = gift; [2] pagan = person not holding any of the major religious beliefs of the world (irreligious); creed = belief; [3] lea = an open meadow; [4] In Greek myth Proteus, the "Old Man of the Sea," rises from the sea at midday and can be forced to tell the future by anyone who holds him as he changes into many frightening forms. Triton is the son of Neptune, god of the sea. The sound of Triton's horn calms the waves.

The Lake Isle of Innisfree

ℐ William Butler Yeats

Learning Goals

- apply strategies to define unfamiliar vocabulary
- write a theme statement
- compare language, imagery, and theme to another poem
- write a comparison-contrast essay and original poem

I will arise and go now, and go to Innisfree,
And a small cabin build there, of clay and wattles made:
Nine bean-rows will I have there, a hive for the honey-bee,
And live alone in the bee-loud glade.

And I shall have some peace there, for peace comes dropping slow,
Dropping from the veils of the morning to where the cricket sings;
There midnight's all a glimmer, and noon a purple glow,
And evening full of the linnet's wings.

I will arise and go now, for always night and day
I hear lake water lapping with low sounds by the shore;
While I stand on the roadway, or on the pavements gray,
I hear it in the deep heart's core.

ℐ   William Butler Yeats was a leader of the Celtic revival and a founder of the Abbey Theatre in Dublin. Early poems, such as "The Lake Isle of Innisfree," were romantic and lyrical. Later books of poetry include *The Wild Swans at Coole* (1917) and *The Winding Stair* (1929). He received the Nobel Prize for Literature in 1923. *(Born Dublin, Ireland 1865; died 1939)*

(Responding Activities pp. 78–79)

Dover Beach

☙ Matthew Arnold

Learning Goals

- analyze changes in mood and relate them to meaning
- trace patterns of imagery
- write a critical analysis of a parody
- compare the poem to a modern song

The sea is calm tonight.
The tide is full, the moon lies fair
Upon the straits—on the French coast the light
Gleams and is gone; the cliffs of England stand,
Glimmering and vast, out in the tranquil bay.
Come to the window, sweet is the night air!
Only, from the long line of spray
Where the sea meets the moon-blanched land,
Listen! you hear the grating roar
Of pebbles which the waves draw back, and fling,
At their return, up the high strand,
Begin, and cease, and then again begin,
With tremulous cadence slow, and bring
The eternal note of sadness in.

Sophocles long ago
Heard it on the Aegean, and it brought
Into his mind the turbid ebb and flow
Of human misery; we
Find also in the sound a thought,
Hearing it by this distant northern sea.

The Sea of Faith
Was once, too, at the full, and round earth's shore
Lay like the folds of a bright girdle furled.
But now I only hear
Its melancholy, long, withdrawn roar,
Retreating, to the breath
Of the night wind, down the vast edges drear
And naked shingles of the world.

Ah, love, let us be true
To one another! for the world, which seems
To lie before us like a land of dreams,
So various, so beautiful, so new,
Hath really neither joy, nor love, nor light,
Nor certitude, nor peace, nor help for pain;
And we are here as on a darkling plain
Swept with confused alarms of struggle and flight,
Where ignorant armies clash by night.

Matthew Arnold was a major poet and critic of the Victorian era in England. His poems often explored feelings of alienation, despair, and spiritual emptiness. "Dover Beach" is one of his best-known works, published in *New Poems* in 1867. *(Born Middlesex, England 1822; died 1888)*

(Responding Activities pp. 79–80)

We Grow Accustomed to the Dark

❧ Emily Dickinson

Learning Goals

- consider an author's purpose
- examine use of punctuation and tone
- create a visual representation
- write an essay comparing imagery to that in another poem

We grow accustomed to the Dark—
When Light is put away—
As when the Neighbour holds the Lamp
To witness her Goodbye—

A Moment—We uncertain step
For newness of the night—,
Then—fit our Vision to the Dark—
And meet the Road—erect—

And so of larger—Darkness—
Those Evenings of the Brain—
When not a Moon disclose a sign—
Or Star—come out—within—

The Bravest—grope a little—
And sometimes hit a Tree
Directly in the Forehead—
But as they learn to see—

Either the Darkness alters—
Or something in the sight
Adjusts itself to Midnight—
And life steps almost straight.

❧ Very few of Emily Dickinson's poems were published during her lifetime. Her work became well known only in the twentieth century. Much of the dramatic tension in her short lyrics stems from religious doubt and innovative techniques that influenced many twentieth-century poets. *The Poems of Emily Dickinson* (1955) contains all 1775 known poems. *(Born Amherst, Massachusetts 1830; died 1886)*

(Responding Activities pp. 80–81)

An Ordinary Person

❧ Rabindranath Tagore

Learning Goals

- recognize the key argument in a poem
- assess the poet's choice of language
- write an original poem
- write a comparison-contrast essay

A stick under his arm, a pack on his head,
at dusk a villager goes home along the river.
If after a hundred centuries somehow—
by some magic—from the past's kingdom of death
this peasant could be resurrected, again made flesh,
with his stick under his arm and surprise in his eyes,
then would crowds besiege him on all sides,
everyone snatching every word from his lips.
His joys and sorrows, attachments and loves,
his neighbours, his own household,
his fields, cattle, methods of farming: all
they would take in greedily and still it wouldn't be enough.
His life-story, today so ordinary,
will, in those days, seem charged with poetry.

❧   Rabindranath Tagore was a Bengali mystic, poet, and novelist. He inspired the Bengali literary revival with the poems, short stories, and popular songs he began to publish at the age of 20. He became known to the world when he translated his poems into English with *Gitanjali* ("song offerings") in 1912. In that year, Tagore became the first Asian to receive the Nobel Prize for Literature. (*Born East Bengal 1861; died 1941*)

(Responding Activities p. 81)

Silhouette

Pauline Johnson (Tekahionwake)

Learning Goals

- examine roles of character and landscape in a poem
- analyze imagery and its relationship to meaning
- create a visual representation
- research a poet's career and develop a presentation

The sky-line melts from russet into blue,
Unbroken the horizon, saving where
A wreath of smoke curls up the far, thin air,
And points the distant lodges of the Sioux.

Etched where the lands and cloudlands touch and die
A solitary Indian teepee stands,
The only habitation of these lands,
That roll their magnitude from sky to sky.

The tent poles lift and loom in thick relief,
The upward floating smoke ascends between,
And near the open doorway, gaunt and lean,
And shadow-like, there stands an Indian Chief.

With eyes that lost their lustre long ago,
With visage fixed and stern as fate's decree,
He looks towards the empty west, to see
The never-coming herd of buffalo.

Only the bones that bleach upon the plains,
Only the fleshless skeletons that lie
In ghastly nakedness and silence, cry
Out mutely that naught else to him remains.

Of Mohawk and English ancestry, Pauline Johnson was born on the Six Nations Reserve. She was widely known in the early 1900s for her lyric poetry and narratives, and for her recitals. Her poetry was often political and focused on the position of Aboriginal peoples in society. (*Born Six Nations Reserve 1861; died 1913*)

(Responding Activities p. 82)

Advice to a Girl

✑ Sara Teasdale

Learning Goals

• analyze theme
• assess a poet's
  use of tone
• create an original
  work based on
  the theme in a
  poem
• present a short
  talk comparing a
  modern song to
  the poem

No one worth possessing
Can be quite possessed;
Lay that on your heart,
My young angry dear;
This truth, this hard and precious stone,
Lay it on your hot cheek,
Let it hide your tear.
Hold it like a crystal
When you are alone
And gaze in the depths of the icy stone.
Long, look long and you will be blessed:
No one worth possessing
Can be quite possessed.

✑ Popular during the early twentieth century, American poet Sara Teasdale published numerous
   volumes of poetry, including *Rivers to the Sea* (1915), *Love Songs* (1917), *Flame and Shadow*
   (1920), *Dark of the Moon* (1926), and *Strange Victory* (1933). In 1918, Teasdale was awarded the
   Columbia University Poetry Society Prize (forerunner of the Pulitzer Prize for Poetry) for *Love
   Songs*. (Born St. Louis, Missouri 1884; died 1933)

(Responding Activities pp. 82–83)

RESPONDING ACTIVITIES
Pre- and Early Twentieth Century Lyric Poems (pages 67–76)

Sonnet 55 – William Shakespeare

Meaning

1. In a small group, read the sonnet aloud. Have each person read one quatrain or the couplet. Don't pause at the end of a line unless there is punctuation. After each quatrain and the couplet, stop and paraphrase the idea contained in it. Jot down your group's paraphrase and compare it with the work of another group.

2. What is "this powerful rime" that Shakespeare refers to in the second line? What is he suggesting about the power of art and language? Summarize his theme in a few sentences.

Form and Style

3. *Irony* is created when an author suggests something different from what is actually said. Explain the irony of lines 7 and 8: "Nor Mars his sword nor war's quick fire shall burn / The living record of your memory."

4. The first three quatrains (four rhyming lines) all use the verb "shall," which is future tense. In the last line, Shakespeare changes to the present tense, "You live in this. . . ." What reasons might he have for changing tense? Think about the effect of the tense change on his ideas about immortality.

Creative Extension

5. Write an English or Shakespearean sonnet about something you love or passionately dislike (e.g., a particular type of music, sports, breaking up, chocolate, and so on). Use "Sonnet 55" as a model to structure your work. Depending on your subject, your poem may be very different in tone from Shakespeare's. Present a dramatic reading of your poem.

6. Compare and contrast Shakespeare's "Sonnet 55" to his "Sonnet 65," which begins "Since brass, nor stone, nor earth, nor boundless sea." Use a graphic organizer to make notes on the similarities and differences between the two texts before you begin your essay.

The Good Morrow – John Donne

Meaning

1. a) Who is the speaker in this poem? Who is the speaker addressing? What are his feelings toward this person? Identify a line in the poem to support your interpretation.

   b) How do you think the listener might respond? Why?

   c) *Hyperbole* is a deliberate exaggeration. How does the speaker use hyperbole to flatter his listener?

2. After focusing on beauty and sensory pleasures in stanza one, Donne argues there is more to love in stanza two. Name at least three qualities he asserts true love has. Quote him and paraphrase the lines.

Form and Style

3. List the pronouns Donne uses in stanza one. What pronouns does he use in stanza two? What is the significance of this change?

4. Donne begins his extended metaphor with the line, "love ... makes one little room an everywhere."
    a) What two things is Donne comparing? Why does he make the comparison?
    b) Donne extends this metaphor up until the last three lines of the poem. What related images does he add to extend the comparison? What ideas about love do these images suggest?

Creative Extension

5. In Donne's poem, the listener never has an opportunity to speak. What might she say that morning before they part and go out to face the day? What might her attitude toward love be?

    Take on the persona of a Renaissance woman. Write a short verse using the first-person point of view and including an extended metaphor to describe your attitude toward love. Your poem can be rhyming or in free verse and can be in Modern English. However, the time period must remain in the Renaissance.

6. Present a dramatic reading of your poem. Use pitch, pace, volume, gestures, and facial expression to reinforce your ideas about love from the woman's point of view. Use sustained eye contact to emphasize the key lines of the poem that help the reader discover one of your themes.

Lake Isle of Innisfree – Wm. Yeats;
The World is Too Much With Us – Wm. Wordsworth
(A comparison)

Meaning

1. Find the meanings of any unfamiliar words in the poems (e.g., wattles, linnet, sordid, boon, pagan, creed, lea, forlorn). With a partner, consider the lines in which these words appear and discuss your interpretations.

2. As a class or in small groups, answer the 5W questions (*who, when, where, what happened, why did the author write this?*) for each poem. Then consider *how* Wordsworth and Yeats present their ideas (the literary techniques used). Lastly, discuss themes or ideas they want to communicate to the reader. Develop theme statements for each poem and discuss the themes within your group.

Form and Style

3. Develop a graphic organizer to compare and contrast "The World is Too Much with Us" and "The Lake Isle of Innisfree." Fill in the organizer with information from your discussions in question 2 and from your own close reading of the poems.

4. The use of metaphor is central to the poet's ability to go beyond the ordinary limitations of language. In the reader, the metaphor calls for an imaginative leap. List two metaphors from each poem. Describe the thoughts and feelings the metaphor creates for you as the reader and explain why you think the poet chose it.

Creative Extension

5. Write an essay comparing and contrasting "The World is Too Much with Us" and "The Lake Isle of Innisfree." Consider what ideas Wordsworth and Yeats develop about the relationship between human beings and nature.

6. Write a poem or paragraph about a time when you have felt "out of tune" with the world around you, and you have longed for "some peace." Describe where you would rather be and what is happening in your special place.

Dover Beach – Matthew Arnold

Meaning

1. a) What is the dominant mood of stanza one? What creates this mood?
   b) Where in the stanza does the mood begin to change? By the time we reach stanza two, what has happened to the mood? Refer to the poem to support your answer.

2. a) Discuss in a small group what you think this author believes about the power of love. Refer to the poem to support your opinions.
   b) In stanza two, the poet alludes to Sophocles, a writer of Greek tragedies. Why does the poet compare himself to a writer of tragedies? How does this allusion contribute to your understanding of the poem?

Form and Style

3. a) What are the three seas referred to in this poem? How is the metaphorical sea in stanza three connected to the seas described in stanzas one and two?
   b) Note specific examples of how the sounds of words and line lengths recreate the movement of the seas. Explain how the movement of the waves reflects the movement of the narrator's emotions.

4. Trace the references to light in the poem. What does the light represent? When does the poet introduce darkness? Why?

5. Read the following parody of "Dover Beach." A *parody* is an imitation designed to ridicule or satirize.

    That Ghastly Night in Dover

    The sea was calm, and sweet the night air,
    but what a bore! One whiff of ocean breeze
    started him blathering all night long, I swear—
    stuff about naked shingles and Sophocles.

    Katherine McAlpine

    What is being parodied or satirized in this poem? In other words, what is the author ridiculing? Is the ridicule justified? Why or why not?

6. Poets, writers, and artists throughout time have dealt with the theme of love. Research a modern song that presents a similar or different view of love from that in Arnold's poem. Compare the attitudes to love in the two selections. Refer to the mood, use of imagery, sound effects (this could be musical effects), and other techniques the writers use to express their ideas.

We Grow Accustomed to the Dark – Emily Dickinson

Meaning

1. What events do you think might have inspired Emily Dickinson to write this poem? Support your opinion.

2. a) Which stanza of the poem is the darkest? How do you know?
    b) What do the Dark and Darkness represent? Why does Dickinson capitalize the words?
    c) What would Dickinson advise individuals who are dealing with dark difficulties or dark moods to do? Is this good advice? Support your opinion.

Form and Style

3. What is the effect of all the dashes in this poem? Explain.

4. Overall, is the tone of this poem pessimistic or optimistic? What phrases or images support your answer?

Creative Extension

5. Create a visual representation of "We Grow Accustomed to the Dark." You could create a painting, sketch, or a collage, for example. Include images from the poem and use layout, style, and colour to convey the narrator's feelings and attitudes about the dark and what it symbolizes. In a written analysis, explain how you used particular techniques to reinforce the narrator's tone and the symbolic meanings of the poem.

6. Compare and contrast Dickinson's "We Grow Accustomed to the Dark" to Arnold's "Dover Beach" in an essay. How do these authors use light and dark imagery and how does it influence their tone? Which author is more optimistic? What techniques contribute to the optimism or pessimism?

An Ordinary Person – Rabindranath Tagore

Meaning

1. a) In lines 3 through 8, Tagore presents the main argument of his poem. In your own words summarize his main idea, supporting points, and conclusion.
   b) What key words in lines 3 to 8 signal that the poet is presenting an argument? Do you agree or disagree with his argument? Support your opinion.

2. A good introduction should provide background information and get the attention of the reader. Evaluate Tagore's poem by reading the information we are given in the opening two lines.

Form and Style

3. Usually, we expect poetry to use language in unique ways and to present vivid and precise images. In lines 9 through 11, Tagore gives us a very general description of the man's life: "His joys and sorrows, attachments and loves, / His neighbours, his own household, / his fields, cattle, methods of farming." Describe the language in these lines. Why does Tagore use this language?

4. Tagore condenses his argument in the last two lines of his poem: "His life-story; today so ordinary, / will, in those days, seem charged with poetry."
   a) What qualities does Tagore imply poetry has? Support your answers with evidence from the poem.
   b) Why does Tagore argue that the everyday ordinary events are suitable subjects for poetry? Do you agree or disagree? Explain your answers. What would Tagore say to the student who says, "I don't have anything to write about?"

Creative Extension

5. Write a poem about an "ordinary" person you know or imagine. Use Tagore's poem as a model. You can change the tone and mood of the poem if you wish and use more modern, colloquial language.

6. Write an essay comparing and contrasting Tagore's poem with another poem in this anthology. Consider Szymborska's "A Speech at the Lost-and-Found" (p. 43), Irving Layton's "Go to the Ant" (p. 30), or Bronwen Wallace's "Common Magic" (pp. 12–13). Address some of the following questions.
   • What is each author's purpose or theme?
   • What is each author's tone or attitude about "ordinary" people and events?
   • How does each author use fantasy, diction, and imagery to develop his or her ideas?
   • How are the same techniques used for different purposes?

Silhouette – Pauline Johnson

Meaning

1. Describe the character of the "Indian Chief" in the poem. List several traits and identify the actions or behaviours that suggest these traits. Use a web or T-chart to record your responses.

2. What role does the landscape play in this poem? Cite specific words and phrases to support your interpretation.

Form and Style

3. a) The silhouette is a powerful image in the poem. Why do you think the poet chose it? What is its significance?
   b) What other images in the poem create a similar effect?

4. Describe the imagery in the final stanza. What is the effect and significance of the final word in the poem

Creative Extension

5. Create a visual representation based on this poem. Incorporate images from the poem and use colour, layout, and style to convey the mood and message. Direct your visual at a modern audience and include a short paragraph explaining the importance of the message for Canadian society today.

6. Research the life and accomplishments of Pauline Johnson. Choose one aspect of her life and develop a multimedia presentation of your findings.

Advice to a Girl – Sara Teasdale

Meaning

1. Who do you think is giving this advice to a girl? Are there any clues to the character of the speaker in the poem to support your opinion? Explain.

2. a) To what does "this truth" refer? Why does Teasdale call "this truth" a "hard and precious stone"?
   b) How does she extend this metaphor? How does the extended metaphor create deeper understanding of "the truth"?
   c) If you were the girl receiving the advice in this poem, how would you respond? Why?

Form and Style

3. a) *Tone* refers to the attitude a writer has toward his or her theme. What is the speaker's tone in this poem? What words in the poem create this tone?
   b) Would this be an effective tone to use if someone were upset? Why or why not?

4. Why does Teasdale use the lines "No one worth possessing / Can be quite possessed" at the beginning and end of the poem?

Creative Extension

5. Write your own advice to a girl or to a boy who has just had a relationship fail. Use Teasdale's poem as a model or choose another form such as a modern song or a short scene in a drama.

6. The theme in Sara Teasdale's poem has been the focus of many modern songs about love. Research a modern love song that expresses a similar message to that in the poem. Give a short talk comparing Teasdale's poem and the modern song lyrics. Present a recording of the song if possible. Discuss what techniques the two writers used to express their key ideas.

Beowulf

Learning Goals

- summarize to show understanding
- recognize characteristics of an epic hero
- analyze purpose and effects of alliteration and diction
- write an elegy and a verse based on a model

Beowulf is a Scandinavian epic poem from the first millennium. For centuries it was passed along orally until scribes in Britain in the eighth century recorded it on paper. The epic, named for its hero Beowulf, tells the life history of this warrior. Beowulf is the ideal Anglo-Saxon hero: he is brave, challenges the fates, seeks glory even if it means courting death, protects his followers, and sacrifices all for honour.

The first display of his bravery comes when he restores the honour of a Danish neighbouring kingdom by killing the monster, Grendel, that has been feasting on the brave warriors of the Danes. He defeats the monster and its mother, saves the tribe, and restores peace. When he returns to his homeland, Beowulf's people revere and honour him. Eventually, Beowulf is raised to the highest position in the tribe of the Geats — he becomes king. The following excerpt tells of the terror Grendel brought to the land and how Beowulf raised his followers to come to the aid of the Danes.

So well lived the warriors   in weal[1] and luxury
Till Hell loosed its hold   of a hideous fiend
Grendel the grim   infamous and gray
As a marsh mist   marking the fenland[2]
Long had he lived   in the land of monsters
Condemned by the Creator   with the race of Cain. . .

Foul in the night-fall   Grendel the fiend
Waited for the Ring-Danes   weary of wassail[3]
To drain their mead-cups   and drop themselves down.
He crept to the high hall   and here he saw heroes
Full from the feast   as they slept on the floor
Senseless to sorrow   of sons of the earth.
Then did the fierce fiend   fume in damned fury.
Gore-greedy and grim   he snatched in his jaws
There of the shield-thanes   to the number of thirty
And flew to the fen   full of his prize.

---

[1] wealth;

[2] marshland;

[3] a drink

Dim in the dawn   the Ring-Danes awaking
Saw the tell-tale blood   the track of the monster.
As once they had given   great joy to the wassail,
So now they lamented   the loss of their comrades,
And Hrothgar the hero[4]   heart-smitten with sorrow
Mourned for his men   murdered unmanfully .
And gazed in his grief   on the tracks of grim Grendel.
Too hateful that struggle,   strenuous and too long

But the dire Grendel   determined on slaughter
Fared forth in the evening   each night for the feast.
Once men knew malice   lurked near the mead-hall
Wisdom it was   for those who were weary
To seek for their shelter   in a safer house
And lie in a bed   less exposed to the mere[5]
Now that they noted   how near Grendel was.
He fled far off   who escaped the fiend.

Alone against all others   did Grendel prevail,
Vaunting to victory   invincible evil
Until Hrothgar's hall   was emptied of heroes.
Twelve years of torment   the lord of the Scyldings
Hopeless of succour   suffered deep grief
Sad did the news spread   over the swan's bath[6]
How Hrothgar the hardy   was harried by Grendel,
Year after year,   with no yielding in view,
For the price of Grendel's peace   no Dane would pay.
No wisemen dree the doom   darker than death
From the cold killer   who keeps black ambush
On misty moors   against old men and young
When dark mists draw   the day and devils glide
Hither from Hell   but where they hie
In their world wandering   no one can tell.

---

[4] King of the Danes

[5] lake

[6] the sea

Horrible humility   on Hrothgar's people
Inflicted this fiend   fierce from the fen,
Harrying with hatred   the hall of Heorot,
In the night noises   knowing his hour.
One place at his peril   was pure from his touch,
The chief throne of honour   where the Scyld chieftain
Gave gifts to his men   as God gives of His grace.
No evil can ever   over giving prevail.
Often the chief of the Scyld-Danes   shrouded in sorrow
Summoned in secret   his sages to council.
Oft did they dispute   the best way to deal with
The horrible stealth   of the sudden attacks.
Sometimes they sacrificed,   saying long prayers,
Asking the demons to aid them   the devil to doom,
Turning their hearts to Hell,   the hope of the heathen,
For little they'd learned   of the one true Lord,
Maker of men   and judge of man's deeds,
And none of them knew   of the Omnipotent
God in His glory   grateful for praise.
Woe-full is the word   of the wicked
Who thrust forever   flaming into Hell
Sin-sick and hopeless   their immortal souls.
But good is the goal   of the God-seeking man.
He finds eternal bliss   in his Father's bosom.

This king Hrothgar,   kinsman of Healfdene,
Worried his wits   with the woe of his times
But wise though he was   still his grief remained.
No country could conquer   nor council assail
The power that preyed   on his people,
Horrible and hideous   out of the night's hell.
Too hateful that struggle,   strenuous and too long.

News of these deeds   done by grim Grendel
Came back to Beowulf   brave thane of the Geats.
Hale in the mead-hall   and high in his breeding,
Stalwart he stood   the strongest of men.
He fitted a stout ship   for the sea's buffeting,
Well-oared and thick-decked,   to his kin declaring
That he would ride the swan-road   to rescue Hrothgar,
Renowned among Spear-Danes,   in his need for men.
All of his liege-men   loyal in their love
Talked not of terrors   to turn him aside
But inspecting the omens   for weal and for woe
They bade Beowulf   blithe on his voyage
Fare with his fourteen   fine men of his choosing,
Picked for their fierceness   from the fiery Geats.
Skilled as a sea-man   he set out for his ship,
Steering by safe ways   his men down to the shore.

An engraving depicts the death of Beowulf after an encounter with a dragon later in the epic poem.

(Responding Activities p. 101)

The Listeners

Walter de la Mare

Learning Goals

- make inferences from cues in a poem
- analyze mood
- consider symbolic interpretations
- create a visual representation and an original poem

"Is there anybody there?" said the Traveller,
    Knocking on the moonlit door;
And his horse in the silence champed the grasses
    Of the forest's ferny floor:
And a bird flew up out of the turret,
    Above the Traveller's head:
And he smote upon the door again a second time;
    "Is there anybody there?" he said.
But no one descended to the Traveller;
    No head from the leaf-fringed sill
Leaned over and looked into his gray eyes,
    Where he stood perplexed and still.
But only a host of phantom listeners
    That dwelt in the lone house then
Stood listening in the quiet of the moonlight
    To that voice from the world of men:
Stood thronging the faint moonbeams on the dark stair
    That goes down to the empty hall,
Hearkening in an air stirred and shaken
    By the lonely Traveller's call.
And he felt in his ear their strangeness,
    Their stillness answering his cry,
While his horse moved, cropping the dark turf,
    'Neath the starred and leafy sky;
For he suddenly smote on the door, even
    Louder, and lifted his head:—
"Tell them I came, and no one answered,
    That I kept my word," he said.
Never the least stir made the listeners,
    Though every word he spake

Fell echoing through the shadowiness of the still house
    From the one man left awake:
Ay, they heard his foot upon the stirrup,
    And the sound of iron on stone,
And how the silence surged softly backward,
    When the plunging hoofs were gone.

Walter de la Mare wrote poems for children, as well as poems about childhood for adults. His first volume, the *Songs of Childhood*, was published in 1902. Other well-known volumes are *Peacock Pie* (1913) and *The Burning Glass and Other Poems* (1945). He is buried in St. Paul's Cathedral. (*Born Kent, England 1873; died 1956*)

(*Responding Activities p. 102*)

The Titanic

E. J. Pratt

Learning Goals

- analyze meaning using the 5W questions

- analyze how and why specific literary techniques are used

- examine use of specialized vocabulary

- present a dramatic reading

- write a research report

In 1912, the cruiseship Titanic *hit an iceberg and sank off the coast of Newfoundland. The event shocked the world. The* Titanic *was supposed to be unsinkable, a state-of-the-art vessel. In this excerpt from his epic poem, Newfoundland poet E. J. Pratt relates the dramatic events of that fateful day.*

11:45 P.M.

A signal from the crow's nest. Three bells pealed:
The look-out telephoned—*Something ahead,*
Hard to make out, sir; looks like . . .iceberg dead
On starboard bow!

MURDOCH HOLDING THE BRIDGE-WATCH

> *Starboard your helm:* ship heeled
To port. From bridge to engine-room the clang
Of the telegraph. *Danger. Stop.* A hand sprang
To the throttle; the valves closed, and with the churn
Of the reverse the sea boiled at the stern.
Smith hurried to the bridge and Murdoch closed
The bulkheads of the ship as he supposed,
But could not know that with those riven floors
The electro-magnets failed upon the doors.
No shock! No more than if someone alive
Had brushed her as she passed. The bow had missed.
Under the vast momentum of her drive
She went a mile. But why that ominous five
Degrees (within five minutes) of a list?

IN A CABIN

'What was that, steward?'

> 'Seems like she hit a sea, sir.'

'But there's no sea; calm as a landlocked bay
It is; lost a propellor blade?'
                'Maybe, sir.'
'She's stopped.'
            'Just cautious like, feeling her way,
There's ice about. It's dark, no moon tonight,
Nothing to fear, I'm sure, sir.'
                      For so slight
The answer of the helm, it did not break
The sleep of hundreds: some who were awake
Went up on deck, but soon were satisfied
That nothing in the shape of wind or tide
Or rock or ice could harm that huge bulk spread
On the Atlantic, and went back to bed.

CAPTAIN IN WIRELESS ROOM

'We've struck an iceberg—glancing blow: as yet
Don't know extent; looks serious; so get
Ready to send out general call for aid;
I'll tell you when—having inspection made.'

REPORT OF SHIP'S CARPENTER AND FOURTH OFFICER

A starboard cut three hundred feet or more
From foremast to amidships. Iceberg tore
Right at the bilge turn through the double skin:
Some boiler rooms and bunkers driven in;
The forward five compartments flooded—mail
Bags floating. Would the engine power avail
To stem the rush?

                Titanic, C.Q.D.
Collision: iceberg: damaged starboard side:
Distinct list forward. (Had Smith magnified
The danger? Over-anxious certainly.)
The second (joking)—*'Try new call, maybe*
Last chance you'll have to send it.'

S.O.S.

Then back to older signal of distress.

On the same instant the *Carpathia* called,
The distance sixty miles—*Putting about,*
And heading for you; Double watch installed
In engine-room, in stokehold and look-out.
Four hours the run, should not the ice retard
The speed; but taking chances: Coming hard!

THE BRIDGE

As leaning on her side to ease a pain,
The tilted ship had stopped the captain's breath:
The inconceivable had stabbed his brain,
This thing unfelt—her visceral wound of death?
Another message—this time to report her
Filling, taxing the pumps beyond their strain.
Had that blow rent her from the bow to quarter?
Or would the aft compartments still intact
Give buoyancy enough to counteract
The open forward holds?
                              The carpenter's
Second report had offered little chance,
And panic—heart of God—the passengers,
The fourteen hundred—seven hundred packed
In steerage—seven hundred immigrants!
Smith thought of panic clutching at their throats,
And feared that Balkan scramble for the boats.

No call from bridge, no whistle, no alarm
Was sounded. Have the stewards quietly
Inform the passengers: no vital harm,
Precautions merely for emergency;
Collision? Yes, but nature of the blow
Must not be told: not even the crew must know:

Yet all on deck with lifebelts, and boats ready,
The sailors at the falls, and all hands steady.

• • •

And was there not the *Californian*?
Many had seen her smoke just over there,
But two hours past—it seemed a harbour span—
So big, so close, she could be hailed, they said;
She must have heard the signals, seen the flare
Of those white stars and changed at once her course.
There under the *Titanic*'s foremast head,
A lamp from the look-out cage was flashing Morse.

No ship afloat, unless deaf, blind and dumb
To those three sets of signals but would come.
And when the whiz of a rocket bade men turn
Their faces to each other in concern
At shattering facts upon the deck, they found
Their hearts take reassurance with the sound
Of the violins from the gymnasium, where
The bandsmen in their blithe insouciance
Discharged the sudden tension of the air
With the fox-trot's sublime irrelevance.

The fo'c'sle had gone under the creep
Of the water. Though without a wind, a lop
Was forming on the wells now fathoms deep.
The seventy feet—the boat deck's normal drop—
Was down to ten. Rising, falling, and waiting,
Rising again, the swell that edged and curled
Around the second bridge, over the top
Of the air-shafts, backed, resurged and whirled
Into the stokehold through the fiddley grating.

Under the final strain the two wire guys
Of the forward funnel tugged and broke at the eyes:
With buckled plates the stack leaned, fell and smashed
The starboard wing of the flying bridge, went through

The lower, then tilting at the davits crashed
Over, driving a wave aboard that drew
Back to the sea some fifty sailors and
The captain with the last of the bridge command.

Out on the water was the same display
Of fear and self-control as on the deck—
Challenge and hesitation and delay,
The quick return, the will to save, the race
Of snapping oars to put the realm of space
Between the half-filled lifeboats and the wreck.
The swimmers whom the waters did not take

With their instant death-chill struck out for the wake
Of the nearer boats, gained on them, hailed
The steersmen and were saved: the weaker failed
And flagged and sank. A man clutched at the rim
Of a gunwale, and a woman's jewelled fist
Struck at his face: two others seized his wrist,
As he released his hold, and gathering him
Over the side, they staunched the cut from the ring.
And there were many deeds envisaging
Volitions where self-preservation fought
Its red primordial struggle with the 'ought,'
In those high moments when the gambler tossed
Upon the chance and uncomplaining lost.

Aboard the ship, whatever hope of dawn
Gleamed from the *Carpathia*'s riding lights was gone,
For every knot was matched by each degree
Of list. The stern was lifted bodily
When the bow had sunk three hundred feet, and set
Against the horizon stars in silhouette
Were the blade curves of the screws, hump of the rudder.
The downward pull and after buoyancy
Held her a minute poised but for a shudder
That caught her frame as with the upward stroke
Of the sea a boiler or bulkhead broke.

Climbing the ladders, gripping shroud and stay,
Storm rail, ringbolt or fairlead, every place
That might befriend the clutch of hand or brace
Of foot, the fourteen hundred made their way
To the heights of the aft decks, crowding the inches
Around the docking bridge and cargo winches.
And now that last salt tonic which had kept
The valour of the heart alive—the bows
Of the immortal seven that had swept
The strings to outplay, outdie their orders, ceased.
Five minutes more, the angle had increased

From eighty on to ninety when the rows
Of deck and port-hole lights went out, flashed back
A brilliant second and again went black.
Another bulkhead crashed, then following
The passage of the engines as they tore
From their foundations, taking everything
Clean through the bows from 'midships with a roar
Which drowned all cries upon the deck and shook
The watchers in the boats, the liner took
Her thousand fathoms journey to her grave.

The poetry of E. J. Pratt is generally regarded as Canada's most important narrative poetry. *Towards the Last Spike* (1952) deals with the building of the transcontinental railway in Canada. Many of the poems, like *The Titanic* (1935), echo central Victorian themes such as the conflict between humans and nature. (*Born Western Bay, Newfoundland 1882; died 1964*)

(*Responding Activities pp. 102–103*)

Doctor's Journal Entry *for August 6, 1945*

♪ Vikram Seth

Learning Goals

- analyze character of a narrator
- examine point of view and its effects
- understand effects of rhythm
- write a comparison-contrast essay

The morning stretched calm, beautiful, and warm.
Sprawling half clad, I gazed out at the form
Of shimmering leaves and shadows. Suddenly
A strong flash, then another, startled me.
I saw the old stone lantern brightly lit.
Magnesium flares? While I debated it,
The roof, the walls and, as it seemed, the world
Collapsed in timber and debris, dust swirled
Around me—in the garden now—and, weird,
My drawers and undershirt had disappeared.
A splinter jutted from my mangled thigh.
My right side bled, my cheek was torn, and I
Dislodged, detachedly, a piece of glass,
All the time wondering what had come to pass.
Where was my wife? Alarmed, I gave a shout,
'Where are you, Yecko-san?' My blood gushed out.
The artery in my neck? Scared for my life,
I called out, panic-stricken, to my wife.
Pale, bloodstained, frightened, Yecko-san emerged,
Holding her elbow. 'We'll be fine,' I urged—
'Let's get out quickly.' Stumbling to the street
We fell, tripped up by something at our feet.
I gasped out, when I saw it was a head:
'Excuse me, please excuse me—' He was dead:
A gate had crushed him. There we stood, afraid.
A house standing before us tilted, swayed,
Toppled, and crashed. Fire sprang up in the dust,
Spread by the wind. It dawned on us we must
Get to the hospital: we needed aid—
And I should help my staff too. (Though this made
Sense to me then, I wonder how I could
Have hoped, hurt as I was, to do much good.)

My legs gave way. I sat down on the ground.
Thirst seized me, but no water could be found.
My breath was short, but bit by bit my strength
Seemed to revive, and I got up at length.
I was still naked, but I felt no shame.
This thought disturbed me somewhat, till I came
Upon a soldier, standing silently,
Who gave the towel round his neck to me.
My legs, stiff with dried blood, rebelled. I said
To Yecko-san she must go on ahead.
She did not wish to, but in our distress
What choice had we? A dreadful loneliness
Came over me when she had gone. My mind
Ran at high speed, my body crept behind.
I saw the shadowy forms of people, some
Were ghosts, some scarecrows, all were wordless dumb—
Arms stretched straight out, shoulder to dangling hand;
It took some time for me to understand
The friction on their burns caused so much pain
They feared to chafe flesh against flesh again.
Those who could, shuffled in a blank parade
Towards the hospital. I saw, dismayed,
A woman with a child stand in my path—
Both naked. Had they come back from the bath?
I turned my gaze, but was at a loss
That she should stand thus, till I came across
A naked man—and now the thought arose
That some strange thing had stripped us of our clothes.
The face of an old woman on the ground
Was marred with suffering, but she made no sound.
Silence was common to us all. I heard
No cries of anguish, or a single word.

(Responding Activities pp. 103–104)

᠗ Poet, novelist, and travel writer Vikram Seth's collections include *The Humble Administrator's
Garden* (1985), *The Golden Gate* (1986), and *All You Who Sleep Tonight* (1990), which contains
"Doctor's Journal Entry 1945." He also wrote *A Suitable Boy* (1993), a novel about families
living in a turbulent post-Independence India. *(Born Calcutta, India 1952)*

Coyote Goes to Toronto

⁊ Thomas King

Learning Goals

- understand the trickster character
- interpret symbols
- consider an author's use of upper case letters
- create a storyboard and an original verse

Coyote went to Toronto
        to become famous.
It's TRUE
        that's what she said.

She walked up and down those
        FAMOUS streets,
And she stood on those
        FAMOUS corners.

Waiting.

But nothing happened.

so.
Coyote got hungry and went
        into a restaurant
        to EAT.

But there was a long line
        and Coyote could see it was
        because the restaurant was
        painted a BEAUTIFUL green.

so.
Coyote painted herself GREEN
        and she went back to the rez
        to show the people what an
        UP-TO-DATE Coyote she was.

And she stood on the rez
    and waited.
So that RAIN came along.
So that WIND came along.
So that HAIL came along.
So that SNOW came along.

And that PAINT began to peel
    and pretty soon the people
    came along and says,
HEY, that's Coyote, by golly
    she's not looking too good.

And the women brought her FOOD.
And the men brushed her COAT
    until it was shiney.
And the children PLAYED with
    their friend.

I been to Toronto Coyote tells
    the people.
Yes, everybody says,
We can SEE that.

Of Cherokee and Greek ancestry, Thomas King was raised in California but has spent much of his adult life in Canada as a Canadian citizen. King's short stories, some of which are collected in *One Good Story, That One* (1993), often employ coyote trickster figures and Aboriginal storytellers. His second novel, *Green Grass, Running Water* (1993), was shortlisted for a Governor General's Award, as was his children's book *A Coyote Columbus Story* (1992). *(Born Sacramento, California 1943)*

(Responding Activities p. 104)

RESPONDING ACTIVITIES
Narrative and Dramatic Poems (pages 84–100)

Beowulf – Anglo-Saxon Epic

Meaning

1. With a partner, summarize the essence of each verse paragraph. Then retell the story in your own words.

2. How is Beowulf described in the excerpt? What ideals of a great hero does he exemplify? Support your answer with direct references from the text.

Form and Style

3. a) *Alliteration* is one of the most obvious literary devices found in this excerpt. Work in groups of four. Assign verses 1 and 2, 3 and 4, 5 and 6, 7 and 8 to each member of your group. Each group member becomes an expert on his or her assigned piece and lists the three strongest examples of alliteration from his or her section. Keep in mind that the examples you choose must contribute a sound, image, or create clarity.

   b) Rewrite the three examples you chose without the alliteration. Which would be easier to remember if you were a storyteller in Viking times? Why would it be an asset if lines were easier to remember?

4. Examine the first two verse paragraphs. What words and images describe the Danish warriors? What words and images describe the characteristics of the monster Grendel? How do these descriptions set the stage for the events that follow in this excerpt?

Creative Extension

5. With the introduction of Beowulf, the poem begins a cycle of vengeance. Beowulf will exact revenge from Grendel for the 12 years of terror he reigned on Hrothgar's hall, and then Grendel's mother will exact her revenge. Create your own 12- to 16-line verse paragraph following the Anglo-Saxon style. In those lines continue the general progression of the narrative or recount the battle with Grendel.

6. Write an *elegy* for Beowulf to be read at his sending off. Remember as you write that he was a grand hero, one who saved a neighbouring tribe and died trying to save his tribe from dragons some 40 years later. The choice of language should be formal and elevated in tone and structure. Present a dramatic reading of your elegy or record it on audiotape for others to hear.

The Listeners – Walter de la Mare

Meaning

1. a) Who do you think the listeners are? What details in the poem lead you to this conclusion? Who are the people referred to as "them" in line 27?
    b) Why do you think the Traveller goes to the place where the listeners are?
    c) What is the effect of so many uncertainties in this poem?

2. Describe the dwelling place of the listeners, inside and outside. What mood is created by the description of the setting? Explain your answer.

Form and Style

3. What sounds describe the Traveller's activities and his horse's activities? What sounds describe the listener's activities? What mood is created by the contrast?

4. An *allegory* is a narrative in which the characters, events, and sometimes the setting have both a literal and symbolic meaning. Revisit your answers to question 1 above. What are the literal answers? What could they symbolize? Is this poem an allegory? Support your opinion.

Creative Extension

5. Create a visual representation of "The Listeners." Include images from the poem and use the layout, style, and colour of your art to convey the mood and symbolic meanings. Design a one- to two-page written analysis of your visual explaining how you used various techniques to express the meaning and mood of the poem.

6. Write the reply from the listeners to the Traveller. Use setting, sounds, and behaviours of the characters to create a consistent mood in your poem. Although Walter de la Mare uses the third-person, use the first-person point of view and assume the role of one of the listeners. Some of the questions your poem might explore are:
    •   Why don't they answer the door?
    •   Why don't they speak?
    •   What is their relationship to the people the traveller refers to as them?
    •   Is the Traveller as mysterious to the listeners as the listeners are to him?
    •   How do they see and perceive him?
    Present a dramatic reading of your poem.

The Titanic – E. J. Pratt

Meaning

1. As a class or in small groups, answer the questions Who? Where? When? and What happened? for each stanza of the poem. Make point-form notes of your answers.

2. Discuss why the author wrote this poem? What themes and ideas did he want to communicate to the reader?

Form and Style

3. Choose one section of the poem. Identify specific techniques the poet uses to communicate the theme and action (e.g., metaphors, similes, different types of sentences or length of lines, use of punctuation). For each technique you identify, explain its effects on meaning and on you as a reader.

4. E. J. Pratt uses a number of special terms related to ships and the sea. Identify five of these terms and explain their meaning, either from the context or by looking them up in a dictionary. Explain how the term contributes to the meaning of the passage in which it occurs. Why do you think Pratt used these terms?

Creative Extension

5. Prepare and present a dramatic reading of a section from the poem. Use pitch, pace, volume, gestures, facial expressions, and sustained eye contact to emphasize the mood and theme of your section.

6. Research the facts on the sinking of the *Titanic*. Which facts did Pratt incorporate in his poem? What facts did he change, delete, or add? Speculate on the purposes for the changes that he made. Write a report on your findings.

Doctor's Journal Entry 1945 – Vikram Seth

Meaning

1. a) Just after the narrator and his wife decide it is best she go ahead without him, he says, "A dreadful loneliness / Came over me when she had gone. My mind / Ran at high speed, my body crept behind." What thoughts do you think ran through his mind at high speed? What makes you think this?

b) The narrator quotes his own speech only three times in the poem. What do the phrases he quotes tell you about his character?

2. Why does the poem conclude with an emphasis on silence? "The face of an old woman on the ground / Was marred with suffering, but she made no sound. / Silence was common to us all. I heard / No cries of anguish, or a single word."

Form and Style

3. Why does the poet use the first-person point of view? What effect does his assuming the role of a doctor during this event have on the tone of the poem?

4. Choose a six-line segment from the poem and describe the rhythm of the lines. How does the rhythm contribute to the meaning? What effect does the rhythm have on you as the reader? Read the lines aloud as you consider your answer.

Creative Extension

5. Write an essay comparing and contrasting Seth's poem, "Doctor's Journal Entry" with Joy Kogawa's "Hiroshima Exit" (pp. 60–61). How do these authors use point of view, symbolism, and stylistic devices such as dialogue and questions to develop their ideas about the bombing of Hiroshima?

6. Present a dramatic reading of this poem. Use pitch, pace, volume, gestures, and facial expression to reinforce the mood and the characterization of the doctor. Use sustained eye contact to emphasize the key lines of the poem. Consider adding sound effects and music.

Coyote Goes to Toronto – Thomas King

Meaning

1. How would you describe the character of Coyote in this poem? List several traits and identify the actions or behaviours that suggest these traits. Use a web or T-chart to record your responses.

2. What role does the rez (reserve) community play in this poem?

Form and Style

3. a) What purpose do the natural elements—rain, wind, hail, and snow—have in the middle of the poem?
   b) What does the green paint symbolize? Why do you think King chose green and not some other colour? Support your interpretations.

4. List the words that appear in all upper case letters throughout the poem. What might King's reasons have been for putting these words in upper case?

Creative Extension

5. With a partner, create a storyboard for King's poem. Use camera angles, movements, composition, and a variety of camera shots to convey King's satiric portrayal of Coyote. Choose music to reinforce the tone, and incorporate sound effects. Write a covering memo explaining how the techniques you used reflect your interpretation of the message and tone of King's poem.

6. Write your own legend in verse using an animal to satirize human follies and weaknesses. Select an animal carefully, noting its characteristics and how those could be exaggerated to shed light on frailties and foibles found in human personalities. Present a dramatic reading of your poem.

Journeys

❧

Can a journey change us so much that we never feel at home again?

Journeys, and the experiences we have on them, can sometimes change us for life. How can we deal with these experiences? How do they change us? In this Echo, poems, a song, a painting, a prologue to a modern novel, and an illustrated map offer several perspectives on these universal questions.

Learning Goals

- analyze presentation of theme in a variety of genres
- recognize how differences in form and style influence response
- create original texts in response to a variety of works

Ulysses

❧ *Alfred Lord Tennyson*

In the following poem, Tennyson imagines the young Greek hero Ulysses as an aging warrior. Ulysses' great adventures, originally told in Homer's poem The Odyssey, *are a distant memory. Ulysses is discontent with his present role as king of Ithaca and tries to persuade his Mariners to leave Ithaca and join him in his search for new adventures and experiences.*

> It little profits that an idle king,
> By this still hearth, among these barren crags,
> Matched with an aged wife,[1] I mete and dole
> Unequal laws unto a savage race,
> That hoard, and sleep, and feed, and know not me.
> I cannot rest from travel; I will drink
> Life to the lees. All times I have enjoy'd

---

[1] wife = Penelope

Greatly, have suffer'd greatly, both with those
That loved me, and alone; on shore, and when
Through scudding drifts the rainy Hyades[2]
Vexed the dim sea. I am become a name;
For always roaming with a hungry heart
Much have I seen and known,—city of men
And manners, climates, councils, governments,
Myself not least, but honoured of them all—
And drunk delight of battle with my peers,
Far on the ringing plains of windy Troy.
I am a part of all that I have met;
Yet all experience is an arch wherethrough,
Gleams that untravelled world whose margin fades
For ever and for ever when I move.
How dull it is to pause, to make an end,
To rust unburnished, not to shine in use!
As though to breathe were life! Life piled on life
Where all too little, and of one to me
Little remains; but every hour is saved
From that eternal silence, something more,
A bringer of new things; and vile it were
From some three suns to store and hoard myself,
And this gray spirit yearning in desire
To follow knowledge like a sinking star,
Beyond the utmost bound of human thought.

    This is my son, mine own Telemachus,
To whom I leave the scepter and the isle—
Well-loved of me, discerning to fulfill
This labour, by slow prudence to make mild
A rugged people, and through soft degrees
Subdue them to the useful and the good.
Most blameless is he, centred in the sphere
Of common duties, decent not to fail
In offices of tenderness, and pay
Meet adoration to my household gods,
When I am gone. He works his work, I mine.

---

[2] Hyades = stars whose setting marked the beginning of rainy weather

There lies the port; the vessel puffs her sail;
There gloom the dark, broad seas. My mariners,
Souls that have toiled, and wrought, and thought with me—
That ever with a frolic welcome took
The thunder and the sunshine, and opposed
Free hearts, free foreheads,—you and I are old;
Old age hath yet his honour and his toil.
Death closes all; but something ere the end,
Some work of noble note, may yet be done,
Not unbecoming men that strove with Gods.
The lights begin to twinkle from the rocks;
The long day wanes; the slow moon climbs; the deep
Moans round with many voices. Come, my friends,
'Tis not too late to seek a newer world.
Push off, and sitting well in order smite
The sounding furrows; for my purpose holds
To sail beyond the sunset, and the baths
Of all the western stars, until I die.
It may be that the gulfs will wash us down;
It may be we shall touch the Happy Isles,
And see the great Achilles,[3] whom we knew.
Though much is taken, much abides; and though
We are not now that strength which in old days
Moved earth and heaven, that which we are, we are—
One equal temper of heroic hearts,
Made weak by time and fate, but strong in will
To strive, to seek, to find, and not to yield.

Alfred Lord Tennyson is one of the best-known English poets of the Victorian Age. He is famous for the majestic and musical quality of his verse and for such narrative and dramatic poems as "The Charge of the Light Brigade," "The Lady of Shalott," and "Idylls of the King," a series of 12 poems based on the legends of King Arthur and his Knights. "Ulysses" was written in 1842. Tennyson was poet laureate of Great Britain from 1850 to 1892. *(Born England 1809; died 1892)*

---

[3] Achilles = a great Greek hero in the Trojan War

RESPONDING

Meaning

1. In groups, discuss the meaning of the following lines. Take into account the context within which these words are spoken.
   a) I will drink life to the lees
   b) Yet all experience is an arch
   c) As though to breathe were life!
   d) Old age hath yet his honour and his toil.

2. What is Ulysses' attitude toward:
   a) his son, Telemachus
   b) his wife, Penelope
   c) himself
   d) his people
   e) foreign lands

Form and Style

3. This poem is a *dramatic monologue*, in which one person speaks to a silent listener at a critical moment in his or her life and unintentionally reveals his or her character. What are some of those unintentionally revealed character traits? Provide proof in your response.

4. Tennyson creates clear similes and metaphors to help the reader visualize Ulysses, Telemachus, and the planned voyage. If you were to create a visual to represent each of the three verse paragraphs, around what line/lines would each focus? Describe in words the visual representation you imagine, or create an actual sketch or collage.

Creative Extension

5. Assume the character of Telemachus, Ulysses' son, and create your own interpretation of his reaction to his father's leaving.

6. Assign one verse paragraph to each member of a three-person team. As preparation to read aloud in sequence to the class, practice the oral reading of your assigned section. Be aware of tone, punctuation, voice expression, and gestures as you practice. Pay attention to how all of these elements can help to convey meaning.

The Forbidden City

ꏳ *William Bell*

This excerpt is from the Prologue of a contemporary novel written by Canadian author William Bell. The main character Alex accompanies his father, a photographer for the CBC, to China to record a state visit. Instead, Alex and his father become embroiled in the Tiannamen Square massacre and the experience has a profound effect on Alex.

Prologue

We studied a poem in English class last spring and, believe it or not, I've been thinking about it a lot lately. It's about a young soldier-king named Ulysses who sails off to fight a long bitter war in a far away country. On his sea-journey home he gets battered off course a few times and endures many adventures. When he finally drags himself out of the waves and onto his own shores he's a lot older than he was the day he left. In more ways than one.

The thing is, he doesn't fit anymore. His adventures have changed him so much that the island kingdom he missed so much seems like a pile of rock. His wife and son are strangers. His subjects don't understand him.

I know how Ulysses felt. How relieved he was at first that it was all over and he was safe. How messed up and alienated and alone he must have felt after he had been back for a while.

I'm not saying that what I've written here is like the poem. This is just what I put together from a journal I was keeping when life was pretty calm, and from the notes and tapes I made when everything began to blow apart.

Dad was pretty worried that night when I sort of went mental for a few hours. He seems to think that writing this will help me re-adjust to normal life. I don't know. Maybe he's right.

I can't help thinking about Ulysses, though. Because, at the end of the poem, he takes off. He never did fit in again.

William Bell is a well-known Canadian author of books for young adults. His works include *Crabbe*, *Metal Head*, and *Absolutely Invincible!* He taught in China for two years. Currently, he is a teacher of English and History in Orillia, Ontario.

Connecting

1. How does Alex describe the effects of Ulysses' experiences?
2. Why does Alex identify with Ulysses?
3. Review the first paragraph of this excerpt and the first verse paragraph of "Ulysses." How would you describe the tone of each of these openings? What specific words from each contribute to the tone?
4. The last line of this excerpt, "He never did fit in again"—simple though it is— is very effective. In a reflective journal entry, apply the idea of this sentence to another Echo piece in this section or to another poem in this anthology.

The Quest for Ulysses

In 1986 National Geographic devoted a lengthy section to "The Quest for Ulysses." In this article, twentieth century adventurers describe how they reenacted what they believed to be the actual journey taken by Ulysses. This map creatively represents their travels.

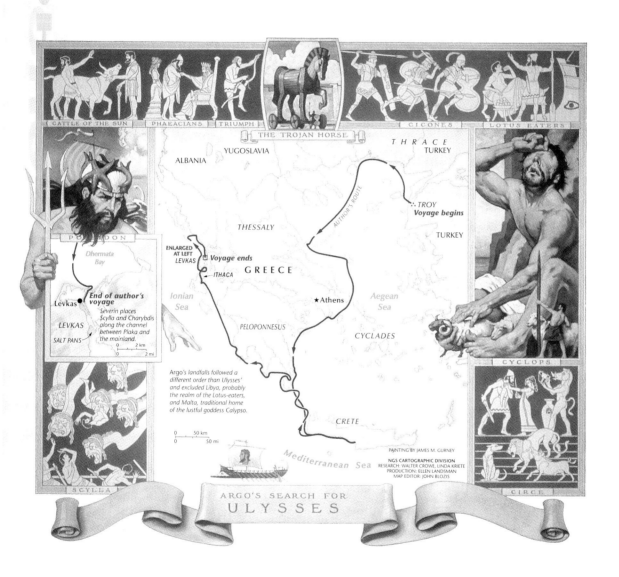

The modern traveller, writer, and filmmaker Tim Severin has launched several expeditions that have shed new light on voyages and adventures from the past. He has crossed the Atlantic in a leather boat to prove that the Irish monk St. Brendan reached North America, he has followed the voyages of mythical heroes Sinbad and Jason of the Golden Fleece, and he has retraced the path of the early Crusaders. His voyages have been recorded in several issues of *National Geographic* and he is the author of many best-selling books.

Connecting

1. Because Ulysses offended one of his gods, he was not permitted to return from the "ringing plains of Troy" until his infant son had become a man. For over a decade he travelled the Mediterranean. Trace his journey on the map. Read the rest of the map including the visuals on the border. How does the map differ from the maps you commonly read? What is the editor's purpose in creating such a map?

2. Research one of the episodes captured within the border of this map. Summarize it and be prepared to assume the persona of Ulysses and 'tell' the class of your adventure and its effects on you.

3. Assume you are one of the *National Geographic* adventurers. In a paragraph or short audio or video recording, explain why you chose "the Quest for Ulysses" assignment.

4. Does your new understanding of Ulysses' actual physical journey affect your view of his character and struggles in Tennyson's poem? If so, how? Explain.

Tales of Brave Ulysses

Eric Clapton and Martin Sharp

This modern song by the British Blues band Cream does not tell a story with a definite beginning and end. It presents instead flashes of powerful and evocative images based on Ulysses' journey.

You thought the leaden winter would bring you down forever,
But you rode upon a steamer to the violence of the sun.

And the colours of the sea blind your eyes with trembling mermaids,
And you touch the distant beaches with tales of brave Ulysses:
How his naked ears were tortured by the sirens sweetly singing,
For the sparkling waves are calling you to kiss their white-laced lips.

And you see a girl's brown body dancing through the turquoise,
And her footprints make you follow where the sky loves the sea.
And when your fingers find her, she drowns you in her body,
Carving deep blue ripples in the tissues of your mind.

The tiny purple fishes run laughing through your fingers,
And you want to ask her with you to the hard land of the winter.

Her name is Aphrodite and she rides a crimson shell,
And you know you cannot leave her for you touched the distant sands
With tales of brave Ulysses; how his naked ears were tortured
By the sirens sweetly singing.

The tiny purple fishes run laughing through your fingers,
And you want to take her with you to the hard land of the winter.

In his early career, contemporary British rock singer Eric Clapton was most interested in Blues music. He formed the Blues band Cream in 1968, which became known for its original music compositions and Clapton's stunning guitar improvisations. Clapton went on to pursue a solo career in 1970. The "Tales of Brave Ulysses" is recorded on the album *The Best of Cream*, Universal Music 2000. *(Born England 1945)*

Connecting

1. Read the lyrics of the song and then in an informal group, discuss the overall mood. What words and phrases contribute to this mood? Then, if possible, listen to the recording of this song and compare your interpretation of the mood created by the words with the effects created by the music.

2. What are the dominant images in this song? What impressions do they create of the journey at the heart of the poem?

3. Scan Tennyson's poem "Ulysses." Which of the images are repeated or at least echoed in the song? What images are different and how are they different?

4. Unlike Tennyson's poem, this song is not presented from a first-person point of view. How does the different voice affect your response to the song?

Ulysses and the Sirens

J.W. Waterhouse

This painting represents the episode in Ulysses' journey when he listens to the tantalizing and hypnotic music of the Sirens who were known to lure ships into the dangerous waters around their island.

The English artist John Waterhouse found the adventures of Ulysses intriguing and based an entire series of paintings on Ulysses' experiences. He also painted scenes from Tennyson's "Lady of Shalott." Waterhouse was influenced by the Pre-Raphaelite school of painters who often focused on literary subjects. *(Born England 1849; died 1917)*

Connecting

1. View the painting with at least two other students. Together decide:
   a) what the focal point of the painting is and who or what it represents
   b) what is happening in this scene
   c) why the dominant colour was chosen and how the colours affect the mood of the painting
   d) what the body language and facial expressions of characters suggest about the artist's interpretation of this scene

2. The artist used paint to elicit an audience response. Use words, and list five adjectives that would prompt a similar response.

3. In Tennyson's poem, Ulysses states, "I am part of all I have met." Carefully view this painting and in a journal entry, explain how those words find expression in this visual. Speculate further to suggest how these words could be applied to Ulysses' life experience.

Penelope's Despair

Yannis Ritsos

While her husband Ulysses experiences life outside of Ithaca for 20 years, his wife Penelope rules his kingdom and is forced to rely on herself and her wits to survive in a man's world. The journey she undertakes is different from his, but it is just as powerful.

Not that she didn't recognize him in the dim light of the fire;
it wasn't that he was disguised, wearing rags like a beggar.
No. There were clear signs:
the scar on the knee-cap, his strength, the cunning look.
Frightened, leaning against the wall, she sought for some excuse,
a delay, to avoid answering so as not to give herself up.
Was it for him she had wasted twenty years waiting and dreaming?
Was it for this wretched stranger, soaked in blood, with his white beard?
She fell speechless on a chair.
She looked closely at the slaughtered suitors on the floor
as if looking at her own dead desires
and she said 'welcome'
her voice sounding to her as if coming from a distance, as if belonging to
    someone else.
Her loom in the corner cast shadows across the ceiling like a cage,
the birds she had woven with bright red threads among green leaves
suddenly turned gray and black
flying low on her flat sky.

Translation: Nikos Stangos

Yannis Ritsos is one of the most celebrated of modern Greek poets. He has published over 40 volumes of poetry and translations. Because of his leftist politics, he was imprisoned for long periods of time in his native Greece and was also forced into exile. (Born 1909)

Connecting

1. This poem presents a modern view of Penelope. How does the poem portray Ulysses' wife? Support your answer.

2. What is the dominant image in this poem? How effective is this image in the characterization of Penelope and her journey? Explain.

3. Do some research to find out more about the actual character of Penelope in the original Greek myth. Then in a paragraph of 50–70 words, contrast the mythical wife with the Penelope in this poem.

4. Recall Ulysses' description of his wife and his attitude toward her in Tennyson's poem. If Ritsos had written this poem in Tennyson's time (the Victorian Age), how do you think it would have been different? Why?

REFLECTING ON THE ECHO

1. You have read and studied various artists' interpretations of Ulysses' journey and how it changed him. Choose another work (poem, article, painting, etc.) that in your view provides another perspective on the journeys theme. Write a short interpretation of this selection. Discuss the techniques the artist or writer uses to express the theme and their effect on you as a reader or viewer.

2. In your library or on the Internet, research other works in the Ulysses series by J. W. Waterhouse. Which of these would you have chosen to include in this Echo section? Why?

3. Imagine you are an editor of *National Geographic* and you could commission a similar map to the one in this Echo section based on a literary journey. What would that journey be? What visuals would you weave around the border of the map? Think about stories, novels, or poems you have read. Sketch out a plan or layout for your chosen map.

Ladybird *(a memory of my mother)*

Ingrid Jonker

Learning Goals

• analyze effective use of comparisons

• interpret tone and attitude

• recognize how techniques such as euphony and dissonance affect meaning

• design a poster and write a comparison-contrast essay

Gleam ochre
and a light breaks
out of the sea.
In the backyard
somewhere among the washing
and a tree full of pomegranates
your laugh in the morning
sudden and small
is like a ladybird
fallen on my hand

South African poet Ingrid Jonker spent time in an orphanage after her mother's death. Her poetry often deals with loss. She is also noted for her love poems. Her most noted work is *Rook en Oker* ("Smoke and Ochre") (1963). English translations of her work appear in *Selected Poems* (1968). *(Born South Africa 1933; died 1965)*

(Responding Activities p. 124)

Sunset

᪗ Oswald Mtshali

Learning Goals

- analyze effective use of comparisons
- interpret tone and attitude
- recognize how techniques such as euphony and dissonance affect meaning
- design a poster and write a comparison-contrast essay

The sun spun like
a tossed coin.
It whirled on the azure sky,
it clattered into the horizon,
it clicked in the slot,
and neon-lights popped
and blinked 'Time expired,' as on a parking meter.

᪗ Oswald Mtshali's poems often express his political concerns, particularly his rage and frustration over the situation of Black people ghettoized in South Africa especially before the fall of apartheid. His voice was first heard in *The Sound of a Cowhide Drum* (1971), where "Sunset" appeared, and later in *Fireflames* (1980). *(Born Vryheid, South Africa 1940)*

(Responding Activities p. 124)

histles

Ted Hughes

Learning Goals

- analyze patterns of imagery
- relate imagery to development of theme
- recognize effective use of different sentence lengths
- write a review and original poem

Against the rubber tongues of cows and the hoeing hands of men
Thistles spike the summer air
Or crackle open under a blue-black pressure.

Every one a revengeful burst
Of resurrection, a grasped fistful
Of splintered weapons and Icelandic frost thrust up

From the underground stain of a decayed Viking.
They are like pale hair and the gutturals of dialects.
Every one manages a plume of blood.

Then they grow grey, like men
Mown down, it is a feud. Their sons appear,
Stiff with weapons, fighting back over the same ground.

Ted Hughes was named Poet Laureate of England in 1984. He published his first collection, *Hawk in the Rain* in 1957, one year after he married well-known American poet Sylvia Plath. Subsequent collections include *Crow* (1970) and *Moortown* (1979). He also wrote children's books and plays for children and adults. (*Born Yorkshire, England 1930; died 1998*)

(Responding Activities pp. 124–125)

ands

ℰ Lorna Crozier

Learning Goals

- assess the impact of images and metaphors
- examine the use of foreshadowing
- consider the effects of personification
- create a collage or a video

1

Hands are always travelling.
See the maps on their palms,
forks in the road,
migratory crossings.

When the lights go out
in the neighbourhood,
they go off in the rain
without an umbrella.

They head into a blizzard
with no weather report,
no survival kit.

So what if their shoes
are full of holes,
they don't need them.

In the middle of the night,
blind and naked,
they go their way.

2

Where are they going?
To the place where their lifelines meet.

Will they come back?
If you leave them a skein of wool,
a water basin, a little colour
for their nails when the moon
goes out.

3

While you sleep, your hands
build a city, a house,
a church with a steeple.
Inside there is a funeral.
One hand preaches, the other
lies in a pocket. Inside
there is a wedding.
One holds a ring,
the other weeps in a closed room.
The right never knows
what the left is doing.

4

In each hand
the sound of the sea,
wind in a hollow
skull, the sound of
a thought beginning.
Cup one to your ear.
It will whisper
what the palm says
to the fortune teller,
what the thumb says
to its family of fingers.

5

They turn so easily
into animals, into shadows
of animals dancing on a wall.
There is a hare, a fox
hunting a hare, a cariboo,
its antlers full of singing birds.

The hands themselves are singing.
Listen: each finger is a choirboy
with a red face, his voice
on the verge of changing.

6

The sky is full of hands:
the five fingers
                    the points of a star,
each nail glowing with its own light,
its own small moon
that never rises.

7

The left hand is a trickster.
From behind your ear
it plucks coins, roses,
memories of another country,
another age. It is always
night, the windows shuttered.
The hand walks the streets
like a soldier,
broad-shouldered and swaggering,
making you stay inside.
You don't know if this is now
or long ago.

8

The right hand is a changeling.
You find it by your door
in a willow basket.
Its nails are pink.
Someone has scraped away
its fingerprints.
It is as innocent
as anything
you've ever seen.

9

Two hands.
Open   close,
come together.

Closer to the dead,
the living,
            than you.
They cut the birth cord,
they wash the body.

They tie the laces
of your first
            your last
pair of shoes.

The poems of Lorna Crozier combine humour, craft, and accessibility. Both *The Garden Going on Without Us* (1985) and *Angels of Flesh, Angels of Silence* (1989) were nominated for Governor General's Awards. *Inventing the Hawk* (1992) received a Governor General's Award. "Hands" appears in *Angels of Flesh, Angels of Silence. (Born Swift Current, Saskatchewan 1941)*

(Responding Activities pp. 125–126)

Knister's Plowman in Winter

ᔑ Robert Gibbs

Learning Goals

- paraphrase meaning
- recognize how form affects content
- create an illustration or cartoon
- write a short comparison-contrast essay

Someday, someday be sure
I shall turn the furrow of all my hopes
But I shall not, doing it, look backward.
                    Raymond Knister

The bright skier chalking up his errors
            in and out the charcoal marks of trees
must wish at times to leave his snows
            as they fell
            unmarked
must at times reverse
            the film his friends have made and see
himself back crazily
            up and off his hills
racing to erase himself
            and yet
there must be that too in front of him
            to think about
the clean new hills of snows on snows
unfallen.

ᔑ   Robert Gibbs has long been associated with the prestigious Canadian literary journal *The Fiddlehead*. He taught English at the University of New Brunswick until his retirement. His subtle and witty poetry collections include *The Road From Here* (1968) and *Earth Aches* (1991). He published "Knister's Plowman in Winter" in *Earth Charms Heard So Early* (1970). He also writes short stories and edits anthologies. *(Born Saint John, New Brunswick 1930)*

(Responding Activities p. 126)

RESPONDING ACTIVITIES
Metaphor And Imagery (pages 116–123)

Ladybird – Ingrid Jonker; Sunset – Oswald Mtshali
(a comparison)

Meaning

1. Both of these poets use unusual comparisons that are fresh and memorable. What is compared in each poem? What qualities do the two things being compared share?

2. What is the purpose of the poet's comparison? (Hint: Think about what Mtshali's simile might say about the apartheid system).

Form and Style

3. a) What aspects of nature and human activities are connected in each poem?
   b) What is the poet's attitude toward nature?
   c) What is the poet's attitude toward human nature?
   d) What words or images support your interpretation of the poet's tone or attitude?

4. a) What sounds are repeated throughout Jonker's poem? How does this *euphonic* sound reinforce the author's meaning?
   b) Define *dissonance*. What dissonant sounds are repeated throughout Mtshali's poem? How does this reinforce the author's meaning?

Creative Extension

5. Design a poster of "Sunset" or "Ladybird." Draw, paint, or construct a collage. Include images from the poem and use the layout, colour, and style in your art to convey the poet's ideas and feelings. Include a theme statement for the poem and picture. Explain how you have used colour, layout, and style in your visual to develop the theme and tone of the poem.

6. Write an essay comparing and contrasting "Sunset" to "Ladybird." Consider how Mtshali and Jonker use imagery, symbols, and sound to emphasize their ideas (themes) or their feelings (tone).

Thistles – Ted Hughes

Meaning

1. a) List the words and images related to fighting and battle in the poem. After each one, explain why it is appropriate to describe thistles this way. What impression of thistles is created through the extended metaphor?
   b) In a two-column chart, note words or phrases that suggest life and words or phrases that suggest death. How are these related to the thistle in Hughes's poem?

2. Identify a word that, in your opinion, summarizes Hughes's point about thistles. Support your choice with evidence from the poem.

Form and Style

3. Hughes uses a variety of sentence lengths to great effect.
   a) What is the shortest sentence? Why does Hughes use it here?
   b) What is the longest sentence? What effect does it create?

4. List the first three words that start each sentence in the poem. How many different ways does Hughes start his sentences? Why are there so many kinds of sentences in a relatively short poem?

Creative Extension

5. Write a short review of this poem for a school newspaper or class magazine. Summarize your impressions of the poem (the effects it had on you as a reader). Support your views with references to specific techniques the poet used.

6. Write a poem using a different plant or a weed as an extended metaphor (e.g., poison ivy, dandelion, ragweed). Research the plant, list its qualities, and note details about its life cycle. Think about what the traits and life cycle of this plant could reveal about human nature. Which characteristic is one of its key traits? What is your attitude or feeling toward this trait? What words or phrases could you use to describe the plant and at the same time reveal your attitude toward it?

   Write your poem using Hughes's poem as a model. Use the same types of phrases. You may want to begin each line of your poem with the same word Hughes does. Refer to humans or plants in the same places.

Hands – Lorna Crozier

Meaning

1. Quote three parts of this poem that made the strongest impression on you and explain why. A part may be a line, several lines, or a stanza. Identify the image and the metaphor that is at work in each section you chose.

2. a) Work with a partner. For each section of the poem, summarize Crozier's description of hands and the qualities of hands that she emphasizes.
   b) In stanza 9, Crozier reminds us that we take all that hands do for granted by showing how they touch new life and take care of the dead. What lines earlier in the poem best foreshadow this conclusion? Justify your choice.

Form and Style

3. In several sections of the poem, Crozier uses images related to palmistry, fortune telling, and astrology. Note the images, and explain their significance when taken together as a group.

4. Identify at least four examples of *personification* in the poem. Explain why you think the poet uses this technique.

5. Create a collage of Crozier's poem. Include a number of images from the poem and use the layout to convey the poem's form and structure. Use style and colour to convey the narrator's attitudes about hands. Explain how you have used style, colour, and layout, in your illustrations to reinforce Crozier's tone and ideas.

6. Working in a small group, create a video of Crozier's poem. You could include a reading of the poem and as many of Crozier's images as you can. Use music and sound effects along with varied camera shots, movements, and angles to suggest the tone and mood of Crozier's poem.

Knister's Plowman in Winter – Robert Gibbs

Meaning

1. a) Explain the quote by Canadian poet Raymond Knister in your own words. What does it mean to "turn the furrow"?
    b) Paraphrase Gibbs's poem. What does he say about errors, and having friends witness one's errors?

2. a) Explain how each poet's view is a metaphor of life's course.
    b) What metaphor would you create to represent your own life's path?

Form and Style

3. How do both Knister and Gibbs become co-authors of this poem?

4. Describe the layout of Gibbs's poem. What does the layout suggest to you? How does the form of the poem become an extension of the poem's content?

Creative Extension

5. Create an illustration or cartoon of Knister's plowman or Gibbs's skier as a visual representation of your response to question 2 a). Share your interpretation with a partner.

6. In a short essay, compare and contrast the plowman's view of the path to that of the skier's.

rama

Harold Pinter on drama:

I've always maintained that the life of any play consists in its dramatic authenticity, if it's true to itself. Something is being said, but the playwright isn't necessarily saying it. It's the play that's saying it . . . . That's why it's such a delicate enterprise in the first place. All the component parts that have come together, to be integrated: the actors, director, the design, the words, the lighting, the whole structure of the event. When it all comes together, it's thrilling.

Romance and Realism

❧

Does love really conquer all?

The Prioress, one of the most memorable characters in English literature, appeared in *The Canterbury Tales* written by Geoffrey Chaucer in about 1386. This famous character, one of several pilgrims travelling from London to Canterbury, wore a broach imprinted with the Latin motto *"Amor Vincit Omnia"* meaning *"Love conquers all."* This Echo section presents a drama, a cartoon, poems, a newspaper column, and a non-fiction excerpt to explore different perspectives on romance. When we consider loving relationships in our lives, is it important to be realistic? Does love really conquer all?

Learning Goals

- examine a theme from different perspectives
- compare and contrast different forms, styles, and techniques
- relate textual details and organizational patterns to an author's purpose
- create original works based on a theme

Salt-Water Moon

❧ *David French*

In the following excerpt from a David French play, a young man returns from Toronto to Newfoundland in 1926 to win the heart of a young woman, a former girlfriend, who is now engaged to another man. The play interweaves aspects of romance and realism.

The Characters:
Mary Snow
Jacob Mercer

The Place:
The front porch and yard of the Dawe's summer house in Coley's Point, Newfoundland.

The Time:
An August night in 1926.

The front porch of a house that was built in the last half of the nineteenth century, probably by a ship's captain or local merchant. It has a solid feel about it, this porch. You just know that the interior of the house would consist of oak banisters and newel posts, wide halls and high ceilings. And that every timber was hand-chosen and pit-sawn and constructed by men who built houses the way they built boats—to last.

On stage right of the porch is a rocker.

There is not much of a yard, because they built their houses close to the sea in those days to make easy access to the waters where they made their living. In fact, the house stands quite close to a road that runs in front of it, a gravel road skirting the rocky embankment that holds back the sea. Some indication of this road should be on the set, though it need not be realistic.

It is a lovely night in August, 1926. A warm night in this tiny outport at the edge of the sea, a night lit by the full moon and a sky full of stars.

At rise: MARY SNOW is alone on stage. She sits on the front step, training a telescope on the sky. MARY is seventeen, a slender, fine-boned, lovely girl with short black hair. She is wearing a short-sleeved yellow satin dress and black flat-heeled shoes. She wears no makeup except for a slight hint of red on her cheeks. The only jewellery she wears is her engagement ring.

Slight pause. Then MARY rises and crosses into the stage left part of the yard and again peers at the sky through the telescope.

A moment later JACOB MERCER's voice is heard offstage, singing faintly as though he were some distance down the road stage right. His voice carries so faintly, in fact, that MARY spins around and faces that direction, listening intently, not sure whether it is her imagination.
JACOB: *(to the tune of 'Pretty Redwing')*
    'Oh, the moon shines bright on Charlie Chaplin,
    His boots are crackin' for the want of blackin',
    And his baggy trousers they want mendin'
    Before they send him, to the Dardanelles.'

(*MARY stands riveted to the spot, her eyes searching the shadow-pocketed road, almost afraid of what might walk into view, but still straining to listen . . . But the song has ended, and there is only silence. With an inward shrug, she assumes it is imagination—the ghost of last summer—and resumes her study of the stars.*)

(*At that moment JACOB MERCER appears on the road stage right. He is about six months older than MARY, a solidly-built, good-looking young man in a store-bought suit and brown fedora. In his right hand he holds a cardboard suitcase held together with a rope tied in a half-hitch knot. At first sight of MARY, he instinctively sets down the suitcase and removes his hat. He watches her so intently it is as though he is holding his breath . . . Finally, JACOB clears his throat, and MARY whirls around, startled. They stand motionless, staring at one another for a long moment.*)

JACOB: (*finally*) Hello, Mary. (*Then*) Aren't you even going to acknowledge me? (*Pause*) The least you could do is make a fist.

MARY: (*beat. Quietly*) It was you I heard . . .

JACOB: What? Just now?

MARY: I heard your voice on the road, and I said to myself, No, it couldn't be him . . .

• • •

[*Jacob has just returned after being away for some time. He left suddenly while he and Mary were courting. While Jacob was away, Mary became engaged to a young man named Jerome McKenzie, a schoolteacher. Jacob resents Jerome because his father worked on a fishing boat for Jerome's father, Will McKenzie, a well-to-do merchant. Jacob's father got into an argument with the captain of the boat. When the boat came back with a poor catch, Will McKenzie blamed Jacob's father and forced him to sit on the McKenzie's porch and rock a cradle with his foot from morning till dark until his work term was done. To Jacob, his father was a proud hero who had served his country in World War I and won a medal. He did not deserve to be shamed.*

As the action resumes, Mary has gone into the house. Jacob is outside the door.]

Jacob Mercer, in a production of *Salt-Water Moon* by Rising Tide Theatre, St. John's, Newfoundland.

• • •

JACOB: (*to himself*) By the Christ, Jacob, that's some wonderful girl. . . . (*He removes his coat and sets it on the railing. Smoothing down his hair, he walks to the door and knocks*) Mary! (*Then*) Mary Snow from Hickman's Harbour! Come out, Mary, and look at the moon! There's never been a night like this before, and there'll never be another! (*He listens. Then he walks down the steps into the yard and faces the house*) Come on out, Mary. Don't be like that. Sometimes I gets carried away, that's all. I'm no different from you in that respect . . . . You're prob'bly peeking t'rough the curtains right this very minute, wondering to yourself, What's that fool up to now? Where do he get the gall to be standing in the yard of the Right Honourable Henry Dawe, Member of Parliament, waking up the half of Coley's Point that isn't at the wake? . . . And won't Lady Emma be some cross, once she finds out the girl she's had in service for four years is causing a disturbance loud enough to start old Bob Foote knocking on his casket? . . . (*Peers in the window*) And poor Jerome, let's not forget him. He might be persuaded to call off the wedding, once he discovers that Mary Snow was carrying on with an old flame . . . (*Walks farther into the yard*) So you decide for yourself, Mary, 'cause I'm not budging. I'll just make myself at home, till Jerome comes driving down the road, innocent as the day he was born. Won't it give him a lesson in life, to find a wolf

in the yard and the lamb cowering behind the curtains? . . . (*He crosses quickly to the porch and sits in the rocker. Begins to sing 'Wedding in Renews'*)
'There's going to be a jolly time,
I'll have you all to know,
There's me and Joe and Uncle Snow
Invited for to go.
I have the list here in my fist,
So I'll read out the crews,
There's going to be a happy time
At the wedding in Renews.

(*louder*) 'There's Julia Farn, from Joe Batt's Arm,
She's coming in a hack;
And Betsy Doyle from old Cape Broyle,
She'll wear her Sunday sack;
And Prudence White, she's out of sight,
She'll wear her dancing-shoes.
We'll dance all night till the broad daylight
At the wedding in Renews.'

(*The door bursts open, and MARY comes striding out*)

MARY: Will you stop that! My God, what's wrong with you? I never would've said hello in the first place had I knowed you'd carry on like this! Now go home!

JACOB: (*rises from the rocker*) Suit yourself, maid. It's just that I t'ought you might like to see what I brought you all the way from Toronto. It's in my suitcase.

MARY: I don't want it, whatever it is. Just go.

[*Jacob presents Mary with a pair of stockings for her and her sister Dot. Mary refuses to take them. She also tells Jacob she can't give a pair to her sister because Dot is in a home with very strict rules and she can wear only a plain uniform. Mary once took her sister one of her dresses, but Dot was not allowed to have it.*]

MARY: I can't accept gifts from you now, Jacob. It's not right.

JACOB: Well, I can't be taking them home, can I? Mother would crack me across the skull if I walked in the door with these on my arm.

MARY: Yes, and what would Jerome say if he heard I'd taken those? Has that crossed your mind?

JACOB: Jerome? The hell with him. If he can bring you oranges last year, I can bring you stockings now.

MARY: That was different.

JACOB: What's different about it?

MARY: I wasn't spoken for last year, that's what's different.

JACOB: We was keeping company, wasn't we? That's almost the same. Did that stop him from slouching in that rocker there, darting a look at you every time he sucked his pipe?

MARY: You make it sound as if we couldn't get rid of him. He may have dropped in once a week, if that.

JACOB: Once was enough. For all the notice he took of me, I might've been one of his students he stuck in a corner and forgot. (*Mockingly*) Tapping his Briar pipe in that pit of his hand. Pointing the stem at the sky. 'Look, Mary, there's the evening star, now. Venus.'

MARY: What odds? I was no more taken with Jerome last summer than the Man in the Moon. What's happened since is your own fault and no one else's.

JACOB: Sure. Rub salt in the wound.

MARY: It's true, isn't it?

JACOB: For Christ's sake, Mary, I was seventeen at the time. Seventeen!

MARY: That's no excuse! You was old enough to lure me up to Jenny's Hill, wasn't you? And two months older when you kept me waiting for the sound of your boots on the road, and me still here when Mr. Dawe was ready to blow out the lamp!

JACOB: That was wrong, I admit.

MARY: The next day I walked down to your house. 'Oh, he left,' your mother said. 'Sure, didn't he tell you? Took the train to Port aux Basques this morning. You must've just missed him.'

JACOB: She had it wrong. I didn't go straight to Port aux Basques. I got off in St. John's. I worked unloading the steamers, till I had enough for my passage and Travelling Certificate. . . .

MARY: I walked up the road that morning, and every step of the way I could feel your mother's eyes on my back. I went straight to Mrs. Dawe. 'I wants to go up to Toronto, Mrs. Dawe,' I said. 'There's somet'ing I have to do there.' 'What?' she said. 'I can't tell you,' I said, 'but it's important.' 'Well, I'm sorry, Mary, but you can't go. You still owes us twenty-four dollars for that bridge you had put in.' 'I won't go for good,' I said. 'Just for a week or two.' 'No,' she said, 'it's out of the question.'

JACOB: What was it you had to do, Mary? Why just a week or two?

MARY: It would've taken me that long to hunt you down. Then I would've put on my prettiest dress and knocked on your door. And when you stuck your head out, I would've slapped your face so hard it would've knocked you into the next room. But at least I'd have had the satisfaction of saying goodbye.

JACOB: I'm sorry. I wanted to tell you goodbye. I tried to, two nights before I left here. . . .

MARY: Two nights before? Yes, I noticed how hard you tried two nights before. The way you sat on the step and looked at your fingers. The way you shuffled off home without a backward glance.

JACOB: The words wouldn't come. . . .

MARY: That must've been a first, mustn't it?

JACOB: Perhaps.

MARY: You'd been so upset the past week. Ever since your father came home from the Labrador. Always working late at Taylor's tinsmith shop.

JACOB: I couldn't go home till he was fast asleep. I didn't want him to have to see me. . . .

MARY: It never occurred to me I was the one on your mind that night. All along I supposed it was him, your father.

JACOB: It was the both of you.

MARY: No mistake.

JACOB: It was. There was a moment there when the boat pulled out of Port aux Basques for North Sydney, for Canada, when I almost jumped over the side.

MARY: (pained) Why didn't you?

JACOB: I can't swim.

MARY: That's not funny, Jacob.

JACOB: I wasn't being funny. . . . I stood on the stern of the Caribou, looking back at land for the longest time. . . . It was a grand day, too, the sun shining, the breeze making t'umbprints on the blue water. It almost felt good to be alive. . . .

MARY: I suppose you never gave a second t'ought to me, did you?

JACOB: Indeed I did.

MARY: Out of sight, out of mind.

JACOB: It wasn't like that at all. It's just that . . .

MARY: What?

JACOB: It's just that I couldn't forget my father's face. The look on his face that day as he raised his head on Will McKenzie's porch and caught me passing. I never wanted a son of mine to see such shame in his father's eyes. Nor a wife of mine to have to look on me with such pity. The way my mother looked, later on, as we all sat down to supper, him with his eyes on his plate, hardly able to swallow a mouthful. . . . The broken look on those two faces made me turn and walk to the bow of the boat that was pointed for another country. . . .

(JACOB pauses, and without looking at MARY, walks to the suitcase. He folds in the stockings. Closes the suitcase and ties the rope. All the time MARY watches him)

MARY: *(finally)* So I didn't count, is that it? What was I, Jacob? Just the girl you frolicked with one night on the cliffs of home?

JACOB: That's not true, now.

MARY: Don't say it's not true, it is true. The simple truth is your father mattered more. It was what you saw on that summer porch, wasn't it, that drove you away from here?

JACOB: Well, it's no whim that's carried me back, I guarantee.

MARY: I never believed it was.

JACOB: And don't suppose I haven't tried to forget you since, because I have. I tried to shut you out as best I could, but . . .

MARY: But what?

JACOB: Somehow you'd always . . . always creep back in. . . . Then I heard about you and Jerome. . . . *(He sets the suitcase on the ground)*

MARY: Who told you?

JACOB: Mother wrote. For a minute I figured she'd become feeble-minded. 'Not Jerome McKenzie,' I said to Sam Boone. 'She must mean another Jerome.'

MARY: What if it had been someone else? Would that have made any odds? *(Then)* Would it?

JACOB: No. Not a bit.

MARY: I wonder . . .

JACOB: I sat on my bed that day and read the letter, and when I come to the part about you and Jerome, the words made my ears ring. I had to go to the window for air. . . . It was like . . .

MARY: Like what?

JACOB: Almost like . . . like I'd swallowed a hook lodged so deep inside it was there for good. For the first time I felt what a fish must feel, with a foot on his head and his guts being ripped out. . . . I quit my job. I tramped the streets from the crack of dawn. Up one street, and down the other, till my soles wore out. I got in a fight with a fellow on Yonge Street. He come at me with an ice-pick. I put my hands behind my back and I said, 'Go on, buddy, put it right there!' I said. (*He smacks his heart*) 'Come on!' I said. 'Do it! I won't make a move to stop you!'. . . He backed off and looked at me like I'd just escaped from a straight-jacket. Dropped the ice-pick and took off up the street. . . . I went back to Sam Boone's that night and packed my bag. I said to his wife, 'Lucy,' I said, 'I t'ink it's time I went home . . .'

(*Slight pause*)

MARY: Well, you ought to have saved yourself the trip. What you ought to have done, Jacob, is had your shoes cobbled and took to the streets again. Till you walked me out of your system.

JACOB: Once was enough. All I got was blisters.

MARY: What did you expect I'd do, boy? Cancel the wedding next month? Hurt someone the way you hurt me? Did you imagine I was pining away that much? My God, you must t'ink a lot of yourself, don't you? All you have to do is walk across the Klondike into Coley's Point, and I'm expected to feel the same? Expected to feel grateful?

(*Slight pause*)

JACOB: Do you love him?

MARY: What odds to you? He's a good man, Jerome. He's quiet and kind, he's smart and dependable, and once he builds his own house in Country Road, we're taking Dot to live with us.

JACOB: That's not what I asked, Mary. He may be all of those t'ings you said, and more. I don't give a damn if he's wise like Solomon or strong

like Samson. I don't care if he builds ten houses in Country Road for
you and your sister. I only asked if you loved him.

MARY: Why wouldn't I love him? I'm marrying him, aren't I? *(She turns away)*

JACOB: That still don't answer my question. Look at me, Mary. . .

MARY: What for? . . .

JACOB: Look me in the eye and tell me you loves him, and I'll walk out of
this yard and never come back.

MARY: You made one promise tonight you never kept. You can't be trusted.

JACOB: Try me once more. Tell me you loves Jerome McKenzie, and you'll
never see the dust of my feet again.

MARY: All right, and I'm holding you to it. *(She turns and stares straight
at him)*

(Slight pause)

JACOB: You can't say it, can you? *(Then)* Can you?

MARY: I loves him. There. I said it.

JACOB: *(beat)* No odds. I don't believe you. *(He walks away)*

MARY: No, you wouldn't believe the Devil if he snuck up behind and
jabbed you with his fork.

JACOB: That I wouldn't.

MARY: No. All you believes is what you wants to believe.

JACOB: No, I believes in what's real. I believes in flesh and blood.
I believes in a young girl trembling at my breath on her neck.
That's what I believes in.

MARY: What young girl?

JACOB: There's only one in the yard that I can see.

MARY: And just when was I trembling?

JACOB: When? I'll tell you when. When you pointed out the blue star of
Vega tonight, and I stood behind you. I could feel you shaking under
your dress like a young bride at the altar.

MARY: It's chilly out!

JACOB: Indeed it's not chilly out, or where's your shawl to? . . . Your heart
was pounding, wasn't it? *(Then)* Wasn't it?

MARY: Next you'll be telling me you could hear it.

JACOB: No, but I could see the pulse in your neck, Mary, beating like a
tom-tom.

MARY: The Bible's got it all wrong. It's not the women who are the vain ones, it's the men.

(*Slight pause*)

JACOB: You ought to wear yellow more often, mind. It really do become you. Suits your black hair and fair complexion.

MARY: Is that what you did the past year up in Toronto? Sweet talk the girls?

JACOB: What girls?

MARY: 'What girls?' he says.

JACOB: There wasn't any girls, sure.

MARY: No, and autumn don't follow summer, I suppose?

JACOB: (*beat*) All right, perhaps there was one or two girls . . .

MARY: One or two? Is *that* all?

JACOB: T'ree or four at most.

MARY: You don't need to exaggerate. And you calls Jerome a blowhard for boasting of somet'ing he never claimed to be in the first place?

JACOB: He claimed to be potent, didn't he?

MARY: That's all he claimed to be, not'ing more. And he said it as a joke, more or less.

JACOB: More or less?

MARY: I'm sorry I ever told you, now.

JACOB: He's in the wrong place, Jerome is. He ought to try Toronto. The girls up there haven't set eyes on a decent man since the day I left.

MARY: Yes, and I suppose all four was waving you off at the station? Running down the tracks? Blowing you kisses? 'Don't forget us, now! Come back soon!'

JACOB: No. Only the two.

MARY: Two, my foot.

JACOB: All right, one then. One in particular.

MARY: Oh?

JACOB: Her name was Rose, and she looked like you. In fact, she might've been your spitting image, except for her gentle manner.

MARY: (*beat*) I'm gentle. . . .

JACOB: The odd time.

MARY: I'm not like this with another soul but you. I've never met anyone who makes me cross as a hornet half the time.

JACOB: Rose was gentle *all* the time. She said I brought out the best in her.

MARY: There was no Rose. You're making it up. What was her last name?

JACOB: I'm not much with last names. Rose of Sharon, I called her. 'How beautiful are thy feet with shoes, O prince's daughter!'. . .

MARY: (*beat*) What did you do together, you and this . . . this Rose?

JACOB: Oh, the odd time we'd go dancing at the Palace Pier. That's a dancehall down by Lake Ontario. Once we took a midnight cruise to Niagara Falls and back. There was a band playing.

MARY: I don't believe a word of it.

JACOB: Mostly we'd go to a picture show. My favourite (*last syllable rhymes with 'night'*) was always Tom Mix.

MARY: Tom Mix? Who in the world is he?

JACOB: What? You've never heard of the 'King of the Cowboys', the most famous Western actor alive?

MARY: No, and I still haven't seen a picture show. I don't have the time or money for such t'ings.

JACOB: Then I'll take you, maid! Right now!

MARY: Take me where?

JACOB: To the pictures, Mary. I'll take you to see Tom Mix in 'The Lucky Horseshoe'. (*He sits on the step and pats the area beside him*) Here. Sit down on the step.

MARY: (*suspiciously*) What's you up to now?

JACOB: (*all innocence*) I'm not up to a blessed t'ing. . . .

(*MARY still regards him with mistrust*)

. . . Come on, sit down. I won't bite. . . . Will you hurry up, we'll be late for the picture . . .

(*MARY reluctantly sits down, though she sits as a discreet distance from JACOB*)

. . . All right, now it's a Friday night in Toronto, and we'm at the picture house. We just slipped into the last row of the Christie T'eatre on St. Clair. You comfortable?

MARY: Yes. Only why are we sitting so far back? Why don't we sit in the front?

JACOB: Why? 'Cause all the front seats are taken, that's why. Jesus, we just sat down, and already you'm complaining.

Jacob tells Mary the story of Tom Mix in *The Lucky Horseshoe.*

MARY: I just wondered why we had to sit in the last row.

JACOB: I told you, didn't I? These are the only two seats left. Count yourself lucky to get 'em. . . . All right, now, the next is important. There are t'ree t'ings, Mary, that a fellow who takes his sweetheart—

MARY: I'm not your sweetheart.

JACOB: Suit yourself.

MARY: Just remember that.

JACOB: Hush up. The picture's about to begin. . . . No, it's just the newsreel. . . . Now as I was saying, there are t'ree t'ings that a fellow who takes a girl to the pictures always does in a picture house. And if he don't do all t'ree to his satisfaction, he don't get his fifteen cents worth.

MARY: What's that?

JACOB: First off, he lights up a cigarette, if he happens to have a tailor-made. That's number one: a Sweet Caporal.

MARY: What's number two?

JACOB: Number two is he cocks his feet on the seat of the fellow ahead, and if the fellow looks back, you stares at him like Tom Mix in 'The

Lucky Horseshoe'. A smirky sort of look that makes him slink low in his seat. . . . Be quiet now. The picture's just begun. . . . Look, there's Tom now, riding up the road on his horse named Tony. That's some wonderful black horse, boy. See how his mane is permed and his tail all combed. And look how smart Tom looks in his same old get-up: silver spurs on the heels of his boots, that leather fit-out over his pants they calls chaps, that hanky knotted around his neck, and that tall hat with the wide brim and the crown stove in on both sides. See how straight Tom sits in the saddle, Mary.

MARY: You said there was t'ree t'ings a fellow did in a picture show. You never mentioned the last.

JACOB: I was getting to that. Saving the best for later. . . . Now there always comes a time in the picture show, Mary, when the fellow you'm with gets the sense . . . the sense that the time is right.

MARY: The time for what?

JACOB: Well, say it's me, now. I'd glance out of the corner of my eye and see you sitting there with your hair all washed, your hands folded in your lap, looking all soft and lovely and smelling as fresh as the wind, and I'd sort of lean back in my seat like this and slip my arm around you . . .

(JACOB does. MARY knocks his arm away and springs to her feet)

MARY: *(indignantly)* So this is what you've been doing, is it, in the picture house with Rose?

JACOB: There is no Rose.

MARY: I don't believe you!

JACOB: I made her up.

MARY: Liar!

JACOB: Look, will you sit down and watch the picture? This is one of the best Tom ever made. He rides right into a wedding chapel and snatches the bride from under the nose of the groom. *(He grins)*

MARY: I suppose you finds that funny?

JACOB: It made me stand up, maid, and cheer.

MARY: That's the most brazen t'ing I ever heard of. Why did he do it in the first place?

JACOB: Why? 'Cause the girl was being married against her will, why else. Tom rode to the rescue.

MARY: What if she wasn't marrying against her will? What then?

JACOB: Then there would've been no picture. Besides, she had to be getting married against her will. If you saw the slouch of a bridegroom, you wouldn't have to ask.

MARY: No odds. He might be full of himself, this . . . this Mr. Tom Mix, but that don't give him the right to barge in and take what's not his.

JACOB: Go on with you. Sure, even the horse looked pleased. He stood there on the carpet, Tony, all sleek and smug. Tom was sitting in the saddle, clutching the bride on his hip, the train of her gown brushing the floor. All eyes was on Tom. The Maids of Honour in their summer hats all gazed up at him, puzzled, and the minister looked on with his t'umb in the Bible, waiting to see what happened next.

MARY: What did the groom do? I suppose he just stood by and never lifted a finger?

JACOB: What could he do, the fool, against the likes of Tom Mix? He raised himself to his full height and gave Tom a dirty look, and Tom gazed right back down at him with that little smirk on his lips, as much as to say, 'Too bad, buddy. Better luck next time.'

(Slight pause)

MARY: Well, Tom Mix had best climb back on his horse and ride off into the night. This is one bride he won't be stealing.

JACOB: No?

MARY: No. And he better ride off soon, too, before Mr. and Mrs. Dawe return from the wake.

JACOB: Nobody puts the run on Tom Mix.

MARY: Tom Mix is a fool.

JACOB: No more than you, if you expects me to swallow another one of your lies.

MARY: What lie's that?

JACOB: 'What lies's that?' she says, knowing full well the Right Honourable and Lady Emma won't be home soon.

MARY: Indeed they will. They'll be home any minute now.

JACOB: Indeed they won't. They won't be home till sunrise. Not till Mrs. Foote has had a good night's sleep and can sit vigil at the coffin. I heard 'em say so. . . .

(MARY says nothing)

. . . So it looks like it's just us, Mary. Just you and me and the moon. You and me and the moon that was meant for Jerome. . . .

(*MARY crosses to the porch and picks up the telescope*)

. . . And isn't she a lovely one, too? As white as the wafer in Holy Communion.

MARY: (*crosses into the yard*) I'm not speaking to you after this, Jacob. From now on you can talk to yourself, for all the good it'll do. . . . (*She trains the telescope on the sky, ignoring him*)

JACOB: That's no way to be, Mary. Rose always liked the way I talked. She said it was . . . oh, what was her word? . . . quaint.

(*MARY doesn't react*)

Sing me a song, Jacob, my son, she'd always say. No one can handle a song like you. (*Beat*) Sing me a verse of 'Newfoundland Love Song'. The verse that goes—(*Recites very simply*)—

'Meet me when all is still
   My Annie fair!
Down by the up-line grove,
   My Annie fair!
Near to the silent grove,
I'll tell you how I love,
While the stars shine above,
   My Annie fair!'

(*MARY turns and regards him with reproach*)

'I can't sing you that one, Rose,' I say. 'That song belongs to a girl back home.'

MARY: I don't care if you had ten Roses, and you sang all the songs up your sleeve. What odds to me? (*She returns to the telescope*)

JACOB: That's right. What odds to you? You have Jerome McKenzie to comfort you now. And what a comfort he'll be on a winter's night, with his knobby knees and cold feet. . . . The wind screeching like a broken heart, and him in the dark, wondering why his wife is turned to the wall, wondering to himself, 'Why is Mary like that? Why is her heart as cold as my feet? . . .

(MARY walks to another part of the yard and turns her back on him, lifting the telescope to the sky)

What do you suppose Jerome's up to right now? Prob'ly sitting on Isaac Tucker's step, whilst Doctor Babcock's inside with Betty. Him and Isaac smoking their pipes, their chins to the sky. 'Look, Isaac, there's King Charles' Wain.' 'King Charles' Wain?' says Isaac. 'Where?'...

(Mary reacts. She lowers the telescope but doesn't look around)

...'Right there,' says Jerome. 'Right over Spaniard's Bay. See? Some calls it the Plough. Most calls it the Big Dipper. But its real name is Ursa Major. U-r-s-a. Ursa Major. That means the Great Bear in a dead language.'

MARY: *(turning)* Why, you...!

JACOB: *(quickly)* Why did you ever agree to it, Mary? Why would you marry someone like that? It don't make sense.

MARY: Where did you learn so much about the Dipper? Standing there, earlier on, pretending not to know a blessed t'ing!

JACOB: Sam Boone taught me this winter. He knows the stars like his own hand. Now will you answer my question?

MARY: What question?

JACOB: You've so much steel inside you, maid. So much fire in your spirit. Why would you waste it on a weak little flame like Jerome? It's not fair to him, and it's not fair to yourself.

MARY: *(vehemently)* Fair? What's fair got to do with it? Is it fair that my sister has to live in a Home with an iron fence around it? A fourteen-year-old girl sleeping in a bed with a number on it, her initials inside her shoes in ink? Is that fair?

JACOB: No, of course not—

MARY: Well then!

JACOB: What's that got to do with what I asked?

MARY: A lot more than you imagines.

JACOB: Well, there's no need to snap my head off, is there?

MARY: You any idea how many girls live at the Home? More than a hundred. All between six and sixteen. Sometimes twenty-one girls to a room. The big girls like Dot get up at five o'clock and make bread. At six she lights the Quebec heater with the galvanized boiler attached. Sometimes it's hard to light, the wood might be wet.

JACOB: So?

MARY: So the Matron will come in and put her hand on the boiler. 'This is not hot enough,' she says. 'I couldn't light it, Miss,' says Dot. 'The wood's wet.' And the Matron will knock her to the floor and put her foot on her.

JACOB: Who told you that?

MARY: Dot did. Back in June.

JACOB: *(under his breath)* Jesus Christ! . . .

MARY: There's a lot more, but I won't go into it. Dot made me promise not to complain to the Home, the Matron would only make it worse. She can't say a word in her letters, either, or they won't be mailed. . . . I went to see her the day we left St. John's this summer. I walked up to Hamilton Avenue and rang the bell. They let me into the sitting-room, then Dot came in. . . . There was a smudge of stove polish on her cheek. She'd been cleaning the stoves with blackening, and the Matron had struck her. She'd wiped the sting away with her hand, forgetting her fingers was black with polish. I said, 'Dot, go get dressed. I'm taking you out for the day.' And when she came back, she was wearing a pair of laced-up boots, a dark blue hat with elastic under the chin, those navy blue kneesocks turned down, and an old tweed coat with no lining. . . . We went back to Mrs. Dawe's and up to my room. I said, 'Take off those clothes, Dot, we're going out.' She looked frightened to death. I said, 'What's wrong?' She said, "I don't want to take my clothes off." I said, 'Don't you want to wear this pretty blue dress?' She said, 'I can't take my clothes off, Mary. Don't make me.' 'I won't make you,' I said.

MARY: Then we . . . went out and walked the streets. I pointed out the drugstore where Tommy Ricketts was now the druggist, and we went inside and looked at him. He had the shyest smile and the kindest eyes, and him so brave in the War. The youngest soldier in the British Army to win a Victoria Cross. I almost asked if he remembered Jim Snow, but I was too in awe to speak. . . . Once outside, I told Dot who he was, and how she had to be like him. Brave like him and Father, only brave in a different way. I told her the Matron was a coward, and like all cowards, I said, she was cruel, so the next time she puts her foot on you, Dot, I said, don't make a sound: don't even cry out, 'cause she'll only grind her heel into you all the harder. Just look into her eyes, I said, and let her know that no odds how often she knocks you down, no odds how hard she steps on you, the one t'ing she'll never destroy is your spirit. And maybe, just maybe she'd stop doing it, 'cause it's a funny t'ing, I said, about cruel people like the Matron, they only respect one kind of person in the long run, and that's the ones they can't break. . . . That night at the station, Mr. Dawe tried to buy me a ticket in Second Class. He always did that. Him and Mrs. Dawe would sit in First Class and he'd buy me a ticket in Second; once we was out of St. John's and the conductor had punched the tickets, he'd come back and say, 'All right, Mary, you can come in First Class now.'. . . Only this time I wouldn't let him. I said, 'No, Mr. Dawe, and that you won't! I wants a ticket in First Class, and I don't care if I have to pay the extra twenty cents myself!'

JACOB: Good for you.

MARY: He bought me the ticket, too, and I sat on the train and looked out the window, vowing I'd get Dot out from behind that iron fence one way or another. . . . There's not much more to tell. . . . Before too long Jerome was stopping by, all dressed up, with a bag of sweets. Only this time I didn't discourage him. I took the sweets that night, and the oranges the next, and when he showed up one night with a ring in his pocket, I took that, too. That's it.

(Pause)

JACOB: No, that's not it. That's not it by a long shot. Not as far as I'm concerned.

MARY: Please, will you just go now? I'd sooner be left alone. I don't want to hear about Tom Mix on his black horse, or girls you went out with called Rose. . . .

JACOB: There was no Rose. You was right the first time. I never took a soul to the picture show and I never went to Niagara Falls.

MARY: I don't care if you did. . . .

JACOB: Not that I couldn't have, mind. Sam Boone had a niece that used to pester me half to death.

MARY: Sam Boone has only one niece. Her name is Rachel. She's two years old and lives in Corner Brook.

(Slight pause)

JACOB: Well, it was Sam and Lucy who saw me off at Union Station. That much is true. Before I boarded the train, I said to him, 'Sam,' I said, 'what would you do if you had a girl back home that might still be smitten with you but prob'bly couldn't let on? What advice would you give?' You want to know what he said, Mary?

MARY: What?

JACOB: He said, 'Jacob, did you ever hear tell of the Society girl from St. John's who let it be known she'd marry the first Blue Puttee to win a Victoria Cross? Every time they went over the top, the single boys would yell:—(*Raises his arm in a fist*)—'JENNY SAUNDERS OR A WOODEN LEG!'

MARY: Keep your voice down, for goodness sake! . . .

JACOB: The best battle cry I ever heard, that.

MARY: Well, I'm no Society Girl, and you're no Blue Puttee. So there.

JACOB: (*beat*) 'Besides,' Lucy said, 'if she's still mooning over you, my son, she'll let you know somehow. It's as simple as that.'

MARY: It's not as simple as that, and you knows it. There's one member of the wedding you forgot to mention, Jacob, when you told about Tom Mix riding in to steal the bride. What about him?

JACOB: Who?

MARY: Who? The father of the groom, as if you forgot. What was he doing that day, bent over with laughter? Or was he standing off to one side, burning up with shame?

JACOB: I never noticed.

MARY: You noticed a lot else.

JACOB: Is that what you suppose this is, Mary? An eye for an eye? You t'ink I rode t'ousands of miles by train and boat, all to get back at Will McKenzie?

MARY: I'm asking *you* that.

JACOB: (*flaring up*) Well, if that's what you really believes, Mary, then you'm right: I am a stranger. More of a stranger than you realizes. And if that's the sort of man you imagines me to be, then the hell with you, Mary Snow! Keep your star-gazing fiancé with his bald spot and bag of candies! (*He slips on his suit jacket and picks up the suitcase*)

MARY: (*pursuing him*) Why shouldn't I wonder that? The same question will be on everyone else's lips tomorrow.

JACOB: I don't give a damn what others t'ink! It wouldn't bother me if the preacher denounced me from the pulpit! It's what you t'inks that matters! You and no one else! (*He starts to exit*)

MARY: There's no call to carry on like this . . .

JACOB: Isn't there? You stand there and tell me straight to my face I'm no better than the Matron—as cruel as her or Will McKenzie—and you expect me not to raise my voice?

MARY: I never meant it the way you took it. . . .

JACOB: Do you really believe I'd ever set out to hurt you? That I'd use you, just to settle accounts with someone else?

MARY: Are you telling me it never crossed your mind? Maybe the night you packed your bag. Maybe the day you walked t'rough Customs at North Sydney. Maybe on the deck of the boat or in your seat on the train to here. Wouldn't it be a slap in the face for Jerome's father to have his son left high and dry at the altar? Be honest!

JACOB: All right. Yes, it crossed my mind. For as long as a shooting star takes. A flash. A flick of a second. I can't help that, can I? . . . But I never came home the avenging angel, the smell of blood in my nostrils. And if you still don't know why I'm standing here in a store-bought suit, with stockings in my suitcase, then I might as well walk out of this yard, and the sooner the better! All I'm doing is making a fool of myself! (*He starts off*)

MARY: I suppose you expect me to stop you?

JACOB: (*stops and turns*) And that I don't. For all I cares, you can sit in that rocker and polish your ring. . . . I won't be troubling you again, Mary. So goodnight to you. (*He starts off again*)

MARY: (*pursuing him*) Not goodnight, Jacob! Goodbye!

JACOB: Suit yourself. Goodbye then. At least now you won't have to slap my face.

(*He exits down the road stage left, leaving behind a sudden, terrible silence. MARY takes a step or two after him, then begins to quickly chant the words of the song we first heard JACOB singing. The tone is defiant, as though she were thumbing her nose at him*)

MARY: 'Oh, the moon shines bright on Charlie Chaplin,
His boots are crackin' for the want of blackin'
And his baggy trousers they want mending. . .'

(*And suddenly the words choke in her throat and she sobs into her hands all the feelings she has stored inside her for the past year. Her hands try to stifle the sobs as if her soul were rushing from her mouth and she was trying to push it back inside. . . . It is a sudden short-lived burst of emotion. She raises her head and looks down the road. She takes another step or two*)

MARY: *(tentatively)* Jacob. . . . *(Louder)* Jacob! . . . *(Then she lets out a cry that splits apart the night)* JAAACOOOB!

(MARY stands looking down the road, her eyes straining to see, her eyes almost listening. . . . but there is only the empty road, the moonlight, the silence. . . . She composes herself and returns to the porch step. She sits gazing at some middle distance, absently turning her engagement ring on her finger)

(At that moment JACOB walks quietly back onto the road, still carrying his suit-case, his fedora cocked at a jaunty angle. There is no grin on his face, however, as he stands staring at MARY for a long moment, waiting for her to notice him. . . . Finally, she does. She rises, but remains standing on the porch, looking at him)

JACOB: You had me worried there. I t'ought for a minute you wasn't going to call. *(Now he grins)*

MARY: Oh, you. . .! *(She raises her elbow and clenches her fist in a parody of a threatening gesture. A gesture that is not coy but more the gesture of exasperation a woman might feel who is taken for granted)*

JACOB: Now she makes a fist. Took you long enough, maid. . . .

(MARY turns away)

. . . And such a little fist, too. Wouldn't bruise a humming-bird, let alone the King of the Cowboys. . . .

MARY: *(still turned away)* So sure of yourself, aren't you, Tom? A real lady-killer, that's you.

JACOB: Tom has a modest nature, Mary. He don't like to boast. Not like some I could name. *(He walks a few feet closer. Sets the suitcase down in the yard and stands beside it)* On a night like this he'd sooner howl at the moon. One last shout of joy for old Bob Foote. *(He lifts his face to sky and cups his hands around his mouth)*

MARY: Don't you dare! You've already woke up half of Conception Bay as it is. . . .

(JACOB drops his hands to his sides, but remains gazing at the sky. Pause)

JACOB: God, you can't beat the mystery of it, can you? It's some wonderful sight. With or without a spyglass.

MARY: Yes. *(She sits and looks up at the heavens)* There are stars up there that Father was watching the night before Beaumont Hamel. The light those stars gave off that night is just reaching us now.

JACOB: Imagine.

MARY: There are other stars whose light won't reach here till long after we're gone. Hundreds of years or more. T'ousands.

JACOB: Jesus, don't get morbid on me. Old Bob wouldn't want that, would he? (*He glances at MARY. She returns his glance*)

(*Slight pause*)

MARY: Was there really a Rose?

JACOB: Yes.

MARY: There was not.

JACOB: All right, there wasn't.

(*Slight pause*)

MARY: There was, wasn't there?

JACOB: No. (*Beat*) Besides, the past is best forgotten, someone once said. Leave it buried. . . .

(*MARY looks away in mild exasperation*)

. . . It's the future that counts, Mary. And the future is here. It's here in this yard right now. It's you and me and that battered old suitcase.

MARY: Yes, held together with a piece of rope. Some future.

(*JACOB kneels down in the yard and unties the rope on the suitcase. He looks over at MARY*)

JACOB: Don't be fooled by appearances, Mary. I've got more than songs up my sleeve. I've got your future and mine, all neatly folded on top of my plaid shirts and diamond socks. (*He lifts the top of the suitcase and removes a pair of silk stockings, draping them over his arm*) All you have to do, Mary, is reach out, and old Bob can rest tonight with a grin on his face. (*Then*) Well?

MARY: (*beat*) What about my sister? Are you forgetting her?

JACOB: I'm not forgetting.

(*MARY rises from the steps. She crosses slowly into the road, but remains well away from JACOB. She stands looking out front as though her eyes are on a distant star. Finally, she speaks*)

MARY: (*evenly, with great seriousness*) In the years to come, Jacob Mercer,—

and this is no idle t'reat, mind—in the years to come, if you ever mentions Rose of Sharon, even in your sleep, I'll make you regret the night you knelt in this yard with those stockings in your hand and the moon for a witness. Do you understand me? (*She turns and stares at JACOB*) Do you?

JACOB smiles up at the serious face of his lovely young girl. His smile becomes a grin, until it is splitting his face from ear to ear.

Blackout

End of Play

ᔕ David French is one of Canada's best-known playwrights. He began writing stories and poems in Grade 8, studied acting after graduating from high school, and established himself as a playwright with the very popular production of *Leaving Home* in 1972. *Salt-Water Moon* was written in 1984 and has won several awards including the Dora Mavor Moore Award for Outstanding New Play in 1985 and the Hollywood Drama-Logue Critics Award in 1987. *(Born Coley's Point, Newfoundland 1939)*

RESPONDING

Meaning

1. *Character foils* are characters who contrast in traits, opinions, behaviours, and attitudes. Find evidence in the play to show that Jacob Mercer and Jerome McKenzie are character foils.

2. What motives does Mary have for accepting Jerome McKenzie's marriage proposal? Does she prefer Jacob to Jerome? Present evidence to support your view.

Form and Style

3. Discuss stories, films, and television programs you would classify as romances. List characters, settings, conflicts, and endings that often occur in romances. How is *Salt-Water Moon* similar to these romances? How is it different?

4. Jacob playfully retells the story of a Tom Mix movie. Identify similarities and differences between the plot of the Tom Mix movie, *The Lucky Horseshoe*, and the plot of *Salt-Water Moon*. Which is the more romantic plot? Which plot includes more realism? Why do you think the Tom Mix story is included?

Creative Extension

5. View a television soap opera and compare the portrayal of characters, the plot, and aspects of the setting with those in *Salt-Water Moon*. Use a Venn diagram to chart similarities and differences. Then write a short summary of your findings.

6. Assume the role of Jacob or Mary 10 years after the conclusion of the play. Write a journal entry telling about your present life and your thoughts and feelings about the past 10 years. Are you still in love? How is your life different? Has your way of looking at things changed? If so, how and why? Alternatively, you could write a short dramatic scene.

Is there someone else, Narcissus?

✑ *Charles Addams*

This ironical cartoon was created by cartoonist Charles Addams and published in The New Yorker *magazine. It takes a playful look at an aspect of love and romance.*

"Is there someone else, Narcissus?"

© The New Yorker Collection 1974 Charles Addams from cartoonbank.com. All Rights Reserved.

Famed cartoonist Charles Addams began his career with *The New Yorker* in 1935. Known for his macabre drawings and caustic wit, his characters caught on quickly and his most popular creations became the characters in the television series *The Addams Family*. Addams was also a successful author and his book of collected cartoons made the bestseller list. He received the Yale Humour Award in 1954 and he also won an award from the Mystery Writers of America. *(Born 1912, died 1988)*

Connecting

1. Explain how the cartoon's meaning depends upon an *allusion* to Greek mythology. Besides the name "Narcissus," what other details in the cartoon suggest the Greek myth?

2. Identify the *irony* in the young woman's question. Does this cartoon present a realistic aspect of romance? Support your views.

3. How does the view of love and romance in this cartoon compare with that presented in *Salt-Water Moon*? In your judgement, does Mary consider Jacob to be somewhat narcissistic? Why or why not?

Pie-In-The-Sky-Guy

 Sandra Shamas

Canadian comedian Sandra Shamas wrote this newspaper column in response to an invitation to various men and women. The invitation asked them to describe their perfect mate.

Let me introduce you to a man who used to live in my head. He is known by many names: The One, Mr. Perfect, but I like to call him, Pie-in-the-Sky-Guy. It's got a nice ring to it doesn't it, Pie-in-the-Sky-Guy? This man, in my mind, is perfect, and I know this to be true because I made him myself. Let me explain.

I'm a six-year-old girl, living in Sudbury, Ont., and I'm addicted to television. I love television, I love the distraction, mostly, I love how perfect the world of television is, so unlike the real world in which I live. Perfect world, perfect people, perfect relationships.

I am secretly head-over-heels in love with Little Joe Cartwright. Every Sunday night CBC (which was all we got) showed *Ed Sullivan*, and then *Bonanza*. The Cartwright family, three sons and a dad, lived on a ranch called the Ponderosa, and every Sunday meant a new episode of their lives. Nine p.m. was late. I knew it was late, I knew it was bedtime, I knew there was school tomorrow, I knew it all, and I still begged my Mom to stay up, hoping to see Little Joe.

When you're in love, everything seems so perfect, and the object of your deep affection can do no wrong.

So it was with Little Joe. He was beautiful to look at, cute as a button, rode a two-toned horse, and seemed to be the only one in his family with a genuine sense of humour. OK, his brother Hoss was funny in his own way, but not like Joe. Occasionally, Hoss and Joe got themselves into funny situations that made their Pa very cross with both of them, but Joe didn't seem to care. Even as their Dad was yelling at them both, Joe seemed to have the most trouble keeping an impish smile off his face. What's not to love? Joe's gorgeous, funny, rides a horse and lives in the TV so I always know where he is. Besides, by the time *Bonanza* went off the air, I had Joe so deeply embedded in my brain, I was happily in reruns for years. That's how Pie-in-the-Sky-Guy got his start.

There's a lot to be said for early childhood development; what and how we learn in our formative years can have far-reaching implications into our adult lives. Pie-in-the-Sky-Guy was a safe, virtual site in my mind. I knew he wasn't real, I knew I would never meet him, in fact his longevity was due to that very fact; he was the unreal.

So, I went out into the world, met real live men (I *was* even married *to* one for a time), had real life interactions that smacked heavily of real life— and you know how heavy real life can be. In hindsight, I plainly see that in the realm of relationships, my early

training came from the vacuum of television, and my preference in men ran toward the unreal. Unbeknownst to me in those past times, I compared the real men in my life to Pie-in-the-Sky-Guy. When they didn't measure up (how could they?), my interest in them would come under serious question, and the relationship would end. Of course, I blamed them. Never occurred to me to take any responsibility and that I was in fact, using Pie-in-the-Sky-Guy as a handy wedge between me and the guy and as a buffer so I could keep one foot out the door.

There's a line in a Blue Rodeo song that says, "It's sad when you discover, that what keeps you going, keeps you all alone." Driving, listening, that line hit home. After much contemplation, soul searching and an honest assessment of my past emotional life, I decided if I wanted to be close to my own happiness, I had to give Pie-in-the-Sky-Guy his walking papers.

He took it well. I explained we were living in two different worlds, and that he had different ideas about relating. I went on to say that I hoped we could stay friends, but that there would be an awkward period of adjustment, and that I just couldn't really see him for a long while. He shuffled a bit, played with the brim of his hat, but he took the parting well. Why wouldn't he, he's perfect.

I'm not quite sure what's left to say. Let's see, have I told you who the perfect mate is? Someone told me once that in this life, you get who you are, not what you want. If that's true, and I believe it is, becoming everything you want to see in someone else acts as a kind of beacon, drawing toward you someone who is or will be the perfect mate for you.

Sandra Shamas is most widely known for her monologues on relationships and their patterns. She studied improvisation at Second City in 1982 and joined its touring company. In 1987 she performed at the Edmonton Fringe Festival where she received national attention and critical acclaim for her performance of *My Boyfriend's Back and There's Going to be Laundry*. This inspired her to write a book of monologues under the same title. *My Boyfriend's Back* was nominated for the Stephen Leacock Award and a Governor General's Award. *(Born Sudbury, Ontario 1957)*

Connecting

1. Identify the characteristics that made Joe Cartwright appealing to the author. How do these characteristics relate to those in many other film and television romances?

2. Quote a sentence in which the author indicates the dangers of "Pie-in-the-Sky-Guys" to meaningful relationships. List another danger to relationships that the author might have noted.

3. The author concludes with advice about attracting "the perfect mate." Summarize her advice. How valid is this advice? Why? Do the tone and style of this piece make you more or less inclined to entertain the author's advice? Explain.

4. a) Summarize how this selection combines aspects of romance and realism. How do these aspects compare with those in *Salt-Water Moon*?
   b) How might Sandra Shamas answer the question: "Does love really conquer all?"

When I Was One-and-Twenty

A.E. Housman

This poem was written in 1896, but its message is timeless. It presents a young man's experience with romance.

When I was one-and-twenty
I heard a wise man say
"Give crowns and pounds and guineas
But not your heart away;
Give pearls away and rubies

ECHO

But keep your fancy[1] free."
But I was one-and-twenty,
No use to talk to me.

When I was one-and-twenty
I heard him say again,
"The heart out of the bosom
Was never given in vain;
'Tis paid with sighs a plenty
And sold for endless rue."[2]
And I am two-and-twenty,
And oh, 'tis true, 'tis true.

---

[1] fancy = imagination or spirit; [2] rue = bitter consequence

British poet and scholar A.E. Housman published his first book of poems *A Shropshire Lad* (1896) at his own expense. The book contained nostalgic verses, many spoken by a soldier or farm boy, and it became immensely popular during World War I. Housman's *Collected Poems* was published in 1939. *(Born 1859; died 1936)*

Connecting

1. Would you describe Housman's poem as romantic or realistic? Why?

2. Comment on the tone of voice of the wise man in the poem and the differing tones of the young man. Why are these tones of voice important in the poem?

3. How might the young man at 22 years of age respond to the Tom Mix movie described in *Salt-Water Moon*? Why? Support your response.

Separations

Leona Gom

This contemporary poem focuses on separation and explores the complexities and tensions in relationships. It presents a realistic perspective on romance.

at first I think I can't take it
that he has to leave, worse
than something final like death or divorce,
an interruption I have to live through,

a commercial going on for hours
after I'm hooked on the program.

the kitchen table fills up
with his letters, every time
I sit down I read a page
but it doesn't satisfy, is like a
meal without protein. I
drift thinly from room to room,
a vapour, pressing up against windows,
almost invisible. when the light
outside drains away, the nights
scratch at the walls, know I
am alone. I prop chairs
under the door handles.

I cannot live this way. I have
grown into him the way barbed wire
grows into a fencepost, it isn't fair
to move the boundaries now, but it
happens, it has to be dealt with.
I remember my mother and grandmothers,
alone in the wilderness, how they
waited for their men
to come back from war, work,
the adventure of absence, how they
packed the new space around themselves
with their own survival: a truth
left out of the history books,
a dangerous secret.

I start by breaking rules.
I park in the middle of the carport,
leave my underwear
on the floor of the bathroom.
I stitch myself back into

old friendships, they feel like
clothes I almost threw away
but fit me now better than ever.
we tell each other stories, where
we have been and how much
we paid for the trip. I have
a party and we all bring ice cream
and wine and break the high heels
off someone's shoes. we promise
not to drift apart again.

then he comes home.
the first few days there are
open suitcases everywhere,
traps we keep stepping into.
the cat thinks one is a litterbox.
we have careful arguments
until everything is unpacked,
we remember how to divide by two.
we are nervous around each other,
not sure who missed who more
or why it is important, not sure
how much we can each be changed
before it is too risky.
one thing we know,
and it frightens us both:
I could live without him again.

Leona Gom is a teacher, an editor, and a writer of both poetry and prose. She spent her university career at the University of Alberta, where she studied for her B.Ed and MA. She won the CAA Award for Best Book of Poetry for *Land of Peace* in 1980 and the Ethel Wilson Fiction Prize for *Housebroken* in 1986. (Born 1946)

Connecting

1. In groups, identify four striking figurative images from the poem. What thoughts and emotions are implied by these images?

2. Poems often conclude with a surprising detail or an ironic twist. Is this true of the conclusion of "Separations"? Explain.

3. Describe or draw a four- or five-part storyboard based on "Separations." Which key concepts in the poem does your storyboard depict? Why did you focus on these concepts?
4. Identify at least one similarity and one difference in the realistic portrayal of romance in "Separations" and *Salt-Water Moon.*

Changing Concepts of Marriage and Family

   ♂ *Noriko Kamachi*

This informational text, excerpted from Culture and Customs of Japan (1999), *discusses changing marriage customs in contemporary Japanese society. It provides a different perspective on relationships with a focus on facts and some general trends.*

Before 1947, two-thirds of marriages in Japan were arranged. In the latter half of the 1960s, the proportion dropped to less than half. According to a government survey in 1997, only 9.6 percent of the couples who married between 1992 and 1997 considered their marriages arranged. Of those who were united by a "love marriage," most met each other at work (33.6%), through the introduction of friends or siblings (27.1%), or at school (10.4%). According to the same survey, the average length of courtship was 3.4 years, and the average age of the women at their first marriage was 26.1 years. This is somewhat higher than the average age of women at their first marriage in the United States.

A growing number of men and women in Japan are putting off marriage until their late twenties. In 1992, the average age of marriage was 28.4 for first-time grooms and 26.0 for first-time brides. It has been a trend among Japanese women to marry late and to have fewer children, if any. When the government announced in 1990 that the total fertility rate (overall number of children born to women in their childbearing years) had dropped to 1.57, this news shocked the nation, because it meant that the population of Japan was on the decline and that the proportion of the elderly had greatly increased in the total population.

Another fact revealed in the 1990 census which startled the public was the increase of the proportion of men and women who had never married. Fully 11.7 percent of men between age 40 and 44, and 13.9 percent of women between age 30 and 34, were reported to have never married. Over 4 percent of men and women between age 50 and 54 were never married. Because more women now earn enough to support themselves, they do not have to resort to marriage as a means of financial security. This fact makes them less willing to marry someone who does not meet their expectations.

Connecting

1. From the text, identify three specific points about marriage customs in contemporary Japan.

2. Arranged marriages, i.e. marriage partners selected by parents or family members, are mentioned in the article. What are some advantages of arranged marriages? Why do you think the number of arranged marriages is declining in Japan?

3. What marriage trends described in the article would you expect to be similar to those in Canada? Which are different? You might like to check the Statistics Canada Web site or other sources of demographic information for a statistical comparison of trends described in Kamachi's informational text.

4. Identify one sentence from the text that clearly connects to topics explored in *Salt-Water Moon*. Defend your choice.

REFLECTING ON THE ECHO

1. You have considered various interpretations of romance related to the question "Does love really conquer all?" Choose another text in any genre or medium (poem, television program, print advertisement, etc.) Write a short interpretation about how romance is presented in your selected text.

2. Create a written or representational text (visual image, tableau, etc.) that captures your ideals about love, or create a written or visual text that presents an ironical statement about loving relationships.

3. Choose two or three selections in this Echo section and write an essay comparing and contrasting the view of romance presented in each text. Include notes on how the authors use their particular form and stylistic devices to convey their ideas.

Once Upon a Greek Stage

❧ Beth McMaster

Learning Goals

- examine characteristics of tragedy
- explore the purpose and effects of comic elements
- analyze aspects of style
- present a representation of a scene and write a short essay

Characters:

Chorus

Audience *(female)*

Three actors: Protagonist *who plays* Antigone, Tiresias, *and* Messenger
Deuteragonist *who plays* Creon
Tritagonist *who plays* Ismene, Sentry, *and* Haemon
Flutist *(non-speaking part)*

Costumes:

Because Greek costumes are draped, they can be created easily using sheets or lengths of fabric. Character changes can be achieved by changing the mantle, headdresses, and props.

Time:

Anytime

Playing space:

The play works best if the playing space is on the same level as the audience. Upstage centre, a neutral, freestanding backdrop can be used, with three low cubes in front of it for the actors. Place Chorus on a high stool down right, the Flutist on a lower stool slightly up and to the left of Chorus, and Audience on a low stool down left. Place a rack for costumes and a table for props up left almost in a "wings" position.

Pronunciation Guide:

ANTIGONE: *AnTIGahNEE*
CREON: *CREEon*
ETEOCLES: *ETEEahCLEES*
EURYDICE: *YuRIDisee*
HAEMON: *HAYmon*
ISMENE: *ISmenee*
POLYNICES: *PAULiNYsees*
THEBES: *Theebs*
TIRESIAS: *TyREEseeAS*

Scene from the Young Actor's Company production of *Once Upon a Greek Stage,* 1999.

Just before opening AUDIENCE *enters and sits downstage left. The* FLUTIST *leads the rest of the cast as they enter through the audience. The flute introduction continues until the actors are in their places on stage. The speaking chorus begins.*

THREE ACTORS and CHORUS: Theatre, theatre, is it a dream?
PROTAGONIST: Is it lies?
TRITAGONIST: Is it life or illusion supreme?
DEUTERAGONIST: Who's going to answer a question like that?
ALL:
  All down through the ages man's asked where it's at.
  We're with you today with a story to tell,
  A story that's old and famous as well.
CHORUS: The tale's of Antigone and Creon the king,
ALL:
  And the tragic results a conflict can bring;
  Our story is Greek—fifth century B.C.
  Right now we are Chorus, but we won't always be,

PROTAGONIST: For each of us has a part to play,
TRITAGONIST: And some more than one—

Actors sit.

CHORUS:
But I'm going to stay,
For Chorus I'll be throughout the show
Chorus is very important, you know.
AUDIENCE: I wouldn't say that!
CHORUS: And who are you?

AUDIENCE rises.

AUDIENCE: I'm Audience, and me you can't do without.
CHORUS: (*moves centre*)
You, important as Chorus?
Now that I must doubt!
Chorus is interpreter; Chorus points up action.
AUDIENCE: Audience is sounding board; Audience is reaction.
CHORUS: Chorus always is the backbone of the show.
AUDIENCE: There wouldn't even be a play if Audience didn't go!
CHORUS: Chorus is informant.
AUDIENCE: Audience is response.

CHORUS and AUDIENCE speak their next lines over one another.

CHORUS: Chorus is—
AUDIENCE: Audience is—

THREE ACTORS jump to their feet.

THREE ACTORS:
Stop! We really don't need either one of you,
It has been said and we know it is true,
That if theatre is what you want to do,
A platform and a passion, maybe two,
Is all you really need. Let's not delay—
We have the stage, the passion—now the play!

THREE ACTORS *sit and face upstage. This freeze is held unless they are part of the action.* CHORUS *signature: this group of notes will be played by the* FLUTIST *to introduce* CHORUS *each time he or she speaks.*

CHORUS: Yes—now—this story is very old. It comes from Greek mythology. It's about Creon, King of Thebes and his niece, Antigone. Creon believed that laws set by the state must be obeyed, no matter what. Antigone believed that family affection and obligations were more important.

AUDIENCE: I can see that a conflict like that could become really dicey.

CHORUS: You're right. It did. Antigone was a princess. Her father had been king of Thebes. There were four children in the royal family— Antigone's sister, Ismene, and two brothers, Polynices and Eteocles, who were twins. When the king died, the twin sons were both eligible to succeed him, and both of them wanted to rule.

AUDIENCE: (*to audience*) In this Greek mythology there's always something like twins thrown in to complicate life.

CHORUS: Well, this time they came up with what seemed like a reasonable solution. Eteocles was to rule for one year and Polynices for the next. Whichever one was having his year off was to leave Thebes.

AUDIENCE: I can see all kinds of loopholes in that deal.

CHORUS: You're right. It didn't work. When Eteocles' year of ruling was over, he decided he didn't want to give up the throne. Polynices wasn't about to let him away with that, so he gathered together an army and attacked Thebes. Somehow in the scuffle, he and Eteocles got into a hand-to-hand fight right at the edge of the city and killed each other.

AUDIENCE: So Antigone became queen and they all lived happily ever after. End of play!

CHORUS: No, no, no! Women didn't rule in those days. That's when Creon, the uncle, came into the picture. Although he didn't really want the throne, Creon became king. And they certainly didn't live happily ever after.

AUDIENCE: I knew it couldn't be that simple. What did happen?

CHORUS: Creon decided that Eteocles should have a state funeral with all the get-up and pizazz, and that Polynices, because he had attacked the city, should be left unburied.

AUDIENCE: Unburied?

CHORUS: Unburied.

AUDIENCE: Isn't Greece a rather hot country?

CHORUS: Very hot.

AUDIENCE: And the body was to lie around in the heat, stinking and rotting and—?

CHORUS: Stop! Don't get into the details. Let's just say Polynices was to be left unburied because he had attacked the city. And Creon put some teeth into his decree by saying that anyone who tried to bury him was to be put to death.

AUDIENCE: I'd call those real sharp teeth.

CHORUS: Antigone was very upset. She felt Polynices, like his brother, should be given the dignity of burial.

AUDIENCE: I agree with Antigone. Whew! the smell—(*to audience*) and right at the edge of the city. Think of the effect on the tourist trade. (*to* CHORUS) And wouldn't there be vultures?

CHORUS: Well, yes, now that you mention it. A body lying in the sun is bound to attract vultures.

AUDIENCE: And dogs, too?

CHORUS: And stray dogs, too.

AUDIENCE: What a gross story this is!

CHORUS: Well, you could leave. Actually, in the early days of Greece, women weren't allowed in the theatre because often the stories were, as you say, "gross" and they couldn't handle it.

AUDIENCE: I can handle it. Let's get on with it.

CHORUS: Very well then, our play begins. Antigone is talking to her sister, Ismene, about Creon's decree.

> ANTIGONE *and* ISMENE *have risen and become part of the action at the beginning of* CHORUS' *speech.* CHORUS *sits on stool at right.*

ANTIGONE: Ismene, have you heard? Uncle Creon has said that Polynices is not to be buried.

ISMENE: Yes, Antigone, I've heard. It's so sad.

ANTIGONE: What are we going to do about it?

ISMENE: Do about it?

ANTIGONE: We've got to do something about it.

ISMENE: But Antigone, there's nothing we can do.

ANTIGONE: We can bury him.

ISMENE: But we can't. Creon has said that anyone who buries the body will be executed.

ANTIGONE: Ismene—this isn't "the body." This is our brother.

ISMENE: But Creon is king and an order from the king—

ANTIGONE: An order from the king that disregards decency and honour is an order to be ignored.

ISMENE: Antigone, we can't—

ANTIGONE: I can. Will you help me?

ISMENE: This is insanity!

ANTIGONE: Will you help me?

ISMENE: I'm afraid. What if we're caught?

ANTIGONE: I hope we are. Then Creon will realize what a despicable thing he has done.

ISMENE: I can't do it, Antigone.

ANTIGONE: Then I'll do it alone. I will not see my brother's body left for the vultures and stray dogs. *(She turns and exits quickly.)*

ISMENE: Don't Antigone! Please don't!

ISMENE *runs after* ANTIGONE. *Both sit on stools upstage.* CHORUS *signature.*

CHORUS: Well, the stage is set. Antigone has stated her case. It doesn't look like she can count on much help from Ismene, does it? Next, we're going to hear from Creon. (CREON *stands and turns to become part of the play.*) That's Creon over there. The sentry that was guarding Polynices' body is going to give a report.

DEUTERAGONIST *begins to change to become* SENTRY.

AUDIENCE: A report on what? The number of vultures?

CHORUS: No, not that.

AUDIENCE: Well, let's get on with it. We want to see what happens.

CHORUS: Just be patient. I want to tell you that in Greek theatre of the fifth century B.C., they didn't use a lot of actors. In fact, the play had only three actors. I say actors and I mean actors. Women were never, but *never*, allowed in a play.

AUDIENCE: I didn't say I wanted in the play. I said I wanted to get on with the play.

CHORUS: The actors all wore masks and each took several parts. When they wanted to change characters, they just changed masks. Today we're going to use slight costume changes instead of masks for the different characters. You can see Ismene is now changing into the sentry. He's going to bring a report to Creon and he's mighty nervous about what Creon's reaction might be.

CREON *stands.* SENTRY *moves to him.*

SENTRY: Sire, I've—
CREON: What is it?
SENTRY: Sire, I've come running—
CREON: I can see that. What is it? What is it?
SENTRY: Sire, I've come running to report to you, Sire.
CREON: To report what?
AUDIENCE: To report a report, Sire.
CREON: Well then, report it, you blockhead!
SENTRY: Well, it's about the burial, Sire.
CREON: Whose burial?
SENTRY: Polynices' burial, Sire.
CREON: Polynices is having no burial.
SENTRY: That's what I said, Sire. That's what I told the other guards. I said, "King Creon says, says he, that Polynices will not be buried."
CREON: Then why are you reporting gossip among the guards to me?
SENTRY: Because he is.
CREON: Who is? What is? Will you speak up, you bungling idiot! Say what you have to say!
SENTRY: Polynices has been buried.
CREON: Impossible.
SENTRY: No, Sire—I mean, yes, Sire—I mean he hasn't been properly buried, but someone has sprinkled dirt on the body. Not much dirt, mind you, but I must say it's helping to keep the smell down.
CREON: One more stupid statement out of you and there'll be a new body out there, smelling up the atmosphere.
SENTRY: Yes, Sire.
CREON: Who put the earth on the body?
SENTRY: I don't know, Sire.

CREON: Are you telling me that all you guards sat around and let someone cover the body and didn't see who it was?

SENTRY: Yes, Sire. I'm afraid that's what I'm telling you. I didn't want to tell you, Sire, but we drew lots to see who got stuck—I mean, assigned, with the job, and I lost—I mean, I won—I mean, I was chosen.

CREON: (*furiously grabbing him*) Get back to the body, you imbecile! Get back and don't leave the post until you find out who has defied a king's order. If you should fail in this task, then I shall assign a new guard and put a fresh body out to see if the culprit returns to bury it. Do you have any idea where that fresh body might come from?

SENTRY: Yes, Sire!

CREON: Then get out and find this person who has defied a ruler's order!

> SENTRY *hurries out.* CREON *and* SENTRY *move stools and freeze.* CHORUS *signature.*

CHORUS: Well, there you have a worried man, and I don't blame him one bit.

AUDIENCE: So what did he do?

CHORUS: I'll tell you in a minute. Now you've met the three actors in the play and, as you already know, I'm Chorus.

AUDIENCE: Glad to know you, Chorus. But what about the play? Let's get on with something important.

CHORUS: Important! You say important? The most important thing in a Greek play is the chorus.

AUDIENCE: We know. We know. You've already told us that.

CHORUS: We've been around longer than any other aspect of theatre. Why, drama began with a chorus. This dialogue thing—you know, characters speaking to one another in plays—it sprang from the chorus. We used to take turns stepping forward and giving the lines for all the characters. There weren't even actors at that time.

AUDIENCE: Some play it would be without actors!

CHORUS: Then there was a period when the chorus's task was to get the listeners stirred up so that when the tragic hero appeared, they saw him almost as a vision—

AUDIENCE: Look! Up in the sky! It's a bird, it's a plane, it's super hero!

CHORUS: Ah, those were the glorious days of the chorus! But now that's all changed. Someone decided that the chorus wasn't all that important —that we were only here for effect—and ZAPPO—they did away with us one by one, till now there's just me. My job, they say, is to bring the audience closer to the stage. (AUDIENCE *moves her stool closer to* CHORUS.) No, no, they don't mean physically closer. They mean to acquaint you more closely with the events on stage.

AUDIENCE: We can't get acquainted with the events on stage because there are no events on stage.

CHORUS: Ah, yes, we were doing a play, weren't we. Now, where were we?

AUDIENCE: Creon had just told the sentry to find out who buried the body or else.

CHORUS: Oh, yes. Well, we're about to see a very relieved sentry. He got the culprit.

CREON *turns on his stool but remains seated with eyes lowered.* SENTRY *and* ANTIGONE *have gone to the side of the playing area and enter from there.*

SENTRY: But, Sire, she—

CREON *grabs* SENTRY.

CREON: You complete idiot! Can't you get one thing right?

ANTIGONE: Stop, Creon! The man is right.

CREON: But, Antigone, he says you—

ANTIGONE: I did, Uncle. I buried Polynices.

CREON: You—(*to* SENTRY) Get out of here. (SENTRY *exits and begins costume change for* ISMENE.) Antigone, why?

ANTIGONE: Polynices was my brother.

CREON: But didn't you know I had forbidden his burial?

ANTIGONE: I knew.

CREON: You purposely defied my order?

ANTIGONE: He was my brother.

CREON: But it was a state order.

ANTIGONE: I had to do it. I couldn't bear to have my brother's soul wander eternally and find no rest. Polynices deserved a decent burial. If you wouldn't do it, I had to.

CREON: You're a fool, Antigone. You defied the king's order. You've made it difficult for me to get you out of this mess.

ANTIGONE: I don't need you to get me out of it.

CREON: Then what will you do?

ANTIGONE: Nothing.

CREON: Are you looking for a way to test me?

ANTIGONE: No, Creon. I have done the decent thing—buried my brother who was left to rot.

CREON: But my order was—

ANTIGONE: Your order was outrageous!

CREON: I am King of Thebes, Antigone. I have a duty as a monarch. You leave me no choice but to carry out the punishment.

ANTIGONE: I expected you to do that, Uncle. I am prepared to die.

Enter ISMENE.

ISMENE: Antigone, how could you? (*sees* CREON) Uncle, I helped Antigone bury Polynices.

ANTIGONE: She did not.

ISMENE: I did, Uncle. We did it together.

ANTIGONE: There's no need to say that, Ismene. Creon knows.

CREON: I certainly hope I don't have a second niece as mad as Antigone.

ANTIGONE: Ismene had nothing to do with it. I did it alone. I'm ready to die.

CREON: I think you are.

ISMENE: But Creon, not Antigone. She's your niece.

CREON: A broken law is a broken law and lawbreakers must be punished. Antigone will be no exception. You will be put into a cave outside the gates of Thebes. The entrance will be sealed. That cave will be your tomb.

ISMENE: Antigone, beg for forgiveness! Tell him you're sorry!

ANTIGONE: I am not sorry.

ANTIGONE *walks away.* ISMENE *turns to* CREON.

ISMENE: Please, Creon, please! Not my sister! (CREON *walks away.*) Not my sister!

All three move to stools and freeze. CHORUS *signature.*

CHORUS: Well, there you have it. As the writer of one version of the play *Antigone* said, the spring is wound up tight, ready to uncoil. Creon isn't going to back down and neither is Antigone. She's a brave girl.

AUDIENCE: She's an idiot.

CHORUS: You may think so. I disagree.

AUDIENCE: Look, if she was going to die to save someone's life, I'd go along with it. But to get yourself killed to bury someone who's already dead—that's not bravery, that's insanity!

CHORUS: I disagree. Often truly courageous people can't completely justify their actions. There is a logic of the heart that has little to do with the logic of the brain.

AUDIENCE: There's no logic in her thinking. Creon gave her every chance to change her stand.

CHORUS: But Antigone's stand was based on instinct and that is too deep within us to change.

AUDIENCE: Then you're on Antigone's side?

CHORUS: Not necessarily. She is compelled by family loyalty and I can certainly understand that. Families are important, don't you agree?

AUDIENCE: Sure they are.

CHORUS: And Creon, as ruler of Thebes, has made a promise to the people to enforce its laws. A ruler must keep his promises, don't you agree?

AUDIENCE: Well, of course—

CHORUS: Then there's something to be said for both sides?

AUDIENCE: I can see that. But I want to know who wins. Let's get on with it and see.

TRITAGONIST *begins to change to* HAEMON.

CHORUS: That's just what we're going to do. But first, I forgot to tell you that Antigone is engaged to Haemon, who is Creon's son. Ismene is going to play the part of Haemon. Haemon is just getting into his tragic boots. See the thick soles? Tragic boots were used in Greek theatre to make a character taller. Height was associated with importance and rank, so in order for the sentry to be raised up to a crown prince, we really need tragic boots. So this is Haemon, Antigone's fiancé. As you can imagine, Haemon is extremely upset over this whole thing. Perhaps he can change his father's mind.

HAEMON: Father, what have you done with Antigone?

CREON: Antigone must die, Haemon.

HAEMON: But Father, she is the girl I'm to marry.

CREON: Haemon, someday you'll be king. A bad example such as allowing a lawbreaker, especially a relative, to go free could affect your whole reign. A king's word is law. If his subjects think there are exceptions to these laws, you'll have open rebellion on your hands. Am I not right?

HAEMON: Yes, you're right, Father. But in this case the law is a bad one. You must listen to the people. Everyone is saying that Antigone should be freed, that her stand is worthy of praise, that Polynices should have been buried.

CREON: And you would give your loyalty to those who rebel against the laws of the state?

HAEMON: I give my loyalty to what is right.

CREON: And you believe Antigone is right?

HAEMON: I do.

CREON: You are wrong, Haemon.

HAEMON: I am not!

CREON: You are wrong.

HAEMON: (*very angry by now*) You are wrong, Father! Punishing Antigone will be your ruin!

Exit HAEMON *quickly.* CREON *follows. Both sit in freeze.* CHORUS *signature.*

CHORUS: Those are strong words, Haemon.

AUDIENCE: I don't think they did any good at all.

PROTAGONIST *begins to change to* TIRESIAS.

CHORUS: You're right, they didn't, but we have one more character who might be able to persuade Creon. Antigone is changing for the part now. It's Tiresias the prophet. He's blind and very old but a very wise person. He makes burnt offerings to the gods and can tell the future from the things that appear in the smoke. Early Greeks placed a lot of faith in messages from the gods. Tiresias has got some advice for Creon. Maybe it will sway him.

CREON *moves into action. Enter* TIRESIAS.

CREON: Welcome, Tiresias.

TIRESIAS: Creon, you have been a good king—good for Thebes and good for her people.

CREON: Thank you, Tiresias.

TIRESIAS: But I must warn you that you are presently heading down a dangerous path.

CREON: What do you mean?

TIRESIAS: This morning at my altar I made a burnt offering. The smoke exploded in the air and my boy told me in its midst he saw birds tearing at one another—tearing the flesh from each other's bodies.

CREON: What does it mean?

TIRESIAS: It means the gods are rejecting our prayers. The state is sick and I know it is your decision not to bury Polynices that has caused it.

CREON: You can't scare me, Tiresias. I don't believe your prophecies.

TIRESIAS: You've become a cruel tyrant, Creon.

CREON: Don't forget who you're speaking to, Tiresias. I am ruler.

TIRESIAS: Yes, you are ruler and I would prefer not to have to tell you, but I must. The signs are all there, Creon. You have angered the gods. This deed, this denial of burial to Polynices, will be avenged. It will come back to haunt you and yours for generations.

Exit TIRESIAS. CREON *sits and ponders.* CHORUS *signature.*

CHORUS: That's pretty scary stuff, eh? Surely Creon won't ignore it. Early Greeks didn't make light of a message from the gods.

AUDIENCE: Well, at least he's thinking about it. I just don't see why this denial of burial thing is causing so much trouble. After all, the smell would eventually die down and—

CHORUS: Early Greeks believed very strongly that if someone wasn't buried his soul would wander forever and never be at peace.

CREON *moves to call* MESSENGER. PROTAGONIST *has been changing to become* MESSENGER.

AUDIENCE: I see. So what will he do now?

CHORUS: He's calling the messenger. Antigone is taking the messenger's part too. He just has to put on his mantle and his headdress. See the laurel leaves he's putting on his head? Messengers always wore laurel leaves.

AUDIENCE: Sh-sh. I want to hear what Creon's decided.

CHORUS: The messenger is ready. Let's hear.

MESSENGER: Sire?

CREON: Jason, go to the sentry that guards Polynices' body.

MESSENGER: Yes, Sire.

CREON: Give him this message: "The King has decreed that Polynices shall be buried with full honours due to the dead."

MESSENGER: Gladly I'll do that, Sire.

CREON: Then go to the cave where Antigone is imprisoned and free her.

MESSENGER: I'll go in haste, Sire.

CREON: No, wait. Come with me. I shall look after this myself.

Both exit.

AUDIENCE: Hurray! Hurray!

CHORUS: Don't cheer too soon, dear Audience. You haven't seen the end of our story.

AUDIENCE: Well, he's gone to rescue Antigone, hasn't he? And then he'll get on to the burial, and boy! will that make a difference in the air around Thebes. And Antigone will marry Haemon and—

CHORUS: Ah, but there's more to the story. Here's Ismene and here's the messenger back. He's going to talk to Ismene.

ISMENE has moved downstage. MESSENGER enters.

ISMENE: Jason, have you heard the wonderful news? Antigone is to be freed!

MESSENGER: Ismene—

ISMENE: What is it, Jason? What is it?

MESSENGER: I have some sad news for you.

ISMENE: It's Antigone, isn't it? Something has happened to Antigone. Tell me!

MESSENGER: Antigone is dead.

ISMENE: Dead? What happened? How? Creon was to free her.

MESSENGER: The King buried Polynices and then we went to the cave to free Antigone. Haemon went with us. We found Antigone dead—hanged by a noose made from her dress. When Haemon saw her he was so distraught he drew his sword and tried to kill Creon. I pulled Creon aside and before I could stop Haemon, he turned the sword on himself and died at Antigone's feet.

ISMENE: Oh no! So many deaths—Why? Why?

Exit ISMENE. *She sits in freeze.*

MESSENGER: Now I must go and tell Haemon's mother.

Exit MESSENGER. *He sits in freeze.* CHORUS *signature.* AUDIENCE *is looking distraught.*

CHORUS: I warned you the stage was set for tragedy.

AUDIENCE: Well, I've had it! Creon's as stupid as Antigone.

CHORUS: What do you mean?

AUDIENCE: Why would he bury Polynices before going to free Antigone? After all, Polynices was already dead, so what difference—

CHORUS: You must understand that, in spite of what Creon said, Tiresias' prophecy would be a very frightening thing for him. No one, especially a king, fooled around when a message came from the gods.

AUDIENCE: I thought you were on Antigone's side?

CHORUS: I'm on nobody's side. In Greek tragedy you don't have to take sides. There are no good guys and bad guys. There is always weakness on both sides. And even now in our story the last note of tragedy hasn't been sounded.

AUDIENCE: What else can possibly go wrong?

CHORUS: The messenger has gone to tell Eurydice. Now Eurydice was Haemon's mother and, of course, Creon's wife. We hadn't mentioned her up until now because she was a quiet woman and didn't involve herself in Creon's decisions. She was very close to Haemon though, and his death is going to be a blow to her. (CREON *and* ISMENE *move into action.*) Oh, here comes Creon.

CREON: Eurydice is dead. Eurydice is dead.

ISMENE: Dead? How?

CREON: She took poison.

ISMENE: You! You did all this! You caused these deaths.

CREON: I know. But everything I did, I did for Thebes. It was my duty.

ISMENE: You say that causing all these deaths was your duty?

CREON: I didn't want to be king. You know that, Ismene. But as king, I had to enforce the laws. I had no choice. As soon as I took the crown, my role was set.

CREON *and* ISMENE *move to freeze.* CHORUS *signature.*

CHORUS: His role was set.

AUDIENCE: That's really sad. In their theatre, these Greeks really went to extremes to drive home their point.

CHORUS: Strong conflict makes good drama. Greek theatre reflects life as it is, and life isn't always fun and happy times.

AUDIENCE: Especially not with someone like Creon around.

CHORUS: Don't be too hard on Creon. He has the very difficult task of being a leader. Don't ever underestimate the heartbreaking decisions that have to be made by leaders.

AUDIENCE: I guess you're right. It's tough. I really can't decide who was at fault in the whole mess. As you said, it's impossible to label the good guys and the bad guys.

CHORUS: And as I said, there were weaknesses on both sides. Isn't that the case in 'most any conflict?

AUDIENCE: Hey, I think you're right. Anyway, it makes for a good play.

CHORUS: Ah, then you agree with the great philosopher Aristotle. He said that drama is a fine way of teaching a universal truth.

The THREE ACTORS *turn to join the action.*

ALL: Theatre, theatre, is it a dream?

ISMENE: Is it lies? Is it life? Or illusion supreme?

ANTIGONE: Antigone right and—

CREON: Creon all wrong?

ISMENE: Who was the weak—

CHORUS: And who was the strong?

AUDIENCE: Each had his values, isn't it true?

ALL:
  We hope that our play had a message for you.
  Pleasure and learning, tied into one,

CHORUS: Theatre can be instructive—

AUDIENCE: And fun!

ALL:

Theatre, theatre, is it a dream?

Is it lies? Is it life?

Or illusion supreme?

*Voices fade toward end. Heads drop. On "illusion supreme," the flute sounds
the final notes.*

Beth McMaster has been writing for the stage since 1969. Her works include mystery thrillers
and plays for children. Several of her plays have won national awards. She was named for the
Maggie Bassett Award for outstanding contribution to theatre in Ontario. She lives near Peterborough, Ontario. *(Born 1935)*

RESPONDING

Meaning

1. a) *Once Upon a Greek Stage* is a modern retelling of the ancient Greek tragedy
        Antigone. Explain the conflict between Antigone and Creon. Make a written
        list of the different values that each of these characters holds, values that
        are central to the conflict.
    b) Is the conflict resolved? Explain.

2. Near the end of the play, the Chorus quotes the Greek philosopher Aristotle who
    said that "drama is a fine way of teaching a universal truth." In your opinion,
    what universal truth is revealed by the story in *Once Upon a Greek Stage*?

Form and Style

3. *Once Upon a Greek Stage* includes many comic lines. Cite two examples. What
    is the effect of these lines? Why do you think the playwright includes comic lines
    in a tragedy?

4. The play is written in an informal or colloquial style. Why do you think the play-
    wright chose this style? Provide specific examples to support your opinion.

Creative Extension

5. Working in groups, choose a short segment from the play. Draw a sketch of the
    stage showing your interpretation of the placement of actors and props. Carefully
    read the lines and add more detailed stage directions for movement, gestures,
    and tone of voice. Stage the scene or record it on videotape.

6. Near the conclusion of the play, the Chorus says, "In Greek tragedy you don't
    have to take sides. There are no good guys and bad guys." Choose a modern
    television drama that you watch regularly. Write a short essay on whether this
    statement applies to the television drama. Suggest reasons for your conclusions.

The Confession of Many Strangers

✑ Lavonne Mueller

The Confession of Many Strangers is a one-act, one-character play based on the life of the man who piloted the Enola Gay, *the plane that dropped the atomic bomb on Hiroshima, Japan, during World War II. The playwright imagines the pilot on the 50th anniversary of the bombing, visiting the* Enola Gay *exhibit in the Smithsonian Air and Space Museum. In the following monologue taken from the end of the play, the pilot reflects back on that fatal moment.*

Learning Goals

- explore historical context in a text
- examine how character is revealed through monologue
- assess effects of irony and symbols
- research and present an oral report
- compare and contrast two different text forms

[*A beat.*]

It was just beginning to get light. I broke open a little pack of Zinnia seeds Mom gave me and tossed them under my seat for good luck. Everything was smooth and steady. When we came to Iwo Jima, I took the controls. Our standby plane swerved away from us and landed.

[*A beat.*]

We were now three hours away from our possible targets—either Hiroshima, Kokura, or Nagasaki. We were proceeding smoothly, waiting anxiously for instructions from the three weather plane. What would be our target? Oppenheimer said Hiroshima was the best because it had flat terrain that would allow the bomb to "run out." I climbed to 30,700 feet, our bombing altitude. Orders were for a visual drop only. No radar sighting. If we suddenly got bad weather, we were to return to Tinian with Parsons disarming the bomb on the way home.

[*A beat.*]

People always wanted to know what I was thinking when I was only moments away from dropping the first A-Bomb. What were my deepest, innermost thoughts? It's hard to remember. In a sense, that man is an illusion to me. He is many illusions. Looking back, which one do I remember? I don't wish to change the thoughts of somebody who is no longer here to defend himself. After all, who I am *now* is not that pilot who has disappeared into history. I was probably thinking about the flights of WWI, and how opposing pilots could lean out of their wood-and-rag planes and fire revolvers at each other. A flying surface was once as human as the flying carpet of the Arabian Nights. Now everything is precision and electronic navigation.

[*A beat.*]

When the target was in range, it was procedure at that time for the pilot to remove his hands from the controls and turn the ship over to the bombardier. Technically, I wasn't even at the helm when the pneumatic bomb-bay doors opened and "Little Boy" dropped. I felt cheated. The only human experience was the explosion and the victims. The days of Earl Ebberly and *The Wilma* when a man hunched down inside the cockpit and let the plane get inside of him were long gone. Now, a pilot simply steps up and climbs inside the plane. Spots used to talk about his farmer friend, Sig Mosley, who got up one morning and drove his tractor all the way to the coast, then pushed that tractor into the ocean. Said he wanted things to get back to the way they were.

[*Into radio:*]
Straight Flush. Come in. This is *Enola Gay.* [*A beat.*] Y-3, B-2, C-1. Code received. Roger and out.

[*A beat.*]

Attention crew. [*A beat.*] The name of our target has just been transmitted from *Straight Flush.* [*A beat.*] It's . . . Hiroshima!

[*On interphone:*] Pilot to Bombardier. What is the status of "Little Boy?" Bomb is alive. Roger.

[*To crew:*]
The city is coming into view. Be prepared for Initial Point, 15 miles east of target. Sighted—eight large ships in the harbor below. No flak visible.

[*A beat.*]

We are approaching our primary. Secure your goggles on your forehead and prepare to use them at bomb release. Do not look into the flash. [*A beat.*] All crew, if you agree, please verify by saying after me: "This . . . is Hiroshima." [*A beat.*] Hiroshima. Check. [*A beat.*] 9:15 and 17 seconds.

Hiroshima time 8:15 and 17 seconds. [*A beat.*] Bombardier, take over the aircraft. [*He holds up his hands away from the controls and moves back in his chair. A beat.*] Bomb-bay doors opening. "Little Boy". . . falling. [*After a brief pause, he takes over the controls again.*] Prepare for break-away dive!

> [*Now stripped to his trousers and sleeveless khaki-undershirt and bare feet, he holds up the chair and turns it sharply to the right in the break-away dive.*]

> [*He speaks the following monologue while he holds the plane in the break-away dive:*]

A mushroom foams up at me in a churling mass of spiking mauve gray. Buds of raw green illuminate on every side. The earth's history blooms and exaggerates itself into the atmosphere: Stalks of lamp black and coal tar, stems of sienna, plants of brittle skin gold . . . shimmering-black leaves . . . yellow arsenic blossoms. I hear Oppie quoting Montaigne: "And if you have lived one day, you have seen everything. One day is equal to all days. There is no other light, there is no other darkness. The whole disposition of the heavens is the same." Now Montaigne is wrong. It's Oppenheimer's science rotting to the knowable. Today will never be like another day. I have made another light. I have made another darkness. I've changed the Heavens. [*He now begins shaking from the plane's turbulence.*] A fierce boiling red orb, five miles wide, rages towards me at a hundred million degrees. I throw the sun!

American playwright Lavonne Mueller has written several monologues for the stage. Her plays have been produced in Japan, England, Scotland, and the United States. She has also travelled around the world as an Arts America speaker. In 1992, she was awarded the Roger Stevens Playwriting Award at the Kennedy Center.

RESPONDING

Meaning

1. The pilot says he doesn't quite know how to answer people's questions about his innermost thoughts moments before the dropping of the A-bomb. How does he explain this uncertainty? Is his explanation convincing? Why or why not?

2. At one point during the mission, the pilot opens a package of Zinnia seeds his mother had given him, and for good luck he tosses the seeds under his seat in the cockpit. Explain the *irony* in this action.

Form and Style

3. In a *monologue*, characters often reveal their innermost thoughts, emotions, and motives—sometimes unintentionally. Choose three quotations and discuss what they reveal about the pilot's character and motives.

4. At one point, the pilot tells the story of Sig Mosley, a farmer who drove his tractor into the ocean in hopes that with the tractor gone, things would return to the way they were. How does this story-within-a-story relate to the bombing of Hiroshima?

5. How does the pilot's final speech emphasize the significance of the Hiroshima bombing? What is the emotional impact of this final speech? Refer to specific words and images in your answer.

Creative Extension

6. Research, through the Internet and other sources, songs written to protest the use of nuclear weapons. Present a short oral report giving your interpretation of two or three songs. If possible, play recorded performances of the songs and discuss how the musical effects contribute to the songwriter's message.

7. Read or reread the poem "Hiroshima Exit" by Joy Kogawa on pages 60–61. Compare and contrast the ideas, images, and techniques in the poem with those in the monologue above.

One Ocean

✑ Betty Quan

Learning Goals

- explore personal response to a key theme
- examine use of symbolic motifs in literature
- analyze transitions in a radio drama
- adapt a folktale into a radio play

Cast:

Father: Chinese, 50s

Daughter: Chinese, plays ages 18 and a more mature, undetermined age

NOTE: Both also play the parts of the folk story as indicated in the scenes, e.g., Jingwei, Sea God, Emperor. Chinese accents are discernible, but not strong.

Female English Voice, on PA system (can be played by daughter)

Scene 1: Narration, inside memory

MUSIC Establish theme, fade under:

DAUGHTER (*older*): A long time ago. It was my favourite. A story. No, our story. Just a Chinese folktale. Yes. About the Jingwei bird and why she is always dropping sticks and stones in the ocean. When I was small, I used to pretend I was that little bird. I would soar through our communal courtyard with arms for wings. That was when you were still allowed to enjoy our stories, (*becomes overwhelmed*) to tell our stories, before, before. . . (*controls herself*) Bah-bah. Father. Do you remember like I do? Father. Tell me about the Jingwei. Yes, like you used to when I was small. You told me that story when I left Hong Kong for Canada. Do you remember? I was sad. We were both sad. Like a bird in your hand I was until you set me free across the sky, across the ocean. Such a long time ago, yet so close I can still see it unfolding before me. Father? Tell me a story. Like you used to do. (*as if repeating what she hears, in memory*) "A long time ago." It seems like yesterday. A long time ago. But that is how we begin our stories, isn't it? We begin with "a long time ago."

Scene 2: Folktale Remembered

MUSIC Begins, continues under:

FATHER: A long time ago there was an emperor who had a young daughter. They loved each other very much.

DAUGHTER (*older*): But although his power could touch all corners of the land, the emperor could see only as far as the shoreline that divided his kingdom with the sea.

FATHER: Beyond that shoreline, his vision was limited, like a kite held high in a strong breeze—he could see the shape, but not the colours.

MUSIC Fades under the SFX and out

SFX Birds, breeze, ocean under:

DAUGHTER (*as Jingwei*): Father, look at the waves, so tall they must be hiding something behind them. I will take my boat for a ride.

FATHER (*as Emperor*): Not so far, not so far.

DAUGHTER (*as Jingwei*): Don't worry, Father. I'll be careful.

FATHER (*as Emperor*): Why don't you wait a while? I'll join you. We can journey to the horizon together, where the sea meets the sun.

DAUGHTER (*as Jingwei*): When? When can we do this? (*laughs*) You're always promising such things, Father! I'll go out on my own first. On my own adventure. Then, I'll show you what I've seen.

FATHER (*as Emperor*): (*laughs*) When?

DAUGHTER (*as Jingwei*): What does that matter? We have all the time in the world.

DAUGHTER (*older*): The sun was warm upon the little girl's face—

FATHER: —and the salty breeze off the water tempted her to travel farther and farther. To see what hid behind the tall waves of the sea.

DAUGHTER (*older*): Far far far away she went, when suddenly—

SFX Thunder and rainstorm

FATHER (*as Sea God*): —Who dares come this far upon the ocean of my reign?

DAUGHTER (*older*): The Sea God's bad temper came upon the little girl.

SFX/BIZ DAUGHTER/JINGWEI screaming as the waves engulf her

FATHER: The water became a blanket that covered her. And the little girl died.

SFX All suddenly end

DAUGHTER (*older*): Died? I don't remember her dying. Is that right? I thought the water changed her into a bird. Like magic.

FATHER: I would tell you that when you were small. When you didn't understand death.

DAUGHTER (*older*): Like I do now.

FATHER: It is only a story. (*continues*) The little girl's soul became a small bird called a Jingwei.

MUSIC Begins

DAUGHTER (*older*): Father, I died that day you sent me away.

FATHER: No, child, you were reborn. Now, continue the story.

DAUGHTER (*older*): Angry was the spirit in that bird, angry at the sea it was for taking her away from her beloved father. And every day the jingwei would carry in her beak stones and twigs from the mountains of the east and flying west ahead drop her small stones and twigs into the sea. And the Sea God finally noticed what the jingwei was trying to do.

MUSIC Ends

SFX Ocean. Close: the wings of a bird in motion

FATHER (*as Sea God*): (*laughing*) Silly creature, my sea is wider and deeper than your limited imagination. You can never fill me up in a million years.

DAUGHTER (*as Jingwei*): But I can. Every day for a million years I will do this. Every day until one day. Until one day. . . (*begins to fade down*) Until one day. . . Until one day. . .

SFX Fades down

FATHER: And the small bird flew back to land—

TOGETHER: —only to return with another small stone or

with DAUGHTER (*older*): twig to drop into the sea.

DAUGHTER (*older*): And the jingwei said: "One day, there will be a bridge between me and my father. One day, even if it takes a million years to build it." (*she no longer speaks as the jingwei*) Soon, father. I will see you again. Soon.

SFX Fade down

Scene 3: Airport

SFX Airplane's acceleration and ascent. Fades into airport interior: Chinese PA system etc. Close: a swallow singing

FATHER: Yes, yes, sing a goodbye song to my daughter. Here's a sunflower seed.

DAUGHTER: I don't think pets are allowed here.

FATHER: This is not just a pet, eh my little friend? Now keep your bag in full sight. Many pickpockets. There is more freedom here in Hong Kong, but that doesn't mean there is less danger. Here's your ticket. Show it to that man over there. Where's your passport?

DAUGHTER: I don't want to go to Vancouver, father. Why me?

FATHER: Your big brother has a family now. You will go first, then settle down. Then we can join you.

DAUGHTER: When?

FATHER: Soon. Soon. Look at us now. We used to have a fine house and good food to eat. First the Japanese and the war, now Mao[1]. Remember, just a few years ago, Mao decided China must have its Great Leap Forward? And the country went two steps forward and five steps back?

Scene 4: Narration, inside memory

MUSIC (Perhaps the theme, but more percussive here) Fades under:

DAUGHTER *(older)*: Mosquitoes, flies, rats, and sparrows: Mao called these the "four pests." 1958: it was the year I turned sixteen. *(bitter laugh)* Do you remember? Mao believed grain production was down because the swallows were feeding on the backs of the people. Families were armed with pots and pans. We were to scare the sparrows out of the trees so they would eventually drop dead from exhaustion. Six hundred million of us, running under trees, in the countryside, in the cities, making enough noise to waken the dead. Yes, the swallows ate the grain, but they also ate the insects. Without the swallows, no one could control the insects. The sky would rain the corpses of little birds to join the corpses of 300 million people, dead of starvation.

---

[1] Mao Zedong (also spelled Mao Tse-tung) was the Chairman of the Communist Party in the People's Republic of China from 1949–1976. Some people who did not agree with the Communist regime attempted to leave China during this period.

Scene 5: Airport

SFX Airport interior. Close: the swallow singing

FATHER: You know how lucky we were to get out of China?

DAUGHTER: I know.

FATHER: How can we Chinese have luck if we are killing birds!? This is why it is good we are here now. No more death. No more hunger. No more sacrificing our own symbols of fortune and happiness. Maybe my good luck has returned right here in this cage. Maybe now we will all have good luck.

DAUGHTER: Maybe's, nothing but maybe's.

FATHER: You have a chance now, can't you see? To start a new life in a new place.

DAUGHTER: Let me finish school first.

FATHER: *(joking)* Maybe, you'll find a rich Canadian and marry him.

DAUGHTER: I'm 18 years old; I don't need a husband. I can try to find a job here, in Hong Kong.

FATHER: Just a temporary thing, you'll see. Your mother, your brother, me. We'll be a family again. We're relying on you. Work hard. Stay out of trouble. Be a citizen your new country can be proud of. When you're settled, you'll sponsor us to come. We'll join you later.

DAUGHTER: Please don't make me go, father.

FATHER: Who is the parent here? Who makes the decision?

DAUGHTER: Please—father—don't make me go all alone.

FATHER: Look, my jingwei. Yes, you have always been like a little bird to me. If I could, I would always try to protect you, away from bad things. But this—this—is a good thing.

DAUGHTER: I don't want to go!

FATHER: Believe me, it's for the best. You'll like it in Canada.

DAUGHTER: Don't you want me to stay here, with you?

FATHER: It doesn't matter what I want. It's what I want for you.

ENGLISH FEMALE: *(over PA, filtered)* Last boarding call for Flight 973 departing for Vancouver, Canada. *(repeats this in Cantonese)*

DAUGHTER: I've never been in a plane before, Father. Have you?

FATHER: No. Not yet. But in time, no?

DAUGHTER: Yes, in time.

Scene 6: Airfield, Ext.

SFX Airport exterior. Plane accelerating and ascending. Closer: the swallow's song.

FATHER: Goodbye! *(to himself)* Goodbye.

SFX Swallow singing.

FATHER: What's that? What are you singing about?

SFX Swallow singing. Metal clink of the cage being opened.

FATHER: Come on, there. No, it's not a trick. Out. Yes. Fly, go on, fly. Fly.

SFX Close: the acceleration of a bird's wings. Heard under:

FATHER: Build a bridge between me and my daughter. Make our ocean one.

Scene 7: Narration, inside memory

MUSIC Begins and continues under:

DAUGHTER *(older)*: You broke your promise. You never came. You let me leave you behind. I waited for you, Father. For the family. A long time ago. Where are you? Are you here, with me? Did you follow on the shadow of the airplane's wings? *(voice begins to break)* Did I fly away like a kite in the breeze? So high up you can see the shape, but not the colours? Can you see me? I'm so far away, but all you have to do is pull me home. Father. Father. When I finish building a bridge, will you cross it? Even if the stones are loose, and the twigs are breaking. Will you cross it? Father? *(beat)* Bah-bah? How big is the ocean?

MUSIC Ends

SFX Exterior: airfield. Plane's acceleration and ascent crosses into that of birds in flight, their wings in motion. Fade into ocean, of water lapping a beach. Up and out.

Betty Quan is a playwright whose work spans stage, television, and radio. A graduate of the University of British Columbia, her plays have been featured on CBC Radio, most notably *Mr. Sandman* and *Echo Location*. *One Ocean* was expanded into a play entitled *Mother Tongue* (1995), which was a finalist for the Governor General's Award for Drama in 1996.

RESPONDING

Meaning

1. *One Ocean* interprets the experiences of some Canadian immigrants. Identify one specific experience depicted in the drama. In a personal journal entry, reflect on your response to this experience. What thoughts and emotions does it evoke? Why? How does it relate to the theme of the drama?

2. How effective is the opening monologue as an introduction to this drama? Consider themes, mood, images, foreshadowing, character development, and other elements in your response.

Form and Style

3. *Motifs* are recurrent elements that take on a particular significance in a text—recurrent images, phrases, events, actions, or story patterns, for example. How does the Jingwei bird motif become symbolic in this drama? Identify another symbolic bird motif in the play and comment on its significance.

4. This drama interweaves past and present, a traditional folktale and current experience. In addition, the same characters play more than one role. Examine the play and note the techniques the author uses to make the transitions between past and present, and between character roles. In what other ways might these transitions be enhanced in the audio version of the play? Would you have chosen different characters for the roles or done anything differently in the production of the drama? Support your responses.

Creative Extension

5. Select another text from this anthology or a piece of your own writing that employs a motif. Briefly report on how the motif conveys ideas, emotions, and experiences in the text.

6. Choose a short folktale you know well and rewrite it as a radio play. Decide on the characters, key themes, number and content of scenes, appropriate music, and use of sound effects. Then script the dialogue. Record your radio play on audiotape complete with music and sound effects.

Short Fiction

Alice Munro on short fiction:

I don't go into a story to find out what happens. . . . [As a reader I think] you go in to find yourself in a certain environment, a certain climate. What I want from a story is a kind of texture, a created world. What is happening in the story, the content—you say, this story is about this and this—that isn't what I'm interested in. I'm interested in the world it creates for me, and I would think that a lot of readers read that way.

The Leap

ᘐ Louise Erdrich

Learning Goals

- analyze characterization and an author's choice of title
- examine techniques that create suspense
- evaluate narrative point of view
- present a dramatic reading and create a shooting script

My mother is the surviving half of a blindfold trapeze act, not a fact I think about much even now that she is sightless, the result of encroaching and stubborn cataracts. She walks slowly through her house here in New Hampshire, lightly touching her way along walls and running her hands over knicknacks, books, the drift of a grown child's belongings and castoffs. She has never upset an object or as much as brushed a magazine onto the floor. She has never lost her balance or bumped into a closet door left carelessly open.

It has occurred to me that the catlike precision of her movements in old age might be the result of her early training, but she shows so little of the drama or flair one might expect from a performer that I tend to forget the Flying Avalons. She has kept no sequined costume, no photographs, no fliers or posters from that part of her youth. I would, in fact, tend to think that all memory of double somersaults and heart-stopping catches had left her arms and legs were it not for the fact that sometimes, as I sit sewing in the room of the rebuilt house in which I slept as a child, I hear the crackle, catch a whiff of smoke from the stove downstairs, and suddenly the room goes dark, the stitches burn beneath my fingers, and I am sewing with a needle of hot silver, a thread of fire.

I owe her my existence three times. The first was when she saved herself. In the town square a replica tent pole, cracked and splintered, now stands cast in concrete. It commemorates the disaster that put our town smack on the front page of the Boston and New York tabloids. It is from those newspapers, now historical records, that I get my information. Not from my mother, Anna of the Flying Avalons, nor from any of her in-laws, nor certainly from the other half of her particular act, Harold Avalon, her first husband. In one news account it says, "The day was mildly overcast, but nothing in the air or temperature gave any hint of the sudden force with which the deadly gale would strike."

I have lived in the West, where you can see the weather coming for miles, and it is true that out here we are at something of a disadvantage.

When extremes of temperature collide, a hot and cold front, winds gener-ate instantaneously behind a hill and crash upon you without warning. That, I think, was the likely situation on that day in June.

People probably commented on the pleasant air, grateful that no hot sun beat upon the striped tent that stretched over the entire centre green. They bought their tickets and surrendered them in anticipation. They sat. They ate caramelized popcorn and roasted peanuts. There was time, before the storm, for three acts. The White Arabians of Ali-Khazar rose on their hind legs and waltzed. The Mysterious Bernie folded himself into a painted cracker tin, and the Lady of the Mists made herself appear and disappear in surprising places. As the clouds gathered outside, unnoticed, the ringmaster cracked his whip, shouted his introduction, and pointed to the ceiling of the tent, where the Flying Avalons were perched.

They loved to drop gracefully from nowhere, like two sparkling birds, and blow kisses as they threw off their plumed helmets and high-collared capes. They laughed and flirted openly as they beat their way up again on the trapeze bars. In the final vignette of their act, they actually would kiss in midair, pausing, almost hovering as they swooped past one another. On the ground, between bows, Harry Avalon would skip quickly to the front rows and point out the smear of my mother's lipstick, just off the edge of his mouth. They made a romantic pair all right, especially in the blindfold sequence.

That afternoon, as the anticipation increased, as Mr. and Mrs. Avalon tied sparkling strips of cloth onto each other's face and as they puckered their lips in mock kisses, lips destined "never again to meet," as one long breathless article put it, the wind rose, miles off, wrapped itself into a cone, and howled. There came a rumble of electrical energy, drowned out by the sudden roll of drums. One detail not mentioned by the press, perhaps unknown—Anna was pregnant at the time, seven months and hardly showing, her stomach muscles were that strong. It seems incredible that she would work high above the ground when any fall could be so danger-ous, but the explanation—I know from watching her go blind—is that my mother lives comfortably in extreme elements. She is one with the con-stant dark now, just as the air was her home, familiar to her, safe, before the storm that afternoon.

From opposite ends of the tent they waved, blind and smiling, to the crowd below. The ringmaster removed his hat and called for silence, so that the two above could concentrate. They rubbed their hands in chalky powder, then Harry launched himself and swung, once, twice, in huge calibrated beats across space. He hung from his knees and on the third swing stretched wide his arms, held his hands out to receive his pregnant wife as she dove from her shining bar. It was while the two were in midair, their hands about to meet, that lightning struck the main pole and sizzled down the guy wires, filling the air with a blue radiance that Harry Avalon must certainly have seen through the cloth of his blindfold as the tent buckled and the edifice toppled him forward, the swing continuing and not returning in its sweep, and Harry going down, down into the crowd with his last thought, perhaps, just a prickle of surprise at his empty hands.

My mother once said that I'd be amazed at how many things a person can do within the act of falling. Perhaps, at the time, she was teaching me to dive off a board at the town pool, for I associate the idea with midair somersaults. But I also think she meant that even in that awful doomed second one could think, for she certainly did. When her hands did not meet her husband's, my mother tore her blindfold away. As he swept past her on the wrong side, she could have grasped his ankle, the toe-end of his tights, and gone down clutching him. Instead, she changed direction. Her body twisted toward a heavy wire and she managed to hang on to the braided metal, still hot from the lightning strike. He palms were burned so terribly that once healed they bore no lines, only the blank scar tissue of a quieter future. She was lowered, gently, to the sawdust ring just underneath the dome of the canvas roof, which did not entirely settle but was held up on one end and jabbed through, torn, and still on fire in places from the giant spark, though rain and men's jackets soon put that out.

Three people died, but except for her hands my mother was not seriously harmed until an overeager rescuer broke her arm in extricating her and also, in the process, collapsed a portion of the tent bearing a huge buckle that knocked her unconscious. She was taken to the town hospital, and there she must have hemorrhaged, for they kept her, confined to her bed, a month and a half before her baby was born without life.

Harry Avalon had wanted to be buried in the circus cemetery next to the original Avalon, his uncle, so she sent him back with his brothers.

The child, however, is buried around the corner, beyond this house and just down the highway. Sometimes I used to walk there just to sit. She was a girl, but I rarely thought of her as a sister or even as a separate person really. I suppose you could call it the egocentrism of a child, of all young children, but I considered her a less finished version of myself.

When the snow falls, throwing shadows among the stones, I can easily pick hers out from the road, for it is bigger than the others and in the shape of a lamb at rest, its legs curled beneath. The carved lamb looms larger as the years pass, though it is probably only my eyes, the vision shifting, as what is close to me blurs and distances sharpen. In odd moments, I think it is the edge drawing near, the edge of everything, the unseen horizon we do not really speak of in the eastern woods. And it also seems to me, although this is probably an idle fantasy, that the statue is growing more sharply etched, as if, instead of weathering itself into a porous mass, it is hardening on the hillside with each snowfall, perfecting itself.

It was during her confinement in the hospital that my mother met my father. He was called in to look at the set of her arm, which was complicated. He stayed, sitting at her bedside, for he was something of an armchair traveller and had spent his war quietly, at an air force training grounds, where he became a specialist in arms and legs broken during parachute training exercises. Anna Avalon had been to many of the places he longed to visit—Venice, Rome, Mexico, all through France and Spain. She had no family of her own and was taken in by the Avalons, trained to perform from a very young age. They toured Europe before the war, then based themselves in New York. She was illiterate.

It was in the hospital that she finally learned to read and write, as a way of overcoming the boredom and depression of those weeks, and it was my father who insisted on teaching her. In return for stories of her adventures, he graded her first exercises. He bought her her first book, and over her bold letters, which the pale guides of the penmanship pads could not contain, they fell in love.

I wonder if my father calculated the exchange he offered: one form of flight for another. For after that, and for as long as I can remember, my mother has never been without a book. Until now, that is, and it remains the greatest difficulty of her blindness. Since my father's recent death, there is no one to read to her, which is why I returned, in fact, from my failed life where the land is flat. I came home to read to my mother, to read out loud, to read long into the dark if I must, to read all night.

Once my father and mother married, they moved onto the old farm he had inherited but didn't care much for. Though he'd been thinking of moving to a larger city, he settled down and broadened his practice in this valley. It still seems odd to me, when they could have gone anywhere else, that they chose to stay in the town where the disaster had occurred, and which my father in the first place had found so constricting. It was my mother who insisted upon it, after her child did not survive. And then, too, she loved the sagging farmhouse with its scrap of what was left of a vast acreage of woods and hidden hay fields that stretched to the game park.

I owe my existence, the second time then, to the two of them and the hospital that brought them together. That is the debt we take for granted since none of us asks for life. It is only once we have it that we hang on so dearly.

I was seven the year the house caught fire, probably from standing ash. It can rekindle, and my father, forgetful around the house and perpetually exhausted from night hours on call, often emptied what he thought were ashes from cold stoves into wooden or cardboard containers. The fire could have started from a flaming box, or perhaps a buildup of creosote inside the chimney was the culprit. It started right around the stove, and the heart of the house was gutted. The babysitter, fallen asleep in my father's den on the first floor, woke to find the stairway to my upstairs room cut off by flames. She used the phone, then ran outside to stand beneath my window.

When my parents arrived, the town volunteers had drawn water from the fire pond and were spraying the outside of the house, preparing to go inside after me, not knowing at the time that there was only one staircase and that it was lost. On the other side of the house, the superannuated extension ladder broke in half. Perhaps the clatter of it falling against the walls woke me, for I'd been asleep up to that point.

As soon as I wakened, in the small room that I now use for sewing, I smelled the smoke. I followed things by the letter then, was good at memorizing instructions and so I did exactly what was taught in the second-grade home fire drill. I got up, I touched the back of my door before opening it. Finding it hot, I left it closed and stuffed my rolled-up rug beneath the crack. I did not hide under my bed or crawl into my closet. I put on my flannel robe, and then I sat down to wait.

Outside, my mother stood below my dark window and saw clearly that there was no rescue. Flames had pierced one side wall, and the glare of the fire lighted the massive limbs and trunk of the vigorous old elm that had probably been planted the year the house was built, a hundred years ago at least. No leaf touched the wall, and just one thin branch scraped the roof. From below, it looked as though even a squirrel would have had trouble jumping from the tree onto the house, for the breadth of that small branch was no bigger than my mother's wrist.

Standing there, beside Father, who was preparing to rush back around to the front of the house, my mother asked him to unzip her dress. When he wouldn't be bothered, she made him understand. He couldn't make his hands work, so she finally tore it off and stood there in her pearls and stockings. She directed one of the men to lean the broken half of the extension ladder up against the trunk of the tree. In surprise, he complied. She ascended. She vanished. Then she could be seen among the leafless branches of late November as she made her way up and, along her stomach, inched the length of a bough that curved above the branch that brushed the roof.

Once there, swaying, she stood and balanced. There were plenty of people in the crowd and many who still remember, or think they do, my mother's leap through the ice-dark air toward that thinnest extension, and how she broke the branch falling so that it cracked in her hands, cracked louder than the flames as she vaulted with it toward the edge of the roof, and how it hurtled down end over end without her, and their eyes went up, again, to see where she had flown.

I didn't see her leap through air, only heard the sudden thump and looked out my window. She was hanging by the backs of her heels from the new gutter we had put in that year, and she was smiling. I was not surprised to see her, she was so matter-of-fact. She tapped on the window. I remember how she did it, too. It was the friendliest tap, a bit tentative, as if she was afraid she had arrived too early at a friend's house. Then she gestured at the latch, and when I opened the window she told me to raise it wider and prop it up with a stick so it wouldn't crush her fingers. She swung down, caught the ledge, and crawled through the opening. Once she was in my room, I realized she had on only underclothing, a bra of the heavy stitched cotton women used to wear and step-in, lace trimmed drawers. I remember feeling light-headed, of course, terribly relieved, and then embarrassed for her to be seen by the crowd undressed.

I was still embarrassed as we flew out the window, toward earth, me in her lap, her toes pointed as we skimmed toward the painted target of the fire fighter's net.

I know that she's right. I knew it even then. As you fall there is time to think. Curled as I was, against her stomach, I was not startled by the cries of the crowd or the looming faces. The wind roared and beat its hot breath at our back, the flames whistled. I slowly wondered what would happen if we missed the circle or bounced out of it. Then I wrapped my hands around my mother's hands. I felt the brush of her lips and heard the beat of her heart in my ears, loud as thunder, long as the roll of drums.

ᕉ Louise Erdrich is best known for her fiction and poetry, which often draw on her Chippewa heritage. Her books include *Love Medicine* (1984) and *Tracks* (1988). "The Leap" first appeared in *Harper's Magazine* in 1990. She won the Academy of American Poets Prize in 1975, the Pushcart prize for "Indian Boarding School," and the National Magazine Award for Fiction in 1983. (*Born Little Falls, Minnesota 1954*)

RESPONDING

Meaning

1. a) Characterization is an important element in this story. Using specific evidence from the story, develop a character sketch of Anna Avalon. Note which qualities the narrator particularly admires about her mother.
    b) Describe the character of the narrator. How does the reader learn about her? Support your responses with direct evidence from the text.

2. The author's choice of title refers to events in the story, but also has a greater significance. In your opinion, what is its significance beyond alluding to occurrences in the plot? Provide reasons for your interpretation.

Form and Style

3. a) Identify an example of *foreshadowing* in the story. How does the author build suspense throughout the story until the true nature of the events she suggests are revealed?
    b) The author repeatedly makes use of *contrast*. Describe an example of contrast and explain why you think the author uses it. Do you think the author has used it effectively? Support your answer.

4. Describe your response to the *first-person narration* of the story, and explain whether or not you feel the choice of a first-person narrator is an effective one. How might the choice of a different point of view have affected the story?

Creative Extension

5. Choose a segment from the story and present it as a dramatic reading or readers' theatre. Pay particular attention to your tone of voice and use pitch, pace, volume, gestures, and facial expressions to emphasize major events and emotions. Following your reading, write a short commentary on how it affected your understanding and interpretation of the scene.

6. Create a shooting script for a particular episode in the story. Use music and sound effects along with varied camera shots, movements, and angles to capture the action and mood of the segment. Refer to pages 510–511 in this anthology for an example of a shooting script.

The Lottery Ticket

❧ Anton Chekhov

Learning Goals

• examine character revelation

• analyze satire

• examine tone and its effects

• write a review and create an original interpretation of a theme

Ivan Dmitritch, a middle-class man who lived with his family on an income of twelve hundred a year and was very well satisfied with his lot, sat down on the sofa after supper and began reading the newspaper.

"I forgot to look at the newspaper today," his wife said to him as she cleared the table. "Look and see whether the list of drawings is there."

"Yes, it is," said Ivan Dmitritch, "but hasn't your ticket lapsed?"

"No, I took the interest on Tuesday."

"What is the number?"

"Series 9499, number 26."

"All right . . . we will look . . . 9499 and 26."

Ivan Dmitritch had no faith in lottery luck, and would not, as a rule, have consented to look at the lists of winning numbers, but now, as he had nothing else to do and as the newspaper was before his eyes, he passed his fingers downwards along the column of numbers. And immediately, as though in mockery of his scepticism, no further than the second line from the top, his eye was caught by the figure 9499! Unable to believe his eyes, he hurriedly dropped the paper on his knees without looking to see the number of the ticket, and just as though someone had given him a douche of cold water, he felt an agreeable chill in the pit of his stomach, tingling and terrible and sweet!

"Masha, 9499 is there!" he said in a hollow voice.

His wife looked at his astonished and panic-stricken face, and realized that he was not joking.

"9499?" she asked, turning pale and dropping the folded tablecloth on the table.

"Yes, yes . . . it really is there!"

"And the number of the ticket?"

"Oh yes! There's the number of the ticket too. But stay . . . wait! No, I say! Anyway, the number of our series is there! Anyway, you understand. . . ."

Looking at his wife, Ivan Dmitritch gave a broad, senseless smile, like a baby when a bright object is shown it. His wife smiled too; it was as pleasant to her as to him that he only mentioned the series, and did not try to find out the number of the winning ticket. To torment and tantalize oneself with hopes of possible fortune is so sweet, so thrilling!

"It is our series," said Ivan Dmitritch, after a long silence. "So there is a probability that we have won. It's only a probability, but there it is!"

"Well, now look!"

"Wait a little. We have plenty of time to be disappointed. It's on the second line from the top, so the prize is seventy-five thousand. That's not money, but power, capital! And in a minute I shall look at the list, and there—26! Eh? I say, what if we really have won?"

The husband and wife began laughing and staring at one another in silence. The possibility of winning bewildered them; they could not have said, could not have dreamed, what they both needed that seventy-five thousand for, what they would buy, where they would go. They thought only of the figures 9499 and 75 000 and pictured them in their imagination, while somehow they could not think of the happiness itself which was so possible.

Ivan Dmitritch, holding the paper in his hand, walked several times from corner to corner, and only when he had recovered from the first impression began dreaming a little.

"And if we have won," he said—"why, it will be a new life, it will be a transformation! The ticket is yours, but if it were mine I should, first of all, of course, spend twenty-five thousand on real property in the shape of an estate; ten thousand on immediate expenses, new furnishings . . . travelling . . . paying debts, and so on. . . . The other forty thousand I would put in the bank and get interest on it."

"Yes, an estate, that would be nice," said his wife, sitting down and dropping her hands in her lap.

"Somewhere in the Tula or Oryol provinces. . . . In the first place we shouldn't need a summer villa, and besides, it would always bring in an income."

And pictures came crowding on his imagination, each more gracious and poetical than the last. And in all these pictures he saw himself well-fed, healthy, felt warm, even hot! Here, after eating a summer soup, cold as ice, he lay on his back in the burning sand close to a stream or in the garden under a lime tree.

It is hot. . . . His little boy and girl are crawling about near him, digging in the sand or catching ladybirds in the grass. He dozes sweetly, thinking of nothing, and feeling all over that he need not go to the office today, tomorrow, or the day after. Or, tired of lying still, he goes to the hayfield, or to the forest for mushrooms, or watches the peasants catching fish with a net. When the sun sets he takes a towel and soap and saunters to the bathing shed, where he undresses at his leisure, slowly rubs his bare chest with his hands, and goes into the water. And in the water, near the opaque soap circles, little fish flit to and fro and green water-weeds nod their heads. After bathing there is tea with cream and milk rolls. . . . In the evening a walk or vint with the neighbours.

"Yes, it would be nice to buy an estate," said his wife, also dreaming, and from her face it was evident that she was enchanted by her thoughts.

Ivan Dmitritch pictured to himself autumn with its rains, its cold evenings, and its St. Martin's summer. At that season he would have to take longer walks about the garden and beside the river, so as to get thoroughly chilled, and then drink a big glass of vodka and eat a salted mushroom or a soused cucumber, and then—drink another. . . . The children would come running from the kitchen-garden, bringing a carrot and a radish smelling of fresh earth. . . . And then, he would lie stretched full length on the sofa, and in leisurely fashion turn over the pages of some illustrated magazine, or, covering his face with it and unbuttoning his waistcoat, give himself up to slumber.

The St. Martin's summer is followed by cloudy, gloomy weather. It rains day and night, the bare trees weep, the wind is damp and cold. The dogs, the horses, the fowls—all are wet, depressed, downcast. There is nowhere to walk; one can't go out for days together; one has to pace up and down the room, looking despondently at the grey window. It is dreary!

Ivan Dmitritch stopped and looked at his wife.

"I should go abroad, you know, Masha," he said.

And he began thinking how nice it would be in late autumn to go abroad somewhere to the South of France . . . to Italy . . . to India!

"I should certainly go abroad too," his wife said. "But look at the number of the ticket!"

"Wait, wait! . . ."

He walked about the room and went on thinking. It occurred to him: what if his wife really did go abroad? It is pleasant to travel alone, or in the society of light, careless women who live in the present, and not such as think and talk all the journey about nothing but their children, sigh, and tremble with dismay over every farthing. Ivan Dmitritch imagined his wife in the train with a multitude of parcels, baskets, and bags; she would be sighing over something, complaining that the train made her head ache, that she had spent so much money. . . . At the stations he would continually be having to run for boiling water, bread and butter. . . .

She wouldn't have dinner because of its being too dear. . . .

"She would begrudge me every farthing," he thought, with a glance at his wife. "The lottery ticket is hers, not mine! Besides, what is the use of her going abroad? What does she want there? She would shut herself up in the hotel, and not let me out of her sight. . . . I know!"

And for the first time in his life his mind dwelt on the fact that his wife had grown elderly and plain, and that she was saturated through and through with the smell of cooking, while he was still young, fresh, and healthy, and might well have got married again.

"Of course, all that is silly nonsense," he thought; "but . . . why should she go abroad? What would she make of it? And yet she would go, of course. . . . I can fancy. . . . In reality it is all one to her, whether it is Naples or Klin. She would only be in my way. I should be dependent upon her. I can fancy how like a regular woman, she will lock the money up as soon as she gets it. . . . She will look after her relations and grudge me every farthing."

Ivan Dmitritch thought of her relations. All those wretched brothers and sisters and aunts and uncles would come crawling about as soon as they heard of the winning ticket, would begin whining like beggars, and fawning upon them with oily hypocritical smiles. Wretched, detestable people! If they were given anything, they would ask for more; while if they were refused, they would swear at them, slander them, and wish them every kind of misfortune.

Ivan Dmitritch remembered his own relations, and their faces, at which he had looked impartially in the past, struck him now as repulsive and hateful.

"They are such reptiles!" he thought.

And his wife's face, too, struck him as repulsive and hateful. Anger surged up in his heart against her and he thought malignantly:

"She knows nothing about money, and so she is stingy. If she won it she would give me a hundred roubles, and put the rest away under lock and key."

And he looked at his wife, not with a smile now, but with hatred. She glanced at him too, and also with hatred and anger. She had her own day-dreams, her own plans, her own reflections; she understood perfectly well what her husband's dreams were. She knew who would be the first to try to grab her winnings.

"It's very nice making daydreams at other people's expense!" is what her eyes expressed. "No, don't you dare!"

Her husband understood her look; hatred began stirring again in his breast, and in order to annoy his wife he glanced quickly, to spite her, at the fourth page on the newspaper and read out triumphantly: "Series 9499, number 46! Not 26!"

Hatred and hope both disappeared at once, and it began immediately to seem to Ivan Dmitritch and his wife that their rooms were dark and small and low-pitched, that the supper they had been eating was not doing them good, but lying heavy on their stomachs, that the evenings were long and wearisome. . . .

"What the devil's the meaning of it?" said Ivan Dmitritch, beginning to be ill-humoured. "Wherever one steps there are bits of paper under one's feet, crumbs, husks. The rooms are never swept! One is simply forced to go out. Damnation take my soul entirely! I shall go and hang myself on the first aspen-tree!"

❧   Anton Chekhov began writing plays, short stories, and comic sketches as a medical student in Russia. He started writing primarily for personal pleasure, but was encouraged by a friend to pursue his talent. Today, he is considered a master of the short story and of modern drama. His major plays are *Uncle Vanya* (1899) and *The Three Sisters* (1901). The short-story collection *Particoloured Stories* (1886) consolidated his reputation. *(Born Taganrog, Russia 1860; died 1904)*

RESPONDING

Meaning

1. Explain why, in your opinion, Ivan Dmitritch's musings over winning the lottery do or do not reveal his true character and feelings towards others.

2. a) Chekhov's story can be considered as a *satire*. What is this story satirizing? Support your interpretations.
    b) Explain the *irony* of the ending.

Form and Style

3. a) In what *tone* does the narrator tell this story? How is this tone established?
    b) What effect does this tone have on the reader's response to the story? Support your answer.

4. Near the end of the story, Chekhov switches the perspective from Ivan to that of his wife. Explain why you think this technique is or is not effective.

Creative Extension

5. Write a review of this story for an on-line magazine or book club newsletter. In your review, state your interpretations of the story and how successful you believe Chekhov is in his satire. Support your opinions with specific references to the text and to the literary devices the author uses.

6. At one point in the story, Ivan muses, "To torment and tantalize oneself with hopes of possible fortune is so sweet, so thrilling!" Consider other situations in which people might be tantalized or tormented by future possibilities. Choose a genre (short dramatic scene, dramatic monologue, visual representation, advertisement, short narrative, etc.) and create your own interpretation of this theme. Attach an analysis of why you chose your particular genre and what techniques you used to convey your ideas.

Wing's Chips

ॐ Mavis Gallant

Learning Goals

• understand the historical context of a story

• analyze a narrator's bias and perspective

• examine irony and use of contrast

• write an essay and present a dramatic monologue

Often, since I grew up, I have tried to remember the name of the French-Canadian town where I lived for a summer with my father when I was a little girl of seven or eight. Sometimes, passing through a town, I have thought I recognized it, but some detail is always wrong, or at least fails to fit the picture in my memory. It was a town like many others in the St. Lawrence Valley—old, but with a curious atmosphere of harshness, as if the whole area were still frontier and had not been settled and cultivated for three hundred years. There were rows of temporary-looking frame and stucco houses, a post office in somebody's living room, a Chinese fish-and-chip store, and, on the lawn of the imposing Catholic church, a statue of Jesus, arms extended, crowned with a wreath of electric lights. Running straight through the centre of the town was a narrow river; a few leaky rowboats were tied up along its banks, and on Sunday afternoons hot, church-dressed young men would go to work on them with rusty bailing tins. The girls who clustered giggling on shore and watched them wore pastel stockings, lacy summer hats, and voile dresses that dipped down in back and were decorated low on one hip with sprays of artificial lilac. For additional Sunday divertissement, there was the cinema, in an old barn near the railway station. They had no sound track; airs from "My Maryland" and "The Student Prince" were played on a piano and there was the occasional toot of the suburban train from Montreal while on the screen ladies with untidy hair and men in riding boots engaged in agitated, soundless conversation, opening and closing their mouths like fish.

Though I have forgotten the name of this town, I do remember with remarkable clarity the house my father took for that summer. It was white clapboard, and surrounded by shade trees and an untended garden, in which only sunflowers and a few perennials survived. It had been rented furnished and bore the imprint of Quebec rural taste, running largely to ball fringes and sea-shell-encrusted religious art. My father, who was a painter, used one room as a studio—or, rather, storage place, since he worked mostly out-of-doors—slept in another, and ignored the remaining seven, which was probably just as well, though order of a sort was kept by a fierce-looking local girl called Pauline, who had a pronounced moustache and was so ill-tempered that her nickname was *P'tit-Loup*—Little Wolf.

Pauline cooked abominably, cleaned according to her mood, and asked me questions. My father had told her that my mother was in a nursing home in Montreal, but Pauline wanted to know more. How ill was my mother? Very ill? Dying? Was it true that my parents were separated? Was my father *really* my father? "*Drôle de père*," said Pauline. She was perplexed by his painting, his animals (that summer his menagerie included two German shepherds, a parrot, and a marmoset, which later bit the finger of a man teasing it and had to be given away to Montreal's ratty little zoo, where it moped itself to death), and his total indifference to the way the house was run. Why didn't he work, like other men, said Pauline.

I could understand her bewilderment, for the question of my father's working was beginning to worry me for the first time. All of the French-Canadian fathers in the town worked. They delivered milk, they farmed, they owned rival hardware stores, they drew up one another's wills. Nor were they the only busy ones. Across the river, in a faithful reproduction of a suburb of Glasgow or Manchester, lived a small colony of English-speaking summer residents from Montreal. Their children were called Al, Lily, Winnie, or Mac, and they were distinguished by their popping blue eyes, their excessive devotion to the Royal Family, and their contempt for anything even vaguely Gallic. Like the French-Canadians, the fathers of Lily and Winnie and the others worked. Every one of them had a job. When they were not taking the train to Montreal to attend to their jobs, they were crouched in their gardens, caps on their heads, tying up tomato plants or painting stones to make multicoloured borders for the nasturtium beds. Saturday night, they trooped into the town bar-and-grill and drank as much Molson's ale as could be poured into the stomach before closing time. Then, awash with ale and nostalgia, they sang about the maid in the clogs and shawl, and something else that went, "Let's all go down to the Strand, and 'ave a ba-na-ar-na!"

My father, I believe, was wrong in not establishing some immediate liaison with this group. Like them, he was English—a real cabbage, said Pauline when she learned that he had been in Canada only eight or nine years. Indeed, one of his very few topics of conversation with me was the

England of his boyhood, before the First World War. It sounded green, sunny, and silent—a sort of vast lawn rising and falling beside the sea; the sun was smaller and higher than the sun in Canada, looking something like a coin; the trees were leafy and round, and looked like cushions. This was probably not at all what he said, but it was the image I retained— a landscape flickering and flooded with light, like the old silents at the cinema. The parents of Lily and Winnie had, presumably, also come out of this landscape, yet it was a bond my father appeared to ignore. It seemed to me that he was unaware of how much we had lost caste, and what grievous social errors we had committed, by being too much identified with the French. He had chosen a house on the wrong side of the river. Instead of avoiding the French language, or noisily making fun of it, he spoke it whenever he was dealing with anyone who could not understand English. He did not attend the English church, and he looked just as sloppy on Sundays as he did the rest of the week.

"You people Carthlic?" one of the fathers from over the river asked me once, as if that would explain a lot.

Mercifully, I was able to say no. I knew we were not Catholic because at the Pensionnat Saint-Louis de Gonzague, in Montreal, which I attended, I had passed the age at which children usually took the First Communion. For a year and more, my classmates had been attending morning chapel in white veils, while I still wore a plain, stiff, pre-Communion black veil that smelled of convent parlours, and marked me as one outside the limits of grace.

"Then why's your dad always around the frogs?" asked the English father.

Drôle de père indeed. I had to agree with Pauline. He was not like any father I had met or read about. He was not Elsie's Mr. Dinsmore, stern but swayed by tears. Nor did he in the least resemble Mr. Bobbsey, of the Bobbsey Twins books, or Mr. Bunker, of the Six Little Bunkers. I was never scolded, or rebuked, or reminded to brush my teeth or say my prayers. My father was perfectly content to live his own summer and let me live mine, which did not please me in the least. If, at meals, I failed to drink my milk, it was I who had to mention this omission. When I came home from swimming with my hair wet, it was I who had to remind him that, because of some ear trouble that was a hangover of scarlet fever, I was supposed to wear a bathing cap. When Lon Chaney in *The Hunchback of Notre Dame* finally arrived at the cinema, he did not say a word about my not going, even though Lily and Winnie and many of the French-Canadian children were not allowed to attend, and boasted about the restriction.

Oddly, he did have one or two notions about the correct upbringing of children, which were, to me, just as exasperating as his omissions. Somewhere in the back of his mind lingered a recollection that all little girls were taught French and music. I don't know where the little girls of the English of his childhood were sent to learn their French—presumably to France—but I was placed, one month after my fourth birthday, in the Pensionnat, where for two years I had the petted privilege of being the youngest boarder in the history of the school. My piano lessons had also begun at four, but lasted only a short time, for, as the nun in charge of music explained, I could not remember or sit still, and my hand was too small to span an octave. Music had then been dropped as one of my accomplishments until that summer, when, persuaded by someone who obviously had my welfare at heart, my father dispatched me twice a week to study piano with a Madame Tessier, the convent-educated wife of a farmer, whose parlour was furnished entirely with wicker and over whose household hung a faint smell of dung, owing to the proximity of the outbuildings and the intense humidity of summer weather in the St. Lawrence Valley. Together, Madame Tessier and I sweated it out, plodding away against my lack of talent, my absence of interest, and my strong but unspoken desire to be somewhere else.

"*Cette enfant ne fera jamais rien,*" I once heard her say in despair.

We had been at it four or five weeks before she discovered at least part of the trouble; it was simply that there was no piano at home, so I never practised. After every lesson, she had marked with care the scales I was to master, yet, week after week, I produced only those jerky, hesitant sounds that are such agony for music teachers and the people in the next room.

"You might as well tell your father there's no use carrying on unless you have a piano," she said.

I was only too happy, and told him that afternoon, at lunch.

"You mean you want me to get you a *piano*?" he said, looking around the dining room as if I had insisted it be installed, then and there, between the window and the mirrored china cabinet. How unreasonable I was!

"But you make me take the lessons," I said. How unreasonable *he* was!

A friend of my father's said to me, years later, "He never had the faintest idea what to do with you." But it was equally true that I never had the faintest idea what to do with him. We did not, of course, get a piano, and Madame Tessier's view was that because my father had no employment to speak of (she called him a *flâneur*), we simply couldn't afford one—the depth of shame in a town where even the milkman's daughters could play duets.

No one took my father's painting seriously as a daily round of work, least of all I. At one point during that summer, my father agreed to do a pastel portrait of the daughter of a Madame Gravelle, who lived in Montreal. (This was in the late twenties, when pastel drawings of children hung in every other sitting room.) The daughter, Liliane, who was my age or younger, was to be shown in her First Communion dress and veil. Madame Gravelle and Liliane drove out from Montreal, and while Liliane posed with docility, her mother hung about helpfully commenting. Here my father was neglecting to show in detail the pattern of the lace veil; there he had a wrong shade of blue for Liliane's eyes; again, it was the matter of Liliane's diamond cross. The cross, which hung from her neck, contained four diamonds on the horizontal segment and six on the vertical, and this treasure he had reduced to two unimpressive strokes.

My father suggested that Madame Gravelle might be just as happy with a tinted photograph. No, said Madame Gravelle, she would not. Well, then, he suggested, how about a miniature? He knew of a miniaturist who worked from photographs, eliminating sittings, and whose fee was about four times his own. Madame Gravelle bore Liliane, her cross, and her veil back to Montreal, and my father went back to painting around the countryside and going out with his dogs.

His failure weighed heavily on me, particularly after someone, possibly Pauline, told me that he was forever painting people who didn't pay him a cent for doing it. He painted Pauline, moustache and all; he painted some of the French-Canadian children who came to play in our garden, and from whom I was learning a savory French vocabulary not taught at Pensionnat Saint-Louis de Gonzague; he very often sketched the little Wing children, whose family owned the village fish-and-chip store.

The Wing children were solemn little Chinese, close in age and so tangled in lineage that it was impossible to sort them out as sisters, brothers, and cousins. Some of the adult Wings—brothers, and cousins—ran the fish-and-chip shop, and were said to own many similar establishments throughout Quebec and to be (although no one would have guessed it to see them) by far the richest people in the area. The interior of their store smelled wonderfully of frying grease and vinegar, and the walls were a mosaic of brightly painted tin signs advertising Player's Mild, Orange Crush, Sweet Marie chocolate bars, and ginger ale. The small Wings, in the winter months, attended Anglican boarding schools in the west, at a discreet distance from the source of income. Their English was excellent and their French-Canadian idiom without flaw. Those nearest my age were Florence, Marjorie, Ronald, and Hugh. The older set of brothers and cousins—those of my father's generation—had abrupt, utilitarian names: Tommy, Jimmy, George. The still older people—most of whom seldom came out from the rooms behind the shop—used their Chinese names. There was even a great-grandmother, who sat, shrunken and silent, by the great iron range where the chips swam in a bath of boiling fat.

As the Wings had no garden, and were not permitted to play by the river, lest they fall in and drown, it was most often at my house that we played. If my father was out, we would stand at the door of his studio and peer in at the fascinating disorder.

"What does he do?" Florence or Marjorie would say. "What does your father do?"

"He paints!" Pauline would cry from the kitchen. She might, herself, consider him loony, but the privilege was hers. She worked there.

It was late in the summer, in August, when, one afternoon, Florence and Marjorie and Ronald and Hugh came up from the gate escorting, like a convoy, one of the older Wings. They looked anxious and important. "Is your father here?" said the grown-up Wing.

I ran to fetch my father, who had just started out for a walk. When we returned, Pauline and the older Wing, who turned out to be Jimmy, were arguing in French, she at the top of her voice, he almost inaudibly.

"The kids talk about you a lot," said Jimmy Wing to my father. "They said you were a painter. We're enlarging the store, and we want a new sign."

"A sign?"

"I told you!" shrieked Pauline from the dining-room door, to which she had retreated. "*Ce n'est pas un peintre comme ça.*"

"*Un peintre, c'est un peintre,*" said Jimmy Wing, impeturbable.

My father looked at the little Wings, who were all looking up at him, and said, "Exactly. *Un peintre, c'est un peintre.* What sort of sign would you like?"

The Wings didn't know; they all began to talk at once. Something artistic, said Jimmy Wing, with the lettering fat and thin, imitation Chinese. Did my father know what he meant? Oh, yes. My father knew exactly."

"Just 'Wing's Chips'?" my father asked. "Or would you like it in French —'*Les Chips de Wing*'?"

"Oh, *English,*" said all the Wings, almost together. My father said later that the Chinese were terrible snobs.

He painted the sign the next Sunday afternoon, not in the studio but out in the back garden, sitting on the wide kitchen steps. He lacquered it black, and painted—in red-and-gold characters, fat and thin—"Wing's Chips," and under this he put the name of the town and two curly little letters, "P.Q.," for "Province of Quebec."

Tommy and Jimmy Wing and all the little ones came to fetch the sign the next day. The two men looked at it for a long time, while the little ones looked anxiously at them to see if they liked it. Finally, Jimmy Wing said, "It's the most beautiful thing I ever saw."

The two men bore it away, the little Wings trailing behind, and hung it on a horizontal pole over the street in front of their shop, where it rocked in the hot, damp breeze from the river. I was hysterically proud of the sign and, for quite the first time, of my father. Everyone stopped before the shop and examined it. The French-Canadians admitted that it was *pas mal, pas mal du tout,* while the English adults said approvingly that he must have been paid a fine penny for it. I could not bring down our new stature by admitting that he had painted it as a favour, and that it was only after Jimmy and Tommy had insisted that he had said they could, if they liked, pay for the gold paint, since he had had to go to Montreal for it. Nor did I tell anyone how the Wings, burdened with gratitude, kept bringing us chips and ice cream.

"Oh, yes, he was paid an awful lot," I assured them all.

Every day, I went to look at the sign, and I hung around the shop in case anyone wanted to ask me questions about it. There it was, "Wing's Chips," proof that my father was an ordinary workingman just like anybody else, and I pointed it out to as many people as I could, both English and French, until the summer ended and we went away.

Along with Alice Munro, Mavis Gallant is considered one of Canada's premier writers of short fiction. Many of her stories deal with the difficulty of fitting into different cultures. They also display a fine eye for detail and involve the interplay of varying points of view. Gallant left Canada for Europe in 1950, and while living in Paris, published many short stories with *The New Yorker* magazine. She has published two novels and one of her many short-story collections, *Home Truths: Selected Canadian Short Stories* (1981), won the Governor General's Award. She was made a Companion of the Order of Canada in 1993. "Wing's Chips" is from *The Other Paris: Stories* (1986). (Born Montreal, Quebec 1922)

RESPONDING

Meaning

1. a) In small groups, discuss why the narrator's father agreed to paint the sign for the Wing family.

   b) What is the significance of the sign in the story? Why did Mavis Gallant choose to make it the title of the story? Share your interpretations with other groups.

2. a) This story is told primarily from the perspective of the narrator as a young child. Develop a profile of the narrator. How does she view her father and the world around her? What biases does she have and what might account for these biases? Support the character traits you identify with specific evidence from the text.

   b) Looking back as an adult, how might the narrator reassess her father's attitudes and behaviour?

Form and Style

3. At one point in the story, the narrator's father is asked to paint the portrait of a young woman, the daughter of Madame Gravelle, from Montreal. Madame Gravelle was not happy with the portrait. The narrator sees this as a failure on her father's part. Explain the *irony* in the narrator's attitude.

4. Mavis Gallant creates irony through her use of contrasting images. For example, the "leaky rowboats" and "rusty bailing tins" contrast with the description of the delicate clothing worn by the girls on the shore. Find two other examples of this type of ironic contrast and explain how they add to the meaning of the story.

Creative Extension

5. In this story, Mavis Gallant points out the prejudices and stereotypes that have existed amongst social classes and cultural groups in Canada. At the same time, she shows us some characters who did not conform to the "norm." Write an essay on the point you believe Mavis Gallant is making in this story. Consider why she chose to make her narrator a young child, the role of the father, and the issue of social pressures and conformity.

6. Create a dramatic monologue from the father's point of view. Your monologue should give clues about the father's innermost thoughts and feelings, his values, and his attitudes towards his daughter and the other people in the town. Present a reading of your monologue or record it on audio or videotape.

Twins

Eric Wright

Learning Goals

• analyze the relationship between author and reader

• assess an author's use of theme

• examine changes in narrative point of view

• recast a text as a radio play or screenplay

• write a newspaper article

His wife had often criticized his plots for being too complicated, but this one worked.

"I want to get it right," he said. "After making the mistake in the last book about how long it takes to get from Toronto to Detroit, I want this one to be water-tight. So just go along with me until I'm sure that it'll work."

They were standing on the edge of an old mine shaft about ten miles north of Sudbury. The shaft had been sunk in the thirties and they had had to claw their way through dense scrub pine to reach it, and pick the locks on two chain link fences that guarded the hole. At least it was too late in the year for mosquitoes. She wondered how he had found this place.

He seemed to hear what was in her mind. "I found it two years ago," he said. "I came up here hunting with Art. Someone told us we might find a bear along at the garbage dump but we missed the road and came to this place."

He was a writer of detective stories. As far as he could, he liked to "walk the course" of his plots until he was sure they would work. She always went along as a primary test that the story was possible. The stories often took them to some pleasant places, so it was like getting a second holiday, but this time she had come because she needed to know what was in his mind. Sudbury in October is not a popular vacation spot. "Tell me again," she said. "How does he get her to come this far? I wouldn't."

"You just did," he pointed out.

"That was research. Unless you make your villain a writer, you're going to have trouble. What is he, by the way?"

"I haven't decided yet. It's not important. I want to make sure this works, then I can flesh it out."

"Yes, but it doesn't work if the reader can't believe she would stumble through a quarter mile of bush in this godforsaken landscape. You've got to find a good reason."

"I'll find one. Let's get the plot straight, shall we?"

"This isn't the way you usually work. Usually you get the characters first, then let the plot grow out of them. So you say, anyway."

"Yeah, but this plot is ingenious. I mean, the villain thinks it is, so I want to test it before I spend my time creating his world. Okay?"

"Okay, so now he kills her. Right? And drops the body down there." She kicked a small rock over the edge of the hole and listened hard, but there was no "ploomp" or rattle of the sound of the rock reaching the bottom. It must go down hundreds of metres.

"That's right. He throws the gun in after her; he's made sure it's untraceable. Then he drives south to the motel in Parry Sound where they have a reservation. When he gets there it's dark." He looked at the sky turning pink in the west. "He registers as her."

"Where did you get this idea?"

"From us. People are always saying we look alike, as if we're a couple of gerbils."

"Where does he change his clothes?"

"In the car, on a side road, probably the Pickerel River road, somewhere quiet. He doesn't actually have to change much: just put on a blonde wig, lipstick, glasses." He looked down at himself to show what he meant. Both of them were dressed in sneakers, blues jeans, and heavy bush jackets that came well below the waist. "Then he checks in at the motel, as her, 'her' husband is turning the car around or picking up beer or something. The point is the motel people have never seen 'her' and believe that he is there, too. An hour later, he goes to the motel office, as himself, to ask for a wakeup call, so now the motel people have seen 'her' and him. Then, around midnight, the fighting starts. The people in the units on either side hear a hell of a row going on, sounds of someone being smacked around, and it goes on so long they complain to the desk, and the night clerk phones over and asks them to pipe down."

"The row is on tape, right?"

"Right. Then early in the morning the row starts again and there's a lot of door-banging and the neighbours see 'her' leaving, walking away. At breakfast time, he checks out leaving a message in case his wife returns. He tells the clerk she walked out on him during the night. She's probably gone to another motel. His message is that he's not going to wait around; he's gone home."

"So he left the motel in the blonde wig, then came back quietly as himself a bit later. Wasn't he taking a chance?"

"Not really. If anyone saw him, he could always say he had tried to follow his wife, but she disappeared. And that's that. He goes home and when his wife doesn't appear that day he reports it to the police. But in circumstances like these it looks likely that the wife has simply gone off somewhere. It's a few weeks before he can get the police seriously interested."

"And when they do take it seriously, do they find her?" There was not much light left now. In the east the sky was almost black.

"I don't know. It doesn't matter. A few weeks is as good as six months."

"They'll suspect him. After the row."

"But they won't be able to prove anything. When he leaves the motel after breakfast, he checks in with the Ontario Provincial Police in Parry Sound, in case 'she' has checked in with them, and he does the same thing all the way down to Toronto, establishing a solid time trail with no gaps for him to drive back up to Sudbury. Then it's easy to make sure he's covered for the next week in Toronto."

"It might work," she said. "Have you figured out how you are going to solve it? How Porter will, I mean." Gib Porter was the writer's hero.

"Not yet."

"You could start with a hunch. You could find out what time he left Sudbury and why it took him five hours to get to Parry Sound. Did anyone see his car parked along the highway, stuff like that?"

"Why would anyone be suspicious?"

She pondered. "Her father. He never liked the man she married, never trusted him, so he hires Gib Porter." Now it was close to dark. "What about the car? Someone might have seen their car parked along the highway."

"It's rented. Perfectly ordinary rented car. If anyone sees it they won't memorize the licence plate. They'll just assume that it's a couple of hunters. But I haven't seen anyone around, have you?"

"No, I haven't. Who would be wandering around this moonscape?" She had to admit that he seemed to have everything covered. "One last thing," she asked. "Why? What's the reason?"

"Motive you mean?" He shrugged. "Another woman, I guess."

"Come on. This is 1990. That was a motive back when you had to wait seven years for a divorce. People change around all the time now."

"Not if she refuses. The other lady I mean. This guy has fallen in love with someone who refuses to see him unless he is free. She was raised in the Brethren. She loves him, but she believes in the sanctity of marriage."

"Does she indeed. It isn't his wife's fault, then." She turned her back on him and walked towards the road. She needed to know one more thing. "In the meantime, old buddy-boy," she said over her shoulder, "we'd better be getting back."

He reached inside his jacket and pulled out the little handgun he had bought in Detroit. "Don't turn round Lucy," he said. She turned and saw that her last question was answered. It wasn't a game. She said, "It isn't going to work."

"It'll work, all right. It's going to work." He pulled the trigger once, twice, three times.

Everything else went smoothly. His wife had often criticized his plots for being too complicated, but this one worked. Two hours later the night clerk at the Sturgeon Motel in Parry Sound signed in Mrs. Harry Coates, a blonde lady with sunglasses (though it was quite dark), while her husband unloaded the car. During the night the clerk had to call them twice to ask them to pipe down because they were fighting and arguing so loudly that the guests on either side had called to complain. The rowing ended in the early morning with a lot of door-crashing, then Mrs. Coates came to the desk to check out. She still had sunglasses on, but now the clerk thought they were probably covering up a black eye. Her husband, she said, had left her, taken a train or bus back to Toronto, maybe even hitchhiked—she didn't know or care. She left a message for him in case he called. He never did, though.

She drove home and waited for two days for him to return, then she called the police. They made some routine enquiries, but they weren't very interested. The story of the night in the motel was clear, and the guy was almost certainly putting a scare into her by taking off for as long as his money held out, but pretty soon he would use a charge card or something like that, then they would be able to reel him in. They did establish that he had a girlfriend tucked away in a condominium on Sherbourne Street, and they kept an eye on her place but she was as mystified as they were and he certainly never showed up. Nor did he try to call her. A month later the police assumed foul play and sent out a serious enquiry, and she began the process of establishing her legal position if he should have disappeared for good. When the first snow fell she knew they wouldn't find him until spring at the earliest, and then what would they find? A body, with no money in the wallet, and the gun that had killed him. (She had thrown *his* gun, from which she had removed the ammunition the night before they started their trip, when she realized what he was planning, into the French River on her way to Parry Sound.) And what would they conclude? That he had been picked up hitchhiking, robbed and killed and dumped into the mineshaft by a local thug. There was still the very slight risk that someone had seen them when they went into the bush that evening, but it was a chance *he* was prepared to take, so it was pretty small. Since the chance of finding the body in the first place was about ten thousand to one, the further remote chance that someone saw them near the mineshaft was an acceptable risk. All she had to do was nurse her grief for the few weeks while the police made their enquiries.

The plan had been perfect, or pretty good. If she had not long known about the lady in the condominium, and if she had not come across his fishing tackle box with the loaded gun, the wig, and the make-up kit, packed ready to go, while she was searching for a pair of pliers, she would never have wondered what he was up to. After that it was just a matter of getting hold of a gun herself, and giving him every chance to prove her guess was wrong. The rest went exactly as he had planned.

Eric Wright immigrated to Canada from London at the age of 21. Famed for crime and mystery novels featuring Toronto Police Inspector Charlie Salter, Wright has also written the satirical *Moodie's Tale* (1994). *The Nights the Gods Smiled* (1983) won an Arthur Ellis Award and a City of Toronto Book Award. (Born London, England 1929)

RESPONDING

Meaning

1. It has been said that a good detective writer is always honest with the reader. How does Eric Wright provide his readers with clues to the outcome of this story?

2. A common theme in detective fiction is "crime does not pay." In your opinion, is it possible that this story sets up a situation in which crime will go unpunished?

Form and Style

3. *In medias res* is a Latin phrase meaning "in the middle of things." Explain how the term can be applied to the opening of this story and evaluate the author's choice in employing this technique.

4. Describe the difference in narrative style between the two parts of the story. Determine why the author chose each style and the effectiveness of each.

Creative Extension

5. Working in groups, recast this story as a script for a radio play or as a screenplay for a television program. Include music and sound effects, and rewrite some of the descriptive passages as appropriate. If you choose to do a screenplay, describe the action carefully and include directions for camera shots and angles. Dramatize and record at least a segment of your script or screenplay on audio or videotape.

6. Write an article for the local newspaper informing its readers of the details surrounding the discovery of the husband's body. Include quotes from an interview with Lucy, the woman in the story. Outline what direction the police investigation is following and speculate on the outcome.

Cornet at Night

☙ Sinclair Ross

Learning Goals

- interpret meaning through a close examination of text
- examine the effects of figurative language
- analyze techniques used to maintain narrative flow
- write a journal entry and short essay

The wheat was ripe and it was Sunday. "Can't help it—I've got to cut," my father said at breakfast. "No use talking. There's a wind again and it's shelling fast."

"Not on the Lord's Day," my mother protested. "The horses stay in the stables where they belong. There's church this afternoon and I intend to ask Louise and her husband home for supper."

Ordinarily my father was a pleasant, accommodating man, but this morning his wheat and the wind had lent him sudden steel. "No, today we cut," he met her evenly. "You and Tom go to church if you want. Don't bother me."

"If you take the horses out today I'm through—I'll never speak to you again. And this time I mean it."

He nodded. "Good—if I'd known I'd have started cutting wheat on Sunday years ago."

"And that's no way to talk in front of your son. In the years to come he'll remember."

There was silence for a moment and then, as if in its clash with hers his will had suddenly found itself, my father turned to me.

"Tom, I need a man to stook for a few days and I want you to go to town tomorrow and get me one. The way the wheat's coming along so fast and the oats nearly ready too I can't afford the time. Take old Rock. You'll be safe with him."

But ahead of me my mother cried, "That's one thing I'll not stand for. You can cut your wheat or do anything else you like yourself, but you're not interfering with him. He's going to school tomorrow as usual."

My father bunched himself and glared at her. "No, for a change he's going to do what I say. The crop's more important than a day at school."

"But Monday's his music lesson day—and when will we have another teacher like Miss Wiggins who can teach him music too?"

"A dollar for lessons and the wheat shelling! When I was his age I didn't even get to school."

"Exactly," my mother scored, "and look at you today. Is it any wonder I want him to be different?"

He slammed out at that to harness his horses and cut his wheat, and away sailed my mother with me in her wake to spend an austere half-hour in the dark, hot, plushy little parlour. It was a kind of vicarious atonement, I suppose, for we both took straight-backed leather chairs, and for all of the half-hour stared across the room at a big pansy-bordered motto on the opposite wall: *As for Me and My House We Will Serve the Lord.*

At last she rose and said, "Better run along and do your chores now, but hurry back. You've got to take your bath and change your clothes, and maybe help a little getting dinner for your father."

There was a wind this sunny August morning, tinged with freedom and departure, and from his stall my pony Clipper whinnied for a race with it. Sunday or not, I would ordinarily have had my gallop anyway, but today a sudden welling-up of social and religious conscience made me ask myself whether one in the family like my father wasn't bad enough. Returning to the house, I merely said that on such a fine day it seemed a pity to stay inside. My mother heard but didn't answer. Perhaps her conscience too was working. Perhaps after being worsted in the skirmish with my father, she was in no mood for granting dispensations. In any case I had to take my bath as usual, put on a clean white shirt, and change my overalls for knicker corduroys.

They squeaked, those corduroys. For three months now they had been spoiling all my Sundays. A sad, muted, swishing little squeak, but distinctly audible. Every step and there it was, as if I needed to be oiled. I had to wear them to church and Sunday-school; and after service, of course, while the grown-ups stood about gossiping, the other boys discovered my affliction. I sulked and fumed, but there was nothing to be done. Corduroys that had cost four-fifty simply couldn't be thrown away till they were well worn-out. My mother warned me that if I started sliding down the stable roof, she'd patch the seat and make me keep on wearing them.

With my customary little bow-legged sidle I slipped into the kitchen again to ask what there was to do. "Nothing but try to behave like a Christian and a gentleman," my mother answered stiffly. "Put on a tie, and shoes and stockings. Today your father is just about as much as I can bear."

"And then what?" I asked hopefully. I was thinking that I might take a drink to my father, but dared not as yet suggest it.

"Then you can stay quiet and read—and afterwards practise your music lesson. If your Aunt Louise should come she'll find that at least I bring my son up decently."

It was a long day. My mother prepared the midday meal as usual, but, to impress upon my father the enormity of his conduct, withdrew as soon as the food was served. When he was gone, she and I emerged to take our places at the table in an atmosphere of unappetizing righteousness. We didn't eat much. The food was cold, and my mother had no heart to warm it up. For relief at last she said, "Run along and feed the chickens while I change my dress. Since we aren't going to service today we'll read Scripture for a while instead."

And Scripture we did read, Isaiah, my mother in her black silk dress and rhinestone brooch, I in my corduroys and Sunday shoes that pinched. It was a very august afternoon, exactly like the tone that had persisted in my mother's voice since breakfast time. I think I might have openly rebelled, only for the hope that by compliance I yet might win permission for the trip to town with Rock. I was inordinately proud that my father had suggested it, and for his faith in me forgave him even Isaiah and the plushy afternoon. Whereas with my mother, I decided, it was a case of downright bigotry.

We went on reading Isaiah, and then for a while I played hymns on the piano. A great many hymns—even the ones with awkward sharps and accidentals that I'd never tried before—for, fearing visitors, my mother was resolved to let them see that she and I were uncontaminated by my father's sacrilege. But among these likely visitors was my Aunt Louise, a portly, condescending lady married to a well-off farmer with a handsome motor-car, and always when she came it was my mother's vanity to have me play for her a waltz or reverie, or *Holy Night* sometimes with variations. A man-child and prodigy might eclipse the motor-car. Presently she roused herself, and pretending mild reproof began, "Now, Tommy, you're going wooden on those hymns. For a change you'd better practise *Sons of Liberty*. Your Aunt Louise will want to hear it, anyway."

There was a fine swing and vigour in this piece, but it was hard. Hard because it was so alive, so full of youth and head-high rhythm. It was a march, and it did march. I couldn't take time to practise at the hard spots slowly till I got them right, for I had to march too. I had to let my fingers sometimes miss a note or strike one wrong. Again and again this afternoon I started carefully, resolving to count right through, the way Miss Wiggins did, and as often I sprang ahead to lead my march a moment or two all dash and fire, and then fall stumbling in the bitter dust of dissonance. My mother didn't know. She thought that speed and perseverance would eventually get me there. She tapped her foot and smiled encouragement, and gradually as the afternoon wore on began to look a little disappointed that there were to be no visitors, after all. "Run along for the cows," she said at last, "while I get supper ready for your father. There'll be nobody here, so you can slip into your overalls again."

I looked at her a moment, and then asked: "What am I going to wear to town tomorrow? I might get grease or something on the corduroys."

For while it was always my way to exploit the future, I liked to do it rationally, within the limits of the sane and probable. On my way for the cows I wanted to live the trip to town tomorrow many times, with variations, but only on the explicit understanding that tomorrow there was to be a trip to town. I have always been tethered to reality, always compelled by an unfortunate kind of probity in my nature to prefer a bare-faced disappointment to the luxury of a future I have no just claims upon.

I went to town the next day, though not till there had been a full hour's argument that paradoxically enough gave all three of us the victory. For my father had his way: I went; I had my way: I went; and in return for her consent my mother wrung a promise from him of a pair of new plush curtains for the parlour when the crop was threshed, and for me the metronome that Miss Wiggins declared was the only way I'd ever learn to keep in time on marching pieces like the *Sons of Liberty*.

It was my first trip to town alone. That was why they gave me Rock, who was old and reliable and philosophic enough to meet motor-cars and the chance locomotive on an equal and even somewhat supercilious footing.

"Mind you pick somebody big and husky," said my father as he started for the field. "Go to Jenkins' store, and he'll tell you who's in town. Whoever it is, make sure he's stooked before."

"And mind it's somebody who looks like he washes himself," my mother warned, "I'm going to put clean sheets and pillowcases on the bunkhouse bed."

By the time they had both finished with me there were a great many things to mind. Besides repairs for my father's binder, I was to take two crates of eggs each containing twelve dozen eggs to Mr. Jenkins' store and in exchange have a list of groceries filled. And to make it complicated, both quantity and quality of some of the groceries were to be determined by the price of eggs. Thirty cents a dozen, for instance, and I was to ask for coffee at sixty-five cents a pound. Twenty-nine cents a dozen and coffee at fifty cents a pound. Twenty-eight and no oranges. Thirty-one and bigger oranges. It was like decimals with Miss Wiggins, or two notes in the treble against three in the bass. For my father a tin of special blend tobacco, and my mother not to know. For my mother a box of face powder at the drug-store, and my father not to know. Twenty-five cents from my father on the side for ice-cream and licorice. Thirty-five from my mother for my dinner at the Chinese restaurant. And warnings, of course, to take good care of Rock, speak politely to Mr. Jenkins, and see that I didn't get machine oil on my corduroys.

It was three hours to town with Rock, but I don't remember them. I remember nothing but a smug satisfaction with myself, an exhilarating conviction of importance and maturity—and that only by contrast with the sudden sag to embarrassed insignificance when finally old Rock and I drove up to Jenkins' store.

For a farm boy is like that. Alone with himself and his horse he cuts a fine figure. He is the measure of the universe. He foresees a great many encounters with life, and in them all acquits himself a little more than creditably. He is fearless, resourceful, a bit of a brag. His horse never contradicts.

But in town it is different. There are eyes here, critical, that pierce with a single glance the little bubble of his self-importance, and leave him dwindled smaller even than his normal size. It always happens that way. They are so superbly poised and sophisticated, these strangers, so com-pletely masters of their situation as they loll in doorways and go saunter-ing up and down Main Street. Instantly he yields to them his place as measure of the universe, especially if he is a small boy wearing squeaky corduroys, especially if he has a worldly-wise horse like Rock, one that knows his Main Streets, and will take them in nothing but his own slow philosophic stride.

We arrived all right. Mr. Jenkins was a little man with a freckled bald head, and when I carried in my two crates of eggs, one in each hand, and my legs bowed a bit, he said curtly, "Well, can't you set them down? My boy's delivering, and I can't take time to count them now myself."

"They don't need counting," I said politely. "Each layer holds two dozen, and each crate holds six layers. I was there. I saw my mother put them in."

At this a tall, slick-haired young man in yellow shoes who had been standing by the window turned around and said, "That's telling you, Jenkins —he was there." Nettled and glowering, Jenkins himself came round the counter and repeated, "So you were there, were you? Smart youngster! What did you say was your name?"

Nettled in turn to preciseness I answered, "I haven't yet. It's Thomas Dickson and my father's David Dickson, eight miles north of here. He wants a man to stook and was too busy to come himself."

He nodded, unimpressed, and then putting out his hand said, "Where's your list? Your mother gave you one, I hope!"

I said she had and he glowered again. "Then let's have it and come back in half an hour. Whether you were there or not, I'm going to count your eggs. How do I know that half of them aren't smashed?"

"That's right," agreed the young man, sauntering to the door and looking at Rock. "They've likely been bouncing along at a merry clip. You're quite sure, Buddy, that you didn't have a run-away?"

Ignoring the impertinence I staved off Jenkins. "The list, you see, has to be explained. I'd rather wait and tell you about it later on."

He teetered a moment on his heels and toes, then tried again. "I can read too. I make up orders every day. Just go away for a while—look for your man—anything."

"It wouldn't do," I persisted. "The way this one's written isn't what it really means. You'd need me to explain—"

He teetered rapidly. "Show me just one thing I don't know what it means."

"Oranges," I said, "but that's only oranges if eggs are twenty-nine cents or more—and bigger oranges if they're thirty-one. You see, you'd never understand—"

So I had my way and explained it all right then and there. What with eggs at twenty-nine and a half cents a dozen and my mother out a little in her calculations, it was somewhat confusing for a while; but after arguing a lot and pulling away the paper from each other that they were figuring on, the young man and Mr. Jenkins finally had it all worked out, with mustard and soap omitted altogether, and an extra half-dozen oranges thrown in. "Vitamins," the young man overruled me, "they make you grow"—and then with a nod towards an open biscuit box invited me to help myself.

I took a small one, and started up Rock again. It was nearly one o'clock now, so in anticipation of his noonday quart of oats he trotted off, a little more briskly, for the farmers' hitching-rail beside the lumber-yard. This was the quiet end of town. The air drowsed redolent of pine and tamarack, and resin simmering slowly in the sun. I poured out the oats and waited till he had finished. After the way the town had treated me it was comforting and peaceful to stand with my fingers in his mane, hearing him munch. It brought me a sense of place again in life. It made me feel almost as important as before. But when he finished and there was my own dinner to be thought about I found myself more of an alien in the town than ever, and felt the way to the little Chinese restaurant doubly hard. For Rock was older than I. Older and wiser, with a better understanding of important things. His philosophy included the relishing of oats even within a stone's throw of sophisticated Main Street. Mine was less mature. I went, however, but I didn't have dinner. Perhaps it was my stomach, all puckered and tense with nervousness. Perhaps it was the restaurant itself, the pyramids of oranges in the window and the dark green rubber plant with the tropical-looking leaves, the man behind the counter and the dusky smell of last night's cigarettes that to my prairie nostrils was the orient itself, the exotic atmosphere about it all with which a meal of meat and vegetables and pie would have somehow simply jarred. I climbed on to a stool and ordered an ice-cream soda.

A few stools away there was a young man sitting. I kept watching him and wondering.

He was well-dressed, a nonchalance about his clothes that distinguished him from anyone I had ever seen, and yet at the same time it was a shabby suit, with shiny elbows and threadbare cuffs. His hands were slender, almost a girl's hands, yet vaguely with their shapely quietness they troubled me, because, however slender and smooth, they were yet hands to be reckoned with, strong with a strength that was different from the rugged labour-strength I knew.

He smoked a cigarette, and blew rings towards the window.

Different from the farmer boys I knew, yet different also from the young man with the yellow shoes in Jenkins' store. Staring out at it through the restaurant window he was as far away from Main Street as I with plodding old Rock and my squeaky corduroys. I presumed for a minute or two an imaginary companionship. I finished my soda, and to be with him a little longer ordered lemonade. It was strangely important to be with him, to prolong a while this companionship. I hadn't the slightest hope of his noticing me, nor the slightest intention of obtruding myself. I just wanted to be there, to be assured by something I had never encountered before, to store it up for the three hours home with old Rock.

Then a big, unshaven man came in, and slouching on to the stool beside me said, "They tell me across the street you're looking for a couple of hands. What's your old man pay this year?"

"My father," I corrected him, "doesn't want a couple of men. He just wants one."

"I've got a pal," he insisted, "and we always go together."

I didn't like him. I couldn't help making contrasts with the cool, trim quietness of the young man sitting farther along. "What do you say?" he said as I sat silent, thrusting his stubby chin out almost over my lemonade. "We're ready any time."

"It's just one man my father wants," I said aloofly, drinking off my lemonade with a flourish to let him see I meant it. "And if you'll excuse me now—I've got to look for somebody else."

"What about this?" he intercepted me, and doubling up his arm displayed a hump of muscle that made me, if not more inclined to him, at least a little more deferential. "My pal's got plenty, too. We'll set up two stooks any day for anybody else's one."

"Not both," I edged away from him. "I'm sorry—you just wouldn't do."

He shook his head contemptuously. "Some farmer—just one man to stook."

"My father's a good farmer," I answered stoutly, rallying to the family honour less for its own sake than for what the young man on the other stool might think of us. "And he doesn't need just one to stook. He's already got three already. That's plenty other years, but this year the crop's so big he needs another. So there!"

"I can just see the place," he said, slouching to his feet and starting towards the door. "An acre to two of potatoes and a couple of dozen hens."

I glared after him a minute, then climbed back on to the stool and ordered another soda. The young man was watching me now in the big mirror behind the counter, and when I glanced up and met his eyes he gave a slow, half-smile little nod of approval. And out of all proportion to anything it could mean, his nod encouraged me. I didn't flinch or fidget as I would have done had it been the young man with the yellow shoes watching me, and I didn't stammer over the confession that his amusement and appraisal somehow forced from me. "We haven't three men— just my father—but I'm to take one home today. The wheat's ripening fast this year and shelling, so he can't do it all himself."

He nodded again and then after a minute asked quietly, "What about me? Would I do?"

I turned on the stool and stared at him.

"I need a job, and if it's any recommendation there's only one of me."

"You don't understand," I started to explain, afraid to believe that perhaps he really did. "It's to stook. You have to be in the field by seven o'clock and there's only a bunkhouse to sleep in—a granary with a bed in it—"

"I know—that's about what I expect." He drummed his fingers a minute, then twisted his lips into a kind of half-hearted smile and went on, "They tell me a little toughening up is what I need. Outdoors, and plenty of good hard work—so I'll be like the fellow that just went out."

The wrong hands: white slender fingers, I knew they'd never do—but catching the twisted smile again I pushed away my soda and said quickly, "Then we'd better start right away. It's three hours home, and I've still some places to go. But you can get in the buggy now, and we'll drive around together."

We did. I wanted it that way, the two of us, to settle scores with Main Street. I wanted to capture some of old Rock's disdain and unconcern; I wanted to know what it felt like to take young men with yellow shoes in my stride, to be preoccupied, to forget them the moment that we separated. And I did. "My name's Philip," the stranger said as we drove from Jenkins' to the drugstore. "Philip Coleman—usually just Phil," and companionably I responded, "Mine's Tommy Dickson. For the last year, though, my father says I'm getting big and should be called just Tom."

That was what mattered now, the two of us there, and not the town at all. "Do you drive yourself all the time?" he asked, and nonchalant and off-hand I answered, "You really don't have to drive old Rock. He just goes, anyway. Wait till you see my chestnut three-year-old. Clipper I call him. Tonight after supper if you like you can take him for a ride."

But since he'd never learned to ride at all he thought Rock would do better for a start, and then we drove back to the restaurant for his cornet and valise.

"Is it something to play?" I asked as we cleared the town. "Something like a bugle?"

He picked up the black leather case from the floor of the buggy and held it on his knee. "Something like that. Once I played a bugle too. A cornet's better, though."

"And you mean you can play the cornet?"

He nodded. "I play in a band. At least I did play in a band. Perhaps if I get along all right with the stooking I will again sometime."

It was later that I pondered this, how stooking for my father could have anything to do with going back to play in a band. At the moment I confided, "I've never heard a cornet—never even seen one. I suppose you still play it sometimes—I mean at night, when you've finished stooking."

Instead of answering directly, he said, "That means you've never heard a band either." There was surprise in his voice, almost incredulity, but it was kindly. Somehow I didn't feel ashamed because I had lived all my eleven years on a prairie farm, and knew nothing more than Miss Wiggins and my Aunt Louise's gramophone. He went on, "I was younger than you are now when I started playing in a band. Then I was with an orchestra a while—then with the band again. It's all I've done ever since."

It made me feel lonely for a while, isolated from the things in life that mattered, but, brightening presently, I asked, "Do you know a piece called *Sons of Liberty*? Four flats in four-four time?"

He thought hard a minute, and then shook his head. "I'm afraid I don't —not by name anyway. Could you whistle a bit of it?"

I whistled two pages, but still he shook his head. "A nice tune, though," he conceded. "Where did you learn it?"

"I haven't yet," I explained. "Not properly, I mean. It's been my lesson for the last two weeks, but I can't keep up to it."

He seemed interested, so I went on and told him about my lessons with Miss Wiggins, and how later on they were going to buy me a metronome so that when I played a piece I wouldn't always be running away with it, "Especially a march. It keeps pulling you along the way it really ought to go until you're all mixed up and have to start at the beginning again. I know I'd do better if I didn't feel that way, and could keep slow and steady like Miss Wiggins."

But he said quickly, "No, that's the right way to feel—you've just got to learn to harness it. It's like old Rock here and Clipper. The way you are, you're Clipper. But if you weren't that way, if you didn't get excited and wanted to run sometimes, you'd just be Rock. You see? Rock's easier to handle than Clipper, but at his best he's a sleepy old plow-horse. Clipper's harder to handle—he may even cost you some tumbles. But finally get him broken in and you've got a horse that amounts to something. You wouldn't trade him for a dozen like Rock."

It was a good enough illustration, but it slandered Rock. And he was listening. I know—because even though like me he had never heard a cornet before, he had experienced enough to accept it at least with tact and manners.

For we hadn't gone much farther when Philip, noticing the way I kept watching the case that was still on his knee, undid the claps and took the cornet out. It was a very lovely cornet, shapely and eloquent, gleaming in the August sun like pure and mellow gold. I couldn't restrain myself. I said, "Play it—play it now—just a little bit to let me hear." And in response, smiling at my earnestness, he raised it to his lips.

But there was only one note—only one fragment of a note—and then away went Rock. I'd never have believed he had it in him. With a snort and plunge he was off the road and into the ditch—then out of the ditch again and off at a breakneck gallop across the prairie. There were stones and badger holes, and he spared us none of them. The egg-crates full of groceries bounced out, then the tobacco, then my mother's face powder. "Whoa, Rock!" I cried, "Whoa, Rock!" but in the rattle and whir of wheels I don't suppose he even heard. Philip couldn't help much because he had his cornet to hang on to. I tried to tug on the reins, but at such a rate across the prairie it took me all my time to keep from following the groceries. He was a big horse, Rock, and once under way had to run himself out. Or he may have thought that if he gave us a thorough shaking-up we would be too subdued when it was over to feel like taking him seriously to task. Anyway, that was how it worked out. All I dared to do was run round to pat his sweaty neck and say, "Good Rock, good Rock—nobody's going to hurt you."

Besides there were the groceries to think about, and my mother's box of face powder. And with his pride and reputation at stake, Rock had made it a runaway worthy of the horse he really was. We found the powder smashed open and one of the egg-crates cracked. Several of the oranges had rolled down a badger hole, and couldn't be recovered. We spent nearly ten minutes sifting raisins through our fingers, and still they felt a little gritty. "There were extra oranges," I tried to encourage Philip, "and I've seen my mother wash her raisins." He looked at me dubiously, and for a few minutes longer worked away trying to mend the egg-crate.

We were silent for the rest of the way home. We thought a great deal about each other, but asked no questions. Even though it was safely away in its case again I could still feel the cornet's presence as if it were a living thing. Somehow its gold and shapeliness persisted, transfiguring the day, quickening the dusty harvest fields to a gleam and lustre like its own. And I felt assured, involved. Suddenly there was a force in life, a current, an inevitability, carrying me along too. The questions they would ask when I reached home—the difficulties in making them understand that faithful old Rock had really run away—none of it now seemed to matter. This stranger with the white, thin hands, this gleaming cornet that as yet I hadn't even heard, intimately and enduringly now they were my possessions.

When we reached home my mother was civil and no more. "Put your things in the bunkhouse," she said, "and then wash here. Supper'll be ready in about an hour."

It was an uncomfortable meal. My father and my mother kept looking at Philip and exchanging glances. I told them about the cornet and the runaway, and they listened stonily. "We've never had a harvest-hand before that was a musician too," my mother said in a somewhat thin voice. "I suppose, though, you do know how to stook?"

I was watching Philip desperately and for my sake he lied, "Yes, I stooked last year. I may have a blister or two by this time tomorrow, but my hands will toughen up."

"You don't as a rule do farm work?" my father asked.

And Philip said, "No, not as a rule."

There was an awkward silence, so I tried to champion him. "He plays his cornet in a band. Ever since he was my age—that's what he does."

Glances were exchanged again. The silence continued.

I had been half-intending to suggest that Philip bring his cornet into the house to play it for us, I perhaps playing with him on the piano, but the parlour with its genteel plushiness was a room from which all were excluded but the equally genteel—visitors like Miss Wiggins and the minister —and gradually as the meal progressed I came to understand that Philip and his cornet, so far as my mother was concerned, had failed to qualify.

So I said nothing when he finished his supper, and let him go back to the bunkhouse alone. "Didn't I say to have Jenkins pick him out?" my father stormed as soon as he had gone. "Didn't I say somebody big and strong?"

"He's tall," I countered, "and there wasn't anybody else except two men, and it was the only way they'd come."

"You mean you didn't want anybody else. A cornet player! Fine stooks he'll set up." And then, turning to my mother, "It's your fault—you and your nonsense about music lessons. If you'd listen to me sometimes, and try to make a man of him."

"I do listen to you," she answered quickly. "It's because I've had to listen to you now for thirteen years that I'm trying to make a different man of him. If you'd go to town yourself instead of keeping him out of school—and do your work in six days a week like decent people. I told you yesterday that in the long run it would cost you dear."

I slipped away and left them. The chores at the stable took me nearly an hour; and then, instead of returning to the house, I went over to see

Philip. It was dark now, and there was a smoky lantern lit. He sat on the only chair, and in a hospitable silence motioned me to the bed. At once he ignored and accepted me. It was as if we had always known each other and long outgrown the need of conversation. He smoked, and blew rings towards the open door where the warm fall night encroached. I waited, eager, afraid lest they call me to the house, yet knowing that I must wait. Gradually the flame in the lantern smoked the glass till scarcely his face was visible. I sat tense, expectant, wondering who he was, where he came from, why he should be here to do my father's stooking.

There were no answers, but presently he reached for his cornet. In the dim, soft darkness I could see it glow and quicken. And I remember still what a long and fearful moment it was, crouched and steeling myself, waiting for him to begin.

And I was right: when they came the notes were piercing, golden as the cornet itself, and they gave life expanse that it had never known before. They floated up against the night, and each for a moment hung there clear and visible. Sometimes they mounted poignant and sheer. Sometimes they soared and then, like a bird alighting, fell and brushed earth again.

It was *To the Evening Star*. He finished it and told me. He told me the names of all the other pieces that he played: an *Ave Maria*, *Song of India*, a serenade—all bright through the dark like slow, suspended lightning, chilled sometimes with a glimpse of the unknown. Only for Philip there I could not have endured it. With my senses I clung hard to him—the acrid smell of his cigarettes, the tilted profile daubed with smoky light.

Then abruptly he stood up, as if understanding, and said, "Now we'd better have a march, Tom—to bring us back where we belong. A cornet can be good fun, too, you know. Listen to this one and tell me."

He stood erect, head thrown back exactly like a picture in my reader of a bugler boy, and the notes came flashing gallant through the night until the two of us went swinging along in step with them a hundred thousand strong. For this was another march that did march. It marched us miles. It made the feet eager and the heart brave. It said that life was worth the living and bright as morning shone ahead to show the way.

When he had finished and put the cornet away I said, "There's a field right behind the house that my father started cutting this afternoon. If you like we'll go over now for a few minutes and I'll show you how to stook. . . .

You see, if you set your sheaves up on top of the stubble they'll be over again in half an hour. That's how everybody does at first but it's wrong. You've got to push the butts down hard, right to the ground—like this, so they bind with the stubble. At a good slant, see, but not too much. So they'll stand the wind and still shed water if it rains."

It was too dark for him to see much, but he listened hard and finally succeeded in putting up a stook or two that to my touch seemed firm enough. Then my mother called, and I had to slip away fast so that she would think I was coming from the bunkhouse. "I hope he stooks as well as he plays," she said when I went in. "Just the same, you should have done as your father told you, and picked a likelier man to see us through the fall."

My father came in from the stable then, and he, too, had been listening. With a wondering, half-incredulous little movement of his head he made acknowledgement.

"Didn't I tell you he could?" I burst out, encouraged to indulge my pride in Philip. "Didn't I tell you he could play?" But with sudden anger in his voice he answered, "And what if he can! It's a man to stook I want. Just look at the hands on him. I don't think he's ever seen a farm before."

It was helplessness, though, not anger. Helplessness to escape his wheat when heat was not enough, when something more than wheat had just revealed itself. Long after they were both asleep I remembered, and with a sharp foreboding that we might have to find another man, tried desperately to sleep myself. "Because if I'm up in good time," I rallied all my faith in life, "I'll be able to go to the field with him and at least make sure he's started right. And he'll maybe do. I'll ride down after school and help till supper time. My father's reasonable."

Only in such circumstances, of course, and after such a day, I couldn't sleep till nearly morning, with the result that when at last my mother wakened me there was barely time to dress and ride to school. But of the day I spent there I remember nothing. Nothing except the midriff clutch of dread that made it a long day—nothing, till straddling Clipper at four again, I galloped him straight to the far end of the farm where Philip that morning had started to work.

Only Philip, of course, wasn't there. I think I knew—I think it was what all day I had been expecting. I pulled Clipper up short and sat staring at the stooks. Three or four acres of them—butts down hard into the stubble. I sat and stared till Clipper himself swung round and started for home. He wanted to run, but because there was nothing left now but the half-mile ahead of us, I held him to a walk. Just to prolong a little the possibility that I had misunderstood things. To wonder within the limits of the sane and probable if tonight he would play his cornet again.

When I reached the house my father was already there, eating an early supper. "I'm taking him back to town," he said quietly. "He tried hard enough —he's just not used to it. The sun was hot today; he lasted till about noon. We're starting in a few minutes, so you'd better go out and see him."

He looked older now, stretched out limp on the bed, his face haggard. I tiptoed close to him anxiously, afraid to speak. He pulled his mouth side-wise in a smile at my concern, then motioned me to sit down. "Sorry I didn't do better," he said. "I'll have to come back another year and have another lesson."

I clenched my hands and clung hard to this promise that I knew he couldn't keep. I wanted to rebel against what was happening, against the clumsiness and crudity of life, but instead I stood quiet a moment, almost passive, then wheeled away and carried out his cornet to the buggy. My mother was already there, with a box of lunch and some ointment for his sunburn. She said she was sorry things had turned out this way, and thanking her politely he said that he was sorry too. My father looked uncom-fortable, feeling, no doubt, that we were all unjustly blaming everything on him. It's like that on a farm. You always have to put the harvest first.

And that's all there is to tell. He waved going through the gate; I never saw him again. We watched the buggy down the road to the first turn, then with a quick resentment in her voice my mother said, "Didn't I say that the little he gained would in the long run cost him dear? Next time he'll maybe listen to me—and remember the Sabbath Day."

What exactly she was thinking I never knew. Perhaps of the crop and the whole day's stooking lost. Perhaps of the stranger who had come with his cornet for a day, and then as meaninglessly gone again. For she had been listening, too, and she may have understood. A harvest, however lean, is certain every year; but a cornet at night is golden only once.

ॐ Prairie writer Sinclair Ross produced a significant body of work, with novels such as *As for Me and My House* (1941) and short stories collected in *The Lamp at Noon and Other Stories* (1968). Most of his writings feature characters oppressed by societal demands or facing isolation in the rural prairies during the drought and depression of the 1930s. (*Born near Prince Albert, Saskatchewan 1908; died 1996*)

RESPONDING

Meaning

1. Explain the two meanings that the narrator attributes to his mother's words at the end of the story: "Didn't I say that the little he gained would in the long run cost him dear? Next time he'll maybe listen to me—and remember the Sabbath Day." Which of the suggested meanings do you think the mother had in mind? Why?

2. a) Throughout the story the author presents us with a series of contrasts: the mother and the father, hymns and marches; the farm and the town; the boy and the narrator; Rock and Clipper. Create a chart to describe what qualities or ideas are being contrasted in each case.

   b) In light of the information you have collected, suggest the thematic significance of Rock's decision to bolt across the prairie at the sound of the cornet.

Form and Style

3. Choose three examples of figurative language that you found particularly effective, and explain what each image adds to the story.

4. This story has a strong narrative flow. Find two places where the writer catches your interest in what will happen next, and explain the techniques he has used to create this interest.

Creative Extension

5. The author leaves the character of the cornet player shrouded in mystery. Write a journal entry that the boy might have written during the cornet player's stay on the farm. In it, give clues that may shed some light on his identity and background.

6. "Cornet at Night" is a coming-of-age story in which a character gains some important knowledge or insight and grows up in some way. What other stories or poems have you read that could be classified as coming-of-age stories? Are there movies, films, or television programs you have viewed that would fall into this category? Choose one and write a short essay explaining why it can be considered part of this genre. Include an analysis of how the author develops the character and the theme.

The Power of Words

∽

What power do words have over us?

Why do we read stories, watch stories, listen to them, make them up, tell
and retell them again and again? Is it because stories are the pathways that
bring us to shared experiences and to experiences we can only dream of?
Are words and how we use them ever dangerous? In this Echo section, a
short story, a poem, an essay, and a piece of art explore the power of words.

Learning Goals

- analyze presentation of theme in a variety of genres
- recognize how differences in form and style influence response
- create original texts in response to a variety of works

Two Words

∽ *Isabel Allende*

*In this short story, Isabel Allende explores how one woman used words to change her own life and
the course of her country's history. While words are a part of everyday life, they also have a
mysterious power.*

> She went by the name of Belisa Crepusculario, not because she had been
> baptized with that name or given it by her mother, but because she herself
> had searched until she found the poetry of "beauty" and "twilight" and
> cloaked herself in it. She made her living selling words. She journeyed
> through the country from the high cold mountains to the burning coasts,
> stopping at fairs and in markets where she set up four poles covered by a

canvas awning under which she took refuge from the sun and rain to minister to her customers. She did not have to peddle her merchandise because from having wandered far and near, everyone knew who she was. Some people waited for her from one year to the next, and when she appeared in the village with her bundle beneath her arm, they would form a line in front of her stall. Her prices were fair. For five centavos she delivered verses from memory; for seven she improved the quality of dreams; for nine she wrote love letters; for twelve she invented insults for irreconcilable enemies. She also sold stories, not fantasies but long, true stories she recited at one telling, never skipping a word. This is how she carried news from one town to another. People paid her to add a line or two: our son was born; so-and-so died; our children got married; the crops burned in the field. Wherever she went a small crowd gathered around to listen as she began to speak, and that was how they learned about each others' doings, about distant relatives, about what was going on in the civil war. To anyone who paid her fifty centavos in trade, she gave the gift of a secret word to drive away melancholy. It was not the same word for everyone, naturally, because that would have been collective deceit. Each person received his or her own word, with the assurance that no one else would use it that way in this universe or the Beyond.

Belisa Crepusculario had been born into a family so poor they did not even have names to give their children. She came into the world and grew up in an inhospitable land where some years the rains became avalanches or water that bore everything away before them and others when not a drop fell from the sky and the sun swelled to fill the horizon and the world became a desert. Until she was twelve, Belisa had no occupation or virtue other than having withstood hunger and the exhaustion of centuries. During one interminable drought, it fell to her to bury four younger brothers and sisters; when she realized that her turn was next, she decided to set out across the plains in the direction of the sea, in hopes that she might trick death along the way. The land was eroded, split with deep cracks, strewn with rocks, fossils of trees and thorny bushes, and skeletons of animals bleached by the sun. From time to time she ran into families who, like her, were heading south, following the mirage of water. Some had begun the march carrying their belongings on their backs or in small carts, but they could barely move their own bones, and after a while they had to abandon their possessions. They dragged themselves along painfully, their skin turned to lizard hide and their eyes burned by the reverberating glare. Belisa greeted them with a wave as she passed, but she did not stop, because she had no strength to waste in acts of compassion. Many people fell by the wayside, but she was so stubborn that she survived to cross through that hell and at long last reach the first trickles of water, fine, almost invisible threads that fed spindly vegetation and farther down widened into small streams and marshes.

Belisa Crepusculario saved her life and in the process accidentally discovered writing. In a village near the coast, the wind blew a page of newspaper at her feet. She picked up the brittle yellow paper and stood a long while looking at it, unable to determine its purpose, until curiosity overcame her shyness. She walked over to a man who was washing his horse in the muddy pool where she had quenched her thirst.

"What is this?" she asked.

"The sports page of the newspaper," the man replied, concealing his surprise at her ignorance.

The answer astounded the girl, but she did not want to seem rude, so she merely inquired about the significance of the fly tracks scattered across the page.

"Those are words, child. Here it says that Fulgencio Barba knocked out El Negro Tiznao in the third round."

That was the day Belisa Crepusculario found out that words make their way in the world without a master, and that anyone with a little cleverness can appropriate them and do business with them. She made a quick assessment of her situation and concluded that aside from becoming a prostitute or working as a servant in the kitchens of the rich, there were few occupations she was qualified for. It seemed to her that selling words would be an honourable alternative. From that moment on, she worked at that profession, and was never tempted by any other. At the beginning, she offered her merchandise unaware that words could be written outside of newspapers. When she learned otherwise, she calculated the infinite possibilities of her trade and with her savings paid a priest twenty pesos to teach her to read and write; with her three remaining coins she bought a dictionary. She poured over it from A to Z and then threw it into the sea, because it was not her intention to defraud her customers with packaged words.

• • •

One August morning several years later, Belisa Crepusculario was sitting in her tent in the middle of a plaza, surrounded by the uproar of market day, selling legal arguments to an old man who had been trying for sixteen years to get his pension. Suddenly she heard yelling and thudding hoof-beats. She looked up from her writing and saw, first, a cloud of dust, and then a band of horsemen come galloping into the plaza. They were the Colonel's men, sent under orders of El Mulato, a giant known throughout the land for the speed of his knife and his loyalty to his chief. Both the Colonel and El Mulato had spent their lives fighting in the civil war, and their names were ineradicably linked to devastation and calamity. The rebels swept into town like a stampeding herd, wrapped in noise, bathed in sweat, and leaving a hurricane of fear in their trail. Chickens took wing, dogs ran for their lives, women and children scurried out of sight, until the only living soul left in the market was Belisa Crepusculario. She had never seen El Mulato and was surprised to see him walking toward her.

"I'm looking for you," he shouted, pointing his coiled whip at her; even before the words were out, two men rushed her—knocking over her canopy and shattering her inkwell—bound her hand and foot, and threw her like a sea bag across the rump of El Mulato's mount. Then they thundered off toward the hills.

Hours later, just as Belisa Crepusculario was near death, her heart ground to sand by the pounding of the horse, they stopped, and four strong hands set her down. She tried to stand on her feet and hold her head high, but her strength failed her and she slumped to the ground, sinking into a confused dream. She awakened several hours later to the murmur of night in the camp, but before she had time to sort out the sounds, she opened her eyes and found herself staring into the impatient glare of El Mulato, kneeling beside her.

"Well, woman, at last you've come to," he said. To speed her to her senses, he tipped his canteen and offered her a sip of liquor laced with gunpowder.

She demanded to know the reason for such rough treatment, and El Mulato explained that the Colonel needed her services. He allowed her to splash water on her face, and then led her to the far end of the camp where the most feared man in all the land was lazing in a hammock strung between two trees. She could not see his face, because he lay in the deceptive shadow of the leaves and the indelible shadow of all his years as a bandit, but she imagined from the way his gigantic aide addressed him with such humility that he must have a very menacing expression. She was surprised by the Colonel's voice, as soft and well-modulated as a professor's.

"Are you the woman who sells words?" he asked.

"At your service," she stammered, peering into the dark and trying to see him better.

The Colonel stood up, and turned straight toward her. She saw dark skin and the eyes of a ferocious puma, and she knew immediately that she was standing before the loneliest man in the world.

"I want to be President," he announced.

The Colonel was weary of riding across that godforsaken land, waging useless wars and suffering defeats that no subterfuge could transform into victories. For years he had been sleeping in the open air, bitten by mosquitoes, eating iguanas and snake soup, but those minor inconveniences were not why he wanted to change his destiny. What truly troubled him was the terror he saw in people's eyes. He longed to ride into a town beneath a triumphal arch with bright flags and flowers everywhere; he wanted to be cheered, and be given newly laid eggs and freshly baked bread. Men fled at the sight of him, children trembled, and women miscarried from fright; he had had enough, and so he had decided to become President. El Mulato had suggested that they ride to the capital, gallop up to the Palace, and take over the government, the way they had taken so many other things without anyone's permission. The Colonel, however, did not want to be just another tyrant; there had been enough of those before him and, besides, if he did that, he would never win people's hearts. It was his aspiration to win the popular vote in the December election.

"To do that, I have to talk like a candidate. Can you sell me the words for a speech?" the Colonel asked Belisa Crepusculario.

She had accepted many assignments, but none like this. She did not dare refuse, fearing that El Mulato would shoot her between the eyes, or worse still, that the Colonel would burst into tears. There was more to it than that, however; she felt the urge to help him because she felt a throbbing warmth beneath her skin, a powerful desire to touch that man, to fondle him, to clasp him in her arms.

All night and a good part of the following day, Belisa Crepusculario searched her repertory for words adequate for a presidential speech, closely watched by El Mulato, who could not take his eyes from her firm wanderer's legs. She discarded harsh, cold words, words that were too flowery, words worn from abuse, words that offered improbable promises, untruthful and confusing words, until all she had left were words sure to touch the minds of men and women's intuition. Calling upon the knowledge she had purchased from the priest for twenty pesos, she wrote the speech on a sheet of paper and then signaled El Mulato to untie the rope that bound her ankles to a tree. He led her once more to the Colonel, and again she felt the throbbing anxiety that had seized her when she first saw him. She handed him the paper and waited while he looked at it, holding it gingerly between thumbs and fingertips.

"What the sh— does this say," he asked finally.

"Don't you know how to read?"

"War's what I know," he replied.

She read the speech aloud. She read it three times, so her client could engrave it on his memory. When she finished, she saw the emotion in the faces of the soldiers who had gathered round to listen, and saw that the Colonel's eyes glittered with enthusiasm, convinced that with those words the presidential chair would be his.

"If after they've heard it three times, the boys are still standing there with their mouths hanging open, it must mean the thing's damn good, Colonel," was El Mulato's approval.

"All right, woman. How much do I owe you?" the leader asked.

"One peso, Colonel."

"That's not much," he said, opening the pouch he wore at his belt, heavy with proceeds from the last foray.

"The peso entitles you a bonus. I'm going to give you two secret words," said Belisa Crepusculario.

"What for?"

She explained that for every fifty centavos a client paid, she gave him the gift of a word for his exclusive use. The Colonel shrugged. He had no interest at all in her offer, but he did not want to be impolite to someone

ECHO

who had served him so well. She walked slowly to the leather stool where he was sitting, and bent down to give him her gift. The man smelled the scent of a mountain cat issuing from the woman, a fiery heat radiating from her hips, he heard the terrible whisper of her hair, and a breath of sweetmint murmured into his ear the two secret words that were his alone.

"They are yours, Colonel," she said as she stepped back. "You may use them as much as you please."

El Mulato accompanied Belisa to the roadside, his eyes as entreating as a stray dog's, but when he reached out to touch her, he was stopped by an avalanche of words he had never heard before; believing them to be an irrevocable curse, the flames of his desire were extinguished.

During the months of September, October, and November the Colonel delivered his speech so many times that had it not been crafted from glowing and durable words it would have turned to ash as he spoke. He travelled up and down and across the country, riding into cities with a triumphal air, stopping in even the most forgotten villages where only the dump heap betrayed a human presence, to convince his fellow citizens to vote for him. While he spoke from a platform erected in the middle of the plaza, El Mulato and his men handed out sweets and painted his name on all the walls in gold frost. No one paid the least attention to those advertising ploys; they were dazzled by the clarity of the Colonel's proposals and the poetic lucidity of his arguments, infected by his powerful wish to right the wrongs of history, happy for the first time in their lives. When the Candidate had finished his speech, his soldiers would fire their pistols into the air and set off firecrackers, and when finally they rode off, they left behind a wake of hope that lingered for days on the air, like the splendid memory of a comet's tail. Soon the Colonel was the favourite. No one had ever witnessed such a phenomenon: a man who surfaced from the civil war, covered with scars and speaking like a professor, a man whose fame spread to every corner of the land and captured the nation's heart. The press focused their attention on him. Newspapermen came from far away to interview him and repeat his phrases, and the number of his followers and enemies continued to grow.

"We're doing great, Colonel," said El Mulato, after twelve successful weeks of campaigning.

But the Candidate did not hear. He was repeating his secret words, as he did more and more obsessively. He said them when he was mellow with nostalgia; he murmured them in his sleep; he carried them with him on horseback; he thought them before delivering his famous speech; and he caught himself savouring them in his leisure time. And every time he thought of those two words, he thought of Belisa Crepusculario, and his senses were inflamed with the memory of her feral scent, her fiery heat, the whisper of her hair, and her sweetmint breath in his ear, until he began to go around like a sleepwalker, and his men realized that he might die before he ever sat in the presidential chair.

"What's got hold of you, Colonel," El Mulato asked so often that finally one day his chief broke down and told him the source of his befuddlement: those two words that were buried like two daggers in his gut.

"Tell me what they are and maybe they'll lose their magic," his faithful aide suggested.

"I can't tell them, they're for me alone," the Colonel replied. Saddened by watching his chief decline like a man with a death sentence on his head, El Mulato slung his rifle over his shoulder and set out to find Belisa Crepusculario. He followed her trail through all that vast country, until he found her in a village in the far south, sitting under her tent reciting her rosary of news. He planted himself, spraddle-legged, before her, weapon in hand.

"You! You're coming with me," he ordered.

She had been waiting. She picked up her inkwell, folded the canvas of her small stall, arranged her shawl around her shoulders, and without a word took her place behind El Mulato's saddle. They did not exchange so much as a word in all the trip; El Mulato's desire for her had turned to rage, and only his fear of her tongue prevented his cutting her to shreds with his whip. Nor was he inclined to tell her that the Colonel was in a fog, and that a spell whispered into his ear had done what years of battle had not been able to do. Three days later they arrived at the encampment, and immediately, in view of all the troops, El Mulato led his prisoner before the Candidate.

"I brought this witch here so you can give her back her words, Colonel," El Mulato said, pointing the barrel of his rifle at the woman's head. "And then she can give you back your manhood."

The Colonel and Belisa Crepusculario stared at each other, measuring one another from a distance. The men knew then that their leader would never undo the witchcraft of those accursed words, because the whole world could see the voracious-puma eyes soften as the woman walked to him and took his hand in hers.

Isabel Allende, the daughter of a Chilean diplomat, left Chile to live in Bolivia, the Middle East, and Europe. She began her career by working as a journalist, and eventually creating her own television program. The House of the Spirits (1982) is one of her internationally acclaimed novels, a chronicle of several generations of an imaginary family in Chile. The story "Two Words" appears in The Stories of Eva Luna (1989). (Born Peru 1942)

RESPONDING

Meaning

1. What is the significance of "the fly tracks scattered across the page"? How do they change Belisa's life? How do they change the story of her country?

2. In this story, Isabel Allende illustrates the dual nature of the power of language. What is this dual nature and how does the author develop this view? Refer to specific evidence from the text in your response.

Form and Style

3. *Hyperbole* is exaggeration which is both deliberate and obvious.

   a) Identify at least four examples of hyperbole. Choose examples from different sections of the story. Explain the effect of each example and why you think the author has used this literary technique.

   b) In what ways might the use of hyperbole prove both beneficial and detrimental to the development of the story's theme? Share your opinions.

4. a) Like some other modern fiction from Central and South America, "Two Words" is an example of *magic realism*. Based on your reading of the story, how would you describe magic realism? Refer to specific elements from the story in your response.

   b) Look up a definition of magic realism in a dictionary of literary terms or other reliable source. How does your definition compare with the one in the dictionary? What further details do you learn about magic realism?

Creative Extension

5. Assume the role of Belisa Crepusculario and write the speech with which the Colonel won the hearts of the voters. Review rhetorical devices (e.g., repetition, examples, analogies, powerful images, etc.) commonly used in speeches and incorporate them as appropriate, giving careful thought to the effects you want to create. When you have finished the speech, write a short analysis explaining why you chose particular techniques.

6. Write an interior monologue for the Colonel which reveals the "two words" and their ongoing effect on his state of mind. Remember that interior monologues can be stream of consciousness. Conventions of correct grammar, sentence structure, and punctuation may be broken intentionally to reflect thought processes and emotions. Perform your monologue for a partner. Ask for his or her analysis of how successfully you conveyed thoughts and emotions.

Translations

🍂 *Lake Sagaris*

In this short yet very powerful poem, Lake Sagaris explores our need for words, their nature, and their mysterious power over us.

> We need words
> like water
> but both flow in every direction
> sparkle yet poison.
>
> The human shell
> holds a red ocean,
> moved by the fickle moon.
> Hold it to your ear. Listen.
> It stirs in your hand.
> Love.

🍂 Lake Sagaris grew up in Toronto. She has lived in Chile since 1981, working as a writer, editor, and foreign correspondent for many magazines. Writer of three acclaimed books of poetry, she also published the novel *Bone and Dream* in 2000. *Medusa's Children: A Journey from Newfoundland to Chiloé* (1993) contains "Translations." (*Born in Montreal, Quebec 1956*)

Connecting

1. In the first stanza, the poet writes that words "sparkle yet poison." What do you think she means? Explain and suggest examples.

2. a) What is the dominant image in this poem? How is it used in the second stanza? What connections can you identify between the two stanzas of the poem?
    b) How effective is the dominant image in illustrating the poem's message or theme?
    c) What is the effect of the final line, and word, in the poem? Explain your interpretations.

3. How do the views on words in this poem compare with those in Isabel Allende's story? Explain this connection using specific references to Allende's short story.

Always Together

ॐ Philippe Beha

In this selection, the power of words is expressed through visual art. The artist uses collage to present his interpretation of the theme.

ॐ A graduate of "Beaux-Arts" in Strasbourg, France, Phillippe Beha has illustrated more than one hundred children's books around the world. He has received many awards, among them a Governor General's Award and an award from the Art and Design Club of Canada. He currently lives in Québec. *(Born France 1950)*

Connecting

1. Briefly describe in a few sentences what you see in this collage. In your view, what is the artist's message?

2. Why do you think the artist chose a collage to present his message? What are the particular advantages of the collage technique for this theme?

3. How does this collage's message relate to the central motif of this Echo section, "The Power of Words"? Explain how the various materials, shapes, colours, and patterns reinforce the Echo theme.

I Am Writing Blindly

ॐ *Roger Rosenblatt*

In the fall of 2000, a news story broke about the Russian submarine Kursk. *The submarine was trapped under the sea, powerless after a series of explosions. Russian officials claimed that death for the men in the submarine had been instantaneous. This proved to be untrue. In this essay, Roger Rosenblatt considers the final actions of the men on the* Kursk. *He uncovers a basic human impulse to tell our stories.*

Besides the newsworthy revelation of Lieut. Captain Dimitri Kolesnikov's dying message to his wife recovered last week from the husk of the sunken submarine Kursk—that 23 of the 118 crewmen had survived in an isolated chamber for a while, on contradiction to claims by Russian officials that all had perished within minutes of the accident—there was the matter of writing the message in the first place.

In the first place, in the last place, that is what we people do—write messages to one another. We are a narrative species. We exist by story-telling—by relating our situations—and the test of our evolution may lie in getting the story right.

What Kolesnikov did in deciding to describe his position and entrapment, others have also done—in states of repose or terror. When a JAL airliner went down in 1985, passengers used the long minutes of its terrible, spiraling descent to write letters to loved ones. When the last occupants of the Warsaw Ghetto had finally seen their families and companions die of disease or starvation, or be carried off in trucks to extermination camps, and there could be no doubt of their own fate, still they took scraps of paper on which they wrote poems, thoughts, fragments of lives, rolled them into tight scrolls and slipped them into the crevices of the ghetto walls.

Why did they bother? With no countervailing news from the outside world, they assumed the Nazis had inherited the earth; that if anyone discovered their writings, it would be their killers, who would snicker and toss them away. They wrote because, like Kolesnikov, they had to. The impulse was in them, like a biological fact.

So enduring is this storytelling need that it shapes nearly every human endeavour. Businesses depend on the stories of past failures and successes, and on the myth of the mission of the company. In medicine, doctors increasingly rely on a patient's narrative of the progress of an ailment, which is inevitably more nuanced and useful than the data of machines. In law, the same thing. Every court case is a competition of tales told by the prosecutor and defense attorney; the jury picks the one it likes best.

All these activities derive from essential places in us. Psychologist Jerome Bruner says children acquire language in order to tell the stories that are already in them. We do our learning through storytelling processes. The man who arrives at our door is thought to be a salesman because his predecessor was a salesman. When the pattern-making faculties fail, the brain breaks down. Schizophrenics suffer from a loss of story.

The deep proof of our need to spill, and keep on spilling, lies in reflex, often in desperate circumstances. A number of years ago, Jean-Dominique Bauby, the editor of *Elle* magazine in Paris, was felled by a stroke so destructive that the only part of his body that could move was his left eyelid. Flicking that eyelid, he managed to signal letters of the alphabet, and proceeded to write his autobiography, *The Diving Bell and the Butterfly*, with the last grand gesture of his life.

All this is of acute and consoling interest to writers, whose odd existences are ordinarily strung between asking why we do it and doing it incessantly. The explanation I've been able to come up with has to do with freedom. You write a sentence, the basic unit of storytelling, and you are never sure where it will lead. The readers will not know where it leads either. Your adventure becomes theirs, eternally recapitulated in tandem— one wild ride together. Even when you come to the end of the sentence, that dot, it is still strangely inconclusive. I sometimes think one writes to find God in every sentence. But God (the ironist) always lives in the next sentence.

It is this freedom of the message sender and receiver that connects them—sailor to wife, the dying to the living. Writing has been so important in America, I think, because communication is the soul and engine of democracy. To write is to live according to one's terms. If you ask me to be serious, I will be frivolous. Magnanimous? Petty. Cynical? I will be a brazen believer in all things. Whatever you demand I will not give you—unless it is with the misty hope that what I give you is not what you ask for but what you want.

We use this freedom to break the silence, even of death, even when—in the depths of our darkest loneliness—we have no clear idea of why we reach out to one another with these frail, perishable chains of words. In the black chamber of the submarine, Kolesnikov noted, "I am writing blindly." Like everyone else.

Roger Rosenblatt is a journalist, author, playwright, and teacher in New York. He taught writing and modern literature at Harvard and studied in Ireland as a Fulbright Scholar. In June 1999, he was appointed Editor-at-Large of Time, Inc. He has written the memoir *Coming Apart* (1996). "I Am Writing Blindly" is from *Time* magazine, 6 November 2000.

Connecting

1. a) Rosenblatt uses both examples and analogies to illustrate his statement that "We are a narrative species." Choose one example and one analogy and evaluate their effectiveness in supporting Rosenblatt's view.
   b) Explain Rosenblatt's reason for believing that we are all "writing blindly."

2. "Communication is the soul and engine of democracy." Discuss the meaning of this statement. Suggest reasons why the author has used this double metaphor.

3. What does Rosenblatt suggest compels us to tell stories? Summarize his thesis in a sentence. How does his view relate to the views on the power of words expressed by Lake Sagaris in her poem and Isabel Allende in her story?

REFLECTING ON THE ECHO

1. Collect a number of examples from different genres and media of how words can "sparkle" yet be "poison" or have a powerful persuasive effect. Consider current advertisements, segments from poems, dramas, stories, or other works you have read, and quotes from television programs, speeches, or films. Document your sources and explain the context for each example you find. Include a short commentary with each example explaining the effects it has on the reader or viewer (the emotions or ideas it evokes).

2. In small groups, create an advertising campaign for one of the following. Your campaign should contain one poster and one advertisement each for radio, television, and a newspaper or magazine. If possible, tape your radio advertisement and videotape your advertisement for television. Focus your campaign on Roger Rosenblatt's theory that humans are "a narrative species" and that language is power.

    a) a non-profit group promoting literacy

    b) an anthology of short stories by Isabel Allende in which the lead story is "Two Words"

    c) a new book containing the final messages sent out from the submarine *Kursk*

3. Create a collage, painting, illustration, or other form of visual representation to express your interpretation of the power of words and how they influence people in society today. Include a short written analysis explaining why you chose the form you did and how you used particular techniques to convey your ideas.

The Persian Carpet

❧ Hanan Shaykh

Learning Goals

- assess reliability of a narrator's point of view
- evaluate the role of pathos or bathos in a story
- write a different ending to a story
- prepare a research report

When Maryam had finished plaiting my hair into two pigtails, she put her finger to her mouth and licked it, then passed it over my eyebrows, moaning: 'Ah, what eyebrows you have—they're all over the place!' She turned quickly to my sister and said: 'Go and see if your father's still praying.' Before I knew it my sister had returned and was whispering 'He's still at it,' and she stretched out her hands and raised them skywards in imitation of him. I didn't laugh, nor did Maryam; instead, she took up the scarf from the chair, put it over her hair and tied it hurriedly at the neck. Then, opening the wardrobe carefully, she took out her handbag, placed it under her arm and stretched out her hands to us. I grasped one and my sister the other. We understood that we should, like her, proceed on tiptoe, holding our breath as we made our way out through the open front door. As we went down the steps, we turned back towards the door, then towards the window. Reaching the last step, we began to run, only stopping when the lane had disappeared out of sight and we had crossed the road and Maryam had stopped a taxi.

Our behaviour was induced by fear, for today we would be seeing my mother for the first time since her separation by divorce from my father. He had sworn he would not let her see us, for, only hours after the divorce, the news had spread that she was going to marry a man she had been in love with before her family had forced her into marrying my father.

My heart was pounding. This was not from fear or from running but was due to anxiety and a feeling of embarrassment about the meeting that lay ahead. Though in control of myself and my shyness, I knew that I would be incapable—however much I tried—of showing my emotions, even to my mother; I would be unable to throw myself into her arms and smother her with kisses and clasp her head as my sister would do with such spontaneity. I had thought long and hard about this ever since Maryam had whispered in my ear—and in my sister's ear—that my mother had come from the south and that we were to visit her secretly the following day. I began to imagine that I would make myself act exactly as my sister did,

that I would stand behind her and imitate her blindly. Yet I know myself:
I have committed myself to myself by heart. However much I tried to force
myself, however much I thought in advance about what I should and
shouldn't do, once I was actually faced by the situation and was standing
looking down at the floor, my forehead puckered into an even deeper
frown, I would find I had forgotten what I had resolved to do. Even then,
though, I would not give up hope but would implore my mouth to break
into a smile; it would none the less be to no avail.

When the taxi came to a stop at the entrance to a house, where two
lions stood on columns of red sandstone, I was filled with delight and
immediately forgot my apprehension. I was overcome with happiness at
the thought that my mother was living in a house where two lions stood
at the entrance. I heard my sister imitate the roar of a lion and I turned to
her in envy. I saw her stretching up her hands in an attempt to clutch the
lions. I thought to myself: She's always uncomplicated and jolly, her gaiety
never leaves her, even at the most critical moments—and here she was,
not a bit worried about this meeting.

But when my mother opened the door and I saw her, I found myself
unable to wait and rushed forward in front of my sister and threw myself
into her arms. I had closed my eyes and all the joints of my body had
grown numb after having been unable to be at rest for so long. I took in
the unchanged smell of her hair, and I discovered for the first time how
much I had missed her and wished that she would come back and live
with us, despite the tender care shown to us by my father and Maryam.
I couldn't rid my mind of that smile of hers when my father agreed to
divorce her, after the religious sheikh had intervened following her threats
to pour kerosene over her body and set fire to herself if my father wouldn't
divorce her. All my senses were numbed by that smell of her, so well pre-
served in my memory. I realized how much I had missed her, despite the
fact that after she'd hurried off behind her brother to get into the car,
having kissed us and started to cry, we had continued with the games we
were playing in the lane outside our house. As night came, and for the
first time in a long while we did not hear her squabbling with my father,
peace and quiet descended upon the house—except that is for the weeping
of Maryam, who was related to my father and had been living with us in
the house ever since I was born.

Smiling, my mother moved me away from her so that she could hug and kiss my sister, and hug Maryam again, who had begun to cry. I heard my mother, who was in tears, say to her 'Thank you,' and she wiped her tears with her sleeve and looked me and my sister up and down, saying: 'God keep them safe, how they've sprung up!' She put both arms round me, while my sister buried her head in my mother's waist, and we all began to laugh when we found that it was difficult for us to walk like that. Reaching the inner room, I was convinced her new husband was inside because my mother said, smiling: 'Mahmoud loves you very much and he would like it if your father would give you to me so that you can live with us and be his children too.' My sister laughed and answered: 'Like that we'd have two fathers.' I was still in a benumbed state, my hand placed over my mother's arm, proud at the way I was behaving, at having been able without any effort to be liberated from myself, from my shackled hands, from the prison of my shyness, as I recalled to mind the picture of my meeting with my mother, how I had spontaneously thrown myself at her, something I had thought wholly impossible, and my kissing her so hard I had closed my eyes.

Her husband was not there. As I stared down at the floor I froze. In confusion I looked at the Persian carpet spread on the floor, then gave my mother a long look. Not understanding the significance of my look, she turned and opened a cupboard from which she threw me an embroidered blouse, and moving across to a drawer in the dressing table, she took out an ivory comb with red hearts painted on it and gave it to my sister. I stared down at the Persian carpet, trembling with burning rage. Again I looked at my mother and she interpreted my gaze as being one of tender longing, so she put her arms round me, saying: 'You must come every other day, you must spend the whole of Friday at my place.' I remained motionless, wishing that I could remove her arms from around me and sink my teeth into that white forearm. I wished that the moment of meeting could be undone and re-enacted, that she could again open the door and I could stand there —as I should have done—with my eyes staring down at the floor and my forehead in a frown.

The lines and colours of the Persian carpet were imprinted on my memory. I used to lie on it as I did my lessons; I'd be so close to it that I'd gaze at its pattern and find it looking like slices of red watermelon repeated over and over again. But when I sat down on the couch, I would see that each slice of melon had changed into a comb with thin teeth. The clusters of flowers surrounding its four sides were purple coloured. At the beginning of summer my mother would put mothballs on it and on the other ordinary carpets and would roll them up and place them on top of the cupboard. The room would look stark and depressing until autumn came, when she would take them to the roof and spread them out. She would gather up the mothballs, most of which had dissolved from the summer's heat and humidity, then, having brushed them with a small broom, she'd leave them there. In the evening she'd bring them down and lay them out where they belonged. I would be filled with happiness as their bright colours once again brought the room back to life. This particular carpet, though, had disappeared several months before my mother was divorced. It had been spread out on the roof in the sun and in the afternoon my mother had gone up to get it and hadn't found it. She called my father and for the first time I had seen his face flushed with anger. When they came down from the roof, my mother was in a state of fury and bewilderment. She got in touch with the neighbours, all of whom swore they hadn't seen it. Suddenly my mother exclaimed: 'Ilya!' Everyone stood speechless: not a word from my father or from my sister or from our neighbours Umm Fouad and Abu Salman. I found myself crying out: 'Ilya? Don't say such a thing, it's not possible.'

Ilya was an almost blind man who used to go round the houses of the quarter repairing cane chairs. When it came to our turn, I would see him, on my arrival back from school, seated on the stone bench outside the house with piles of straw in front of him and his red hair glinting in the sunlight. He would deftly take up the strands of straw and, like fishes, they'd slip through the mesh. I would watch him as he coiled them round with great dexterity, then bring them out again until he had formed a circle of straw for the seat of the chair, just like the one that had been there before. Everything was so even and precise: it was as though his hands were a machine and I would be amazed at the speed and nimbleness of his fingers. Sitting as he did with his head lowered, it looked as though he were using his eyes. I once doubted that he could see more than vague shapes in front of him, so I squatted down and looked into his rosy-red face and was able to see his half-closed eyes behind his glasses. They had in them a white line that pricked at my heart and sent me hurrying off to the kitchen, where I found a bag of dates on the table, and I heaped some on a plate and gave them to Ilya.

I continued to stare at the carpet as the picture of Ilya, red of face and hair, appeared to me. I was made aware of his hand as he walked up the stairs on his own; of him sitting on his chair, of his bargaining over the price for his work, of how he ate and knew that he had finished every-thing on the plate, of his drinking from the pitcher, with the water flowing easily down his throat. Once at midday, having been taught by my father that before entering a Muslim house he should say 'Allah' before knocking at the door and entering, as a warning to my mother in case she were unveiled, my mother rushed at him and asked him about the carpet. He made no reply, merely making a sort of sobbing noise. As he walked off, he almost bumped into the table and, for the first time, tripped. I went up to him and took him by the hand. He knew me by the touch of my hand, because he said to me in a half-whisper: 'Never mind, child.' Then he turned round to leave. As he bent over to put on his shoes, I thought I saw tears on his cheeks. My father didn't let him leave before saying to him: 'Ilya, God will forgive you if you tell the truth.' But Ilya walked off, steadying himself against the railings. He took an unusually long time as he felt his way down the stairs. Then he disappeared from sight and we never saw him again.

ᓀ Hanan Shaykh is one of the foremost writers of the Arab world. She worked from 1966 to 1975 as a journalist in Beirut before writing fiction. Her novels, which have been translated into English, include *The Story of Zahra* and *Only in London* (2000). Her story collection, *I Sweep the Sun Off Rooftops*, was published in 1999. "The Persian Carpet" appears in *Arabic Short Stories* (1983). She lives in London. *(Born in Beirut, Lebanon 1945)*

RESPONDING

Meaning

1. a) Describe the narrator's feelings toward her mother and the secret meeting. How does the narrator's comparison of herself with her sister reveal some of her inner conflict?

   b) At one point, the narrator states, "I know myself; I have committed myself to myself by heart." Do events in the story support this statement? If not, how might this affect the reader's interpretation of future events?

2. a) Describe the mother's reaction to meeting her children? How does she react when the narrator notices the carpet? What might account for her reaction?

   b) In your opinion, is the narrator's view of events at the end of the story reliable? Why or why not? Support your views.

Form and Style

3. *Pathos* occurs when an author establishes feelings of sympathy for a character. *Bathos* occurs when the pathos is overworked or excessive. In your opinion, what has the author created in her description of Ilya? What role does this play in the story?

4. How does the anecdote about the carpet serve many functions in this story? Consider plot, characterization, and symbolism.

Creative Extension

5. Write an ending to the story that reveals how the visit continued after the narrator's anger is aroused by the memory of the incident over the carpet. This ending should include dialogue between all of the characters present.

6. Arranged marriages are the norm in many countries and cultures. With a partner, find out more about this practice. How is it viewed by those who practise it? How much say do the bride and groom have in their choice of partner? What benefits do arranged marriages bring? If possible, interview someone who is in an arranged marriage. Present your findings in a brief report.

Rich for One Day

❧ Suzanne Jacob

Learning Goals

- compare values and ideas in a text with your own
- examine an author's use of details
- explain the role of literary devices such as irony, metaphor, personification, and symbol
- write and present a dramatic monologue and continuation of the story

Aline decided to open her eyes. She had no idea of the time but by the sounds in the house that came down into her small room in the basement, she knew that just about everyone was well into their day. The theme music of Phil Donahue made its way through the ceiling, four o'clock. Aline grunted with pleasure. Was there anyone else like her who just woke up and for whom four o'clock meant only a delicious nest under a thick white sheepskin, it was most unlikely and Aline felt her good mood grow, she was incredibly lucky, and she took pity on the rest of the world.

Propping herself up on one elbow, she looked around her room. There were lots of crayons, paint bottles of all colours, notebooks, sheets here and there, and photographs, piles of photographs on the large yellow piece of plywood that she had made into a work table. Aline laughed sweetly and scolded herself that she should get serious, that the mess on the table ordered her to hours of work and that one must work to live. She sighed and she laughed as she hid her laughter in her warm pillow. How sweet it is.

Then she remembered, she was rich today. She had eight dollars, a fortune. She could allow herself thousands of things. Sitting up in her bed, she stretched her arms towards the ceiling; acknowledging her hands, she yawned with relish. She pulled her old worn cords and loosely knit sweater towards her and put them on under the sheets to stay warm. She got up.

It was wonderful. She could go to the movies and have popcorn and Coke. The telephone rang, it was Lucien, all excited, he offered her a contract. A designer needed a photographer for his spring collection, would Aline be interested?

"You," said Lucien, "are you sleeping or are you listening?"

Aline told him that she was listening very carefully but that she was not quite awake and that she felt too rich today to give an answer. Lucien sighed, he explained to Aline that she would never be successful if she insisted on not taking things seriously, not jumping at opportunities when they came her way. Aline answered that she agreed totally with Lucien's opinion and that she often berated herself for this flagrant lack of maturity on her part, but that she really just got up and that she couldn't help it, and if he could call back . . . Lucien hung up and Aline put on the *Deep Purple* record already out of its jacket.

It was risky to open the black burlap curtains that held out the light. The sky could be too bright, it could be too much, Aline was careful, she preferred to take the sky outside all at once, not here in this basement. She turned on her work light and poured a glass of orange juice. She kept only orange juice in her room. Usually her friends invited her to eat with them. She wasn't difficult, whatever you say. She examined some of the negatives lying on the table, they could wait. Last Saturday's paper was open to the entertainment page, but Aline preferred to submit herself to the good taste of the schedulers at the Cinéma Outremont, expecting a surprise, she would go there and take her chances. It may be easy to find her capricious, but difficult she was not, she said to herself.

She put on her boots and looked everywhere for her keys. She wrapped herself up warmly and climbed the stairs. The street was full of people hurrying to get home, people who had finished their day, their Thursday. It was their duty to fill each day from morning to evening and to think of her day as perfectly empty; Aline felt like converting the whole world to her style of living. She got to Côte-des-Neiges.

The air was humid, the sidewalks were banked by dirty snow, a swollen sky rolled from one roof to another. Aline felt invulnerable, she was absorbed by a small stubborn happiness that warmed her from inside and her small happy steps carried her home from one storefront to the next. The shop window of Renaud-Bray Books was an old friend of Aline's, always full of new items. Aline decided to go in and browse.

She opened the fat books and fingered them, she caressed and congratulated them. Books were thousands of little heaters, Aline's hands were warm and she felt good. There were other customers, they also moved from one universe to the other with the pages they turned and that made pockets of heat, no doubt about it, Aline thought to herself. It didn't occur to her to buy anything. For years now she had been in the habit of enjoying things that were available to her without feeling like she had to buy them. She didn't need anything.

To get to the movies, she would have to take two buses, the 165 and the 160. The 165 stop was just by the bookstore but there was a line and the first bus, packed, went by without stopping. Aline walked to the next stop at the corner of Lacombe. In her oversized coat and her scarf that was too long, she felt loved and fulfilled, another bus arrived, she let it pass and continued on to the next stop across from the liquor store at the corner of Edouard Montpetit. She didn't really feel like taking a bus. She said to herself that when she was grown up, she would be very, very rich, and that she would have a car and a chauffeur, and that she would have the whole back seat to herself, and that she would be surrounded by very rare things, very beautiful things, and very astonishing things, and she would never cease being astonished at all these things around her. And she would travel, she would spend all her time in this car, and she would stroll over the whole world and not just one or two sidewalks. Because the light is too harsh in buses, Aline didn't like them. There is not much that Aline didn't like and she walked on to the next stop.

It started to snow and Aline hailed a taxi. She said to herself, "This is the way to live," she had the whole back seat all to herself, and the chauffeur drove where Aline wanted to go.

Then she settled herself in a seat at the movies and enjoyed the arrival of other people that came in with hands full of popcorn, gloves, mittens, hats and scarves. The lights went out and Aline started to eat her popcorn. The first image lit up the screen. I love life, thought Aline.

Translated by Susanna Finnell

As well as writing short stories, Québécois author Suzanne Jacob writes poetry, plays, essays, and novels. In 1984, her novel *Laura Laur* won the Prix Paris-Québec and the Governor General's Award. In 1998, she received another Governor General's Award for her collection of poems *La Part de feu*. Many of her works have been translated into English. (*Born Amos, Québec 1943*)

RESPONDING

Meaning

1. "Then she remembered, she was rich today."
   a) In what ways does Aline consider herself "rich"?
   b) Evaluate Aline's life in terms of what you consider important and significant.

2. Sometimes events or details that appear trivial have significant importance. Why has the author included the details about the buses and the taxi?

Form and Style

3. a) Explain the *irony* in the following:
   - "Aline decided to open her eyes."
   - "The first image lit up the screen. I love life, thought Aline."
   b) Examine the placement of these two sentences in the story and evaluate the effectiveness of the author's decision to put the sentences where she has.

4. Identify an example of metaphor, personification, and symbol in the author's description of the books and explain the role each of these literary devices plays in the story as a whole.

Creative Extension

5. Write and present a monologue in which an older Aline looks back over her life. Did she remain happy? How does she feel about the way she chose to live? Record your monologue on audio or videotape.

6. Write a continuation of the story, in which Aline is confronted by a situation that seriously challenges her world view or lifestyle. What might that situation be? How do you think Aline would react? Share and discuss your endings with others in a small group.

The Boat

⌐ Alistair MacLeod

Learning Goals

- explore characterization
- examine use of symbol
- analyze an author's use of language to create atmosphere
- research and analyze art on a similar theme
- write a non-fiction article

There are times even now, when I awake at four o'clock in the morning with the terrible fear that I have overslept; when I imagine that my father is waiting for me in the room below the darkened stairs or that the shore-bound men are tossing pebbles against my window while blowing their hands and stomping their feet impatiently on the frozen steadfast earth. There are times when I am half out of bed and fumbling for socks and mumbling for words before I realize that I am foolishly alone, that no one waits at the base of the stairs and no boat rides restlessly in the waters of the pier.

At such times only the grey corpses on the overflowing ashtray beside my bed bear witness to the extinction of the latest spark and silently await the crushing out of the most recent of their fellows. And then because I am afraid to be alone with death, I dress rapidly, make a great to-do about clearing my throat, turn on both faucets in the sink and proceed to make loud splashing ineffectual noises. Later I go out and walk the mile to the all-night restaurant.

In the winter it is a very cold walk, and there are often tears in my eyes when I arrive. The waitress usually gives a sympathetic little shiver and says, "Boy, it must be really cold out there; you got tears in your eyes."

"Yes," I say, "it sure is; it really is."

And then the three or four of us who are always in such places at such times make uninteresting little protective chit-chat until the dawn reluctantly arrives. Then I swallow the coffee, which is always bitter, and leave with a great busy rush because by that time I have to worry about being late and whether I have a clean shirt and whether my car will start and about all the other countless things one must worry about when one teaches at a great Midwestern university. And I know then that that day will go by as have all the days of the past ten years, for all the call and the voices and the shapes and the boat were not really there in the early morning's darkness and I have all kinds of comforting reality to prove it. They are only shadows and echoes, the animals a child's hands make on the wall by lamplight, and the voices from the rain barrel; the cuttings from an old movie made in the black and white of long ago.

I first became conscious of the boat in the same way and at almost the same time that I became aware of the people it supported. My earliest recollection of my father is a view from the floor of gigantic rubber boots and then of being suddenly elevated and having my face pressed against the stubble of his cheek, and how it tasted of salt and of how he smelled of salt from his red-soled rubber boots to the shaggy whiteness of his hair.

When I was very small, he took me for my first ride in the boat. I rode the half-mile from our house to the wharf on his shoulders and I remember the sound of his rubber boots galumphing along the gravel beach, the tune of the indecent little song he used to sing, and the colour of the salt.

The floor of the boat was permeated with the same odour and in its constancy I was not aware of change. In the harbour we made our little circle and returned. He tied the boat by its painter, fastened the stern to its permanent anchor and lifted me high over his head to the solidity of the wharf. Then he climbed up on the little iron ladder that led to the wharf's cap, placed me once more upon his shoulders and galumphed off again.

When we returned to the house everyone made a great fuss over my precocious excursion and asked, "How did you like the boat?" "Were you afraid in the boat?" "Did you cry in the boat?" They repeated "the boat" at the end of all their questions and I knew it must be very important to everyone.

My earliest recollection of my mother is of being alone with her in the mornings while my father was away in the boat. She seemed to be always repairing clothes that were "torn in the boat," preparing food "to be eaten in the boat" or looking for "the boat" through our kitchen window which faced upon the sea. When my father returned about noon, she would ask, "Well, how did things go in the boat today?" It was the first question I remember asking: "Well, how did things go in the boat today?" "Well, how did things go in the boat today?"

The boat in our lives was registered at Port Hawkesbury. She was what Nova Scotians called a Cape Island boat and was designed for the small inshore fishermen who sought the lobsters of the spring and the mackerel of summer and later the cod and haddock and hake. She was thirty-two feet long and nine wide, and was powered by an engine from a Chevrolet truck. She had a marine clutch and a high-speed reverse gear and was painted light green with the name *Jenny Lynn* stencilled in black letters on her bow and painted on an oblong plate across her stern. Jenny Lynn had been my mother's maiden name and the boat was called after her as another link in the chain of tradition. Most of the boats that berthed at the wharf bore the names of some female member of their owner's household.

I say this now as if I knew it all then. All at once, all about boat dimensions and engines, and as if on the day of my first childish voyage I noticed the difference between a stencilled name and a painted name. But of course it was not that way at all, for I learned it all very slowly and there was not time enough.

I learned first about our house, which was one of about fifty that marched around the horseshoe of our harbour and the wharf that was its heart. Some of them were so close to the water that during a storm the sea spray splashed against their windows while others were built farther along the beach, as was the case with ours. The houses and their people, like those of the neighbouring towns and villages, were the result of Ireland's discontent and Scotland's Highland Clearances and America's War of Independence. Impulsive, emotional Catholic Celts who could not bear to live with England and shrewd, determined Protestant Puritans who, in the years after 1776, could not bear to live without.

The most important room in our house was one of those oblong old-fashioned kitchens heated by a wood- and coal-burning stove. Behind the stove was a box of kindlings and beside it a coal scuttle. A heavy wooden table with leaves that expanded or reduced its dimensions stood in the middle of the floor. There were five wooden homemade chairs which had been shipped and hacked by a variety of knives. Against the east wall, opposite the stove, there was a couch which sagged in the middle and had a cushion for a pillow, and above it a shelf which contained matches, tobacco, pencils, odd fish-hooks, bits of twine, and a tin can filled with bills and receipts. The south wall was dominated by a window which faced the sea and on the north there was a five-foot board which bore a variety of clothes hooks and the burdens of each. Beneath the board there was a jumble of odd footwear, mostly of rubber. There was also, on this wall, a barometer, a map of the marine area and a shelf which held a tiny radio. The kitchen was shared by all of us and was a buffer zone between the immaculate order of ten other rooms and the disruptive chaos of the single room that was my father's.

My mother ran her house as her brothers ran their boats. Everything was clean and spotless and in order. She was tall and dark and powerfully energetic. In later years she reminded me of the women of Thomas Hardy, particularly Eustacia Vye, in a physical way. She fed and clothed a family of seven children, making all of the meals and most of the clothes. She grew miraculous gardens and magnificent flowers and raised broods of hens and ducks. She would walk miles on berry-picking expeditions and hoist her skirts to dig for clams when the tide was low. She was fourteen years younger than my father, whom she had married when she was twenty-six and had been a local beauty for a period of ten years. My mother was of the sea, as were all of her people, and her horizons were the very literal ones she scanned with her dark and fearless eyes.

Between the kitchen clothes rack and barometer, a door opened into my father's bedroom. It was a room of disorder and disarray. It was as if the wind which so often clamoured about the house succeeded in entering this single room and after whipping it into turmoil stole quietly away to renew its knowing laughter from without.

My father's bed was against the south wall. It always looked rumpled and unmade because he lay on top of it more than he slept within any folds it might have had. Beside it, there was a little brown table. An archaic goose-necked reading light, a battered table radio, a mound of wooden matches, one or two packages of tobacco, a deck of cigarette papers and an overflowing ashtray cluttered its surface. The brown larvae of tobacco shreds and the grey flecks of ash covered both the table and the floor beneath it. The once-varnished surface of the table was disfigured by numerous black scars and gashes inflicted by the neglected burning cigarettes of many years. They had tumbled from the ashtray unnoticed and branded their statements permanently and quietly into the wood until the odour of their burning caused the snuffing out of their lives. At the bed's foot there was a single window which looked upon the sea.

Against the adjacent wall there was a battered bureau and beside it there was a closet which held his single ill-fitting serge suit, the two or three white shirts that strangled him and the square black shoes that pinched. When he took off his more friendly clothes, the heavy woollen sweaters, mitts and socks which my mother knitted for him and the woollen and doeskin shirts, he dumped them unceremoniously on a single chair. If a visitor entered the room while he was lying on the bed, he would be told to throw the clothes on the floor and take their place upon the chair.

Magazines and books covered the bureau and competed with the clothes for domination of the chair. They further overburdened the heroic little table and lay on top of the radio. They filled a baffling and unknowable cave beneath the bed, and in the corner by the bureau they spilled from the walls and grew up from the floor.

The magazines were the most conventional: *Time, Newsweek, Life, Maclean's, The Family Herald, The Reader's Digest.* They were the result of various cut-rate subscriptions or the gift subscriptions associated with Christmas, "the two whole years for only $3.50."

The books were more varied. There were a few hardcover magnificents and bygone Book-of-the-Month wonders and some were Christmas or birthday gifts. The majority of them, however, were used paperbacks which came from those second-hand bookstores that advertise in the backs of magazines: "Miscellaneous Used Paperbacks 10¢ Each." At first he sent for them himself, although my mother resented the expense, but in later years they came more and more often from my sisters who had moved to the cities. Especially at first they were very weird and varied. Mickey Spillane and Ernest Haycox vied with Dostoyevsky and Faulkner, and the Penguin Poets edition of Gerard Manley Hopkins arrived in the same box as a little book called *Getting the Most Out of Love.* The former had been assiduously annotated by a very fine hand using a very blue-inked fountain pen while the latter had been studied by someone with very large thumbs, the prints of which were still visible in the margins. At the slightest provocation it would open almost automatically to particularly graphic and well-smudged pages.

When he was not in the boat, my father spent most of his time lying on the bed in his socks, the top two buttons of his trousers undone, his discarded shirt on the ever-ready chair and the sleeves of the woollen Stanfield underwear, which he wore both summer and winter, drawn half way up to his elbows. The pillows propped up the whiteness of his head and the goose-necked lamp illuminated the pages in his hands. The cigarettes smoked and smouldered on the ashtray and on the table and the radio played constantly, sometimes low and sometimes loud. At midnight and at one, two, three and four, one could sometimes hear the radio, his occasional cough, the rustling thud of a completed book being tossed to the corner heap, or the movement necessitated by his sitting on the edge of the bed to roll the thousandth cigarette. He seemed never to sleep, only to doze, and the light shone constantly from his window to the sea.

My mother despised the room and all it stood for and she had stopped sleeping in it after I was born. She despised disorder in rooms and in houses and in hours and in lives, and she had not read a book since high school. There she had read *Ivanhoe* and considered it a colossal waste of time. Still the room remained, like a rock of opposition in the sparkling waters of a clear deep harbour, opening off the kitchen where we really lived our lives, with its door always open and its contents visible to all.

The daughters of the room and of the house were very beautiful. They were tall and willowy like my mother and had her fine facial features set off by the reddish copper-coloured hair that had apparently once been my father's before it turned to white. All of them were very clever in school and helped my mother a great deal about the house. When they were young they sang and were very happy and very nice to me because I was the youngest, and the family's only boy.

My father never approved of their playing about the wharf like the other children, and they were only there when my mother sent them on an errand. At such times they almost always overstayed, playing screaming games of tag or hide-and-seek in and about the fishing shanties, the piled traps and tubs of trawl, shouting down to the perch that swam languidly about the wharf's algae-covered piles, or jumping in and out of the boats that tugged gently at their lines. My mother was never uneasy about them at such times, and when her husband criticized her she would say, "Nothing will happen to them there," or "They could be doing worse things in worse places."

By about the ninth or tenth grade my sisters one by one discovered my father's bedroom, and then the change would begin. Each would go into the room one morning when he was out. She would go in with the ideal hope of imposing order or with the more practical objective of emptying the ashtray, and later she would be found spellbound by the volume in her hand. My mother's reaction was always abrupt, bordering on the angry. "Take your nose out of that trash and come and do your work," she would say, and once I saw her slap my youngest sister so hard that the print of her hand was scarletly emblazoned upon her daughter's cheek while the broken-spined paperback fluttered uselessly to the floor.

Thereafter my mother would launch a campaign against what she had discovered but could not understand. At times, although she was not overly religious, she would bring God to bolster her arguments, saying, "In the next world God will see to those who waste their lives reading useless books when they should be about their work." Or without theological aid, "I would like to know how books help anyone to live a life." If my father were in, she would repeat the remarks louder than necessary, and her voice would carry into his room where he lay upon his bed. His usual reaction was to turn up the volume of the radio, although that action in itself betrayed the success of the initial thrust.

Shortly after my sisters began to read the books, they grew restless and lost interest in darning socks and baking bread, and all of them eventually went to work as summer waitresses in the Sea Food Restaurant. The restaurant was run by a big American concern from Boston and catered to the tourists that flooded the area during July and August. My mother despised the whole operation. She said the restaurant was not run by "our people," and "our people" did not eat there, and that it was run by outsiders for outsiders.

"Who are these people anyway?" she would ask, tossing back her dark hair, "and what do they, though they go about with their cameras for a hundred years, know about the way it is here, and what do they care about me and mine, and why should I care about them?"

She was angry that my sisters should even conceive of working in such a place, and more angry when my father made no move to prevent it, and she was worried about herself and about her family and about her life. Sometimes she would say softly to her sisters, "I don't know what's the matter with my girls. It seems none of them are interested in any of the right things." And sometimes there would be bitter savage arguments. One afternoon I was coming in with three mackerel I'd been given at the wharf when I heard her say, "Well, I hope you'll be satisfied when they come home knocked up and you'll have had your way."

It was the most savage thing I'd ever heard my mother say. Not just the words but the way she said them, and I stood there in the porch afraid to breathe for what seemed like the years from ten to fifteen, feeling the damp, moist mackerel with their silver glassy eyes growing clammy against my leg.

Through the angle in the screen door I saw my father, who had been walking into his room, wheel around on one of his rubber-booted heels and look at her with his blue eyes flashing like clearest ice beneath the snow that was his hair. His usually ruddy face was drawn and grey, reflecting the exhaustion of a man of sixty-five who had been working in those rubber boots for eleven hours on an August day, and for a fleeting moment I wondered what I would do if he killed my mother while I stood there in the porch with those three foolish mackerel in my hand. Then he turned and went into his room and the radio blared forth the next day's weather forecast and I retreated under the noise and returned again, stamping my feet and slamming the door too loudly to signal my approach. My mother was busy at the stove when I came in, and did not raise her head when I threw the mackerel in a pan. As I looked into my father's room, I said, "Well, how did things go in the boat today?" and he was lying on his back and lighting the first cigarette and the radio was talking about the Virginia coast.

All of my sisters made good money on tips. They bought my father an electric razor, which he tried to use for a while, and they took out even more magazine subscriptions. They bought my mother a great many clothes of the type she was very fond of, the wide-brimmed hats and the brocaded dresses, but she locked them all in trunks and refused to wear any of them.

On one August day my sisters prevailed upon my father to take some of their restaurant customers for an afternoon ride in the boat. The tourists with their expensive clothes and cameras and sun glasses awkwardly backed down the iron ladder at the wharf's side to where my father waited below, holding the rocking *Jenny Lynn* in snug against the wharf with one hand on the iron ladder and steadying his descending passengers with the other. They tried to look both prim and wind-blown like the girls in the Pepsi-Cola ads and did the best they could, sitting on the thwarts where the newspapers were spread to cover the splattered blood and fish entrails, crowding to one side so that they were in danger of capsizing the boat, taking the inevitable pictures or merely trailing their fingers through the water of their dreams.

All of them liked my father very much and, after he'd brought them back from their circles in the harbour, they invited him to their rented cabins which were located high on a hill overlooking the village to which they were so alien. He proceeded to get very drunk up there with the beautiful view and the strange company and the abundant liquor, and late in the afternoon he began to sing.

I was just approaching the wharf to deliver my mother's summons when he began, and the familiar yet unfamiliar voice that rolled down from the cabins made me feel as I had never felt without really knowing it, and I was ashamed yet proud, young yet old and saved yet forever lost, and there was nothing I could do to control my legs which trembled nor my eyes which wept, for what they could not tell.

The tourists were equipped with tape recorders and my father sang for more than three hours. His voice boomed down the hill and bounced off the surface of the harbour, which was an unearthly blue on that hot August day, and was then reflected to the wharf and the fishing shanties, where it was absorbed amidst the men who were baiting lines for the next day's haul.

He sang all the old sea chanteys that had come across from the old world and by which men like him had pulled ropes for generations, and he sang the East Coast sea songs that celebrated the sealing vessels of Northumberland Strait and the long liners of Boston Harbor, Nantucket and Block Island. Gradually he shifted to the seemingly unending Gaelic drinking songs with their twenty or more verses and inevitable refrains, and the men in the shanties smiled at the coarseness of some of the verses and at the thought that the singer's immediate audience did not know what they were applauding nor recording to take back to staid old Boston. Later as the sun was setting he switched to the laments and the wild and haunting Gaelic war songs of those spattered Highland ancestors he had never seen, and when his voice ceased, the savage melancholy of three hundred years seemed to hang over the peaceful harbour and the quiet boats and the men leaning in the doorways of their shanties with their cigarettes glowing in the dusk and the women looking to the sea from their open windows with their children in their arms.

When he came home he threw the money he had earned on the kitchen table as he did with all his earnings but my mother refused to touch it, and the next day he went with the rest of the men to bait his trawl in the shanties. The tourists came to the door that evening and my mother met them there and told them that her husband was not in, although he was lying on the bed only a few feet away, with the radio playing and the cigarette upon his lips. She stood in the doorway until they reluctantly went away.

In the winter they sent him a picture which had been taken on the day of the singing. On the back it said, "To Our Ernest Hemingway" and the "Our" was underlined. There was also an accompanying letter telling him how much they had enjoyed themselves, how popular the tape was proving and explaining who Ernest Hemingway was. In a way, it almost did look like one of those unshaven, taken-in-Cuba pictures of Hemingway. My father looked both massive and incongruous in the setting. His bulky fisherman's clothes were too big for the green and white lawn chair in which he sat, and his rubber boots seemed to take up all of the well-clipped grass square. The beach umbrella jarred with his sunburned face and because he had already been singing for some time, his lips, which chapped in the winds of spring and burned in the water glare of summer, had already cracked in several places, producing tiny flecks of blood at their corners and on the whiteness of his teeth. The bracelets of brass chain which he wore to protect his wrists from chafing seemed abnormally large and his broad leather belt had been slackened and his heavy shirt and underwear were open at the throat, revealing an uncultivated wilderness of white chest hair bordering on the semi-controlled stubble of his neck and chin. His blue eyes had looked directly into the camera and his hair was whiter than the two tiny clouds that hung over his left shoulder. The sea was behind him and its immense blue flatness stretched out to touch the arching blueness of the sky. It seemed very far away from him or else he was so much in the foreground that he seemed too big for it.

Each year another of my sisters would read the books and work in the restaurant. Sometimes they would stay out quite late on the hot summer nights and when they came up the stairs my mother would ask them many long and involved questions which they resented and tried to avoid. Before ascending the stairs they would go into my father's room, and those of us who waited above could hear them throwing his clothes off the chair before sitting on it, or the squeak of the bed as they sat on its edge. Sometimes they would talk to him a long time, the murmur of their voices blending with the music of the radio into a mysterious vapour-like sound which floated softly up the stairs.

I say this again as if it all happened at once and as if all my sisters were of identical ages and like so many lemmings going into another sea, and again, it was of course not that way at all. Yet go they did, to Boston, to Montreal, to New York with the young men they met during the summers and later married in those far-away cities. The young men were very articulate and handsome and wore fine clothes and drove expensive cars and my sisters, as I said, were very tall and beautiful with their copper-coloured hair, and were tired of darning socks and baking bread.

One by one they went. My mother had each of her daughters for fifteen years, then lost them for two and finally forever. None married a fisherman. My mother never accepted any of the young men, for in her eyes they seemed always a combination of the lazy, the effeminate, the dishonest and the unknown. They never seemed to do any physical work and she could not comprehend their luxurious vacations and she did not know whence they came nor who they were. And in the end she did not really care, for they were not of her people and they were not of her sea.

I say this now with a sense of wonder at my own stupidity in thinking I was somehow free and would go on doing well in school and playing and helping in the boat and passing into my early teens while streaks of grey began to appear in my mother's dark hair and my father's rubber boots dragged sometimes on the pebbles of the beach as he trudged home from the wharf. And there were but three of us in the house that had at one time been so loud.

Then during the winter that I was fifteen he seemed to grow old and ill all at once. Most of January he lay upon the bed, smoking and reading and listening to the radio while the wind howled about the house and the needle-like snow blistered off the ice-covered harbour and the doors flew out of people's hands if they did not cling to them like death.

In February, when the men began overhauling their lobster traps, he still did not move, and my mother and I began to knit lobster trap headings in the evenings. The twine was as always very sharp and harsh, and blisters formed upon our thumbs and little paths of blood snaked quietly down between our fingers while the seals that had drifted down from distant Labrador wept and moaned like human children on the ice-floes of the Gulf.

In the daytime my mother's brother, who had been my father's partner as long as I could remember, also came to work upon the gear. He was a year older than my mother and was tall and dark and the father of twelve children.

By March we were very far behind and although I began to work very hard in the evenings I knew it was not hard enough and that there were but eight weeks left before the opening of the season on May first. And I knew that my mother worried and my uncle was uneasy and that all of our very lives depended on the boat being ready with her gear and two men, by the date of May the first. And I knew then that *David Copperfield* and *The Tempest* and all of those friends I had dearly come to love must really go forever. So I bade them all good-bye.

The night after my first full day at home and after my mother had gone upstairs he called me into his room, where I sat upon the chair beside his bed. "You will go back tomorrow," he said simply.

I refused then, saying I had made my decision and was satisfied.

"That is no way to make a decision," he said, "and if you are satisfied I am not. It is best that you go back." I was almost angry then and told him as all children do that I wished he would leave me alone and stop telling me what to do.

He looked at me a long time then, lying there on the same bed on which he had fathered me those sixteen years before, fathered me his only son, out of who knew what emotions when he was already fifty-six and his hair had turned to snow. Then he swung his legs over the edge of the squeaking bed and sat facing me and looked into my own dark eyes with his of crystal blue and placed his hand upon my knee. "I am not telling you to do any-thing," he said softly, "only asking you."

The next morning I returned to school. As I left, my mother followed me to the porch and said, "I never thought a son of mine would choose useless books over the parents that gave him life."

In the weeks that followed he got up rather miraculously, and the gear was ready and the *Jenny Lynn* was freshly painted by the last two weeks of April when the ice began to break up and the lonely screaming gulls returned to haunt the silver herring as they flashed within the sea.

On the first day of May the boats raced out as they had always done, laden down almost to the gunwales with their heavy cargoes of traps. They were almost like living things as they plunged through the waters of the spring and manoeuvred between the still floating icebergs of crystal-white and emerald green on their way to the traditional grounds that they sought out every May. And those of us who sat that day in the high school on the hill, discussing the water imagery of Tennyson, watched them as they passed back and forth beneath us until by afternoon the piles of traps which had been stacked upon the wharf were no longer visible but were spread about the bottoms of the sea. And the *Jenny Lynn* went too, all day, with my uncle tall and dark, like a latter-day Tashtego standing at the tiller with his legs wide apart and guiding her deftly between the floating pans of ice and my father in the stern standing in the same way with his hands upon the ropes that lashed the cargo to the deck. And at night my mother asked, "Well, how did things go in the boat today?"

And the spring wore on and the summer came and school ended in the third week of June and the lobster season on July first and I wished that the two things I loved so dearly did not exclude each other in a manner that was so blunt and too clear.

At the conclusion of the lobster season my uncle said he had been offered a berth on a deep-sea dragger and had decided to accept. We all knew that he was leaving the *Jenny Lynn* forever and that before the next lobster season he would buy a boat of his own. He was expecting another child and would be supporting fifteen people by the next spring and could not chance my father against the family that he loved.

I joined my father then for the trawling season, and he made no protest and my mother was quite happy. Through the summer we baited the tubs of trawl in the afternoon and set them at sunset and revisited them in the darkness of the early morning. The men would come tramping by our house at four a.m. and we would join them and walk with them to the wharf and be on our way before the sun rose out of the ocean where it seemed to spend the night. If I was not up they would toss pebbles to my window and I would be very embarrassed and tumble downstairs where my father lay fully clothed atop his bed, reading his book and listening to his radio and smoking his cigarette. When I appeared he would swing off his bed and put on his boots and be instantly ready and then we would take the lunches my mother had prepared the night before and walk off toward the sea. He would make no attempt to wake me himself.

It was in many ways a good summer. There were few storms and we were out almost every day and we lost a minimum of gear and seemed to land a maximum of fish and I tanned dark and brown after the manner of my uncles.

My father did not tan—he never tanned—because of his reddish complexion, and the salt water irritated his skin as it had for sixty years. He burned and reburned over and over again and his lips still cracked so that they bled when he smiled, and his arms, especially the left, still broke out into the oozing salt-water boils as they had ever since as a child I had first watched him soaking and bathing them in a variety of ineffectual solutions. The chafe-preventing bracelets of brass linked chain that all the men wore about their wrists in early spring were his the full season and he shaved but painfully and only once a week.

And I saw then, that summer, many things that I had seen all my life as if for the first time and I thought that perhaps my father had never been intended for a fisherman physically or mentally. At least not in the manner of my uncles; he had never really loved it. And I remembered that, one evening in his room when we were talking about *David Copperfield*, he had said that he had always wanted to go to the university and I had dismissed it then in the way one dismisses one's father saying he would like to be a tight-rope walker, and we had gone on to talk about the Peggottys and how they loved the sea.

And I thought then to myself that there were many things wrong with all of us and all our lives and I wondered why my father, who was himself an only son, had not married before he was forty and then I wondered why he had. I even thought that perhaps he had had to marry my mother and checked the dates on the flyleaf of the Bible where I learned that my oldest sister had been born a prosaic eleven months after the marriage, and I felt myself then very dirty and debased for my lack of faith and for what I had thought and done.

And then there came into my heart a very great love for my father and I thought it was very much braver to spend a life doing what you really do not want rather than selfishly following forever your own dreams and inclinations. And I knew then that I could never leave him alone to suffer the iron-tipped harpoons which my mother would forever hurl into his soul because he was a failure as a husband and a father who had retained none of his own. And I felt that I had been very small in a little secret place within me and that even the completion of high school was for me a silly shallow selfish dream.

So I told him one night very resolutely and very powerfully that I would remain with him as long as he lived and we would fish the sea together. And he made no protest but only smiled through the cigarette smoke that wreathed his bed and replied, "I hope you will remember what you've said."

The room was now so filled with books as to be almost Dickensian, but he would not allow my mother to move or change them and he continued to read them, sometimes two or three a night. They came with great regularity now, and there were more hardcovers, sent by my sisters who had gone so long ago and now seemed so distant and so prosperous, and sent also pictures of small red-haired grandchildren with baseball bats and dolls, which he placed upon his bureau and which my mother gazed at wistfully when she thought no one would see. Red-haired grandchildren with baseball bats and dolls who would never know the sea in hatred or in love.

And so we fished through the heat of August and into the cooler days of September when the water was so clear we could almost see the bottom and the white mists rose like delicate ghosts in the early morning dawn. And one day my mother said to me, "You have given added years to his life."

And we fished on into October when it began to roughen and we could no longer risk night sets but took our gear out each morning and returned at the first sign of the squalls; and on into November when we lost three tubs of trawl and the clear blue water turned to a sullen grey and the trochoidal waves rolled rough and high and washed across our bows and decks as we ran within their troughs. We wore heavy sweaters now and the awkward rubber slickers and the heavy woollen mitts which soaked and froze into masses of ice that hung from our wrists like the limbs of gigantic monsters until we thawed them against the exhaust pipe's heat. And almost every day we would leave for home before noon, driven by the blasts of the northwest wind coating our eyebrows with ice and freezing our eyelids closed as we leaned into a visibility that was hardly there, charting our course from the compass and the sea, running with the waves and between them but never confronting their towering might.

And I stood at the tiller now, on these homeward lunges, stood in the place and in the manner of my uncle, turning to look at my father and to shout over the roar of the engine and the slop of the sea to where he stood in the stern, drenched and dripping with snow and the salt and the spray and his bushy eyebrows caked in ice. But on November twenty-first, when it seemed we might be making the final run of the season, I turned and he was not there and I knew even in that instant that he would never be again.

On November twenty-first the waves of the grey Atlantic are very high and the waters are very cold and there are no signposts on the surface of the sea. You cannot tell where you have been five minutes before and in the squalls of snow you cannot see. And it takes longer than you would believe to check a boat that has been running before a gale and turn her ever so carefully in a wide and stupid circle, with timbers creaking and straining, back into the face of the storm. And you know that it is useless and that your voice does not carry the length of the boat and that even if you knew the original spot, the relentless waves would carry such a burden perhaps a mile or so by the time you could return. And you know also, the final irony, that your father, like your uncles and all the men that form your past, cannot swim a stroke.

The lobster beds off the Cape Breton coast are still very rich and now, from May to July, their offerings are packed in crates of ice, and thundered by the gigantic transport trucks, day and night, through New Glasgow, Amherst, Saint John and Bangor and Portland and into Boston where they are tossed still living into boiling pots of water, their final home.

And though the prices are higher and the competition tighter, the grounds to which the *Jenny Lynn* once went remain untouched and unfished as they have for the last ten years. For if there are no signposts on the sea in storm, there are certain ones in calm, and the lobster bottoms were distributed in calm before any of us can remember, and the grounds my father fished were those his father fished before him and there were others before and before and before. Twice the big boats have come from forty and fifty miles, lured by the promise of the grounds and strewn the bottom with their traps, and twice they have returned to find their buoys cut adrift and their gear lost and destroyed. Twice the Fisheries Officer and the Mounted Police have come and asked many long and involved questions, and twice they have received no answers from the men leaning in the doors of their shanties and the women standing at their windows with their children in their arms. Twice they have gone away saying: "There are no legal boundaries in the Maine area;" "No one can own the sea;" "Those grounds don't wait for anyone."

But the men and the women, with my mother dark among them, do not care for what they say, for to them the grounds are sacred and they think they wait for me.

It is not an easy thing to know that your mother lives alone on an inadequate insurance policy and that she is too proud to accept any other aid. And that she looks through her lonely window onto the ice of winter and the hot flat calm of summer and the rolling waves of fall. And that she lies awake in the early morning's darkness when the rubber boots of the men scrunch upon the gravel as they pass beside her house on their way down to the wharf. And she knows that the footsteps never stop, because no man goes from her house, and she alone of all the Lynns has neither son nor son-in-law who walks toward the boat that will take him to the sea. And it is not an easy thing to know that your mother looks upon the sea with love and on you with bitterness because the one has been so constant and the other so untrue.

But neither is it easy to know that your father was found on November twenty-eighth, ten miles to the north and wedged between two boulders at the base of the rock-strewn cliffs where he had been hurled and slammed so many many times. His hands were shredded ribbons, as were his feet which had lost their boots to the suction of the sea, and his shoulders came apart in our hands when we tried to move him from the rocks. And the gulls had pecked out his eyes and the white-green stubble of his whiskers had continued to grow in death, like the grass on graves, upon the purple, bloated mass that was his face. There was not much left of my father, physically, as he lay there with the brass chains on his wrists and the seaweed in his hair.

ɕ   Alistair MacLeod grew up in Cape Breton and began publishing stories in Canadian and American journals in the 1960s and 1970s. International recognition came with his publication of "The Boat" in the *Massachusetts Review* in 1968; it was selected to appear in the annual collection *Best American Short Stories* for 1969. MacLeod received this honour again in 1975 with the story "The Lost Salt Gift of Blood." Many of his stories deal with the power of the past over the present. *(Born North Battleford, Saskatchewan 1936)*

RESPONDING

Meaning

1. Briefly summarize the effects of books and reading on the various members of the narrator's family.

2. a) Prove that although the narrator loves his father, he does not idealize him or his way of life. Explain how the narrator's relationship to his father reflects the central conflict he faces in his life.

    b) In a journal entry, speculate about whether the author has fully explored the reasons for the mother's opposition to books and reading. What reasons might exist which have not been explored in the story?

Form and Style

3. a) In literature, a boat is often a *symbol* for the journey through life. How, in this story, has the symbolism of the boat been transformed?

    b) What symbol has replaced the boat, and why, in this story, is it particularly effective? Present your response in a short essay.

4. a) Choose a passage from the story of one to three paragraphs. Copy the passage and annotate it to show how the author uses language to create a distinctive atmosphere. Point out specific verbs, adjectives, metaphors, etc. and their effects. Note how they appeal to the different senses.

    b) Describe your reaction to the detailed description of the narrator's dead father. In your opinion, does this passage provide an effective ending? What are its strengths and weaknesses?

Creative Extension

5. Research works by Canadian artists that deal with some of the same themes and images as those in Alistair MacLeod's story. Check books, CD-ROMs, and Internet Web sites of national and provincial art galleries. Select two pieces and write a short analysis explaining how the artists have used colour, size of images, and other techniques to convey their ideas and to evoke a response from the viewer.

6. "The Boat" provides a considerable amount of information about the way of life of a fisher on the East Coast of Canada in the time of the narrator's childhood. Based on this information, write a short non-fiction magazine article describing this way of life. You may want to include information about how this way of life is changing today.

For Mataji

ᕔ Amita Handa

Learning Goals

• examine the
  relationship
  between
  characters

• analyze an
  author's use of
  parallel incidents
  and a narrative
  hook

• create a free verse
  poem based on a
  text

• write and present
  a eulogy

"It's like going to sleep with your eyes open," she murmured. I didn't understand. Maybe the true meaning was lost because I didn't know all the Punjabi words. It's like Punjabi jokes, they make me laugh until my stomach aches but when I try telling them in English, they're not funny anymore. I fell asleep next to her and dreamt about the brand new vacuum cleaner I wrote on with pen. Oooh was ma ever mad. She slapped me. I felt so grown up because this time I didn't even cry. In the morning ma dressed me in a white dress, kissed me, and rushed off to work. It was early, eight o'clock, and I was feeling quite cranky. I sat at the kitchen table and tried to count all the little marks on the wall which I had made the day before with my crayon set. Mataji told me to drink my juice. It was in my favourite, old scratched-up thick yellow glass. As I picked up the glass my elbow slipped off the table and the juice ran pretty colours all over my dress. Mataji scolded me for being so clumsy and pulled me into my room. She had never dressed me before, it was always ma. She rummaged through the drawers and pulled out a white slip with lace on it. She started putting it on me. "This is a nice dress," she said.

• • •

The nurse came in and fiddled with the I.V. I watched it drip down slowly into the tube. I wondered if she could feel every drop enter her. Her sleep was disturbed. "Were you sitting here all this time?" she asked. "Yeah, I was thinking about when I was little and we lived in Thorncliffe Park." She started to cry. I thought it was nostalgia and sentiment. "I must have done something awful in my last life," she said. "What do you mean?" She was out of breath and couldn't speak. I tried to console her with my hand rubbing hers. "Must have been something horrible," she repeated. "They took me into a room and poked needles in my head. What did I do?" She began to sob. I felt lost, confused, startled. Was she dreaming? Ahh Cat Scan. I thought of her lying on the bed. Doctors and nurses wheeling her into a big room, her protesting in Punjabi. "Now Mrs. Handa, we're going to do a Cat Scan." Only for her, it was blah, blah, blah, poke, poke. I tried to explain the Cat Scan but she fell asleep again. I drifted off too.

• • •

"Mataji!" I yelled, "I can't wear this, it's a slip." I looked at her in frustration and realized there was no use. She was a stubborn woman. I started to cry, but nonetheless off we went across the street to school. My kindergarten teacher looked at me funny. I tried to keep away from the other kids. We had new blocks and puzzles to play with and I soon forgot about the slip. Mataji sat between the double doors like she always did from the time I went into the classroom until noon, when school was over to walk me home, even though we lived in the apartment building right across the street. She always sat on the floor and leaned against the wall and I'd sneak out to visit her. At about ten o'clock, I got bored with the new games and when the teacher left the room, I went to see Mataji but she wasn't there. I felt frantic and went back to the classroom. Where is she? Five minutes passed and I went back. Sure enough there she was. She had gone out for some fresh air. I sat on her lap. She took out some roti and subji (cooked vegetables) which she had wrapped in foil paper and started feeding me. I pressed my cheek against her sari. I could smell the coconut oil in her hair as she rubbed my head with her hand. "When you finish school, we'll go to the Mall," she said. I loved going to the Mall with her. I would always try to count out the change 'cause she didn't know what all the different sized coins stood for. I felt like an adult when I would translate for her and the cashier.

I wasn't hungry anymore so she put the leftovers back in the foil and took out her copy of the *Gita*. It was written in Punjabi. "Mataji, I thought you couldn't read." "I can't," she said, "but I can make out a little bit from years of hearing it being read." I remember once she told me she wasn't allowed to learn how to read. When her brothers were in school she would sit near the school yard and write out the alphabet with her finger in the sand. She would coy the letters from billboards or any other written material around. But she would always get caught. Her brothers would hit her hands with a stick and tell her she was forbidden to write, so she stopped doing so. "How come girls couldn't go to school?" I asked. "Girls weren't looked at in the same way," she said. She told me that with the birth of a son the whole village celebrates, but when a daughter is born there is no such fireworks, mostly just condolences. When I was born in England, Mataji was still in India. She told everyone in Ferozepore I was a boy so she could have a big celebration for me. This was my favourite story. How she tricked everyone! She didn't even tell my grandfather. They must have been so mad when they found out I was a girl.

I heard the teacher's voice in the classroom so I hugged her and went back in. I decided to put together the orange puzzle this time. It was difficult. Too many pieces that wouldn't fit so I pushed hard on them until they would.

• • •

The nurse walked in to monitor the I.V. They did that according to schedule every hour or so. Mataji wasn't wearing a sari, but some kind of nightie. She looked clownish, she had never worn anything but a sari all her life. I looked down to watch her breathe. Each breath was a struggle—her whole body moved on the inhale and she kept on taking the oxygen mask off. "She's only semi-conscious now, it's the pneumonia," the nurse said. Mataji's eyes were closed. I held her hand and squeezed hard, hoping she could feel me. She began muttering something. She opened her eyes wide and stared at the ceiling. The words got louder and she reached out with both hands to claw at something in the air. She looked frightened. "She's just disoriented," the nurse said as she walked out of the room. Maybe she can really see something that we can't, I thought.

• • •

Puzzles are boring I decided. So now it was time to do some work in my colouring book. I would always cross the lines, never being able to stay within them. But I liked it better when I didn't have to worry about doing it right and could just let my crayons go wherever they wanted, wherever I wanted. The teacher came over, glanced at my artwork and kneeled down beside me. "Your grandmother can't come here any more," she said. "But why?" I blurted out. "She can drop you off and pick you up, but that's all." "What did she do wrong, she's not doing any harm," I cried. "I'm sorry," she muttered.

• • •

The phone rang. It was my father telling us to come to the hospital right away. I knew something had happened. We got there as soon as we could and entered the room. Dad was standing beside the bed, eyes closed. "I saw her last breath," he said. She looked really peaceful, just as they say. No more strain in her face, the struggle was gone. We all stood there silently, our eyes closed. The nurse came in, opened the curtains, picked up my grandmother's hand and pressed her fingers to her wrist. She dropped the hand, took out a needle from her pocket, and began to feel around for veins in Mataji's arm. "What are you doing?" my sister gasped. "The doctor ordered to draw some blood," she stated and proceeded to put together the needle. "But she's dead. . . ."

• • •

The bell rang and my teacher walked away. I knew she had already talked to Mataji because she wasn't there any more. The space between the double doors was empty. I tried to open the door but couldn't. I waited until one of the older kids opened it for themselves and quickly leaned my body against it before it shut, so that I could pass through. Maybe Mataji's waiting for me outside, I thought. But she wasn't, I looked everywhere. I approached the street to cross over to the other side. I saw my mom driving by. She sometimes let me ride across the street in the car if she saw me without Mataji on her way home for lunch. I waved and yelled. As she looked over her jaw hung open in embarrassment. She drove right by me. I didn't understand, did she not see me? But she looked right at me. As the wind blew by, I caught a glimpse of cloth. I looked down and remembered about the slip. . . .

Amita Handa was born in England and raised in Toronto, Canada. She has published a series of interviews with South Asian women living in Canada entitled *Caught Between Omissions* (2001). "For Mataji" is from *Fireweed*, February 1990. In a note to the story, Amita Handa wrote: "This is not a story about all South Asian families, about all South Asian grandmothers, mothers, and daughters. This is a story about one family, a story about my grandmother from a pre-industrialized generation and some of the barriers and alienation she faced once she migrated to Canada." *(Born England 1964)*

RESPONDING

Meaning

1. Describe the character of Mataji. How does she attempt to keep her cultural traditions alive in Canada? What barriers does she face?

2. To what degree does the expression, "The acorn doesn't fall far from the tree," apply to the relationship between the narrator and her grandmother?

Form and Style

3. Handa structures her narrative around a series of parallel incidents.
   a) Describe two of these incidents.
   b) How effectively does this structure contribute to our understanding of the story and to our emotional response to Mataji's death?

4. A *narrative hook* is a strategy used by a writer to immediately engage the reader's interest. Evaluate the author's use of culturally specific details in the first paragraph in terms of engaging and keeping the interest of the reader.

Creative Extension

5. Write a free verse poem describing Mataji's thoughts and emotions when she is told by the teacher that she may not wait at the school for her granddaughter.

6. Assume the role of the narrator and present a *eulogy* for Mataji. Be sure to include details from the story and your own ideas about Mataji's life.

The Blues Merchant

♪ Jerome Washington

Learning Goals

- examine effectiveness of setting
- analyze use of varying sentence lengths, sentence structures, and musical effects of language
- create a poem
- develop a storyboard for a short video

Long Tongue, The Blues Merchant, strolls on stage. His guitar rides side-saddle against his hip. The drummer slides onto the tripod seat behind the drums, adjusts the high-hat cymbal, and runs a quick, off-beat tattoo on the tom-tom, then relaxes. The bass player plugs into the amplifier, checks the settings on the control panel and nods his okay. Three horn players stand off to one side, clustered, lurking like brilliant sorcerer-wizards waiting to do magic with their musical instruments.

The auditorium is packed. A thousand inmates face the stage; all anticipate a few minutes of musical escape. The tear gas canisters recessed in the ceiling remind us that everything is for real.

The house lights go down and the stage lights come up. Reds and greens and blues slide into pinks and ambers and yellows and play over the six poised musicians.

The Blues Merchant leans forward and mumbles, "Listen. Listen here, you all," into the microphone. "I want to tell you about Fancy Brown and Mean Lean Green. They is the slickest couple in the East Coast scene."

Thump. Thump. The drummer plays. Boom-chicka-chicka-boom. He slams his tubs. The show is on. Toes tap. Hands clap. Fingers pop. The audience vibrates. Long Tongue finds his groove. He leans back. He moans. He shouts. His message is picked up, translated and understood. With his soul he releases us from bondage, puts us in tune with tomorrow, and the memories of the cold steel cells—our iron houses—evaporate.

Off to one side, a blue coated guard nods to the rhythm. On the up-beat his eyes meet the guard sergeant's frown. The message is clear: "You are not supposed to enjoy the blues. You get paid to watch, not to be human." The message is instantaneously received. The guard jerks himself still and looks meaner than ever.

Long Tongue, The Blues Merchant, wails on. He gets funky. He gets rough. He gets raunchy. His blues are primeval. He takes everybody, except the guards, on a trip. The guards remain trapped behind the prison's walls while, if only for a short time, we are free.

Jerome Washington spent 16 years in American prisons on charges that were dropped after he was released in 1989. An accomplished journalist before he was convicted, Washington founded the Auburn Collective, an award-winning prison newspaper that chronicled prisoners' struggles. He received the 1994 Western States Arts Federation Book Award for Creative Non-Fiction for *Iron House: Stories from the Yard* (1994). *(Born United States 1939)*

RESPONDING

Meaning

1. a) The setting of this story isn't immediately clear. At what point in the story is the setting revealed? How is it revealed? What effect does this have on you, the reader?
    b) The story brings together two contrasting worlds. Explain this contrast.

2. Explain the *irony* of the incident being described in this story. Do you feel that the irony is comic or tragic? Support your interpretation.

Form and Style

3. *Syntax* is the arrangement of words into sentences. It includes sentence structure and sentence length. Describe the author's use of syntax in this story. How does it change? What effect do the author's syntactical choices have on the mood and pace of the description?

4. Like the music the Blues Merchant plays, the story is filled with rhythm and musical sound. Identify specific word choices that help to convey this impression.

Creative Extension

5. Write a poem describing a musical concert. Use syntax and word choice to help convey the sound and rhythm of the music.

6. Adapt this story into a storyboard for a short video. Use a variety of camera shots and angles, choose music to set the mood, and incorporate sound effects. Then write a memo explaining the choices you made to create particular effects. Point out one or two challenges you encountered and the strategies you used to deal with them.

Nanuq, the White Ghost, Repents

♋ Alootook Ipellie

Learning Goals

- examine universal themes presented in a modern myth
- analyze use of parallelism and incongruity
- consider how language, narrative point of view, and imagery establish tone
- recreate a story in a different time and setting
- create an original ballad

The suspersonic speed with which my soul had travelled out of my body denied me the opportunity to fully reflect on the true cause of the death of myself and my father. However, like a dream that one finally remembers later in the day, I found out it wasn't by choice that we had left the planet Earth—but by the violent agony of incredible physical pain.

My father and I had been stalking a ringed seal close to the clutter of ice ridges hugging a small island. We had suddenly heard the hardened snow making crunching sounds behind us. But before we could turn around to see what was making the sounds, a powerful polar bear paw had knocked us down. The great white Nanuq, the King of Arctic wildlife, had come to stake his claim to the very same ringed seal we were after. With a few powerful swipes of its claws and life-ending bites from its hungry jaws, the great White Ghost had cut through our flesh and burst open the bubble of our life-blood!

My father and I spent our last few moments in the physical world engulfed in the violence of the tyrannical beast. Memorable were the gratified eyes of the King, in contrast to our hysterical shrieks and terrified, bulging eyeballs!

It wasn't fair to me and my father that the King never gave us an opportunity to challenge it in battle for supremacy over the Great White Arctic Kingdom. It would have been a call-to-arms pitting the King's natural weapons against our manmade weapons of knives and harpoons. My father and I could only commend the King for its great agility despite its lumbering reputation when walking or running on ice. Its natural instinct as a predator allowed it to do what comes naturally—a couple of well-placed slaps to our bodies—the rest of its job was elementary; sending our souls unceremoniously toward the widening cosmos!

It was from a certain perspective in the sky that I was able to observe what happened next. My older brother, Nuna, who had gone to the other side of the island to watch over one of the other breathing holes, came back to discover a great tragedy. The Great White Ghost was in the act of devouring our bodies when my brother ran up to the towering beast with his harpoon at the ready. He then hurled the powerful darting lance with rage in his eyes. The advancing force of the harpoon became bullet-like as it flew toward its target. My brother's face was so incredibly enraged that I did not recognize him. He looked like a marauder; a tyrannical man, who had suddenly grown long fangs in his madness. I was astonished how a gentle person like Nuna could become so monstrous during a fit of rage, swearing vengeance for a great injustice done to his dear father and brother!

Finally, his tool of death found its victim. Only a Great White Ghost could growl with such distinction as this one did. Its heart splintered like glass. The pupils turned angelic white. The black blood instantaneously jetted out onto the crystallized ice. What a way to pay for taking away the lives of two innocent hungry hunters! What a bloody shame to have wasted such precious human beings. Then again, that was the nature of our precarious lives; both man and beasts'.

In the land of the wild, no individual is ever favoured over another. When the time comes, no individual is ever spared. No law of nature protects or galvanizes the lives of men or beasts alike.

In the end, Nanuq, the Great White Ghost, was forced to repent in front of my dear brother, Nuna.

Alootook Ipellie, one of the best-known Inuit authors and artists in Canada, has been editor of *Kivioq*, as well as a contributor to other northern publications. His first book, *Arctic Dreams and Nightmares* (1993), combines traditional Inuit literary forms with modern themes. "Nanuq, The White Ghost, Repents" is from this book.

RESPONDING

Meaning

1. Nuna swears "vengeance for a great injustice done to his dear father and brother." Why does the narrator consider his and his father's deaths unjust?

2. How does the narrator use *parallelism* to link the killing of the men with the killing of Nanuq?

Form and Style

3. *Incongruity* occurs when an author places together things, events, images, or characters that do not seem to be connected or compatible. Find an example of incongruity in the first paragraph and assess the effectiveness of its use.

4. The author imbues this story with a mythic grandeur. What elements of the story provide this sense of myth or universality? Consider language, narrative point of view, and imagery.

Creative Extension

5. "In the land of the wild, no individual is ever favoured over another. When the time comes, no individual is ever spared." Using this universal statement about life and death as your theme, rewrite this story in a different setting—perhaps a city, or a war zone. What might replace the polar bear as the agent of death? What circumstances might bring death and vengeance in the new setting? Who will be your narrator? Feel free to change the tone, diction, and other details, but maintain as many parallels as possible with the original story line.

6. A *ballad* is a song or poem that tells a dramatic story. Write a song ballad that tells the story of Nanuq. Use the tune from a well-known traditional song of your choice and include a refrain that repeats after each verse.

Personal Writing

Buchi Emecheta on personal writing:

Writing an autobiography should be a fairly easy task. One has simply to look back into oneself, lift the lid off the great past and allow its time-lessness to overflow into the present through the channel of one's pen and paper. But writing my autobiography is not going to be easy. This is because most of my . . . stories are, like my children, too close to my heart. They are too real. They are too me.

Hockey Dreams

David Adams Richards

Learning Goals

• examine meaning
  through a close
  reading of text

• analyze an
  author's choice of
  style and its
  effects

• create original
  written and media
  works based on a
  text

We were all going to make the NHL when I was ten or eleven.

In those years—long ago, the weather was always *more* than it is now. There was more of it—more snow, more ice, more sky—more wind.

More hockey.

We played from just after football season until cricket started sometime after Easter. We played cricket in our little town in the Maritimes, or "kick the can" as we alluded to it, after we put away our waterlogged and mud-soaked hockey sticks. Behind us and down over the bank, the Miramichi River was breaking its ice and freeing itself from another winter. In the piles of disappearing snow, fragments of sticks and tape could be found.

The sun was warm and smoke rested on the fields and grasses.

At Easter, in my mind there always seemed to be a funeral. One year, 1961, just after Easter, there was the funeral of a man who was shot in Foley's Tire Garage, and everyone was excited about it. We were all friends of the Foley boys—there were seven of them. The oldest of them was Paul.

He was the boy who told me that when bigger boys go into the corner after the puck—or after the ball if it was road hockey—always watch and wait patiently just on the outside.

"You're too little," he said. And in a characteristically protective way that other children had with me, he added. "You're also lame. You *can't* use your left arm—so if you just wait, the puck will dribble out to you and you'll have a chance at a goal."

A goal. To score one goal was the height of my ambition.

But looking back, half of us playing, half of us who wanted nothing more than to play in the NHL—which was always to Maritimers some-where else—were going to have at least as much problem as me. Being a Maritimer certainly had a little to do with it.

One of our goalies was a girl. . . .

The brother of my friend who cautioned me about going into the corner was a diabetic—Stafford Foley. Stafford wore a Detroit sweater and in his entire life he never got outside Newcastle. He was a fanatical sports fan all his life.

• • •

In the late fall of long ago, of 1960 when we were all running up and down the outdoor rink, in huge boots, or pavement-dulled skates, in bare heads and kneepads, and a few with helmets that were pulled down over their toque, with ice on our sticks, the sport was Stafford Foley's and mine.

Stafford Foley actually believed we—he and I—would be elevated to the Peewee All-Star team, go on the road trips—one was to Boston like the Bantam As—and be "normal," like the other kids. In my dreams Stafford Foley and I had already made it. Already had scored the winning goals in Boston—there had to be two winning goals; one for him and one for me.

That he was growing blind, and wiped his eyes with a handkerchief in order to see who was on a breakaway, did not deter him. That I had only use of one arm and couldn't skate—especially backwards—did not deter me either, in my dreams. . . .

However my own father was hinting that I should retire from the sport. One day he took me out to the garage and said, "Lift that brick with your right hand."

I lifted it over my head.

"Lift that brick with your left hand."

I could hardly get my fingers over it.

My father then explained to me that I was like a great hockey player who had suffered an injury. I was on the disabled list.

He said the "disabled list" because at that time I would fly into a fury—almost froth at the mouth—if anyone said I was disabled. But he knew that. And so, staring at me, he said, "You're not at all disabled—it's just a disabled LIST."

My father really didn't care if I played hockey until I was 80—or 90. Half the time he forgot that I was "disabled."

• • •

As we grew older we all went our various ways with hockey. It was strange to see boys who were on the ice in high school one year giving it all up to grow their hair long the next, saying, "Hey man—what's happenin'? Get on down, baby."

Of course some of them took up the puck later to play in the gentle-man leagues. (Sometimes the gentleman league on our river was enough to give you cardiac arrest.)

I know at least five people who might have made it to the NHL if they had disciplined themselves. Perhaps, too, and I say this without bitterness, if there had been proper scouts from the big teams here, or more credit was given to the Maritimers themselves. There was the OHL and the Quebec Major Junior—in the Maritimes the boys graduated to Senior hockey and played to sell-out crowds for their home towns.

I don't know how many of us could have made it, but there were some of us who could but didn't. Perhaps they didn't have the breaks; per-haps they didn't have the heart. The real thing the OHL and Quebec Major Junior is, is a journey through hell, at seventeen years old, a thousand miles from home on a snowy road. One only has to talk to anybody who *has* played in those leagues; billeted in houses, travelling all night by bus or car, suffering the scorn of the coach if he was just not quite good enough.

• • •

Even back then "Hockey Night in Canada" came from places that seemed another world, or on another planet—places like Chicago and Detroit and New York—places that most of these children I am writing about never ever got a chance to see.

I don't remember ever *not* thinking something was a little wrong with us or with this: that is, the concept of six teams—four in the United States.

It didn't matter to me, at least not much, that two of these American teams were lousy all through my childhood—that is, Boston and New York —which essentially left four teams, two Canadian and two American. (Of course, I constantly reminded people that they were all Canadian players.)

Nor did any of this matter to my cousin from Boston, who in January 1961 came on a hockey tournament to Canada, and did *not know* that there was an NHL or a team called the Boston Bruins.

That was the first indication to me that "Hockey Night in Canada" was a night that wasn't shown to him. He had no idea that they showed hockey on television. There was something stinkingly wrong with this. But the fact that he did not know there was an NHL threw me for a loop.

I stared at him in incredulity. How could you lace up your skates with nowhere to go? At least I was going to the NHL—with a few turns of good luck. (One of the ideas was that they wouldn't see my left foot which was turned inward, and my left hand which was crippled.)

"Why are there four teams in the United States?" I asked Mr. Foley about that same time.

"'Cause they got the money."

I don't remember why this struck me as not the absolute answer. My idea—and since my cousin did not know about the Boston Bruins or the NHL, it seemed in a way to verify it for me—was that the LOVE of the game had to be everything.

In a way this has been the main pin of my hockey ideas ever since.

Also, there was something more subtle in my conversation with my American cousin that winter day. It was the idea of two cultures sparring and emerging from this sparring with definitive national attitudes about themselves.

I *had not* told my American cousin that there *was* an NHL because I did not want to inflict *my* superior knowledge upon a visitor. I was too polite. I was a Canadian. It's this national trait that has helped sideline our hockey history I'm sure.

Because ten minutes later he came at me with this: "What is the greatest basketball team?" And I said, truthfully, that I didn't know.

"The Harlem Globetrotters," he laughed. "Don't you guys know anything up here? Hockey is not as great a sport as baseball—it doesn't have the statistics," my cousin said sniffing. "Baseball is what everyone watches on television down home. Mickey Mantle, he earns more money than all the hockey players put together probably."

I'd heard of Mickey Mantle. I did not know what a statistic was.

And then he said, "Hockey will never be on TV."

I was in Toronto years later—about the same time I first saw Doug Gilmour live—having dinner with good friends of mine, an American and a Canadian. When they asked if I watched sports I told them that I loved to watch hockey.

My American friend said that she could not follow hockey because she never knew where the puck was. I didn't mind her saying this, for she had never watched a game in her life.

"No one does," the Canadian quipped. "It's poor TV because no one can follow what's going on. That's why Canadians now love baseball."

Of course, that is about as untrue a statement as ever was made about *our* game. Anyone who knows hockey can tell instinctively what is happening on the ice—even away from the camera. You can tell an offside, or a two-line pass in the remotest blink of an eye—just as you can tell a real penalty from a make-believe one. Even when Stafford Foley was almost blind, he could tell this.

But talking to my cousin in 1961, my eyes were being opened to the limits of our game once away from us, to the position of the game as related to spheres other than our own. My eyes were being opened not by light so much as by shiners.

I did not realize at the time that being Canadian was part of the reason why *our game* didn't exist on American networks. It seemed strange to me even then that so few people recognized this oddity or spoke about it as a major problem in Canadian identity.

David Adams Richards is an award-winning author of fiction, non-fiction, stage plays, screenplays, and poetry. He received Governor General's Awards for both his novel *Nights Below Station Street* (1988) and his meditation on the joys of fly fishing, *Lines on the Water* (1998). In 2000 he won the Giller Prize (shared with Michael Ondaatje) for his novel *Mercy Among the Children*. *Hockey Dreams: Memories of a Man Who Couldn't Play* was published in 1996. (Born Newcastle, New Brunswick 1950)

RESPONDING

Meaning

1. As boys, David Adams Richards and his friends dreamed of playing in the NHL. They didn't make it, but their childhood experiences with hockey nevertheless had a vivid and lasting effect on them. What effects did Richards's childhood experiences have on him and his views as an adult? Support your answer.

2. Explain the significance of each of the following lines from the reading.
   a) "You're not at all disabled—it's just the disabled LIST."
   b) "It's this national trait that has helped sideline our hockey history I'm sure."
   c) "My eyes were being opened not by light so much as by shiners."

Form and Style

3. This reading has a conversational quality and uses colloquial language. Provide specific examples of the conversational style and language from the text. In your opinion, do these elements enhance or detract from the message the author wants to convey? Explain your answer in a few sentences.

4. Most of David Adams Richards's books and stories are set along the Miramichi River in New Brunswick, and they evoke a strong sense of place. How does Richards develop a sense of place in this excerpt from *Hockey Dreams*? List specific words, phrases, and sentences. Explain why a sense of place is important in this reading.

Creative Extension

5. Write a short memoir about one of your own memories or dreams from childhood. Choose a style appropriate to your topic and make your memoir as vivid as possible by appealing to two or more of the five senses—taste, touch, smell, hearing, and sight. Consider recording your memoir on audio as an oral text or writing it as a film or video script.

6. Write an editorial on one of the following topics or on another aspect of sports that you feel strongly about. Your editorial should state a clear opinion supported by relevant facts.
    a) media coverage of women in professional or amateur sports
    b) the use of performance-enhancing drugs by amateur or professional athletes
    c) violence in professional hockey
    d) support for the Para-Olympics
    e) salaries and star athletes

Recovering a Lost Past

❧

What value can we find in unlocking the mysteries of our pasts?

We can never know everything about our pasts. Our pasts always contain some mysteries, some people or events we will never know. Nevertheless, people have always felt compelled to investigate their family histories and their heritages—to learn a little more about who they are. Through a family memoir, poems, personal essay, and art, this Echo section presents how a few writers and artists have connected with their pasts and their identities.

Learning Goals

- examine a theme from different perspectives
- analyze how various texts reveal identities and positions
- examine how different forms, techniques, language, and styles affect meaning

The Concubine's Children

❧ Denise Chong

Ever since she was a child, Denise Chong had been curious about an old photograph of two young girls she had found in a family chest. She always knew there might be relatives in China, but the connection with her family there had been lost. It wasn't until 1987, while on a trip to China with her mother, that Denise Chong began slowly to piece together the story of her grandparents' lives. The following excerpt from her family memoir The Concubine's Children *presents an episode from her grandmother's life in China in the early 1900s.*

Chapter Two

May-ying traced a part down the back of her head, bound the hair on each side with a filament of black wire and twisted it into a chignon above each ear. Then she unpinned and combed the curls framing her forehead. She assessed the finished look in the mirror: a girl of seventeen looked in; the reflection was supposed to pass for a woman of twenty-four.

It had been Auntie's advice to wear her hair up to add years to her face. May-ying set her dangling earrings swaying, the tear of jade on each side following the gold ball suspended between the links above. The earrings, along with the jade pendant, had been her mother's; she had taken them off to give to her child when they'd said goodbye forever. In the years since, May-ying had kept them safe. Now that she was leaving her girlhood behind, she knew she should guard no other possessions more carefully. As long as she had her jade and gold near, the souls of her ancestors would do all they could to keep harm from her path.

She stood up, turned away from the mirror, smoothed the *cheong sam* over her girl's body and went to sit for her portrait as the wife of a man she had not yet met.

May-ying had never expected that she would have a say in whom she married; no girl or boy did in traditional Chinese society. Marriage was a union between two families and was too important to be left to the whim of the young. Love was not a consideration; in fact, it was seen as a threat to the husband's family, as undermining the authority of the mother over her new daughter-in-law. Parents, in arranging their children's marriages, were most concerned about avoiding any mismatch between the two family backgrounds that might create problems, envy or embarrassment between the families. That was best ensured by a matchmaker, typically an elderly lady from one of the surrounding villages. As well as asking the gods to pronounce on the auspiciousness of a match, she would act as messenger in negotiations over the dowry (if the girl's family was better off than the boy's), or (if he was the better-off family), the bride-price to be paid.

Auntie was not May-ying's real aunt. Born in 1907 into the Leong family, May-ying came from Nam Hoy, one of four counties that comprised the city of Canton and its outskirts, in the province of Kwangtung in south China. As such, she carried a strain of superiority; the people from these four counties were the original native Cantonese, whose dialect and ways were considered more refined than those of peasants further afield. . . .

May-ying stayed with her family until she was perhaps four; she could remember her mother trying to apply the first bandages to bind her feet. The practice of binding a young girl's growing bones had been dying out in China, especially in the south where the peasant economy needed girls and women to work in the fields. But some clung to the practice as a way for their daughters to escape becoming beasts of burden. Diminutive feet would have elevated May-ying into a social class where women were artful objects. When hard times struck, as they surely would, and the family was without rice, her mother might have hoped to sell her daughter as a child-bride, to have some say over her future husband. It was not to be. Because of May-ying's cries of protest, her feet were unbandaged. "Auntie," a stranger, bought her as a servant.

When May-ying turned seventeen and of marrying age, she was ready to be sold again. Auntie was aware that her girl-servant's looks would command a high bride-price. No man or woman who first came upon May-ying could help but stare fixedly at this tiny figure of a girl, who stood no higher than the average person's chin. Her delicate features, the bright round eyes and the much admired heart-shaped mouth, were set in pale skin that had retained its translucence because Auntie's chores had kept her out of the fields and out of the baking sun. But for her unbound feet, she had the body and features much imitated in Chinese porcelain dolls.

May-ying had been squatting over a basin in the courtyard washing Auntie's clothes when she was summoned inside. A stool was offered, tea poured. May-ying was immediately suspicious; a mistress does not serve her servant.

"*Ah* Ying, I have found you a *ho muen how*," Auntie declared.

A girl expected there to come a day when she would hear these words, announcing a good doorway to another house, that of her future mother-in-law. The question was where; she wondered if she would be staying in Auntie's village.

"Where is it, Auntie?"

Auntie hesitated. "It is in *Gum San*," she said.

"What?!" May-ying could not believe her ears or bite her tongue. "What am I hearing?" Gold Mountain was another continent, a foreign land of white ghosts. Her tone said it was unthinkable that she would be sent to live in North America. "I don't want to go!"

Auntie had expected the news to come as a shock. She herself had been persuaded only when she saw the bride-price offered. She took it as a sign that the claims of prosperity in Gold Mountain were no exaggeration.

"The man is from Heung San," Auntie said, naming the province's county of rice farmers, further south along the Pearl River estuary. "He has been living in *Gum San* for some years. People living in *Gum San* have wealth and riches; they have to push the gold from their feet to find the road." She met May-ying's eyes. "I am only doing what is best for you. I want you to have *on lock cha fan*."

May-ying heard the echo of these words in her head. Her mother had used these same words of farewell. She too had wished her a life of contentment, a life never short of tea or rice. It only reminded May-ying of that tearful parting.

In a flash of temper, May-ying kicked the table legs. He's only a peasant, she said. Why couldn't Auntie find a boy from a decent family near Canton? She shoved the table top, splashing tea. She repeated that she did not want to go, that she did not want to eat rice from a strange land. Auntie was dismayed; she had warned May-ying many times that her quick temper would enslave her to her heart.

Auntie had to shout to make herself heard: "You are not going for good." May-ying glared and waited for what had been held back. "He has a *Dai-po* in Heung San," Auntie continued, "and he wants to have a *chip see* in *Gum San*."

The effect was more cruel than if May-ying had been told no family would have her. Stunned to hear that she was to join the household of a man already married, that she was to be a concubine, at his whim and in the servitude of his wife, May-ying knew it would be taken as a mark against herself. No decent girl became a concubine, married off in shame without wedding or ceremony. . . .

May-ying's ebony eyes flashed a familiar accusing look at Auntie. "Then I might just as well stay in China and be a prostitute," she snapped.

At such a stinging rebuke of ungratefulness, such disrespect for the match she had made, Auntie thundered back, "I will not hear any more of this nonsense. When I say go out the door, you will go!"

෪   Writer and economist Denise Chong published her family memoir *The Concubine's Children* in 1994. The book has since been translated into more than seven different languages, was short-listed for the Governor General's Award, and won the City of Vancouver Book Award. In 1999, she published *The Girl in the Picture: The Kim Phuc Story. (Born Vancouver)*

RESPONDING

Meaning

1. Most stories, whether fiction or non-fiction, present a conflict. What is the central conflict in this selection from *The Concubine's Children*? Has the conflict been resolved by the end of the selection? Explain your answer.

2. a) "May-ying had never expected that she would have a say in whom she married; no girl or boy did in traditional Chinese society." Outline the system of arranged marriages described in the text. Why was May-ying "stunned" that she would become a concubine, a secondary wife?

   b) Many of the aspects of traditional Chinese society described in this reading have changed since the early 1900s, as they have in most other cultures and societies. In your class, share views on how various cultures view arranged marriages today. How has the status of women in society and the control they have over their own lives changed?

Form and Style

3. List the Chinese words and phrases in this reading. For each word or phrase, use the contextual clues the author has provided to write a definition in English. Compare your definitions with those of a partner. State why you think Denise Chong included these Chinese words in her narrative.

4. Describe the *point of view* of the narrator in this excerpt. What advantages does this point of view give the author? Make reference to specific evidence in the text.

Creative Extension

5. Create a monologue based on the reading. Adopt the persona of one of the characters and focus on the emotions associated with one important event in that character's life. Use some of the language from the reading to give your monologue a feeling of authenticity.

6. Denise Chong's memoir could be called a work of *creative non-fiction*. In groups, agree on a definition of this genre and its major characteristics. Refer to aspects of the excerpt from *The Concubine's Children* in your answer. Discuss whether or not you believe a work of creative non-fiction presents an accurate view of the facts. Why would you read or not read other works of creative non-fiction?

Phone Calls

Alice Major

The following poem by Canadian poet Alice Major explores the question of how immigrating to a new land can affect a family's connection with the past and with relatives overseas.

I

The phone calls came at Christmas, rarer
than the pomegranates the children had to share;
more costly, more improbable than strawberries
in December. They were often prearranged
by letters on thin blue paper with a Scottish stamp.
Our mother always neatly headed off the dash
    to answer.

"Oh George, so good to hear your voice. How's Kath?
And Iain—still doing well in school? And Alasdair?"

All of us cupped around the receiver, close
as a stocking round the apple in the toe.

"Och no, May, you know Alasdair. He'll work
no harder than he has to. Here he is."
"Happy Christmas, Auntie May.
    How's Uncle Willie?"
"Hi, Aunt Kath, I got a dress for Christmas."
"And don't you lassies sound like real wee Canadians
now."
    "No we don't."

Then the operator's voice, like the taste
of an orange pip. "Your three minutes are up."

"George, George, we'll have to go. All this money."
"Aye, May, aye. Lovely to hear you all."

Goodbye, goodbye, a chorus of goodbyes. The hiss
of the Atlantic cut as cleanly as a cherry in a slice
of Christmas cake. Our mother would laugh and cry
together, and pick up tangerine peel
from the coffee table.

II

The phone calls came in the sombre hours
of the night, the heavy black receiver
lifted reluctantly.

"It's Dad, May. He went to the cottage hospital
this afternoon, insisted
on walking by himself. He just sat down
in the waiting room and passed away."

"Jean's gone, May. She went quickly
at the end. No, there's no point
in coming for the funeral. It's so expensive
and you've the bairns to think of."

The children wait at the end of the room,
can't imagine fathers, sisters dying,
can't comprehend mothers
crying this way.

Alice Major immigrated to Toronto from Scotland at eight years old. She later attended the University of Toronto and after receiving her degree, went on to work for a newspaper association. This took her to Edmonton in 1981, where she lives today. Her first novel for young adults, *The Chinese Mirror* (1988), won the Alberta Writing for Youth Competition. She continues to write short stories and award-winning poetry books, including *Tales for an Urban Sky* (1999).

Connecting

1. How does this poem convey the emotional tension of feeling a connection with the past on one hand, and having to let go on the other? Quote specific lines and refer to specific images to support your response.

2. Discuss the significance of the final stanza in the poem.

3. Why do you think Alice Major wrote this poem? How do the emotions and experiences expressed in the poem relate to Denise Chong's experiences and the story of her grandmother, May-ying?

Afro-American Fragment

Langston Hughes

In the following poems, American poet Langston Hughes explores his connection with his African heritage. For him, the link with the past seems much more distant and mysterious at first, but he discovers it is nevertheless still a vital part of his identity.

So long,
So far away
Is Africa.
Not even memories alive
Save those that history books create,
Save those that songs
Beat back into the blood—
Beat out of blood with words sad-sung
In strange un-Negro[1] tongue—
So long,
So far away
Is Africa.

Subdued and time-lost
Are the drums—and yet
Through some vast mist of race
There comes this song
I do not understand
This song of atavistic[2] land,
Of bitter yearnings lost
Without a place—
So long,
So far away
Is Africa's
Dark face.

---

[1] Negro is a term no longer commonly used and considered offensive. It was used at the time this poem was written to refer to people of African ancestry.

[2] atavistic—referring to remote ancestors.

The Negro Speaks of Rivers:

I've known rivers:
I've known rivers ancient as the world and older than the
flow of human blood in human veins.

My soul has grown deep like the rivers.
I bathed in the Euphrates when dawns were young.
I built my hut near the Congo and it lulled me to sleep.
I looked upon the Nile and raised the pyramids above it.
I heard the singing of the Mississippi when Abe Lincoln
went down to New Orleans, and I've seen its muddy
bosom turn all golden in the sunset.

I've known rivers:
Ancient, dusky rivers.

My soul has grown deep like the rivers.

ᔓ   American poet, short-story writer, novelist, and playwright Langston Hughes actively partici-
pated in the Harlem Renaissance of the 1920s and 1930s, in which many Black American artists
explored and celebrated their African heritage. Hughes published his first volume of poetry,
The Weary Blues, in 1926. *(Born Joplin, Missouri 1902; died 1967)*

Connecting

1. In the first poem, why does the speaker in Langston Hughes's poem find it difficult
   to recover the details of his past?

2. The poems contain two powerful metaphors—the song and the river. Explain the
   significance of these metaphors. How do they contribute to the message the poet
   wants to convey?

3. The final line of the second poem is "My soul has grown deep like the rivers." What
   does this statement suggest about the value the speaker has found in exploring his
   lost past?

Caribana Dreams

ᔓ *Cecil Foster*

*In this excerpt from a personal essay, author Cecil Foster describes how a celebration connects
people with their heritage and allows them to discover their identities.*

I remember my first year in Canada, how four months after arriving in a new
country and feeling homesick, I went to the Caribana festival in downtown Toronto and instantly felt at home. There, I found the music, the faces,

the people, the accents, the food and the excitement of the Caribbean. Over the years, we would joke that Caribana is the best spiritual tonic for the social and political alienation so many of us feel in Canada, including so many of us born and raised in this country.

One of the great things about this festival is that you never know who you will meet for the first time, or which old friend or acquaintance you will rediscover in the crowd. Perhaps an actor like Lou Gossett Jr. or Billy Dee Williams will show up and mix, excited as little boys at being in such a festival. The parade with its glamorous costumes is secondary to the joyful camaraderie along the parade route. And for the participants, Caribana is not first and foremost about making money, about their festival being reduced to simple balance sheet issues. Caribana is always a renewing of the spirit—more than just dancing, something spiritual.

And over the years, I have noticed how young Black and Caribbean people, especially teenagers, blossom during Caribana. So many of our children seem so lost. They do not know who they are, confused by what they are hearing at school and in their home and church, unsure of their place in a white-dominated society.

With Caribana comes a breaking out. Suddenly, these youths appear free, strong and confident. They are proud of discovering their heritage and exult in it by dancing in the streets, just like their elders. Oh, to see the young people liberated! Could this freedom come about through paying an admission fee and sitting passively while watching some pageant? I don't think so; Caribana's spirituality is fed by spontaneous participation, by the celebration of a way of life.

Now, I think of the times I took my children to Caribana: they were so young they felt overwhelmed by the crowd. But, like so many other parents, I was looking forward to their cultural awakening, when they, too, would discover a festival like Caribana and feel it belongs to them, that it is a festival that makes them special Canadians. A festival that, were it not held, would make the task of helping my children and others to find their place in this society—to discover who they are and what sets them apart culturally and spiritually—so much more difficult.

Caribana is a two-week festival of rhythmic Caribbean and African music, of humour and brotherly and sisterly love openly displayed, of dancing on the streets and meeting new friends, of enjoying exotic foods and, for many businesses, hearing cash registers ring. Caribana is all pageantry and glamour, when men, women, and children abandon themselves to frolicking, to decking out in elaborately designed costumes and parading on a route in downtown Toronto, with the eyes of the world looking on. It is a musical cacophony of different voices and accents; of faces representing the cultures of the world and, in turn, reflecting back a peaceful multicultural Canada to the rest of humanity.

Cecil Foster came to Canada from Barbados in 1978. He earned success as a journalist, culminating in his position as senior editor for *The Financial Post*. He then turned to fiction and gained critical acclaim with *No Man in the House* (1991) and *Sleep On, Beloved* (1995). "Caribana Dreams" is from *A Place Called Heaven: The Meaning of Being Black in Canada* (1996). (*Born Barbados 1954*)

Connecting

1. What, for Cecil Foster, are the most important aspects of the Caribana festival? How does this excerpt suggest that the festival is not only a connection with a heritage, but also of vital importance to the present?

2. Describe the *tone* of this excerpt. How does it compare with the tone of other selections in this Echo section? How might you account for similarities and differences?

3. How does this selection fit in with the theme of "recovering a lost past"? Compare the perspective presented in this excerpt with that in at least one other selection in this Echo section.

Esprit 2000 Spirit

Jane Ash Poitras

In this mixed media piece, artist Jane Ash Poitras explores the connection between past and present.

ᔕ Jane Ash Poitras is at the forefront of a contemporary generation of Aboriginal artists. She holds a degree in microbiology from the University of Alberta and a Master of Fine Arts from Columbia University in New York. Using mixed media, her art explores the spirituality and cultural heritage of Aboriginal peoples and the impact of North American colonization on indigenous peoples. (*Born Fort Chipewyan, Alberta 1951*)

Connecting

1. View this artwork with at least two other students. Together make notes on
   a) how the colours and shadings used create a mood
   b) which images appear in the foreground, which appear in the background, and their significance
   c) what the facial expressions and positions of the two women convey
   Share your notes with other groups.

2. Why do you think Jane Ash Poitras called her painting "Esprit 2000 Spirit"? How does the title of the painting connect with the pictures of the two women and the features of the artwork that you identified?

3. In your own words, provide your interpretation of what Jane Ash Poitras is trying to convey through this artwork. How does your interpretation relate to the theme of recovering a lost past?

REFLECTING ON THE ECHO

1. Identify a poem, artwork, photo, or story that best helps you connect with your past—either your personal past or your cultural heritage. Write a journal entry on what this piece means to you and how it expresses your connection to your past. Then choose a different medium or genre and create an original work to express the same ideas in a different way.

2. Assume the role of a radio or television interviewer. Imagine that you could interview one of the writers or artists featured in this Echo section. Working in groups, draft questions you would ask about the work in this section. Do research to find the answers to as many questions as possible. Speculate on how the writer or artist might answer the other questions. Then role play the interview or record it on audio or videotape.

3. Choose one of the selections in this Echo section and rewrite it as a short fictional narrative or short story. Keep the theme of the Echo, but add characters or other elements if you wish. Share your narratives with a partner or small group.

Within Reach: My Everest Diary

⌐ Mark Pfetzer and Jack Galvin

Learning Goals

- compare personal ideas, values, and perspectives with those in a text
- examine characteristics of diary writing
- analyze style in non-fiction writing
- apply effective research techniques
- create original works including a photo essay and news story

MAY 9, 1996

We're on a steep section of the Lhotse Face when a group coming down from Camp Three shouts for us to get off the rope. I dig my ice ax into the 45-degree slope and watch as a climber and five Sherpas carefully lower a sled-stretcher. The bundled sleeping bag and the bit of twisted face with a froth of icy blood on its beard slides by me. "Fell at Camp Three," the climber explains. "Being unroped up there can get you killed."

"Will he be OK?" I ask.

The climber shakes his head. "Not with his internal injuries. But we gotta try."

The wind starts to pick up as we watch the stretcher's descent. At least he has a shot, I think. Lots of guys die up here, and no one even finds their bodies. Then a season or two later, a body will emerge from the snow as if it swam to the surface, still intact if its flesh hasn't been eaten by birds. There are at least four or five corpses near enough to the routes that you can see them. Maybe someone should bring them down for proper burial. But it's dangerous even to get to them. Like the rescuers who just passed us, I'd help any live climber I could. I'm not going after dead ones. Besides, climbers are left up here out of respect for their love of the mountains.

MAY 10, 1996

I always thought the tough part about climbing was, well, the climbing itself. Now, as we get into higher altitude, I'm beginning to realize that what we have to wear just makes everything so much harder. Over my down pants, jacket, and hood, I put on an oxygen mask, tank, heavy backpack, and goggles. The trouble is the mask. It has an extra-long tube to the tank, under my arms and around my back, which I keep getting twisted. I feel all tied up. Then the oxygen mask hits me just below the eyes, and the overlapping goggles stick out so far I have to bend way over just to see my feet. But if I bend over to see where I'm walking, I pinch the tube and cut off my oxygen supply. If I take the mask off, to get a

Mark Pfetzer with Everest in the background.

breath or to spit because my cold's much worse, the rubber gets wet, and pretty soon I have inch-long icicles hanging off my chin.

Put all that into the environment of the Geneva Spur and a steep, yellow band of rock we have to traverse on the way to Camp Four, and you have high-altitude adventure. Not only do I have trouble breathing, coughing, and seeing, but now we have to angle across bald, slippery rock with crampons. Like trying to cross a steep concrete ramp on ice skates. Only it's covered with shalelike, loose rock, and when you look down, you know that if you fall, you have an express trip 5,000 feet[1] right down the Lhotse Face What we should be wearing are regular hiking boots with good-gripping rubber soles. But even if we had them, we wouldn't risk frost-bite to change. Or even take off the crampons.

Time for patience. Jabion, my Sherpa friend, and I slowly pick our way across, finding footholds for our crampons. We can hear the wind coming from above as if someone is slowly turning up the volume, and we know we'll soon be out of the protection of the Geneva Spur, and the already-swirling snow will be like needles.

---

[1] 1524 metres

Jabion and I finally get free of the Geneva Spur. We're on the long steep section, very tired, when the weather hits like a hurricane in a fog of snow. We still have one more short steep section before Camp Four, which we struggle through OK. I notice that Jabion does not have on his heavy mittens, probably thinking he wouldn't need them because he'd be in camp soon. The wind is blasting too loud for me to ask him; he must be all right.

At Camp Four, tents, maybe twenty of them erected by Sherpas and climbers already up here, are concentrated in one flat, rocky area. All the teams need and have tents up here, the final refuge before the summit, 3,000 feet[1] away.

Camp Four is at 26,000 feet[2]. Above 25,000 feet[3]—known as the "Death Zone"—the temperatures and winds can be so severe, the air so thin, that climbers are in constant danger. Thinking and movement slow down; even a small error like dropping a glove can mean death, because a hand can freeze, become useless. So these tents are vital to survival. Fortunately for Jabion and me, ours are the first tents we come to. I stumble inside, get the mask off, wipe the icicles and slime off my face, and Jabion mumbles something about his hands. They are extremely white. I start yelling at him as if I'm the father and he's the little kid. "Ya shoulda said something back there!"

"Aw," he mumbles. That's all he can think of to say. Possible frostbite —the kind that costs fingers—and all he can say is "Aw"? I put his hands under my armpits for five minutes, give him a high dosage of oxygen, put his heavy mittens on, and Jabion lucks out. A half hour later he's fine. Lost in the moment is my personal altitude record: 26,000 feet. Soon we all crowd into two tents: Neil, Brigeete, Michael, and Graham in one tent. Pemba, Pasang, Jabion, Lhakpa, Ang Tshering, and me in the other. Thirty oxygen bottles, a small stove, and six guys in sleeping bags have us all jammed in. Jabion's arm sticks into my shoulder; I'm next to Pasang, who smells; and, as close as we are, the wind—the train roaring next to your ear now—drowns out the loudest shout. As strange as it may seem, I love it here in this tent. I'm relatively warm, have no headache, am breathing fairly easily, and will summit Everest tomorrow. I am ready. I have worked

---

[1] 915 metres; [2] 7925 metres; [3] 7620 metres

towards this moment since I was thirteen, climbed the highest mountains in South America, reached 25,000 feet on Everest last year, and trained very hard to be here at Camp Four. In spite of all the critics who say a sixteen-year-old has no business on Everest, I am within reach of the summit.

Funny that I should choose to be with the Sherpas, the people who live in the mountains and work as our guides, porters, and cooks. Most climbers keep their distance and have only a work relationship with them. Al Burgess introduced me to the Sherpas when I first came to Nepal three years ago, and so I learned to visit their homes, drink tea with them, help them carry equipment. They, in turn, have taught me that time means so little, that you focus on each day, get up with the sun, eat, work all day, eat, and go to bed when it gets dark.

Over the last three years, I learned what great people the Sherpas are. In fact, Jabion and I became very good friends, so much so that I promised I'd take him to America for the summer after this trip. I already have his visa arranged. The other Sherpas have their orders in for hats and T-shirts. About five o'clock, Neil comes in from the other tent and shouts above the wind, "Henry radioed. Says some of Scott Fischer's climbers might be missing." While we are having difficulty being heard, keeping warm, and eating limp noodles, there are climbers outside in this wind!

Neil's back soon. "Now Henry says Ray's missing!" A veteran climber once told me that one of the most important pieces of equipment a climber uses on Everest is the two-way radio. By calling back and forth, Base Camp people and their climbers, who are spread all over the mountain, can exchange important information about conditions and positions. Our two-way radio has become a lifeline.

Jabion and Pemba bundle up, put on headlamps, and head out into the dark to look for Ray. They will follow the trail down toward Camp Three and hope to find him safely tucked behind a rock. They are soon back. "Can't see." Jabion points to his lamp. We all know what he means: the snow is coming horizontally, so hard that a headlamp is useless, as are the dark lenses of the goggles at night. Without goggles they risk taking the needle-like snow directly at the eyes.

The night goes on, and we have no idea what may be happening outside. As time goes along, we do know that anyone stuck out there will have at least nine more hours of pitch dark, snow driven by winds over a hundred miles an hour[1], and windchill near a hundred below. We doze, we eat, we drink, and slowly all the inevitable questions seep in. Is this just one storm? Has the window of opportunity closed? Are there people hurt? Dead? None of us huddled in our tent know the answers. I begin to feel my cough steal away more and more of my strength. I have to summit soon, before I lose my strength. We're so close—within reach—and all we can do is hang on to this scab of rocks, 26,000 feet up, and hope that daylight will give us new hope to reach our goal.

MAY 11, 1996

Pasang looks out of the tent, sees a star above the South Col, and immediately shoves his stuff into his rucksack and is gone into the thundering wind. Jabion says, "Bad luck to see a star that bright in morning." He may be right. Paul had already gone down from Camp Three. Jabion, Graham, and I decide to go down, too. I still don't know about Ray, who was missing last night. Brigeete, Neil, and Michael plan to wait out the wind and summit tomorrow. Fat chance they'll have to summit.

I get out of the tent, feeling very spaced out and weak after coughing all night, struggle to get crampons on, struggle to get backpack, oxygen mask on. Have to rest after each effort. Shocked to see Pete Athans, one of the best climbers, coming up. How did he get here so early? "Rob Hall's still up there," he says. I look up and see, in the early light, a string of black dots working up the slope. A rescue team. "At least nine people missing. Don't know for sure." He radios to Base Camp that I'm coming down and takes off for the rescue mission. Pete's amazingly strong to go up in that storm. I stand watching him for a moment. Nine people? Who? I look up the mountain, imagine trying to grope through a whiteout with dark coming on, imagine trying to find our tents, the smallest possible needle in the huge haystack of Everest, especially when your brain can hardly function, and I realize how lucky I was to be in a tent.

Jabion and I go back over the Geneva Spur, fighting the wind for balance on each rocky step. How strong that wind is, trying to pluck us off

---

[1] 160 km/h

Coming down from one of the camps.

the mountain with one gust, trying to flatten us with the next. And then, once across, we round a corner and are suddenly wind-free, protected by the spur we just traversed. Soon the sun comes out, we warm up, and, as we descend, off comes the mask, the heavy mittens, the heavy coat.

Haven't had much solid food now for four days. Can't seem to force anything down. Lack of appetite and coughing have weakened me to the point that I can only take about ten steps before I have to rest. Jabion stays with me, and it is very slow going. In fact, a group of climbers from Scott Fischer's team passes me. They look awful, in much worse shape than I am. They tell me they had been caught by the storm, were lucky to make it back to camp. And then one guy tells me Scott is dead. One of the best in the world, a climber who's survived some terrible situations, has died. They don't know exactly what happened. He seemed OK, then they lost sight of him. They leave for Camp Three, some of them frostbitten, all exhausted and devastated by Scott's death. I take ten more steps before resting again.

When Jabion and I get to Camp Three, Fischer's team has already set backpacks into the steep slope and they are sitting on them in the sun. They just lost their great friend and leader, are lucky to be alive themselves, and they just sit there, numb. Neal Beidleman mumbles something about Scott's dying being his fault; the others get on his case, deny there was anything he could have done. I sit with them. The scary pitch of the slope here at Camp Three seems safe now compared to the howling nightmare of Camp Four, but I don't know what to say.

Scott had been friendly to me, invited me over to his tent, helped me with my camera, and now he's dead—same trip, same mountain, not far from me. And I can't think about it now. Everything is so confusing. All the order and scheduling gone, all the acclimatizing, oxygen masks, foot warmers—none of them seem to matter now. It is just the fate of survival as to who makes it. I'm in a tent and make it. Some of them make it back to their tents; others don't. I'm the first climber these tired, beaten people have seen. I should say something consoling but I can't. No way to analyze or talk. Just sit in the sun for a moment, then head down to Base Camp.

My dad was a police officer for years, but he wasn't the one to go to the parents' house at two a.m. to tell them about their kids' accidents. His partner, Jack, did that. Same for me. I just can't talk right now. Neither can they. We all just sit there a while, hacking. We're all gaunt, sunburned, dirty, with constant coughs.

I load up all my equipment: sleeping bag, clothes, oxygen tank, accessories, and the video camera, and start to leave Camp Three. I never even used the video camera up there. National Geographic Special? Forget it. It was enough just to survive. I know there was a lot of time and money invested, and I was expected to get my share of filming done. But right now, I really can't care. I could never film Scott Fischer's people at Camp Three. No way I'm doing that. I'm not intruding on them.

I tell Jabion to go ahead. I'll go down myself. Let momentum pull me.

Hold on to rope, slide down. Rest. I meet David Breashears going up for rescue. He congratulates me. My legs are cramping, my eyes hurt, the roof of my mouth is burning, I'm coughing, my back hurts from the heavy pack, and I'm so weak I can walk only ten steps before resting. Congratulations? He must think I summited. "I didn't summit," I mumble.

"So what," he says. "You're alive." And takes off. I watch him go and think: He's right. Don't feel sorry for yourself. You wanted to be here. Your pilgrimage. And you are still alive. So pay attention and get down the mountain!

That's what I do. I pay attention. Even though I'm really scared for the first time, with crevasses everywhere, alone, unroped, fatigued, I won't let Scott Fischer into my mind; I won't think about falling; I won't panic. I go fast. Have to get to Camp Two.

Into the kitchen tent. Hot orange drink. Someone tells me Ray's OK. He spent the whole awful night outside, lost his backpack with sleeping bag, down suit, glasses—just about everything—stumbled around, turned up at Camp Three. Ray's a tough New Yorker. Last year on our trip to the north side of Everest, he grabbed the wrong rope, fell forty feet[1], landed in snow, wandered around, fell into a crevasse, got out, and showed up later that night. I struggle to our tent, where I find Ray, along with Henry, Paul, and Graham, talking about the rumours, the reports of deaths, the missing climbers. Henry's furious with Brigeete, Neil, and Michael for staying at Camp Four and not becoming involved with the rescue. I send a message to my mom to let her know I'm OK, crawl into my sleeping bag, and go to sleep.

---

[1] 12 metres

Mark Pfetzer was 16 years old when he made his climb of Mount Everest and almost reached the summit in 1996. He started mountain climbing when he was 13 years old. Once he made a decision to pursue a goal or activity, he committed to it. *Within Reach: My Everest Story* was published in 1998 and was written with Jack Galvin.

RESPONDING

Meaning

1. At one point, Mark Pfetzer says: "I always thought the tough part about climbing was, well, the climbing itself." In fact, he discovers that he faces many different challenges—physical, emotional, social, and intellectual. Describe these challenges using specific evidence from the text.

2. Which of these challenges was Mark Pfetzer able to overcome? Which could he not overcome? How do you think his experiences changed him? In a journal entry, speculate on how you might have reacted in a similar situation.

Form and Style

3. This excerpt is written in *diary form*. Define the major characteristics of this form. Why do you think the authors chose it for their book? Discuss the advantages and disadvantages of the diary form for this particular material.

4. Look through this reading for examples of simile and metaphor. Identify at least one example of each. What do the authors accomplish by including these literary devices in this non-fiction narrative?

Creative Extension

5. Search newspapers, magazines, and the Internet for photos of expeditions on Mount Everest. Use copies of the photos to create a picture essay illustrative of a typical climb. Consider including the equipment the climbers use, the different base camps, and at least one photo of the Sherpas who guide the expeditions. Show some of the dangers that the climbers face. Conclude your essay with a photo indicative of the overall message you wish to convey. Provide captions as appropriate and necessary. Alternatively, you could choose to focus your photo essay on a different type of challenging task or expedition.

6. Write a news story based on Mark Pfetzer's experiences on the Everest expedition. Write the news story for a newspaper, newsmagazine, television news show, or Internet news service. Include information and quotations from the text, and add visuals as appropriate. Compare your story with others written for a different medium and explain the differences in form and style.

A Month and a Day: A Detention Diary

Ken Saro-Wiwa

Learning Goals

- compare personal values and ideas with those in a text
- support interpretations with evidence from a text
- analyze an author's purpose and choice of form
- create a computer diary and pamphlet

Ken Saro-Wiwa was a Nigerian writer, journalist, politician, and businessperson. On 10 November 1995 he was hanged in prison for his protests against the Nigerian government and the international oil companies that were destroying his homeland and the homeland of the Ogoni people in the Niger River Delta. He believed the industrial pollution caused by the extraction of oil was turning his homeland into an ecological wasteland and threatening the survival of the Ogoni people. This excerpt is taken from a book Ken Saro-Wiwa wrote during his imprisonment.

CHAPTER ONE

Suddenly, my car screeched to a halt. I raised my head in surprise. Before me was an armed security man flagging the car down, his rifle pointed at my chauffeur's head. Then, just as suddenly, more security men in mufti headed for the rear door of the car, swung it open, and ordered me to get down. I refused to do so. They spoke more gruffly and I remained just as adamant. A superior officer whom I knew well ordered two of the men to get into the empty front seat of the car. They obeyed him. Then they ordered my chauffeur to do a U-turn against the traffic. He obeyed. The superior security officer had turned his own car around and ordered my chauffeur to follow him. Behind us was yet another car which I knew to be a security vehicle crammed with security men. We drove off in a convoy.

It was 21 June 1993. We were at a crossroads in Port Harcourt, at the busy UTC junction on the equally busy expressway linking the city with the town of Aba to the north. The drama took place in front of commuters, and I imagine that many would have guessed that I was being arrested. I, however, knew that for sure. It was my fourth arrest in three months.

As we drove towards the Port Harcourt Club Sports Ground, there was no doubt in my mind as to where we were going: the scrappy offices of the State Security Service (SSS), where I was already a well-known customer, as the saying goes in Nigeria. I chuckled to myself. . . .

In ten minutes we were at the Central Police Station, a place with which I was not unfamiliar. It had been the state headquarters of the Nigerian Police force but when the force's new office buildings were complete, it got turned over to the State Intelligence and Investigation Bureau (SIIB). It was, as usual with public property in Nigeria, in disrepair. The lawn was littered with cars, in different colours and states. Some appeared to have been there for ages, waiting to be used as exhibits for cases that would never be tried.

I was ushered into a little cubicle which served as the office for some investigating police officers, and asked to sit on a wooden bench. I sat there chewing on the stem of my pipe while one of the investigating police officers, who was taking down a statement from an accused person, stared incredulously at me. He might have been star-struck. I had been very much in the news lately, and, as often happens to those who have that misfortune, was considered more as a news item than as a living being with flesh and blood. Seeing me in the latter condition caused my friend's eternal surprise. I understood his agitation and smiled at it.

In another fifteen minutes a form was pushed in front of me and I was asked to write a statement about my activities on election day, 12 June 1993. The Ogoni, under leadership of the Movement of the Survival of the Ogoni People (MOSOP), had boycotted the election. I asked perfunctorily to be allowed to see my lawyer before committing myself to paper. The request, as I expected, was turned down. Without further ado, I whipped out my pen and wrote the required statement, knowing full well that it would never be used. I signed it with a flourish.

A young woman, a senior police officer, soon came in to examine the statement I had written. She read it, seemed satisfied, and then offered me a place on a rickety wooden chair in her curtained office next door. How sweet of her, I thought. She disappeared with the statement. I was left to my pipe. I stoked, lit it, and drew deeply. My mind flew about like a bird on the wing.

The young lady returned and smilingly engaged me in conversation. We spoke about Nigeria, about the suffering of the peoples of Rivers State, of oil and the sorrows it had brought those on whose land it is found, of the social inequities in the country, of oppression and all such. She was an Izon, neighbours of the Ogoni and the fourth largest ethnic group of Nigeria's 200-odd groups; they lived in the main oil-producing area of the country. She fully understood all the arguments I had been making and certainly sympathized with them and with me for the travails I had suffered in recent months. She assured me, like many operatives I had met, and am yet to meet, that she did not mean any harm to me but that she was only doing her duty. I accepted her assertions graciously.

• • •

After what seemed an interminable wait, the senior police officer told me that on election day, 12 June 1993, policemen had been made to frog-march people in Ogoni and there had been disturbances. I let it be known to him that that was news to me, as I had been in Lagos, a thousand kilometres away and nowhere near Ogoni on the day in question. That did not impress him. He then told me that I was under arrest. I thanked him for the information.

A longish silence followed while I digested this. I looked round the room. It was large, big enough for a huge writing desk and a full complement of cushioned chairs and two or three filing cabinets. The man at the desk, I noticed, was pencil-thin with aquiline features. He looked quite ungainly, his bearing undignified. I essayed to speak to him as a way of passing the time.

"Where do you come from?" I asked.

"Sokoto," he replied. . . .

"How long have you been in Rivers State?" I asked. My mind was elsewhere.

"One year." Or something to that effect. I was not listening. I did not care for his answer.

"Do you like it here?"

"Yes."

You bet.

"I gather you're sending me to Lagos."

"Who told you?"

"A bird."

"What?"

"The wind."

"I'm not sending you to Lagos."

Liar. I pulled out my pipe, struck a match and drew. The smoke danced into the air, upwards towards the ceiling.

"I haven't had anything to eat all day," I said.

He drew a kola nut from the folds of his dress, broke it in two and offered me half. I declined. He bit into his half and crunched away. I blew more smoke into the air.

• • •

Everyone except me went to sleep. I thought then of my youth and how I might have been tempted, in those heady days, to jump out of the bus, grab a rifle from one of the sleeping guards, and shoot my way to safety or to adventure and death. I thought also, for a brief moment, of my family: father, mother, brothers and sisters and how they would be feeling. I thought of my children: he that was ill in my house in Port Harcourt; and of the other one, the elegant young boy, fourteen years old, who had been at Britain's premier school, Eton College, and whom I had buried only in March at Eton Wick.

But my main thought went to the Ogoni people and the travails they had been forced to endure for over a century, which travail I was as deter-mined as iron to mitigate in my lifetime. I thought of the tremendous courage they had shown in the six months since I began to stir up things and to raise the questions which no one seemed willing to confront. I wondered what they would do, faced as they were with my arrest. . . .

I was to learn later that Ogoni youths had shown far more solidarity, far more courage, than I had credited them with. Not knowing what had happened to me, they had gone in a group of 500 or more to the offices of the SSS and opened every single door in an effort to trace me. And when they had not found me there, they had gone to the Central Police Station in Port Harcourt, where they engaged the riot police in a struggle. They picked up canisters of tear gas shot by the police before they could explode and threw them back at their tormentors. They tore down a part of the brick wall which fenced off the police station from the rest of the town. And almost all night they lit bonfires along Aggrey Road to place a dis-tance between the brutality of the police and themselves. They made sure that the town of Port Harcourt heard their protest at my arrest. And no one could stop them. My brother Owens, who tried to calm them, was openly accused of having received bribes from the police and he had to leave them to their devices!

• • •

Meanwhile at four o'clock, my captors roused themselves from their sleep and we recommenced our journey. . . . The state of the road irked me. It was one of my overriding concerns. Not the road itself, but the fact that in this rich, oil-bearing area, the roads should be so rickety, while in the north of Nigeria, in that arid part of the country, there were wide express-ways constructed at great cost with the petrodollars which the delta belched forth. The injustice of it cried to the heavens. It was unacceptable. It had to be corrected at no matter what cost. To die fighting to right the wrong would be the greatest gift of life! Yes, the gift of life. And I felt bet-ter. What did a rough bus ride matter in the circumstances? It could be worse. May it be worse. The designers of the iniquitous system be shamed. My spirit would not be broken. Never!...

Ken Saro-Wiwa was instrumental in setting up the Movement of the Survival of the Ogoni People (MOSOP) in his native Nigeria. He received international awards for his work on the Ogoni peoples' peaceful campaign against the international oil companies drilling in his homeland. His memoir, *A Month and a Day: A Detention Diary*, was published posthumously in 1995. *(Born Bori, Nigeria 1941; died 1995)*

RESPONDING

Meaning

1. Ken Saro-Wiwa was persecuted for his attempts to stop the economic exploita-tion of his Ogoni homeland. What current issues are there in Canada for which protestors have been jailed? Are there any issues that you feel strongly about and for which you would risk going to jail? If so, name the issue(s) and explain why you feel so strongly.

2. At the end of the excerpt, Saro-Wiwa says, "My spirit would not be broken. Never!" Quote specific evidence from this excerpt that shows this will to resist and survive.

Form and Style

3. At one point, a police officer tells Ken Saro-Wiwa directly that he is under arrest. Focusing on the segment that begins: "A longish silence followed while I digested this" to "I blew more smoke into the air," describe in detail how Ken Saro-Wiwa's actions, thoughts, and style of writing reflect a sense of tension.

4. The subtitle for Ken Saro-Wiwa's book is *A Detention Diary*, even though, strictly speaking, the book is not written in diary form. Why do you think the author gave his book this title? In what ways is this reading both like and unlike a diary?

Creative Extension

5. Assume the role of a person who has experienced a dramatic event in his or her life. You could choose a photo of an interesting person from a newspaper or magazine and use that person as your imaginary diary writer. Write a computer diary with one week's entries including specific details about events, people, and your diary writer's feelings.

6. Visit the Web site of a major international human rights organization such as Amnesty International, PEN, or the United Nations (which has published a Universal Declaration on the Rights of Indigenous Peoples). In groups, create a pamphlet aimed at explaining the mandate, major goals, and key actions of the organization to your classmates.

Letters Across Centuries

Learning Goals

- analyze thoughts and emotions conveyed through letters
- compare tone and style in two different letters
- write a letter describing an experience
- rewrite a letter in e-mail format

The following letters were written 200 years apart and are very different in tone and style. The first was written by Marie Antoinette, who was deposed as Queen of France at the time of the French Revolution. She was about to be guillotined when she picked up her pen and wrote the last letter of her life. The second letter was written by an Alberta farmer and sent to the CBC radio show Morningside *to be shared with all listeners. Though they are very different, both letters convey strong emotion.*

October 16, 1795

4:30 in the morning

My sister

I am writing to you for the very last time. I have just been condemned to a death that is in no way shameful—since a shameful death is a fate reserved for criminals—but I am going on a journey to meet your brother once again. I hope I will show the same fortitude as he in my last moments.

I am calm, as one always is when one's conscience is clear. I am deeply saddened to abandon my children: you know that I have lived for them alone, as well as for you, my dear and gentle sister, who through your friendship have given everything to be with me.

Where can we find more affection than in the bosom of our families? May my son never forget the undying words of his father, which I have expressly repeated to him: "Never seek to avenge our death."

I have told you things that weigh heavily on my heart. I know how much trouble this boy must cause you: forgive him, my dear sister; remember his youth and how easy it is to speak to a child, yet how hard it is for him to understand you. The day will come, I trust, when he will feel only the worth of your love for the two of them.

Farewell, my good and dear sister; may this letter find its way to you! Think always of me; I embrace you with all my heart, you and my poor, dear children—my God, it is heart-wrenching to leave them forever! Farewell, farewell! I will now give myself up to my spiritual preparation.

MARIE ANTOINETTE

To CBC Morningside:

I first homesteaded in this country some twenty-five years ago. I remember one drizzly overcast day in the fall. I had most of my harvest in the bin and I was doing my fall cultivating when I stopped for supper. As I got off the tractor and the world was once again silent and sweet without old John puffing and snorting around the field (old John is my John Deere tractor), I heard what must have been a thousand geese from the sound of them. I ran to the house to get my gun and with some luck perhaps get one for supper. But when I came back out, the geese had not yet arrived. I thought that this must surely be a big flock to be heard from so far off. I stood there for what seemed an eternity, but it could not have been more than five minutes. As I stood there, the noise of all these thousands of snow geese rose to such an intensity that it drowned out any other sound. When they finally came into view, it was not like any flock of geese I have ever seen, but a cloud that darkened the sky. As they passed overhead I stood in awe. I could not bring myself to shoot at such a marvellous sight. The flock was more than a mile long. I know, because my farm is a mile long, and the flock was stretched the full length of the farm. When the last little straggler had finally passed overhead, I wished I had a movie camera to record all this, as surely no one would believe what I had seen, and I didn't shoot even one. But then I would only have to clean it and —well, beans and wieners didn't taste so bad. I had just started cooking my supper when I heard a second flock fly over, and it was as big as the first. I could not believe there were so many geese in the world. This flock was followed by a third flock that was just as big.

During the night as I lay in bed, I heard geese flying overhead as I drifted off to sleep. In the morning when I went out to greet the day, the sun had not yet crested the treetops, and in the pre-dawn light it seemed I was in some magic world, as during the night it froze quite hard and the mist that hung in the air from the day before was now suspended frosty crystals that sparkled and shimmered like a million tiny jewels. As I stood there drinking in this marvellous sight, I thought it must have snowed because my fields looked white, but then it was really hard to see through all those sparkling jewels drifting all about me. I took a step closer so I could see, and then, as if thunder had broken this silent sparkling world, twenty thousand wings of snow geese thundered to get airborne, and with this came the cries of alarm from ten thousand snow geese. For what seemed like only a moment, the world was vibrating with the cries of snow geese and thundering wings. It shook me to my soul. A few minutes later the world was silent once again. The sun broke over the treetops and all the sparkles melted into the sunlight and I stood there wondering if I had really seen this marvellous sight, or was I just dreaming. But as I stood there shivering in my long underwear, I knew that I had seen what perhaps no other man has seen.

Vic Daradick
High Level, Alberta

RESPONDING

Meaning

1. What concerns are foremost in Marie Antoinette's mind prior to her execution? How does she make it clear that these concerns are important to her?

2. What evidence does Vic Daradick give to show that he was profoundly affected by his experience? What was it that most moved him?

Form and Style

3. What words, phrases, and punctuation in Marie Antoinette's letter express the strength of her emotion? What indicates the very personal and private nature of this letter?

4. a) Compare the tone and style of Vic Daradick's letter to Marie Antoinette's letter. Account for the differences.
    b) Cite examples of references to the five senses (touch, hearing, sight, smell, and taste) that enhance the vividness of Vic Daradick's description.

Creative Extension

5. Write a letter to a best friend describing an experience in your life that moved you deeply. Describe the experience using specific, concrete details that will engage one or more of your reader's five senses. At the same time, describe and reflect on the emotions you felt as a result of the experience.

6. Choose one of the letters and rewrite it as a one-paragraph e-mail. Refer to "Dot-com This!" in the Media unit (pp. 513–516) for tips on e-mail style. How much does the letter change when it is rewritten this way? What parts of the letter remain the same?

I Can Speak!™

✐ George Saunders

Learning Goals

- examine the goals and techniques of satire
- analyze the use of the letter form
- identify and explain techniques of humour
- create original works including an editorial and letter

The following selection is a satirical short fiction written in the form of a letter.

Mrs. Ruth Faniglia
210 Lester Street
Rochester, N.Y. 14623

Dear Mrs. Faniglia,

We were very sorry to receive your letter of 23 Feb., which accompanied the I CAN SPEAK!™ you returned much to our disappointment. We here at KidLuv believe that the I CAN SPEAK!™ is an innovative and essential educational tool that, used with proper parental guidance, offers a rare early-development opportunity for babies and toddlers alike. And so I thought I would take some of my personal time (I am on lunch) and try to address the questions you raised in your letter, which is here in front of me on my (cluttered!) desk.

First, may I be so bold as to suggest that your disappointment may stem from your own, perhaps unreasonable, expectations? Because in your letter, what you indicated, when I read it, was that you think and/or thought that somehow the product can read your baby's mind? Our product cannot read your baby's mind, Mrs. Faniglia. No one can read a baby's mind, at least not yet. Although believe me, we are probably working on it! All that I CAN SPEAK!™ can do, however, is respond to aural patterns in a way that makes baby seem older. Say baby sees a peach. If you or Mr. Faniglia (I hope I do not presume) were to loudly say something like "What a delicious peach!" the I CAN SPEAK!™, hearing this, through that little slotted hole near the neck, would respond by saying something like "I LIKE PEACH." Or "I WANT PEACH." Or, if you had chosen the ICS2000 (you chose the ICS1900, which is fine, perfectly good for most babies), the I CAN SPEAK!™ might even respond by saying something like "FRUIT, ISN'T THAT ONE OF THE MAJOR FOOD GROUPS?" Which would be pretty good, for a six-month-old like Derek, your son, don't you think?

But here I must reiterate: That would not in reality be Derek speaking. Derek would not in reality know that a peach is a fruit, or that fruit is a major food group. The I CAN SPEAK™ knows, however, and, from its position on Derek's face, it will give the illusion that Derek knows, by giving the illusion that Derek is speaking out of the twin moving SimuLips. But that is it. That is all we claim.

Furthermore, in your letter, Mrs. Faniglia, you state that the I CAN SPEAK!™ "mask" (your terminology) takes on a "stressed-out look when talking that is not what a real baby's talking face appears like but is more like some nervous middle-aged woman." Well, maybe that is so, but, with all due respect, you try it! You try making a latex face of an actual live baby! Inside are over 5000 separate circuits and 390 moving parts. And as far as looking like a middle-aged woman, we beg to differ: we do not feel that a middle-aged stressed-out woman has (1) no hair on her head and (2) chubby cheeks and (3) fine downy facial hair. The ICS1900 unit is definitely the face of a baby, Mrs. Faniglia. We took over twenty-five hundred photos of different babies and using a computer combined them to make this face, this face we call Male Composite 37 or, affectionately, Little Roger. But what you possibly seem to be unhappy about is that Little Roger's face is not Derek's face? To be frank, Mrs. Faniglia, many of you, our customers, have found it disconcerting that their baby looks different with the I CAN SPEAK!™ on. Which we find so surprising. Did you, we often wonder, not look at the cover of the box? On that cover the ICS1900 is very plainly shown, situated on a sort of rack, looking facewise like Little Roger, albeit Little Roger is a bit crumpled and has a forehead furrow of sorts.

But this is why we came up with the ICS2100. With the ICS2100, your baby looks just like your baby. And, because we do not want anyone to be unhappy with us, we would like to give you a complimentary ICS2100 upgrade!

• • •

And as far as Derek flinching whenever that voice issues forth from him? When that speaker near his mouth sort of buzzes his lips? May I say this is not unusual? What I suggest? Try putting the ICS on Derek for a short time at first, maybe ten minutes a day, then gradually build up his Wearing Time. That is what we did. And it worked super. Now Billy wears his even while sleeping. In fact, if we forget to put it back on after his bath, he pitches a fit. Kind of begs for it! He starts to say, you know, "Mak! Mak!" Which we think is his word for mask. And when we put the mask on and Velcro the Velcro, he says, or rather it says, "GUTEN MORGEN, PAPA!" because we are trying to teach him German, and have installed the German learning module in our ICS2100. Or for example, if his pants are not yet on, he'll say, "HOW ABOUT SLAPPING ON MY ROMPERS SO I CAN GET ON WITH MY DAY!" (I wrote that one.)

My point is, with the ICS2100 Billy is much, much cleverer than he ever was with the ICS1900. He has recently learned, for example, that if he spills a little milk on his chin, his SimuLips will issue a MOO sound. Which he really seems to get a kick out of! I'll be in the living room doing a little evening paperwork and from the kitchen I'll hear, you know, "MOO! MOO! MOO!" And I'll rush in, and there'll be this sort of lake of milk on the floor. And there'll be Billy, pouring milk on his chin until I yank the milk away, at which point he bellows, "DON'T FENCE ME IN." (Ann's contribution—she was raised in Wyoming!)

• • •

Mrs. Faniglia, it is nearly the end of my lunch, and so I must wrap this up, but I hope I have been of service. On a personal note, I did not have the greatest of pasts when I came here, having been in a few scrapes and even rehab situations, but now, wow, the commissions roll in, and I have made a nice life for me and Ann and Billy. Not that the possible loss of my commission is the reason for my concern. Please do not think so. While it is true that, if you decline my upgrade offer and persist in your desire to return your ICS1900, my commission must be refunded, by me, to Mr. Ames, it is no big deal, I have certainly refunded commissions to Mr. Ames before, especially lately. I don't quite know what I'm doing wrong. But that is not your concern, Mrs. Faniglia. Your concern is Derek. My real reason for writing this letter, on my lunch break, is that, hard as we all work at KidLuv to provide innovative and essential development tools for families like yours, Mrs. Faniglia, it is always sort of a heartbreak when our products are misapprehended. Please do accept our offer of a free ICS2100 upgrade. We at KidLuv, really love what kids are, Mrs. Faniglia, which is why we want them to become something better as soon as possible! Baby's early years are so precious, and must not be wasted, as we are finding out, as our Billy grows and grows, learning new skills every day.

Sincerely yours,

Rick Sminks
Product Service Representative
KidLuv, Inc.

George Saunders writes humorous and satirical collections of short stories about contemporary American life. *CivilWarLand In Bad Decline* was a finalist for the 1996 PEN/Hemingway Award and a *New York Times* Notable Book for that year. His stories have appeared in *The New Yorker*, *Harper's*, and *Story*, and he has won two National Magazine Awards. "I Can Speak!™" appeared in *The New Yorker*.

RESPONDING

1. What is the "I Can Speak!" device? What is the author satirizing by writing this mock letter about the device?

2. List Mrs. Faniglia's specific concerns with the "I Can Speak!" How does Rick Sminks respond to these concerns? How do his responses contribute to the satire?

Form and Style

3. a) What is the *tone* of this letter? Is it appropriate to a business letter?
   b) What personal information do we learn about Rick Sminks through his letter? Is this information appropriate in a formal letter? Why is it included?

4. This satirical story uses several techniques to achieve its humour. Identify and provide an example of three methods the author uses.

Creative Extension

5. Write an editorial in which you state your opinion about the introduction and marketing of the "I Can Speak!" device.

6. Write your own fictional letter that reveals two characters (the writer and receiver of the letter) and a conflict between them that the letter writer is trying to resolve.

Essays

Cynthia Ozick on essays:

The essay is gradual and patient. The article is quick, restless, and brief. The essay reflects on its predecessors, and spirals organically out of a context, like a green twig from a living branch. The article rushes on, amnesiac, despising the meditative. . . . Essays, like articles, can distort and lie, but because essays are under the eye of history, it is a little harder to swindle the reader.

The Thrill of the Crowd

How can being part of a crowd change our behaviour?

Have you ever found that you feel freer to "act out" when you are part of a crowd than when you are on your own? How can being part of a crowd affect our personal boundaries and our behaviour? Is there both a positive and negative side to crowd behaviour? Today, one of the most common reasons people gather in crowds is to watch sports. Through a variety of short essays, a poem, a song, and a photo essay, this Echo section explores different perspectives on crowd behaviour and its effects on others.

Learning Goals
- examine a theme from a variety of perspectives
- explore how different forms, techniques, language, and styles convey meaning
- create original works based on a theme

Where the Wild Things Are

Barbara Ehrenreich

In this formal essay, Barbara Ehrenreich considers what motivates modern sports fans to put on a spectacle in the stands. She asks what real connection fans have with the sports they watch, and speculates on the reasons for the behaviour of sports fans in crowds.

Sports fans don't usually attract much attention unless they get violent—hurling missiles at "enemy players," rushing the field, brawling after the game. But in the last three decades, in a trend almost unnoticed by sports commentators and sociologists, fans have been expressing themselves in more colorful and peaceable ways, potentially even upsetting the games themselves. Soccer fans worldwide were generally the trendsetters, having been the first to paint their faces and decorate themselves head to toe in masks, ribbons, scarves, and massive headgear. These fans often bring music to the game—samba bands or African drums—and they sometimes march to stadiums in organized masses or leave in parades of heavily festooned, loudly honking cars. Most spectacularly, they engage in synchronized displays during the game, like the British "synchro-clap," in which the fans, as if schooled in the task, intersperse their songs and chants with precisely timed rhythmic clapping. Spectators don't get much respect, at least compared to athletes, but you can't call them passive anymore.

In the last two decades, the trend toward participation has spread to American sports events, especially football, baseball, and basketball. Take face painting: Only a few years ago, ardent fans had to use magic markers or even housepaint to lend their allegiances epidermal expression. Now there are at least half a dozen purveyors of skin-compatible colored makeup —and spokespersons for these companies describe the business as "really surprising" and "huge."

You can buy "team spirit" kits with colors appropriate to almost every known team, or you can be painted professionally at concessions located at stadium entrances. There are other forms of personal decoration, too, and these now go well beyond the team-colored scarf or sweatshirt to include color-coordinated nail polish, earrings, headgear—Cheeseheads, in the case of Green Bay Packer fans—and a new line of team-colored Afro wigs.

Americans have made their own unique contribution to the spectacle in the form of "the Wave," which was invented in 1981—though where, exactly, is a matter of intense dispute—and moved quickly from football to baseball and basketball. Another distinctly American mode of synchronized crowd display, much criticized by Native Americans, is "the chop" and its accompanying war chant, popularized by fans of the Atlanta Braves.

What motivates fans to become part of the show? Is this a case of team ardor run amok, or could there be deeper psychological forces at work? Sheer exhibitionism might explain some forms of display in their earliest stages—a painted bare chest, for example, can still catch the attention of cameras—but this cannot explain the thousandth painted face or the massed synchronized activities. Nor, in a climate increasingly marked by free agency, is it easy to explain the ever-more flamboyant behavior of fans in terms of mounting team loyalty. With elite players free to market themselves to the highest bidder, and owners free to change line-ups and move teams to new cities, fans may indeed be left with nobody to get excited about—except each other. In fact, Americans have been known to indulge in, say, face painting even when they have no direct stake in the game, as at soccer matches between teams representing foreign nations.

One possibility is that the fans are rebelling, however unconsciously, against their appointed role as spectators in sports that were once much more participatory. Medieval European football pitted whole villages against each other and involved "everyone . . . male and female, adult and child, rich and poor, laity and clergy," as Amherst College sports historian Allen Guttmann has written. He has speculated that today, "as sports become more commercialized and bureaucratized, fans may feel the need to say 'We're part of this, too.'"

But the specific forms of display undertaken by modern fans recall a tradition even broader and more ancient than sports: the organized festivities, both secular and religious, of preindustrial societies throughout the world. Almost universally, these have involved masking, costuming, dancing, and feasting, all of which are in chaotic abundance at today's sports stadiums. Face painting is a form of masking; synchronized motions like the Wave a kind of dance. Medieval Europe boasted an especially robust tradition of communal festivity, with carnivals and other feast days taking up, in some regions, as much as one day out of every four in the year. When commentators complain that today's demonstrative fans are turning the game into a "carnival," they only betray their ignorance of history: Carnival was in fact the traditional setting for medieval sports such as wrestling, bull running, and archery.

Only scattered remnants of the European festive tradition survived into the modern era. Beginning in the 16th century, both secular and religious authorities, representing the Protestant Reformation and the Catholic Counter-Reformation, moved to suppress popular festivities on the grounds that they were disorderly, indecent, un-Christian, and, especially as the Industrial Revolution gained ground, an extravagant waste of time. Feast days were canceled, carnivals denied a venue, raucous celebrations were transformed into sober prayer vigils. Sports, at least the ones seen as plebeian, fell under the same attack: In 1608, a Manchester ordinance prohibited football, complaining of the harm done by a "company of lewd and disordered persons usinge that unlawfulle exercise of playing with the fotebale in ye streets."

The result today is a global culture fairly desolate of joyous communal ritual. Sports enjoyed a revival in the late 19th century, but only because they were seen as a fine source of manly, nationalistic values; later they were encouraged largely as a tame form of "entertainment." In today's multi-billion-dollar sports industry, it no longer takes a village to score a touchdown.

We do a lot of complaining about the lack of "community" in modern societies, but few have noted the absence of public and participatory festivities that can, however briefly, unite total strangers in ecstatic communion. Emile Durkheim called this experience "collective effervescence," which he discerned in the ritual dances of Australian aborigines and postulated to be the emotional basis of all religion. A few religious denominations— Pentecostalism, for example—still offer a collective ecstatic experience, as did rock culture at its height. But the ecstatic religions tend to be marginal, and rock has been tamed for commercial consumption or driven into clubs as "raves." Hence, perhaps, the attempts by fans to transform sports events into an occasion for communal festivity—where else, in a culture of cubicles and malls, can you lose yourself so completely in a transient community of like-minded others?

Unfortunately, English lacks a word, or even a graceful phrase, for the desire for ebullient self-expression and excited merger with the crowd. Call it primitive religiosity or some sort of "carnival instinct:" What today's demonstrative fans are telling us is that it cannot be suppressed forever.

Non-fiction writer Barbara Ehrenreich is a media critic, social activist, and feminist. She became involved in political activism during the Vietnam War and has written professionally ever since. Health care, class, and gender are just some of the issues addressed in her essays and books. Her book *Fear of Falling: The Inner Life of the Middle Class* (1989) was nominated for the National Book Critics Award. *Blood Rites* (1997) is one of her most recent books. Since 1990, she has been an essayist for *Time* magazine, where "Where the Wild Things Are" appeared in 1996. (Born Butte, Montana 1941)

RESPONDING

Meaning

1. Ehrenreich describes different types of sports fan behaviours that have evolved over the last 30 years, and then explains the cause of these behaviours. Make a list in point form of the fan behaviours she writes about in her essay. Then list the possible causes she gives for this behaviour.

2. a) In paragraph 10, Ehrenreich writes that "we do a lot of complaining about the lack of 'community' in modern societies." What does she mean by "community"? How does she feel sports events help provide this sense of community for many people?
   b) Are there other public gatherings or occasions that could fulfil this role? What are they? How do they create a sense of community?

Form and Style

3. This essay is a cause-and-effect expository essay. The only twist is that the author states the effects first, and then the possible causes. How clear was the connection between cause and effect for you as the reader? What other explanations could be offered for fan behaviour? Write a brief review of this essay in which you summarize your thoughts on Ehrenreich's explanation.

4. This essay is written in a formal style. The tone is serious, the sentence structures are at times complex, and the author uses some sophisticated vocabulary. Express in your own words what the author means by the following phrases: massed synchronized activities, chaotic abundance, communal festivity, collective effervescence, ebullient self-expression. Use the context and a dictionary to arrive at the meanings.

Creative Extension

5. Choose one of the fan participation events Ehrenreich mentions in her essay such as soccer, football, baseball, or basketball games. Imagine that you are in the crowd for one of these events. Write an e-mail or letter to a friend describing your experiences. Be sure to focus on physical sensations—sights, sounds, tastes, etc.—and your feelings, whether positive or negative. At the end of your letter, offer some explanation for why people participate in these events.

6. Interview a sports fan who attends local games or watches them on TV. In your interview, focus on finding out what appeals to the fan about these games. Summarize your findings and comment on your own feelings toward this particular form of game.

 # The Sprinters

     ❧ *Lillian Morrison*

In this poem, Lillian Morrison describes the relationship between the crowd and the runners, especially the winner, in a sprint.

The gun explodes them.
Pummeling, pistoning they fly
In time's face.
A go at the limit,
A terrible try
To smash the ticking glass,
Outpace the beat
That runs, that streaks away
Tireless, and faster than they.

Beside ourselves
(It is for us they run!)
We shout and pound the stands
For one to win
Loving him, whose hard
Grace-driven stride
Most mocks the clock
And almost breaks the bands
Which lock us in.

ᘒ   Lillian Morrison writes poems for young readers using rhyme and free verse. She takes a particular interest in sports and is one of the few poets to publish a book consisting entirely of sports
poems. She published *Sprints and Distances: Sports in Poetry and Poetry in Sports* in 1990. She also
compiled the illustrated anthology of baseball poems *At the Crack of the Bat* (1992).

Connecting

1. a) How does the speaker in the poem describe the sprinters in the first verse?
        Identify specific verbs and metaphors, and describe their effects.
    b) The first verse is in third-person; the second is in first-person. Why do you
        think the poet changes point of view? What effect does this have on the poem
        and the reader?

2. Time and clocks are mentioned in both verses. What role does time play in the first
    verse? What role does it play in the second verse?

3. What is the connection between the crowd and the sprinter in this poem? How does
    this connection compare with the relationship between the crowd and athletes in
    Ehrenreich's essay? Support your answer.

Who Killed Benny Paret?

Norman Cousins

This famous essay presents a dark view of the sport-event audience. The topic is boxing. The writer argues that it is audience bloodlust that keeps crowds coming back for more.

Sometime about 1935 or 1936 I had an interview with Mike Jacobs, the prizefight promoter. I was a fledgling reporter at that time; my beat was education, but during the vacation season I found myself on varied assignments, all the way from ship news to sports reporting. In this way I found myself sitting opposite the most powerful figure in the boxing world.

There was nothing spectacular in Mr. Jacobs' manner or appearance; but when he spoke about prizefights, he was no longer a bland little man but a colossus who sounded the way Napoleon must have sounded when he reviewed a battle. You knew you were listening to Number One. His saying something made it true.

We discussed what to him was the only important element in successful promoting—how to please the crowd. So far as he was concerned, there was no mystery to it. You put killers in the ring and the people filled your arena. You hire boxing artists—men who are adroit at feinting, parrying, weaving, jabbing, and dancing, but who don't pack dynamite in their fists—and you wind up counting your empty seats. So you searched for the killers and sluggers and maulers—fellows who could hit with the force of a baseball bat.

I asked Mr. Jacobs if he was speaking literally when he said people came out to see the killer.

"They don't come out to see a tea party," he said evenly. "They come out to see the knockout. They come out to see a man hurt. If they think anything else, they're kidding themselves."

Recently, a young man by the name of Benny Paret was killed in the ring. The killing was seen by millions; it was on television. In the twelfth round, he was hit hard in the head several times, went down, was counted out and never came out of the coma.

The Paret fight produced a flurry of investigations. Governor Rockefeller was shocked by what happened and appointed a committee to assess the responsibility. The New York State Boxing Commission decided to find out what was wrong. The District Attorney's office expressed its concern.

One question that was solemnly studied in all three probes concerned the action of the referee. Did he act in time to stop the fight? Another question had to do with the role of the examining doctors who certified the physical fitness of the fighters before the bout. Still another question involved Mr. Paret's manager; did he rush the boy into the fight without adequate time to recuperate from the previous one?

In short, the investigators looked into every possible cause except the real one. Benny Paret was killed because the human fist delivers enough impact, when directed against the head, to produce a massive hemorrhage in the brain. The human brain is the most delicate and complex mechanism in all creation. It has a lacework of millions of highly fragile nerve connections. Nature attempts to protect this exquisitely intricate machinery by encasing it in a hard shell. Fortunately, the shell is thick enough to withstand a great deal of pounding. Nature, however, can protect man against everything except man himself. Not every blow to the head will kill a man—but there is always the risk of concussion and damage to the brain. A prizefighter may be able to survive even repeated brain concussions and go on fighting, but the damage to his brain may be permanent.

In any event, it is futile to investigate the referee's role and seek to determine whether he should have intervened to stop the fight earlier. That is not where the primary responsibility lies. The primary responsibility lies with the people who pay to see a man hurt. The referee who stops a fight too soon from the crowd's viewpoint can expect to be booed. The crowd wants the knockout; it wants to see a man stretched out on the canvas. This is the supreme moment in boxing. It is nonsense to talk about prizefighting as a test of boxing skills. No crowd was ever brought to its feet screaming and cheering at the sight of two men beautifully dodging and weaving out of each other's jabs. The time the crowd comes alive is when a man is hit hard over the heart or the head, when his mouthpiece flies out, when the blood squirts out of his nose or eyes, when he wobbles under the attack and his pursuer continues to smash at him with poleax impact.

Don't blame it on the referee. Don't even blame it on the fight managers. Put the blame where it belongs, on the prevailing mores that regard prizefighting as a perfectly proper enterprise and vehicle of entertainment. No one doubts that many people enjoy prizefighting and will miss it if it should be thrown out. And that is precisely the point.

🕙   Norman Cousins began his career as an essayist and the editor of the *Saturday Review*. Because of his struggle with a life-threatening disease, he became the author of more than 20 books on the nature of illness. Cousins described his successful battle with the illness ankylosing spondylitis in the popular book *Anatomy of an Illness as Perceived by the Patient* (1979). Other books include *Head First: The Biology of Hope* (1991). *(Born Union Hill, New Jersey 1915; died 1990)*

Connecting

1.   What was the main point Mike Jacobs made in his interview with Norman Cousins? How do Cousins's feelings about the Benny Paret fight support what Jacobs said about boxing 40 years earlier?

2.   Cousins writes that "the primary responsibility is with the people who pay to see a man get hurt." Comment on this statement. Do you agree or disagree? Support your opinion.

3.   This essay shows a very different crowd than that described by Ehrenreich in "Where the Wild Things Are." Using a Venn diagram, compare the different characteristics of the crowd in both essays. Write a brief summary of your findings.

4.   Assuming that the individuals in the crowd at a boxing event don't, in their everyday lives, want to see men get hurt or killed, how does Cousins's essay illustrate that being part of a crowd can change a person's behaviour?

Flying

🕙   *Stan Rogers*

This song, by Canadian Stan Rogers, takes the athletes' point of view. It offers some insight into the effects crowds have on them and what a young striving athlete's life is really like.

It was just like strapping 'em on and starting again.
Coaching these kids to the top and calling them men
I was a third round pick in the NHL
And that's three years of living hell
And going up flying, and going home dying.

My life was over the boards and playing the game.
And every day checking the papers and finding my name.
And Dad would go crazy when the scouts would call;
He'd tell me that I'd have it all
Ninety-nine of us trying, only one of us flying.

And every kid over the boards listens for the sound.
The roar of the crowd is their ticket for finally leaving this town
To be just one more hopeful in the Junior A,
Dreaming of that miracle play.
And going up flying, going home dying.

I tell them to think of the play and not of the fame.
If they got any future at all, it's not in the game
'Cause they'll be crippled and starting all over again
Selling on commission and remembering
When they were flying, remembering dying.

And every kid over the boards listens for the sound;
The roar of the crowd is their ticket for finally leaving this town
To be just one more hopeful in the Junior A,
Dreaming of that miracle play.
And going up flying, and going home dying.

 ♪   Stan Rogers is recognized as one of Canada's most talented folk singers. Many of his songs are about Canada's history and people. He recorded six albums, two that were released after his death. The song "Flying" is from the 1984 album entitled *From Fresh Water*. Rogers died in a plane fire in 1983 at the age of 33. *(Born Hamilton, Ontario 1949; died 1983)*

Connecting

1. "Flying" and "dying" are used repeatedly at the ends of verses in this song. What does Rogers mean by these words? Is he literally speaking of flight and death?

2. Why does the speaker tell the kids he coaches to "think of the play and not of the fame"?

3. What does the roar of the crowd mean for these NHL-hopefuls? How is this relationship between crowd and sport or athletes different from that in Ehrenreich's essay?

4. This song is from the athlete's perspective, so the thoughts of the crowd members must be imagined. Who might be in a small-town hockey audience? What might their feelings be as they watch the game? How might watching temporarily change them?

Playing to Win

Margaret A. Whitney

This personal essay describes the effect sports has on a young woman and her family. It offers a very different perspective on the relationship between athletes and spectators.

My daughter is an athlete. Nowadays, this statement won't strike many parents as unusual, but it does me. Until her freshman year in high school, Ann was only marginally interested in sport of any kind. When she played, she didn't swing hard, often dropped the ball, and had an annoying habit of tittering on field or court.

Indifference combined with another factor that did not bode well for a sports career. Ann was growing up to be beautiful. By eighth grade, nature and orthodontics had produced a 5-foot 8-inch 125-pound, brown-eyed beauty with a wonderful smile. People told her, too. And, as many young women know, it is considered a satisfactory accomplishment to be pretty and stay pretty. Then you can simply sit still and enjoy the unconditional positive regard. Ann loved the attention, too, and didn't consider it demeaning when she was awarded "Best Hair," female category, in the eighth-grade yearbook.

So it came as a surprise when she became a jock. The first indication that athletic indifference had ended came when she joined the high school cross-country team. She signed up in early September and ran third for the team within three days. Not only that. After one of those 3.1 mile races up hill and down dale on a rainy November afternoon, Ann came home muddy and bedraggled. Her hair was plastered to her head, and the mascara she had applied so carefully that morning ran in dark circles under her eyes. This is it, I thought. Wait until Lady Astor sees herself. But the kid with the best eighth grade hair went on to finish the season and subsequently letter in cross-country, soccer, basketball, and softball.

I love sports, she tells anyone who will listen. So do I, though my midlife quest for a doctorate leaves me little time for either playing or watching. My love of sports is bound up with the goals in my life and my hopes for my three daughters. I have begun to hear the message of sports. It is very different from many messages that women receive about living, and I think it is good.

My husband, for example, talked to Ann differently when he realized she was a serious competitor and not just someone who wanted to get in shape so she'd look good in a prom dress. Be aggressive, he'd advise. Go for the ball. Be intense.

Be intense. She came in for some of the most scathing criticism from her dad, when, during basketball season, her intensity waned. You're pretending to play hard, he said. You like it on the bench? Do you like to watch while your teammates play?

I would think, how is this kid reacting to such advice? For years, she'd been told at home, at school, by countless advertisements, "Be quiet, Be good, Be still." When teachers reported that Ann was too talkative, not obedient enough, too flighty. When I dressed her up in frilly dresses and told her not to get dirty. When ideals of femininity are still, quiet, cool females in ads whose vacantness passes for sophistication. How can any adolescent girl know what she's up against? Have you ever really noticed intensity? It is neither quiet nor good. And it's definitely not pretty.

In the end, her intensity revived. At half time, she'd look for her father, and he would come out of the bleachers to discuss tough defense, finding the open player, squaring up on her jump shot. I'd watch them at the edge of the court, a tall man and a tall girl, talking about how to play.

Of course, I'm particularly sensitive at this point in my life to messages about trying hard, being active, getting better through individual and team effort. Ann, you could barely handle a basketball two years ago. Now you're bringing up the ball against the press. Two defenders are after you. You must dribble, stop, pass. We're depending on you. We need you to help us. I wonder if my own paroxysms of uncertainty would be eased had more people urged me—be active, go for it!

Not that dangers don't lurk for the females of her generation. I occasionally run this horror show in my own mental movie theatre: an unctuous but handsome lawyer-like drone of a young man spies my Ann. Hmmm, he says, unconsciously to himself, good gene pool, and wouldn't she go well with my BMW and condo? Then I see Ann with a great new hairdo kissing the drone goodbye-honey and setting off to the nearest mall with splendid-looking children to spend money.

But the other night she came home from softball tryouts at six in the evening. The dark circles under her eyes were from exhaustion, not makeup. I tried too hard today, she says. I feel like I'm going to puke.

After she has revived, she explains. She wants to play a particular position. There is competition for it. I can't let anybody else get my spot, she says, I've got to prove that I can do it. Later we find out that she has not gotten the much-wanted third-base position, but she will start with the varsity team. My husband talks about the machinations of coaches and tells her to keep trying. You're doing fine, he says. She gets that I-am-going-to-keep-trying look on her face. The horror show vision of Ann-as-Stepford-Wife fades.

Of course, Ann doesn't realize the changes she has wrought, the power of her self-definition. I'm an athlete, Ma, she tells me when I suggest participation in the school play or the yearbook. But she has really caused us all to rethink our views of existence: her younger sisters who consider sports a natural activity for females, her father whose advocacy of women has increased, and me. Because when I doubt my own abilities, I say to myself, Get intense, Margaret. Do you like to sit on the bench?

And my intensity revives.

I am not suggesting that participation in sports is the answer for all young women. It is not easy—the losing, the jealousy, raw competition, and intense personal criticism of performance.

And I don't wish to imply that the sports scene is a morality play either. Girls' sports can be funny. You can't forget that out on that field are a bunch of people who know the meaning of the word cute. During one game, I noticed that Ann had a blue ribbon tied on her ponytail, and it dawned on me that every girl had an identical bow. Somehow I can't picture the Celtics gathered in the locker room of the Boston Garden agreeing to wear the same colour sweatbands.

No, what has struck me, amazed me, and made me hold my breath in wonder and in hope is both the ideal of sport and the reality of a young girl not afraid to do her best.

I watch her bringing the ball up the court. We yell encouragement from the stands, though I know she doesn't hear us. Her face is red with exertion, and her body is concentrated on the task. She dribbles, draws the defense to her, passes, runs. A teammate passes the ball back to her. They've beaten the press. She heads toward the hoop. Her father watches her, her sisters watch her, I watch her. And I think, drive, Ann, drive.

Margaret Whitney was studying for a doctoral degree in technical communications in Troy, New York, when she wrote this essay. It was first published in the *New York Times Magazine*.

Connecting

1. Why is Ann's interest in athletics and her need to excel startling, yet reassuring, for her mother?

2. Whitney writes "what has struck me, amazed me, and made me hold my breath in wonder and in hope is both the ideal of sport and the reality of a young girl not afraid to do her best." What does Whitney mean by "the ideal of sport"?

3. How have Ann's new-found skills as an athlete changed the members of her family, including herself? Are these transformations temporary (as are those in the crowds described by Ehrenreich) or permanent?

4. Do the audiences described by Whitney sound like those described by Ehrenreich? How might Ehrenreich explain the connection of Ann's audience to her as an athlete?

The Real Sports Connection

♪ *Photo Essay*

In this photo essay, pictures tell the story and present another viewpoint. Consider the point this visual representation makes.

The Thrill of the Crowd

The Drive for Victory

A)

B)

The Spectacle of Sport

A)

B)

Real Courage—Real Admiration

Connecting

1. Consider the title of this photo essay and scan the photos. What question do you believe this photo essay aims to answer? Restate the title as a question.

2. A photo essay, like a written essay, has a carefully thought-out structure. In your own words, summarize the main point in each section of this photo essay.

3. Explain the significance of the final photo, which shows injured Canadian rower Silken Laumann pushing for the finish line in the 1992 Olympics though she did not win a gold medal. What is the concluding idea or thesis of this photo essay?

4. Compare the main idea in this photo essay with that in Barbara Ehrenreich's essay. Which essay is most in line with your own thinking? Support your answer with reasons.

REFLECTING ON THE ECHO

1. You have examined a variety of perspectives on the question of how being part of a crowd can change people's behaviour and the effects of that behaviour on others—whether positive or negative. Which point of view presented in this Echo section is closest to your own? Write an editorial or short persuasive essay presenting your own view on this issue.

2. Working in small groups, identify other selections that could fit into this Echo section. They could be literary, musical, visual, or multimedia. In a short memo, explain why you would recommend them. Then develop four questions to go with each of your selections. Exchange your selections with other groups and consider their answers to your questions.

3. Imagine you are the director of a documentary and are responsible for creating a short film on the topic of crowd behaviour. What would you include in your production? Who would you quote or interview? Create the script for the documentary. See pages 61–64 for an example of a documentary script.

Humans and Other Animals

≼ Bronwen Wallace

Learning Goals

• identify the thesis
  in an essay

• examine the
  effectiveness of
  first-person point
  of view

• evaluate the use
  of quotations

• create and present
  a short speech
  and a media study

There's a poem by Earle Birney called "The Bear on the Delhi Road," in which he describes seeing a huge Himalayan bear being brought down from the mountains by two "men of Kashmir." The men have captured the bear, not to kill him, but "simply to teach him to dance"— to become a dancing bear, in the great markets of Delhi where his owners will earn a living from his performances.

Birney talks about the work it takes for these trainers to wear from the bear's "shaggy body the tranced / wish forever to stay / only an ambling bear / four-footed in berries." And the poem ends by widening that picture of this one bear into a larger image of our relationship to many other animals:

> It is not easy to free
> myth from reality
> or rear this fellow up
> to lurch-lurch with them
> in the tranced dancing of men.

Birney's poem came to mind when I saw Klass Act recently at the local shopping centre. Klass Act, an outfit from Ohio, offered several lionesses performing tricks in a small cage in the parking lot. And inside, another cage held lion and tiger cubs—cute little fellas; you could have your kids' (or your own) picture taken with them.

I find the appearance of Klass Act, like Birney's bear on the Delhi road, disturbing. Seeing those lionesses in that tiny cage and those cubs being picked up for endless photographic sessions gave me that sick feeling that animal acts in the circus often give me—or the appearance of wild animals at a zoo.

I am not talking here about how "well" or how "cruelly" the animals are treated, though that is an important issue. The Klass Act animals had the bored, listless look that the big cats often have when seen through bars. The cubs were even more listless and I couldn't help wondering how they had been rendered "safe" for close-up photos with young children. Still, we are talking about animals born and raised in captivity. Given that, to talk about the specific "cruelty" of Klass Act is to single out one rather tawdry example from a long list. If Klass Act is where we "end up," it is, as far as I'm concerned, different only in degree from the zoo or the circus. Once we have decided, as a species, that other animals can be caged and trained for our entertainment, we have made a decision as well about our relationship to those other animals. It's that relationship I want to explore.

Let me start by saying that I think the relationship between our species and other animals is a very complex one. I think, too, that there is a difference between our relationship to lions and tigers and our relationship to house cats, dogs and horses. For those who want to explore some of the complexities of the latter relationship, I recommend Vicki Hearne's book *Adam's Task* as one particularly challenging viewpoint.

I also believe that the relationship between humans and other animals varies from culture to culture. I've talked before about the work of Hugh Brody, an anthropologist who has lived for many years among the hunting tribes of the Canadian North. In his latest work—*Living Arctic*—Brody explores the complex relationship between these hunters and the animals they hunt. He recognizes that in all these cultures, this relationship is seen as spiritual as well as practical. It is a relationship of dependence, primarily, because the hunter depends on the animal for survival. "Dependence," Brody points out, "entails vulnerability. The relationship between the hunter and the hunted, therefore, has a certain equality. Ultimately, no one can be superior to that upon which he depends."

This spiritual complexity is evident in Native literature, in their religious views, and in the reliance of some peoples (the Athapascan and the Alonquian, for example) on dreams to guide them to the right hunting spots. The sense of interdependency, which is at the centre of this relationship with other animals, also accounts for the fact that these peoples kill only what they need and, in doing so, do not usually deplete the species.

Brody also recognizes the argument often put forward by biologists that northern hunters' belief systems may only take into account one part of a species' cycle and that they may engage in ecologically dangerous practices. But he envisages a situation of "northern hunters and white biologists sitting down together, agreeing about wildlife problems and discovering ways in which these can be ameliorated." Brody also believes that Southern attitudes about meat diets and about hunting in general have fuelled animal-rights campaigns which do not look at the full complexity of these relationships.

Another person who has written extensively about the meaning of our relationship to other animals is John Berger. Berger is an art critic, novelist, and scriptwriter who is best known for a book called *Ways of Seeing*, a series of essays on European art. For the past 20 years, however, he has lived and worked in a peasant village in the south of France. From there he has continued to write essays on art and on the lives of the people around him.

Like Brody, Berger recognizes that the relationship between the peasant farmer and the animals he kills and eats is a spiritual as well as a practical one. Again, he sees it as a relationship of interdependence which those of us who buy our food (be it vegetable or animal) wrapped in plastic at the supermarket cannot understand. Within our culture, perhaps it would be the dairy farmer who comes closest to this understanding of interdependence, this recognition that your life is dependent on the animals you care for—as their lives are dependent on you.

But back to Klass Act. In another essay, "Why Look at Animals," in a book called *About Looking*, Berger explores what has happened to the city-dwellers' relationship to animals—and why shows like Klass Act are such an apt expression of it. As we move further and further away from a life which is directly dependent on animals for survival, we also move further away from an understanding of ourselves in relationship with them. Other animals become simply—animals, beings completely separate from us.

One element in this process is the romanticization of animals. Birney's bear is the forbearer, if you will, of *The Three Bears* and the Teddy Bear and even Yogi Bear. As we become more and more separate from real animals in the real world, their appearance as stuffed toys and nostalgic creatures in books and movies becomes more apparent. This becomes more marked, Berger argues, in the 19th century, as cities grow and the human species loses contact with animals. They become "things we look at," rather than beings with which we are engaged. Zoos—the London Zoo opened in 1828—become more and more popular.

Real animals are rapidly disappearing from our lives. They have become marginalized—whether to egg and poultry farms where the hens never see the sun or to zoos or to displays like Klass Act. They are no longer at the centre of our lives. As well, the people who still relate to animals in a whole way—Native peoples, for example, and peasant cultures—are also marginalized. We think of them as "past" or "primitive," we display their tools in museums as artifacts, we do not think we have anything at all to learn from their way of life.

So we go to see Klass Act. We let our children be photographed with that cute tiger cub who has become as mythical a creature as Santa Claus or the Easter Bunny, whose appearances in shopping centres are also the occasion for photographs. We know nothing, anymore, about real animals.

Meanwhile, at least 20 500 dolphins are killed every year by the tuna industry, a situation allowed by the US Marine Mammal Protection Act. Sometimes as many as 200 dolphins are killed for 10 tuna. They are usually bombed or netted and chopped to pieces.

Meanwhile, Beluga whales in the Gulf of St. Lawrence are producing grotesquely deformed young, if they produce any at all, mainly because of the excessive industrial pollution of the Great Lakes.

Meanwhile, thousands—think of it, *thousands*—of other species become extinct or endangered every year.

When are we going to realize—or remember? We are not on the planet alone. We are in relationship with everything that lives here. And we are only one more species, after all.

Poet and essayist Bronwen Wallace was born in Kingston, Ontario, and educated at Queen's University. Her political activism led her to work with auto workers, to co-found a women's bookstore, and to work in a battered women's shelter. She was also a creative writing teacher and filmmaker. Publications after her death in 1989 include the book of short stories *People You'd Trust Your Life To* (1990). "Humans and Other Animals" is from *Arguments with the World: Essays by Bronwen Wallace* published in 1992. *(Born Kingston, Ontario 1945; died 1989)*

RESPONDING

Meaning

1. We are given the topic of this essay in its title—the relationship between animals and humans. What is the author's *thesis* or controlling idea? Where do we find it in the essay? Justify your answer.

2. Explain the meaning of the following statements:
    a) "Once we have decided, as a species, that other animals can be caged and trained for our entertainment, we have made a decision as well about our relationship to those other animals."
    b) "The relationship between the hunter and the hunted, therefore, has a certain equality. Ultimately, no one can be superior to that upon which he depends."
    c) "Other animals become simply—animals, beings completely separate from us."

Form and Style

3. This essay is written in first-person point of view. Rewrite the third and fourth paragraphs in the third-person point of view. How does this different point of view change the impact of Wallace's ideas on you, the reader? Why did the author choose the first-person point of view?

4. Cite two examples of how Bronwen Wallace uses quotations in this essay. What is the purpose of these quotations? How do they affect you as a reader? Did they help to illustrate the author's point, or would it have been better for her to leave out the literary references? Explain your views.

Creative Extension

5. Bronwen Wallace clearly thinks humans need to be reminded of their intimate relationship with animals. The more distant the human/animal relationship, the more dangerous humans become for the planet. She says this is particularly true for city dwellers, who have very little contact with wild animals. Write and present a short speech that suggests ways humans can re-establish a healthy relationship with animals. Record your speech on audio or videotape.

6. Create a media log by making notes on human/animal relationships you observe on television, in magazines, in newspapers, and in other media over one week. Include copies of any pictures or illustrations you find. Present your findings to the class and state your conclusions on how the media depicts human/animal relationships.

Young People

✑ David Suzuki

Learning Goals

• assess an author's purpose

• examine a distinction between argumentative and persuasive essays

• understand the difference between deductive and inductive reasoning

• create a pamphlet and present a research report

No group has more at stake in the resolution of the global ecocrisis than today's generation of children and youth. Young people are more receptive to new ideas, not having yet invested heavily in the status quo and therefore being able to see with greater clarity. And it is youth in whom we find the greatest ecological activism.

Try this. Take a few discarded car oil containers, store them in a heated room for a day, then pour out the residual oil. That was the science project of David Grassby, a 14-year-old who lives in Thornhill, Ontario. He got the idea while visiting a friend whose father was complaining about not being able to get all of the oil out of a can into his engine. David wondered how much, on average, is left when people throw "empty" containers away.

Like a good scientist, he collected more than 100 discarded containers from trash cans and service stations. After draining 100 of them for two minutes each, David recovered 3.7 litres of oil, an average of 37 millilitres per discard. After phoning several oil companies, he finally managed to glean enough information to calculate that annual sales of passenger car oil in Canada amount to 220 million litres of which 132 million are in one-litre containers (executives of one company told him that is a low estimate). That means over five million litres of oil are wasted and end up contaminating soil and water annually. As well, David calculated that 10 million kilograms of empty plastic receptacles end up in dumps each year.

David then suggested that large drums of motor oil could be kept at each gas station so that motorists could fill up their own reusable container or the oil could be pumped directly into the car like gas. He sent a copy of his study to Petrocan, Shell, Sunoco, and Imperial, receiving a reply only from Petrocan. David also sent his report to the print and electronic media and the radio program *As It Happens*, which arranged for David to meet the president and executives of Esso Petroleum. At the meeting, David suggested the use of large barrels for bulk distribution of oil, but the executives replied that it was impossible because of the wide variety of grades of car oil. David replied that he had read that 90 per cent of all car oil sold was 5W30. The company reps had no response.

Calling this "The Unknown Oil Spill," David printed up a brochure of his results, with suggested solutions and addresses of people to write. Like the child in the parable about the emperor with no clothes, David, with his simple science project (good scientific experiments are usually simple), went straight to the heart of a fundamental issue—unsustainable and unnecessary waste and pollution. He made us confront a number of facts: we are acting as if the environment can absorb our discards, even highly toxic ones, indefinitely; we seem to assume that our resources are so vast that we can waste them; we let the dictates of short-term profit come ahead of long-term ecological costs.

David's project also highlights the enormous cumulative impact of large numbers of tiny incremental effects. Each of us contributes a trivial amount to the planet's load, but the sum of consumption and waste by 5.5 billion of us is enormous.

Young people like David see with embarrassing clarity because they aren't blinded by fear, vested interests in a career, or the allure of rampant consumerism. And they have the most at stake in the future of the environment. All young people today have been exposed to chemicals and toxic environmental agents from conception on, and each successive newborn will have higher exposures than any previous generation. Today's youth will become adults in a world beset with enormous ecological problems that we bequeath to them by our inability to curb the short-sighted and the unsustainable pursuit of endless growth in the economy and consumption. Their world will be radically diminished in the biological diversity that we adults took for granted when we were children.

Youth speak with a power and clarity that only innocence confers, and because we love them, adults *have* to make changes in the way we live.

≼ Geneticist, environmentalist, and broadcaster David Suzuki became a media personality through his popularization of science. He hosted the radio series *The Nature of Things* for 10 years, and his 1985 CBC special "A Planet for the Taking" was one of the most watched shows in CBC history. In 1994, he wrote *Time to Change*. He was named an officer in the Order of Canada in 1977. (*Born Vancouver, British Columbia 1936*)

RESPONDING

Meaning

1. What is David Suzuki's purpose in writing this essay? Support your view with evidence from the text.

2. Suzuki refers to a science project by David Grassby, a 14-year-old high school student. David's project led to a list of suggestions to oil companies for ways to reduce the "unknown oil spill." What were these suggestions? How did the oil companies respond to them?

Form and Style

3. Some writers distinguish between argumentative essays and persuasive essays. Argumentative essays use facts and logical arguments to appeal to the reader's sense of reason. Persuasive essays use emotionally charged language to appeal to the reader's feelings. Both types of essay attempt to convert the reader to the writer's point of view on a given topic. Would you categorize "Young People" as an argumentative essay, a persuasive essay, or a combination of the two? Support your answer with evidence from the text.

4. Define the differences between deductive and inductive reasoning. Which type of reasoning does David Suzuki use? Outline his basic argument to show why it is an example of inductive or deductive reasoning.

Creative Extension

5. David Grassby's project is an example of one of the basic principles of ecological activism: "think globally and act locally." Think of your own local area or neighbourhood and make a list of things that contribute to its pollution. Choose one of the items on your list and decide what you yourself could do to reduce it as a pollutant. Formulate an action plan in five or six clearly expressed steps, then create a pamphlet to clearly outline this plan and motivate others to follow it.

6. Use the Internet and library sources to research an organized group that is active in environmental causes. Present a brief report to your class on the group. Tell when and why it was founded, what cause or causes it specializes in, and what it has managed to accomplish in its fight on behalf of environmental causes. Be sure to outline how people can contact the group or become members of it. Some likely groups include Greenpeace, the Sierra Club, Earth First!, Ducks Unlimited, and Western Canada Wilderness Committee.

Loose Ends

✑ Rita Dove

Learning Goals

- write a précis
- evaluate an author's thesis
- handle difficult vocabulary
- create a dialogue and multimedia presentation

For years the following scene would play daily at our house: Home from school, my daughter would heave her backpack off her shoulder and let it thud to the hall floor, then dump her jacket on top of the pile. My husband would tell her to pick it up—as he did every day—and hang it in the closet. Begrudgingly with a snort and a hrrumph, she would comply. The ritual interrogation began:

"Hi, Aviva. How was school?"

"Fine."

"What did you do today?"

"Nothing."

And so it went, every day. We cajoled, we pleaded, we threatened with rationed ice cream sandwiches and new healthy vegetable casseroles, we attempted subterfuges such as: "What was Ms. Boyers wearing today?" or: "Any new pets in science class?" but her answer remained the same: "I dunno."

Asked, however, about that week's episodes of "MathNet," her favourite series on Public Television's "Square One," or asked for a quick gloss of a segment of "Lois and Clark" that we happened to miss, and she'd spew out the details of a complicated story, complete with character development, gestures, every twist and back-flip of the plot.

Is TV greater than reality? Are we to take as damning evidence the soap opera stars attacked in public by viewers who obstinately believe in the on-screen villainy of Erica or Jeannie's evil twin? Is an estrangement from real life the catalyst behind the escalating violence in our schools, where children imitate the gun-'em-down pyrotechnics of cop-and-robber shows?

Such a conclusion is too easy. Yes, the influence of public media on our perceptions is enormous, but the relationship of projected reality—i.e., TV —to imagined reality—i.e., an existential [real] moment—is much more complex. It is not that we confuse TV with reality, but that we prefer it to reality—the manageable struggle resolved in twenty-six minutes, the witty repartee within the family circle instead of the grunts and silence common to most real families; the sharpened conflict and defined despair instead of vague anxiety and invisible enemies. "Life, my friends, is boring. We must not say so," wrote John Berryman, and many years and "Dream Songs" later he leapt from a bridge in Minneapolis. But there is a devastating corollary to that statement: Life, friends, is ragged. Loose ends are the rule.

What happens when my daughter tells the television's story better than her own is simply this: the TV offers an easier tale to tell. The salient points are there for the plucking—indeed, they're the only points presented—and all she has to do is to recall them. Instant Nostalgia! Life, on the other hand, slithers about and runs down blind alleys and sometimes just fizzles at the climax. "The world is ugly, / And the people are sad," sings the country bumpkin in Wallace Stevens's "Gubinnal." Who isn't tempted to ignore the inexorable fact of our insignificance on a dying planet? We all yearn for our private patch of blue.

ୟ Rita Dove was Poet Laureate of the United States from 1993–1995. Her poetry has earned many awards. She received a Pulitzer Prize for *Thomas and Beulah* (1986), a collection of poems based upon the lives of her grandparents, who came to Ohio in the early twentieth century. *On the Bus with Rosa Parks* (1999) was named a *New York Times* Notable Book of the Year. *(Born Akron, Ohio 1952)*

RESPONDING

Meaning

1. A *précis* is a brief summary, or abstract, of a longer piece of writing in which the most important points are concisely presented in logical order and in a readable form. Write a précis of this essay.

2. a) In the third-to-last paragraph, the author asks if the explanation for her daughter's behaviour is because TV is greater than reality. Then she says that that conclusion is too easy and offers another one (we prefer TV to reality because it is manageable and tidy; this is her thesis). What is your opinion of her conclusion? Would you say it is also "too easy"? Explain.

    b) What do the two final sentences in the essay mean? How do they connect to the author's thesis?

Form and Style

3. Why does the thesis occur so late in this essay? Suggest reasons for your answer.

4. a) This essay contains some difficult but precise vocabulary. Identify words or phrases you did not understand on the first reading. Which could you understand on a second or third reading from the context? Which did you need to look up in a dictionary?

    b) Did you need to understand every word to get the main idea of the essay on first reading? How did your understanding of the vocabulary enhance your understanding of the text on a second and third reading? Explain your answer.

Creative Extension

5. Write a parent/child dialogue about watching TV. Work in ideas from this essay and add your own thoughts on the issue. Avoid stereotypical representations of the parent (stereotypically anti-TV) and child (usually pro-TV).

6. In this essay, Rita Dove writes that "Life, friends, is ragged. Loose ends are the rule." Illustrate this statement in a non-print way such as a multimedia presentation, speech, visuals such as posters or a slide show, a song, poetry reading, video or dramatic performance, etc. Explain why you chose the medium you did.

When Was the Murder of Duncan First Plotted?

❧ A.C. Bradley

Shakespeare's play Macbeth *has intrigued a succession of literary critics through the centuries. In this literary essay, A. C. Bradley explores the motivation of Macbeth and Lady Macbeth to murder Duncan, the King of Scotland. Bradley presents his view of just when the plot was hatched. Was it already planned before the famous opening scene of the play with the three witches?*

Learning Goals

- analyze an author's argument
- examine the use of transition words and phrases
- present a dramatic reading interpreting meaning
- write a literary essay

Did the Macbeths plot Duncan's murder before the meeting with the witches?

A good many readers probably think that, when Macbeth first met the witches, he was perfectly innocent; but a much larger number would say that he had already harboured a vaguely guilty ambition, though he had not faced the idea of murder. And I think there can be no doubt that this is the obvious and natural interpretation of the scene. Only it is almost necessary to go rather further, and to suppose that his guilty ambition, whatever its precise form, was known to his wife and shared by her. Otherwise, surely, she would not, on reading his letter, so instantaneously assume that the King must be murdered in their castle; nor would Macbeth, as soon as he meets her, be aware (as he evidently is) that this thought is in her mind.

But there is a famous passage in *Macbeth* which, closely considered, seems to require us to go further still, and to suppose that, at some time before the action of the play begins, the husband and wife had explicitly discussed the idea of murdering Duncan at some favourable opportunity, and had agreed to execute this idea.

The passage occurs in Act 1, sc. 7, where Lady Macbeth is urging her husband to the deed:

MACBETH: Prithee, peace:
    I dare do all that may become a man;
    Who dares do more is none.

LADY MACBETH: What beast was't then,
 That made you break this enterprise to
   me?
 When you durst do it, then you were a
   man;
 And, to be more than what you were,
   you would
 Be so much more the man. Nor time nor
   place
 Did then adhere, and yet you would
   make both:
 They have made themselves, and that
   their fitness now
 Does unmake you. I have given suck,
   and know
 How tender 'tis to love the babe that
  milks me:
 I would, while it was smiling in my face,
 Have pluck'd my nipple from his bone-
   less gums,
 And dashed the brains out, had I so
   sworn as you
 Have done to this.

Here Lady Macbeth asserts (1) that Macbeth proposed the murder to her; (2) that he did so at a time when there was no opportunity to attack Duncan, no 'adherence' of 'time' and 'place'; (3) that he declared he would *make* an opportunity, and swore to carry out the murder.

Now it is possible that Macbeth's 'swearing' might have occurred in an interview off the stage between scenes 5 and 6 or scenes 6 and 7; and, if in that interview Lady Macbeth had with difficulty worked her husband up to a resolution, her irritation at his relapse, in sc. 7, would be very natural. But, as for Macbeth's first proposal of murder, it certainly does not occur in our play. Nor could it possibly occur in any interview off the stage; for when Macbeth and his wife first meet, 'time' and 'place' *do* adhere; 'they have made themselves.' The conclusion would seem to be, either that the proposal of the murder and probably the oath, occurred in a scene at the very beginning of the play, which scene has been lost or cut out; or else that Macbeth proposed, and swore to execute, the murder at some time prior to the action of the play. The first of these hypotheses is most improbable, and we seem driven to adopt the second, unless we consent to burden Shakespeare with a careless mistake in a very critical passage.

And, apart from unwillingness to do this, we can find a good deal to say in favour of a plan formed at a past time. It would explain Macbeth's start of fear at the prophecy of the kingdom. It would explain why Lady Macbeth, on receiving his letter, immediately resolves on action; and why, on their meeting, each knows that murder is in the mind of the other. And it is in harmony with her remarks on his probably shrinking from the act, to which, she had already thought it necessary to make him pledge himself by an oath.

Yet I find it very difficult to believe in this interpretation. It is not merely that the interest of Macbeth's struggle with himself and with his wife would be seriously diminished if we felt he had been through all this before. I think this would be so; but there are two more important objections. In the first place the violent agitation described in the words,

> If good, why do I yield to that suggestion
> Whose horrid image doth unfix my hair
> And make my seated heart knock at my
> ribs,

would surely not be natural, even in Macbeth, if the idea of murder were already quite familiar to him through conversation with his wife, and if he had already done more than 'yield' to it. It is not as if the Witches had told him that Duncan was coming to his house. In that case the perception that the moment had come to execute a merely general design might well appal him. But all that he hears is that he will one day be king—a statement which, supposing his general design, would not point to any immediate action. And, in the second place, it is hard to believe that, if Shakespeare really had imagined the murder planned and sworn to before the action of the play, he would have written the first six scenes in such a manner that practically all readers imagine quite another state of affairs, *and continue to imagine it* even after they have read in scene 7 the passage which is troubling us. Is it likely, to put it otherwise, that his idea was one which nobody seems to have divined till late in the nineteenth century? And for what possible reason could he refrain from making this idea clear to his audience, as he might so easily have done in the third scene? It seems very much more likely that he himself imagined the matter as nearly all his readers do.

But, in that case, what are we to say of this passage? I will answer first by explaining the way in which I understood it before I was aware that it had caused so much difficulty. I suppose that an interview had taken place after scene 5, a scene which shows Macbeth shrinking, and in which his last words were 'we will speak further.' In his interview, I supposed, his wife had so wrought upon him that he had at last yielded and pledged himself by oath to do the murder. As for her statement that he had 'broken the enterprise' to her, I took it to refer to his letter to her—a letter written when time and place did not adhere, for he did not yet know that Duncan was coming to visit him. In the letter, he does not, of course, openly 'break the enterprise' to her, and it is not likely that he would do such a thing in a letter; but if they had had ambitious conversations, in which each felt that some half-formed guilty idea was floating in the mind of the other, she might naturally take the words of the letter as indicating much more than they said; and then in her passionate contempt at his hesitation, and her passionate eagerness to overcome it, she might easily accuse him, doubtless with exaggeration, of having actually proposed the murder. And Macbeth, knowing that when he wrote the letter he really had been think-ing of murder, and indifferent to anything except the question whether murder should be done, would easily let her statement pass unchallenged.

This interpretation still seems to me not unnatural. The alternative (unless we adopt the idea of an agreement prior to the action of the play) is to suppose that Lady Macbeth refers throughout the passage to some interview subsequent to her husband's return, and that, in making her do so, Shakespeare simply forgot her speeches on welcoming Macbeth home, and also forgot that at any such interview 'time' and 'place' did 'adhere'. It is easy to understand such forgetfulness in a spectator and even in a reader; but it is less easy to imagine it in a poet whose conception of the two characters throughout these scenes was evidently so burningly vivid.

A. C. Bradley worked as a professor of literature and philosophy in Oxford, Glasgow, and Liverpool. He is best known for his *Oxford Lectures on Poetry* (1909) and *Shakespearean Tragedy* (1904). *Shakespearean Tragedy* includes a series of lectures in which Bradley examines the personalities of Shakespeare's characters. *(Born Cheltenham, England 1851; died 1935)*

RESPONDING

Meaning

1. List Bradley's arguments in this essay in a T-chart. Note his arguments supporting the idea that Macbeth and his wife plotted Duncan's murder before the play opened on one side, and his arguments against that idea on the other.

2. Explain which argument you support and why.

Form and Style

3. A. C. Bradley uses an interesting technique in this literary essay. He has a particular interpretation of Shakespeare's play *Macbeth*, but argues against it before arguing for it. Why might he do this? What effect does it have on you as a reader?

4. Transition statements and phrases are used by essay writers to help the reader move smoothly from one idea to the next. They frequently occur at the beginnings and ends of paragraphs to ease transition from paragraph to paragraph, but sometimes occur in the middle of paragraphs, as well. List the words, phrases, and sentences that act as transition statements in "When Was the Murder of Duncan First Plotted?"

Creative Extension

5. In pairs, practise reading the critical scene (I. vii.) Bradley cites in his third paragraph. Present two different readings to the class: one that implies Macbeth and Lady Macbeth planned killing Duncan before the play began, and one that implies they planned it after Duncan arrived at their castle. How does this activity affect your acceptance of Bradley's interpretation of the play?

6. Write a literary essay that focuses on character motivation in a novel, story, play, or other work that you have read. Use Bradley's essay as a model. Present the argument you disagree with first, then present the argument that you want to persuade your reader to accept. Incorporate quotations effectively to support your interpretations.

The Truth About Lying

Judith Viorst

Learning Goals

- analyze meaning through a pause and think technique
- examine point of view
- understand the technique of categorization in an essay
- create dramatic skits and a public interest commercial

I've been wanting to write on a subject that intrigues and challenges me: the subject of lying. I've found it very difficult to do. Everyone I've talked to has a quite intense and personal but often rather intolerant point of view about what we can—and can never *never*—tell lies about. I've finally reached the conclusion that I can't present any ultimate conclusions, for too many people would promptly disagree. Instead, I'd like to present a series of moral puzzles, all concerned with lying. I'll tell you what I think about them. Do you agree?

Social Lies

Most of the people I've talked with say that they find social lying acceptable and necessary. They think it's the civilized way for folks to behave. Without these little white lies, they say, our relationships would be short and brutish and nasty. It's arrogant, they say, to insist on being so incorruptible and so brave that you cause other people unnecessary embarrassment or pain by compulsively assailing them with your honesty. I basically agree. What about you?

Will you say to people, when it simply isn't true, "I like your new hairdo," "You're looking much better," "It's so nice to see you," "I had a wonderful time"?

Will you praise hideous presents and homely kids?

Will you decline invitations with "We're busy that night—so sorry we can't come," when the truth is you'd rather stay home than dine with the So-and-sos?

And even though, as I do, you may prefer the polite evasion of "You really cooked up a storm" instead of "The soup"—which tastes like warmed-over coffee—"is wonderful," will you, if you must, proclaim it wonderful?

There's one man I know who absolutely refuses to tell social lies. "I can't play that game," he says; "I'm simply not made that way." And his answer to the argument that saying nice things to someone doesn't cost anything is, "Yes, it does—it destroys your credibility." Now, he won't, unsolicited, offer his views on the painting you just bought, but you don't ask his frank opinion unless you want frank, and his silence at those moments when the rest of us liars are muttering, "Isn't it lovely?" is, for the most part, eloquent enough. My friend does not indulge in what he calls "flattery, false praise, and melifluous comments." When others tell fibs he will not go along. He says that social lying is lying, that little white lies are still lies. And he feels that telling lies is morally wrong. What about you?

Peace-Keeping Lies

Many people tell peace-keeping lies; lies designed to avoid irritation or argument; lies designed to shelter the liar from possible blame or pain; lies (or so it is rationalized) designed to keep trouble at bay without hurting anyone.

I tell these lies at times, and yet I always feel they're wrong. I understand why we tell them, but still they feel wrong. And whenever I lie so that someone won't disapprove of me or think less of me or holler at me, I feel I'm a bit of a coward, I feel I'm dodging responsibility, I feel . . . guilty. What about you?

Do you, when you're late for a date because you overslept, say that you're late because you got in a traffic jam?

Do you, when you forget to call a friend, say that you called several times but the line was busy?

Do you, when you didn't remember that it was your father's birthday, say that his present must be delayed in the mail?

And when you're planning a weekend in New York City and you're not in the mood to visit your mother, who lives there, do you conceal—with a lie, if you must—the fact that you'll be in New York? Or do you have the courage—or is it the cruelty?—to say, "I'll be in New York, but sorry—I don't plan on seeing you"?

(Dave and his wife Elaine have two quite different points of view on this very subject. He calls her a coward. She says she's being wise. He says she must assert her right to visit New York sometimes and not see her mother. To which she always patiently replies: "Why should we have useless fights? My mother's too old to change. We get along much better when I lie to her.")

Finally, do you keep the peace by telling your husband lies on the subject of money? Do you reduce what you really paid for your shoes? And in general do you find yourself ready, willing and able to lie to him when you make absurd mistakes or lose or break things?

"I used to have a romantic idea that part of intimacy was confessing every dumb thing that you did to your husband. But after a couple of years of that," says Laura, "have I changed my mind!"

And having changed her mind, she finds herself telling peace-keeping lies. And yes, I tell them too. What about you?

Protective Lies

Protective lies are lies folks tell—often quite serious lies—because they're convinced that the truth would be too damaging. They lie because they feel there are certain human values that supersede the wrong of having lied. They lie, not for personal gain, but because they believe it's for the good of the person they're lying to. They lie to those they love, to those who trust them most of all, on the grounds that breaking this trust is justified.

They may lie to their children on money or marital matters.

They may lie to the dying about the state of their health.

They may lie about adultery, and not—or so they insist—to save their own hide, but to save the heart and the pride of the men they are married to.

They may lie to their closest friend because the truth about her talents or son or psyche would be—or so they insist—utterly devastating.

I sometimes tell such lies, but I'm aware that it's quite presumptuous to claim I know what's best for others to know. That's called playing God. That's called manipulation and control. And we never can be sure, once we start to juggle lies, just where they'll land, exactly where they'll roll.

And furthermore, we may find ourselves lying in order to back up the lies that are backing up the lie we initially told.

And furthermore—let's be honest—if conditions were reversed, we certainly wouldn't want anyone lying to us.

Yet, having said all that, I still believe that there are times when protective lies must nonetheless be told. What about you?

If your Dad had a very bad heart and you had to tell him some bad family news, which would you choose: to tell him the truth or to lie?

If your dearly beloved brother selected a wife whom you deeply disliked, would you reveal your feelings or would you fake it?

Trust-Keeping Lies

Another group of lies are trust-keeping lies, lies that involve triangulation, with A (that's you) telling lies to B on behalf of C (whose trust you'd promised to keep). Most people concede that once you've agreed not to betray a friend's confidence, you can't betray it, even if you must lie. But I've talked with people who don't want you telling them anything that they might be called on to lie about.

"I don't tell lies for myself," says Fran, "and I don't want to have to tell them for other people." Which means, she agrees, that if her best friend is having an affair, she absolutely doesn't want to know about it.

"Are you saying," her best friend asks, "that if I went off with a lover and asked you to tell my husband I'd been with you, that you wouldn't lie for me, that you'd betray me?"

Fran is very pained but very adamant. "I wouldn't want to betray you, so . . . don't ask me."

Fran's best friend is shocked. What about you?

Do you believe you can have close friends if you're not prepared to receive their deepest secrets?

Do you believe you must always lie for your friends?

Do you believe, if your friend tells a secret that turns out to be quite immoral or illegal, that once you've promised to keep it, you must keep it?

And what if your friend were your boss—if you were perhaps one of the President's men—would you betray or lie for him over, say, Watergate?[1]

As you can see, these issues get terribly sticky.

It's my belief that once we've promised to keep a trust, we must tell lies to keep it. I also believe that we can't tell Watergate lies. And if these two statements strike you as quite contradictory, you're right—they're quite contradictory. But for now they're the best I can do. What about you?

Some say that truth will out and thus you might as well tell the truth. Some say you can't regain the trust that lies lose. Some say that even though the truth may never be revealed, our lies pervert and damage our relationships. Some say . . . well, here's what some of them have to say.

---

[1] Watergate was the political scandal in the United States in which the government and President Richard Nixon tried to cover-up their bugging attempt during the 1972 election campaign. Nixon was impeached for his "lies."

"I'm a coward," says Grace, "about telling close people important, diffi-cult truths. I find that I'm unable to carry it off. And so if something is bothering me, it keeps building up inside till I end up just not seeing them any more."

"I suffer most from the misconception that children can't take the truth," says Emily. "But I'm starting to see that what's harder and more damaging for them is being told lies, is *not* being told the truth."

"I'm afraid," says Joan, "that we often wind up feeling a bit of contempt for the people we lie to."

And then there are those who have no talent for lying.

"Over the years, I tried to lie," a friend of mine explained, "but I was always found out and I always got punished. I guess I gave myself away because I feel guilty about any kind of lying. It looks as if I'm stuck with telling the truth."

For those of us, however, who are good at telling lies, for those of us who lie and don't get caught, the question of whether or not to lie can be a hard and serious moral problem. I liked the remark of a friend of mine who said, "I'm willing to lie. But just as a last resort—the truth's always better."

"Because," he explained, though others may completely accept the lie I'm telling, I don't."

I tend to feel that way too.

What about you?

In addition to books of poetry, Judith Viorst is the author of several works in the fields of psychology and biology including *Imperfect Control* (2000). She has also written more than a dozen children's books. A graduate of the Washington Psychoanalytic Institute, she is the recipient of several awards for her journalism and writings on psychology.

RESPONDING

Meaning

1. Review the essay and jot down your answers to the questions Viorst asks you, the reader, about lying. Is there any contradiction in your responses? Are there any contradictions in her responses? If so, explain how that can be so.

2. Demonstrate your understanding of the distinctions between the four kinds of lies she talks about by explaining them in your own words. Is there any category of lie that Viorst has omitted? Explain.

Form and Style

3. a) Writers of expository essays often choose to use the third-person point of view. Judith Viorst, however, does not, preferring first-person. What effect does her choice have on you, the reader?

   b) In several places in her essay (usually at the end of a paragraph), Viorst does something unusual. She switches from first-person to second-person point of view to address the reader directly: "What about you?" Why do you think she does this?

4. Judith Viorst uses the technique of categorization to organize her essay. Explain how she does this and what she achieves by doing it.

Creative Extension

5. Write four short dramatic skits that demonstrate the four kinds of lies Viorst discusses in her essay. Each skit can be scripted for from one to four characters. When you are finished, perform your skits for the class.

6. Create a "public interest commercial" about lying. First decide whether your commercial is going to be for or against lying, then write a script for a 30-second TV ad. Decide on props and costumes. If you have the equipment, videotape your commercial and present it to the class.

How to Paint a Fresco

✑ Adam Goodheart

Learning Goals

• summarize an
  author's theme
  and purpose

• analyze style
  in an informal
  expository essay

• adapt information
  into a visual
  representation

• write a "how-to"
  expository essay

Although it must be painted in a very short time, a fresco will last a very long time—that is its great advantage. Many of the masterpieces of the golden age of fresco (from the 14th through the 18th centuries) are as brilliant now as when they were first painted. If you want to fresco a cathedral or palazzo today, you may have a few problems—papal and ducal commissions are scarcer than they once were, and the great Renaissance masters are no longer accepting applications for apprenticeships. Fortunately, a few of their trade secrets have come down to us through the ages.

Equipment

Lime

Sand

Water

A trowel

Paper

A needle

A small bag of charcoal dust

The bristles of a white hog

The hair of bears, sables, and martens

The quills of vultures, geese, hens and doves

Ochre, burnt grapevines, lapis lazuli

Egg yolks

Goat's milk

1. *Preparing the wall.* Cennino Cennini, a Tuscan master, advised pupils in 1437 to "begin by decking yourselves with this attire: Enthusiasm, Reverence, Obedience, and Constancy." You'd do better to deck yourself with some old clothes, though, since the first stage of the process is quite messy. Soak the wall thoroughly and coat it with coarse plaster, two parts sand to one part lime, leaving the surface uneven. (Andrea Pozzo, a 17th-century expert, recommended hiring a professional mason to do this, since "the lime makes a foul odour, which is injurious to the head.")

2. *Tracing your design.* You should already have extensive drawings for your fresco—these will be much sought by scholars and collectors in centuries to come. Make a full-size sketch, on sturdy paper, of a section of the fresco that you can paint in a day. Then go over the drawing with a needle, pricking holes along every line. Lay a coat of fine plaster on a section of the wall corresponding to the location, size and shape of the sketch, and press the sketch against the plaster. Fill a loosely woven bag with charcoal dust and strike it lightly all over the surface of the paper. Now peel the sketch off. Your design will be outlined in black dots on the wet plaster, giving you a guide for the day's work.

3. *Painting.* Time is of the essence: You must paint the plaster while it is wet, so that the pigments bind chemically with the lime. That gives you about six hours, although some painters had tricks to prolong drying. (Piero della Francesca packed the plaster with wet rags; problem was, this left indentations that are still visible after 500 years.) Use top-quality brushes. One 17th-century Flemish master recommended those made of "fish hair" (he probably meant seal fur), but most painters made brushes from bear, marten, or sable hairs inserted in hollow quills. Cennini suggested the bristles of a white hog for the coarser work. As for paints, every artist had his own favourite recipes, but all agreed that mineral pigments such as ochre or ground stone mixed with water were best. Avoid white lead. One 14th-century Umbrian used it to paint a nursing infant; the lime turned the white black and, the milky babe into a "devilish changeling." A few pigments, such as dark blue azurite, must be mixed with egg yolk or goat's milk and added after the fresco is dry. Such colours will prove less durable.

   Money is a consideration in choosing materials. When Michelangelo frescoed the Sistine ceiling, expenses came out of his fee, so he used cheap blue malt for the sky. Twenty years later, when he did the *Last Judgement*, Michelangelo used semi-precious lapis lazuli for blue, since the pope was paying for the paint. (He made up for it by using burnt grapevines for black.)

4. *Casualties of style.* Realism, while a worthy goal, has its perils. Spinello Aretino, a 14th-century Tuscan, is said to have painted a fresco that depicted Lucifer with such hideous accuracy that the Evil One himself

came to the artist in a dream and demanded an explanation. Spinello went half-mad with fear and died shortly thereafter. On the other hand, a Florentine woodcut from 1500 depicts a painter who has portrayed the Virgin Mary so skillfully that when he falls off the scaffold, she reaches out of the fresco and saves him.

Warning

Frescoing ceilings can be rough on your back. While working on the Sistine Chapel, Michelangelo wrote a poem complaining: "I've already grown a goiter at this drudgery. . . . With my beard toward heaven . . . I am bent like a bow." Don't be discouraged, though. Bad posture is a small price to pay for immortality.

A detail from Michelangelo's fresco of the Sistine Chapel in Rome, Italy, painted in 1508–1512.

Fresco painting was practised in many parts of the world. This detail is from a fresco painted in Ajunta, India in the Gupta style fourth to late sixth century.

Adam Goodheart is a freelance writer in Washington, DC. He writes book reviews and essays for the *New York Times*, *The Washington Post*, and *Atlantic Monthly*. He is also a columnist for *Civilization Magazine* and a member of the editorial board of the *American Scholar*.

RESPONDING

Meaning

1. Explain what Cennino Cennini meant when he gave the following advice to student fresco painters: "Begin by decking yourself with this attire: Enthusiasm, Reverence, Obedience, and Constancy." What do you think of his advice? What other, current activities might his advice be good for today?

2. The topic of this essay can be found in its title: "How to Paint a Fresco." What do you think the main message or controlling idea of the essay is? Summarize it in one sentence.

Form and Style

3. This expository essay is written in an informal style. Provide specific examples from the essay of diction, sentence structure, and tone that contribute to this style. (*Diction* is the author's choice of words. *Sentence structure* refers to the length and complexity of the sentences the author writes. *Tone* is the overall mood or feeling the author conveys in a piece of writing.)

4. Unlike the essay by Anita Rau Badami, this essay does not use poetic or figurative language and imagery. Why do you think this is so? What is Goodheart trying to accomplish in this essay, and how does the absence of poetic imagery help him to accomplish his objective?

Creative Extension

5. Convert the written information on how to paint a fresco in this essay into visual instructions, as in a flow chart. Create a poster to display your instructions or develop them into a PowerPoint presentation.

6. Choose another skill or activity related to a sport, hobby, art, or craft that you have learned. Write a "how-to" expository essay on this activity or skill. Use Goodheart's essay as a model but do not use all of the same headings. You may also decide to use a different tone.

Wonders of the World

❧

How do different people, in different times and places, define what is wonderful?

If you were asked to list seven wonders of the modern world, what would your list include? What does "wonder" mean to you? Through the centuries, peoples around the world have always identified "wonders" of their world, in their time and place. Through an expository essay, poems, novel excerpt, and photo series, this Echo section explores different perspectives on what "wonder" means.

Learning Goals
- examine a theme from a variety of perspectives
- explore how different forms, techniques, language, and styles convey meaning
- create original works based on a theme

Seven Wonders

❧ *Lewis Thomas*

This expository essay by Lewis Thomas outlines the seven things he thinks "most wonderful" in the modern world. To keep the reader intrigued and entertained, he describes the last six wonders first, and saves his first wonder for last.

A while ago I received a letter from a magazine editor inviting me to join six other people at dinner to make a list of the Seven Wonders of the Modern World, to replace the seven old, out-of-date Wonders. I replied that I couldn't manage it, not on short order anyway, but still the question keeps hanging around in the lobby of my mind. I had to look up the old biodegradable Wonders, the Hanging Gardens of Babylon and all the rest, and then I had to look up that word "wonder" to make sure I understood what it meant. It occurred to me that if the magazine could get seven people to agree on a list of any such seven things you'd have the modern Seven Wonders right there at the dinner table.

Wonder is a word to wonder about. It contains a mixture of messages: something marvellous and miraculous, surprising, raising unanswerable questions about itself, making the observer wonder, even raising skeptical questions like, "I *wonder* about that." Miraculous and marvellous are clues; both words come from an ancient Indo-European root meaning simply to smile or to laugh. Anything wonderful is something to smile in the presence of, in admiration (which, by the way, comes from the same root, along with, of all telling words, "mirror").

I decided to try making a list, not for the magazine's dinner party but for this occasion: seven things I wonder about the most.

I shall hold the first for the last and move along.

My Number Two Wonder is a bacterial species never seen on the face of the earth until 1982, creatures never dreamed of before, living violation of what we used to regard as the laws of nature, things literally straight out of Hell. Or anyway what we used to think of as Hell, the hot unlivable interior of the earth. Such regions have recently come into scientific view from the research submarines designed to descend twenty-five hundred metres or more to the edge of deep holes in the sea bottom, where open vents spew superheated seawater in plumes from chimneys in the earth's crust, known to oceanographic scientists as "black smokers." This is not just hot water, or steam, or even steam under pressure as exists in a laboratory autoclave (which we have relied upon for decades as the surest way to destroy all microbial life). This is extremely hot water under extremely high pressure, with temperatures in excess of 300 degrees centigrade. At such heat, the existence of life as we know it would be simply inconceivable. Proteins and DNA would fall apart, enzymes would melt away, anything alive would die instantaneously. We have long since ruled out the possibility of life on Venus because of that planet's comparable temperature; we have ruled out the possibility of life in the earliest years of this planet, four billion or so years ago, on the same ground.

B.J.A. Baross and J.W. Deming have recently discovered the presence of thriving colonies of bacteria in water fished directly from these deep-sea vents. Moreover, when brought to the surface, encased in titanium syringes and sealed in pressurized chambers heated to 250 degrees centigrade, the bacteria not only survive but reproduce themselves enthusiastically. They can be killed only by chilling them down in boiling water.

And yet they look just like ordinary bacteria. Under the electron microscope they have the same essential structure—cell walls, ribosomes, and all. If they were, as is now being suggested, the original archbacteria, ancestors of us all, how did they or their progeny ever learn to cool down? I cannot think of a more wonderful trick.

My Number Three Wonder is *oncideres*, a species of beetle encountered by a pathologist friend of mine who lives in Houston and has a lot of mimosa trees in his backyard. This beetle is not new, but it qualifies as a Modern Wonder because of the exceedingly modern questions raised for evolutionary biologists about the three consecutive things on the mind of the female of the species. Her first thought is for a mimosa tree, which she finds and climbs, ignoring all other kinds of trees in her vicinity. Her second thought is for the laying of eggs, which she does by crawling out on a limb, cutting a longitudinal slit with her mandible and depositing her eggs beneath the slit. Her third and last thought concerns the welfare of her offspring; beetle larvae cannot survive in live wood, so she backs up a foot or so and cuts a neat circular girdle all around the limb, through the bark and down into the cambium. It takes her eight hours to finish this cabinetwork. Then she leaves and where she goes I do not know. The limb dies from the girding, falls to the ground in the next breeze, the larvae feed and grow into the next generation, and the questions lie there unanswered. How on earth did these three linked thoughts in her mind evolve together in evolution? How could any one of the three become fixed as beetle behaviour by itself, without the other two? What are the odds favouring three totally separate bits of behaviour—like a particular tree, cutting a slit for eggs, and then girdling the limb—happening together by random chance among a beetle's genes? Does this smart beetle know what she is doing? And how did the mimosa tree enter the picture in its evolution? Left to themselves, unpruned, mimosa trees have a life expectancy of twenty-five to thirty years. Pruned each year, which is what the beetle's girdling labour accomplishes, the tree can flourish for a century. The mimosa-beetle relationship is an elegant example of symbiotic partnership, a phenomenon now recognized as pervasive in nature. It is good for us to have around on our intellectual mantelpiece such creatures as this insect and its friend the tree, for they keep reminding us how little we know about nature.

The Fourth Wonder on my list is an infectious agent known as the scrapie virus, which causes a fatal disease of the brain in sheep, goats, and several laboratory animals. A close cousin of scrapie is the C-J virus, the cause of some cases of senile dementia in human beings. These are called "slow viruses," for the excellent reason that an animal exposed to infection today will not become ill until a year and a half or two years from today. The agent, whatever it is, can propagate itself in abundance from a few infectious units today to more than a billion next year. I use the phrase "whatever it is" advisedly. Nobody has yet been able to find any DNA or RNA in the scrapie or C-J viruses. It may be there, but if so it exists in amounts too small to detect. Meanwhile, there is plenty of protein, leading to a serious proposal that the virus may indeed be *all* protein. But protein, so far as we know, does not replicate itself all by itself, not on this planet anyway. Looked at this way, the scrapie agent seems the strangest thing in all biology and, until someone in some laboratory figures out what it is, a candidate for Modern Wonder.

My Fifth Wonder is the olfactory receptor cell, located in the epithelial tissue high in the nose, sniffing the air for clues to the environment, the fragrance of friends, the smell of leaf smoke, breakfast, nighttime and bedtime, and a rose, even, it is said, the odour of sanctity. The cell that does these things, firing off urgent messages into the deepest parts of the brain, switching on one strange unaccountable memory after another, is itself a proper brain cell, a certified neuron belonging to the brain but miles away out in the open air, nosing around the world. How it manages to make sense of what it senses, discriminating between jasmine and anything else non-jasmine with infallibility, is one of the deep secrets of neurobiology. This would be wonder enough, but there is more. This population of brain cells, unlike any other neurons of the vertebrate central nervous system, turns itself over every few weeks; cells wear out, die, and are replaced by brand-new cells rewired to the same deep centres miles back in the brain, sensing and remembering the same wonderful smells. If and when we reach an understanding of these cells and their functions, including the moods and whims under their governance, we will know a lot more about the mind than we do now, a world away.

Sixth on my list is, I hesitate to say, another insect, the termite. This time, though, it is not the single insect that is the Wonder, it is the collectivity. There is nothing at all wonderful about a single, solitary termite, any more than we can imagine a genuinely solitary human being; no such thing. Two or three termites gathered together on a dish are not much better; they may move about and touch each other nervously, but nothing happens. But keep adding more termites until they reach a critical mass, and then the miracle begins. As though they had suddenly received a piece of extraordinary news, they organize in platoons and begin stacking up pellets to precisely the right height, then turning the arches to connect the columns, constructing the cathedral and its chambers in which the colony will live out its life for the decades ahead, air-conditioned and humidity-controlled, following the chemical blueprint coded in their genes, flawlessly, stone-blind. They are not the dense mass of individual insects they appear to be; they are an organism, a thoughtful, meditative brain on a million legs. All we really know about this new thing is that it does its architecture and engineering by a complex system of chemical signals.

The Seventh Wonder of the modern world is a human child, any child. I used to wonder about childhood and the evolution of our species. It seemed to me unparsimonious to keep expending all that energy on such a long period of vulnerability and defencelessness, with nothing to show for it, in biological terms, beyond the feckless, irresponsible pleasure of childhood. After all, I used to think, it is one sixth of a whole human life span! Why didn't our evolution take care of that, allowing us to jump catlike from our juvenile to our adult (and, as I thought) productive stage of life? I had forgotten about language, the single human trait that marks us out as specifically human, the property that enables our survival as the most compulsively, biologically, obsessively social of all creatures on earth, more interdependent and interconnected even than the famous social insects. I had forgotten that, and forgotten that children *do* that in childhood. Language is what childhood is for.

There is another related but different creature, nothing so wonderful as a human child, nothing so hopeful, something to worry about all day and all night. It is *us*, aggregated together in our collective, critical masses. So far, we have learned how to be useful to each other only when we connect in small groups—families, circles of friends, once in a while (although still rarely) committees. The drive to be useful is encoded in our genes. But when we gather in very large numbers, as in the modern nation-state, we seem capable of levels of folly and self-destruction to be found nowhere else in all of Nature.

As a species, taking all in all, we are still too young, too juvenile, to be trusted. We have spread across the face of the earth in just a thousand years, no time at all as evolution clocks time, covering all parts of the planet, endangering other forms of life, and now threatening ourselves. As a species, we have everything in the world to learn about living, but we may be running out of time. Provisionally, but only provisionally, we are a Wonder.

And now the first on my list, the one I put off at the beginning of making a list, the first of all Wonders of the modern world. To name this one, you have to redefine the world as it has indeed been redefined in this most scientific of all centuries. We named the place we live in the *world* long ago, from the Indo-European root *wiros*, which meant man. We now live in the whole universe, that stupefying piece of expanding geometry. Our suburbs are the local solar system, into which, sooner or later, we will spread life, and then, likely beyond into the galaxy. Of all celestial bodies within reach or view, as far as we can see, out to the edge, the most wonderful and marvellous and mysterious is turning out to be our own planet earth. There is nothing to match it anywhere, not yet anyway.

It is a living system, an immense organism, still developing, regulating itself, making its own oxygen, maintaining its own temperature, keeping all its infinite living parts connected and interdependent, including us. It is the strangest of all places, and there is everything in the world to learn about it. It can keep us awake and jubilant with questions for millennia ahead, if we can learn not to meddle and not to destroy. Our great hope is in being such a young species, thinking in language only a short while, still learning, still growing up.

We are not like the social insects. They have only the one way of doing things and they will do it forever, coded for that way. We are coded differently, not just for binary choices, *go* or *no-go*. We can go four ways at once, depending on how the air feels: *go*, *no-go*, but also *maybe*, plus *what the hell let's give it a try*. We are in for one surprise after another if we keep at it and keep alive. We can build structures for human society never seen before, thoughts never thought before, music never heard before.

Provided we do not kill ourselves off, and provided we can connect ourselves by the affection and respect for which I believe our genes are also coded, there is no end to what we might do on or off this planet.

At this early stage in our evolution, now through our infancy and into our childhood and then, with luck, our growing up, what our species needs most of all, right now, is simply a future.

✑   The son of a surgeon, Lewis Thomas was also a medical doctor. He had a distinguished medical career, but always displayed literary ambition and published a number of poems. In 1974, he published the essay collection *The Lives of a Cell: Notes of a Biology Watcher*, which found a sizeable audience and won the National Book Award. Later essay collections include *Late Night Thoughts on Listening to Mahler's Ninth Symphony* (1983). *(Born Flushing, New York 1913; died 1993)*

RESPONDING

Meaning

1. a) List Lewis's seven wonders. What is your opinion of his choices? Do you detect any bias in his choices? Explain.
    b) Make a list of your own seven wonders of the modern world. What biases does your list reveal? Consider the list a friend made. What biases are revealed? What does this tell you about how people choose what is wonderful to them?

2. a) Which of Lewis's wonders most intrigued you? What about his description did you find intriguing? Explain.
    b) Which of Lewis's seven wonders was the easiest to understand? Which was the most difficult? Summarize each one in your own words.

Form and Style

3. Reread the first four paragraphs of this essay. How does Lewis ease the reader into the topic of his essay? Create an outline of the first four paragraphs, then share your findings in small groups. Discuss how effective you find Lewis's introduction and why.

4. a) This is an expository essay that uses listing as an organizational technique. Note the transition phrases and sentences Lewis uses to introduce each wonder. How are these phrases and sentences similar? How are they different? Explain in a few sentences how effective you found these transitions.
    b) In small groups, discuss the purpose of the final four paragraphs in this essay. How does the tone of the essay shift in these paragraphs? Why do you think Lewis included them? Report your interpretations to the class.

Creative Extension

5. Create a Web site that includes information about the seven ancient wonders, some modern wonders, and your seven personal wonders. Include illustrations and short summaries. Add links to already existing sites about the seven ancient wonders and some modern wonders.

6. Prepare a multimedia presentation about the seven ancient wonders, some modern wonders, or your personal wonders. Include speech, visuals, and at least seven different musical selections. Follow up with a written analysis of your presentation, explaining why you chose the visuals and music you did, and what techniques you used to convey your ideas.

Ozymandias

Percy Bysshe Shelley

This sonnet by one of the most famous Romantic poets of the nineteenth century tells the story of a traveller who comes across the ruins of an incredible statue built to commemorate a once-powerful ruler. Ozymandias is another name for Ramses II, an Egyptian pharoah who ruled during the thirteenth century and was given to commissioning statues of himself.

I met a traveller from an antique land
Who said: Two vast and trunkless legs of stone
Stand in the desert . . . Near them, on the sand,
Half sunk, a shattered visage lies, whose frown,
And wrinkled lip, and sneer of cold command,
Tell that its sculptor well those passions read
Which yet survive, stamped on these lifeless things,
The hand that mocked them, and the heart that fed:
And on the pedestal these words appear:
"My name is Ozymandius, king of kings:
Look on my works, ye Mighty, and despair!"
Nothing beside remains. Round the decay
Of that colossal wreck, boundless and bare
The lone and level sands stretch far away.

The English lyric poet Percy Bysshe Shelley was a leading figure in the Romantic movement. He fought all his life for political freedom. This fight is reflected in the early poem *Queen Mab* (1813). He later wrote tragedies, lyric dramas such as the well-known *Prometheus Unbound* (1820), and lyrical poems such as "Ode to the West Wind." He drowned while sailing in Italy. *Ozymandias* was written in 1817. *(Born Sussex, England 1792; died 1822)*

Connecting

1. What is the irony of "Look on my works, ye Mighty, and despair!" given the current condition of Ozymandias's statue?
2. Explain the theme of this poem.
3. Statues of Ramses are not listed among the seven wonders of the ancient world, although his pyramid is. Why do you think this poem is included in this Echo section, which is dedicated to wonders of the world?
4. What natural wonder might this poem be inadvertently celebrating?

The Next Best Thing

John Ralston Saul

The following excerpt from a novel by Canadian writer John Ralston Saul depicts a scene in which a London-based Eastern antiquities expert named Spenser arrives at the ancient religious city of Pagan in Myanmar (formerly Burma). Although he loves and reveres the antiquities he studies, Spenser is there to plunder the site illegally. Nevertheless, he is captured by the wonder of what he sees.

The rest of the morning was spent pounding over the dry countryside of the plain. The roads, paved or not, were a series of pot-holes and dry river beds without bridges. When the sun was at its highest, they opened the rear canvas to let in air and began to skirt south around the rail centre of Thazi on a dirt track. The fields were empty. The land was flat and grey. After a time it became flat and red. In the middle of the afternoon the monotony was disturbed by a dead volcano, Mount Popa, a lone deformation of the plain. Then the flatness rolled up into small hills covered with grape-vines, which were succeeded by sugar-palms. Beyond them the horizon was broken in an irrational manner that could only have been man-made.

Small pagodas and temples began rising like young corn in the fields on either side. This crop grew thicker and the ruins larger until the truck was rolling through a forest of ruins, each of which sat calmly, throwing long evening shadows across the ploughed land. There was no hint of the people they had once served. All the houses, even the palaces, had been built of wood and had disappeared a few years after Pagan was abandoned. The truck stopped because neither the driver nor Eddie knew which way to go. Spenser was sent forward to squeeze into the cabin. He had no need of his map; the plan of the site was fixed in his mind. The dirt track he had directed them on to wound through the ruins aimlessly—he did not say he had chosen it in order to pass by what he would not get another chance to see. They should have noticed it in his eyes or by his silence, because he said not a single word; only raising a finger periodically to point the way, his mind lost among the beauty of the ruins. Eventually he brought them to a halt beneath a large square temple, the Sulamani, which stood like a two-tiered wedding-cake a mile from the core of the site.

A heavy kick broke the rusted chain holding the temple door closed and they all filed into the first corridor. The Shans left their shoes at the entrance, went in to kneel before a large ruined brick buddha, then settled down there in the dust, while Spenser climbed up a narrow flight of stairs to the first terrace, fifty feet[1] above the ground.

The sun was setting beyond the Irrawaddy, which flowed two miles[2] wide and brown at an unhurried pace. On its near bank a cluster of a thousand temples were silhouetted. To either side and behind were thousands more—square and circular players set for an unknown game.

'Where is the museum?'

Spenser did not hear him the first time. He heard nothing extraneous. Blake touched him on the shoulder and repeated the question. Spenser turned to find him examining the buildings through his field-glasses, and Santana, ashen from the effort of the stairs.

'You see the largest building between us and the river?' Spenser pointed. It was a white square of six receding storeys, on top of which sat a golden pagoda that tapered to a pinnacle. 'The museum is 100 yards[3] beyond it and to the right.'

Blake was still examining the white and gold pagoda. Apparently he had not expected anything so extraordinary.

It was Santana who noticed and said, 'That is the Ananda. The most wonderful.'

Spenser broke in without thinking, 'Two hundred and ten feet[4] high, built as a cross, two hundred and ninety feet[5] long each way.' He was chanting an incantation to beauty; to the immortality of perfect form. 'The central cube is an eighty-two foot[6] square, begun by King Kyanzittha in 1091 with the finest workmen of Asia. Inside, there are one thousand five hundred statues sitting untouched in the niches for which he had them sculpted. In the world there is not a building more symmetrical or complete. Or abandoned.'

He hardly noticed the discomfort caused by the impassioned recital and turned away from the two men to sit on the stones of the terrace until

---

[1] 15 m; [2] 3.2 km (one mile = 0.3 km); [3] 91 m; [4] 64 m; [5] 88 m; [6] 25 m

the day was gone and the moon had risen and the golden pinnacles had ceased to reflect light. Now that the jungle was behind and he had the Ananda in sight, within reach, its spires and domes entered into communion with him; they danced for him, dragging in their train all of the temples and the pagodas; the thousands of ruins coming alive with the only living thing that remained in them—the genius of man. No. Not of man. Transmitted through man and free of his temporal human touch the moment the creation was complete. Spenser ceded to the dance for as long as there was light and when all was still on the obscured horizon he rose to his feet to find the other two men no longer there.

☙ John Ralston Saul is a writer of both social criticism and fiction. He was named Canadian Humanist of the Year in 1995 and won the Governor General's Award for Non-Fiction a year later. His articles have appeared in international publications including the *New York Times* and London's *Spectator*. *The Next Best Thing* was published in 1986. (*Born Ottawa, Ontario 1947*)

Connecting

1. What features of the city of Pagan might qualify it as one of the wonders of the ancient world?

2. Why is the Ananda temple "the most wonderful"?

3. How does "There was no hint of the people they had once served" connect with Shelley's poem "Ozymandias"?

4. Reread the last paragraph of this excerpt. How might Spenser define "wonderful" or characterize the wonders of the world? How well do the other wonders mentioned in this Echo section fit Spenser's definition of "wonder"? Explain.

A Grain of Rice

☙ F. R. Scott

This poem by Canadian F. R. Scott alternates images of the earth's "majestic rhythms"—such as weather—with humanity's "tiny disturbances"—such as war. Through these varying images, Scott shows us how wonderful the world is and how humans can appreciate it.

> Such majestic rhythms, such tiny disturbances.
> The rain of the monsoon falls, an inescapable treasure,
> Hundreds of millions live
> Only because of the certainty of this season,
>   The turn of the wind.

The frame of our human house rests on the motion
Of earth and of moon, the rise of continents,
Invasion of deserts, erosion of hills,
     The capping of ice.

Today, while Europe tilted, drying the Baltic,
I read of a battle between brothers in anguish,
     A flag moved a mile.

And today, from a curled leaf cocoon, in the course of its rhythm,
I saw the break of a shell, the creation
Of a great Asian moth, radiant, fragile,
Incapable of not being born, and trembling
     To live its brief moment.

Religions build walls round our love, and science
Is equal of error and truth. Yet always we find
Such ordered purpose in cell and in galaxy,
So great a glory in life-thrust and mind-range,
Such widening frontiers to draw out our longings,
     We grow to one world
     Through enlargement of wonder.

The Canadian poet, law teacher, and social philosopher F. R. Scott studied politics. During his life, he argued major civil-rights cases before the Supreme Court. Through his involvement with Canadian literary figures and journals, he became an important figure in Canadian poetry. His *Selected Poems* (1966) won a Governor General's Award. (*Born Québec City, Québec 1899; died 1985*)

Connecting

1. List the majestic rhythms and tiny disturbances Scott writes about in his poem. How do they exemplify the statement "the frame of our human house rests on the motion of earth and of moon"?

2. What are examples of the "ordered purpose in cell and in galaxy" in the poem? What are some examples from outside the poem?

3. What, based on this poem, does F. R. Scott find wonderful? What does the title of his poem have to do with wonder?

Wonders Through Time

Photo Series

Some Ancient Wonders of the World

Great Pyramid of Ghiza (right)

Among the pyramids of Ghiza in Egypt stands the Great Pyramid, the only one of the original seven wonders of the ancient world still standing. The Great Pyramid is the tomb of Khufu, or Cheops, who began building it in 2560 BCE. The Pyramid took 20 years to build and was a masterpiece of mathematics and stonework. Its sides are oriented to the four compass points and slant upwards at 51 degrees, 51 minutes to the topmost point. It is built of over 2 million blocks of stone, which fit so tightly together on the inside that a fingernail cannot be inserted between them. The sides are so precisely the same length there is less than 0.1% error in their comparative lengths. When originally built, the Great Pyramid was the tallest structure on earth, 145.75 m in height. Inside the Pyramid is the King's chamber and sarcophagus, in addition to a number of corridors, galleries, and escape shafts.

Hanging Gardens of Babylon

Ancient Greek travellers tell us the Hanging Gardens of Babylon were miraculous; they were planted on a series of large terraces or tiers. The tiers were supported at their base by huge arched vaults and columns, so the gardens were literally hoisted in the air above the viewers' heads. The garden tiers overflowed with complicated fountain and irrigation systems, lush flowers, fruit trees, and grass. They were believed to have been built by King Nebuchadnezzar II, who ruled Mesopotamia from the royal city of Babylon between 604 and 562 BCE. He is reputed to have built the gardens to please his wife who was from a mountainous region and missed that landscape and the green vegetation.

Machu Pichu

Machu Pichu is not on the list of the seven ancient wonders of the world originally compiled by the Greeks (who focused on wonders within their world), but it is undoubtedly an ancient wonder. The site of an ancient Incan city in Peru, it is an amazing example of the Incas' building and engineering skills. The city contains running water, drainage systems, food production capability, and very advanced stone structures. Machu Pichu was designated a UNESCO World Heritage Site in 1983.

Some Modern Wonders of the World

Petronas Towers

The Petronas Towers have been listed among the wonders of the modern world. The towers were completed in 1998 in Kuala Lumpur, Malaysia, and are the tallest buildings on the face of the earth. They are matching skyscrapers built of steel, concrete, and glass and are joined by a sky bridge about half way up. Each one is 88 stories tall; the additional architectural point and spire bring their total height to 452 metres. They are supported by a 4.5 metre thick raft foundation which sits on top of concrete pylons. There is some controversy associated with the "world's tallest building" designation and the Petronas Towers may soon be eclipsed. The Shanghai World Financial Centre is expected to top a height of 460 metres. The Petronas Towers are home to the offices of Malaysia's Petronas Oil Company.

The Grand Canyon

The Grand Canyon has been considered one of the modern natural wonders of the world. It is located in the northwest corner of Arizona. It is famous for its red dirt, which lies on the canyon floor, and for being one of the largest—in terms of length, depth and width—canyons in the world. It is 446 km long and ranges in depth up to a maximum of 1829 m from rim to river. It is up to 29 km wide. To appreciate this size without seeing it, you need to know that it takes a person on a mule two full days to go from the rim to the bottom and back again; a person who is walking takes three days. Raft trips from one end of the canyon to the other take two weeks. The Colorado River, which flows a total of 2333 km from the Rocky Mountains to the Gulf of California in Mexico lies at the bottom of the Grand Canyon. The Colorado's flow action, in combination with other, more minor, erosion forces, carved the Canyon over the last five to six million years. The Canyon is famous for its exposure of layers of different kinds and ages of rock.

Connecting

1. What do the ancient wonders tell us about the people who decided they were wonderful? What do they seem to value?

2. The remaining wonders illustrated were all labelled "wonderful" by people in modern times. What does this tell you about the people who labelled them? What might their values be?

3. How well do the places and things in these photographs fit your criteria of "wonder" or "wonderful"? Should they be considered wonders of the world? Are there Canadian "wonders" you would include? Explain.

4. Compare the photo essay wonders to those described in the essay, novel excerpt, and two poems in this Echo section. How are they similar? How are they different?

REFLECTING ON THE ECHO

1. Do research to discover some other things that people consider wonderful, including the modern and natural wonders of the world. Consider everything you have read and seen on the topic while you write an essay that answers the question: How do different people, in different times and places, define what is wonderful?

2. Create a found poem on the topic of wonder that incorporates phrases and images from each of the reading and viewing selections in this Echo section. Present your poem to the class along with an explanation of your writing process.

3. Imagine it is the year 3025 and you have found a time capsule from the year 2000. The time capsule was dedicated to the theme of wonder. In it you find the reading and viewing selections from this Echo section, along with a number of other items. What conclusions do you draw about what people found wonderful in the 21st century? Suggest four other items that could be in the capsule and explain why they are there.

My Canada

ɕ Anita Rau Badami

Learning Goals

- identify an author's theme
- write a summary
- analyze use of figures of speech in non-fiction
- create a narrative essay, photo essay, or travel brochure

Early one morning in June last year, my family and I travelled from Vancouver to Tofino, a small town on the western coast of Vancouver Island. We had come in search of whales, particularly the magnificent orca. If we were lucky, we might even get to see a whole pod of them.

When I was growing up in India, nothing had seemed more remote and exotic to me than these great mammals. I had seen pictures of them in geography texts and wildlife magazines, but the depictions were extremely unsatisfactory. The creatures were generally obscured by water or captured as a dim submarine shape by an underwater camera—sometimes there was merely a spout of water shooting upwards from a brief arc of grey that might well have been the shoulder of a wave. By the time I left India for Canada, the orca had assumed mythical proportions, and a huge desire had ballooned in me to see this whale in its natural habitat.

The trip to Tofino had been inspired by an advertisement for whale-watching tours in a Vancouver paper. "Let's go this weekend," I had said to my husband and son. After several telephone calls to book a room in a hotel, we were on our way.

It was a grey morning when we left to catch the ferry to Victoria. But nothing could keep my hopes down; we were going to see those whales no matter what. The intensity of my longing, I was convinced, would keep the rain away from Tofino. The crossing to Victoria was rough and cold, and by the time we had driven across the island and reached the small coastal town, we could barely see the way through the rain to our hotel. I had encountered rain like this only in India during the monsoons and had come to expect nothing more in this country than the gentle drizzle that was so characteristic of Vancouver. This wild downpour, accompanied by the roar of thunder and the crackle of lightning, was a glimpse of Canada that I had never seen before—the country had been doing a slow dance for me over the nine years I had lived here, showing me tantalizing little bits of itself every now and then.

That first day, we were trapped inside our hotel room with nothing to do but gaze at the Pacific Ocean, which was hurling itself furiously at the beach. But the next morning, to our delight, was bright and sunny, and we rushed down to the jetty where the whale-watching tours began. "Too rough to go out in the open sea," said the tour operator regretfully. "I can take you on calmer waters between islands." A lone orca had been spotted grazing in those channels, and if we were lucky, we might catch a glimpse of it. We drifted in and out of dark green fingers of water whose otherwise still surface was now pocked by the rain that started again. We saw a black bear at the edge of a stand of pines on a tiny island, an eagle gliding on currents of air against the grey sky, otters and stellar seals, but not a single whale. We started our journey home disappointed but determined to come back the next year.

And then it happened. On the ferry from Victoria, a cry went up from the crowd of people strolling the decks. There, cleaving the steely, restless ocean, was a large pod of orca whales—bulls, cows, calves—rolling and diving, sending up plumes of water. I had hoped to see *one* of these creatures, and here I was being treated to a whole family when I least expected it.

Looking for the Canada that has gently seeped into my bloodstream is like looking for those whales. I find her at unexpected moments: in the sudden kindness of a stranger's smile; in the graceful flight of a hundred snow geese; or in the cascading, iridescent shimmer of the aurora borealis lighting up the midnight sky. Several years ago, a friend asked me what I thought of this land of vast, empty spaces, of mountains and trees and snow and water, where almost every person claims ancestry in another culture, another land, and where a hundred different histories mingle to create a new set of memories. I had said that Canada reminded me of a beautiful, enigmatic woman who looks down demurely most of the time, but then surprises the watcher with a sudden glance from a pair of mischievous eyes. A shy coquette, I said, pleased at having found the words to describe a country with which I was just beginning a relationship.

In those early stages, I tried to define Canada in terms of other places, as a series of negatives: not as colourful and noisy as India, not as old as China, not as brash and individualistic as the United States. I would read all the Canadian newspapers and magazines and watch all the Canadian television shows I could (including curling tournaments, even though I am not a sports enthusiast and couldn't see the point of a game that involved a teapot-like object and a broom). I travelled as much as possible into the mountains; breathed the moist air of ancient forests that held secrets of an unknowable past; wandered over the weird, moonlike surface of the Badlands at Drumheller, Alta., marvelling at the skeletal remains of dinosaurs that had roamed there aeons ago; tried skiing and ice-skating and rock climbing, ending up with little more than sore muscles. The more I looked, the less I seemed to see Canada. Until that afternoon on the deck of the ferry, when, as I watched the whales floating in the ocean, it came to me: there was no point in trying to find one fixed image of this land. It would always be an accumulation of events and experiences, smells, sights and sounds. I was, after all, seeing it through so many different lenses: a writer's, an immigrant's, a lover's, a mother's. It was at that moment that I began to think of Canada without any reference to any other country, to love it on its own terms for what it was, rather than what it wasn't.

We came to Canada from India a little more than nine years ago. My husband had woken up one morning and decided that he wanted to reinvent himself. He was tired of his engineering degree and his job in a vast, faceless corporation. Our relatives were alarmed by this sudden decision. They couldn't understand why we wanted to leave good jobs (I was a newspaper journalist) and comfortable lives for an uncertain future. And why Canada of all places, they wanted to know. Wasn't that somewhere near the North Pole? Horribly cold? With bears and wild animals that mauled people to death?

By September 1990, my husband had arrived in Canada and was taking a master's degree in environmental studies at the University of Calgary. By March of the next year, I had cleaned out our flat in the bustling metropolitan city of Bangalore, sold all our furniture and packed most of our other belongings in boxes and trunks to store in my parents-in-law's home. No point in taking everything with us—we would be back in a few years, I told myself and everybody else, resenting this move and quite certain that I would never want to live in a country that I knew basically as a vague band of land between the United States of America and the North Pole. At school we had learned a huge amount about Britain and Europe, and at university, American literature was one of the areas I had opted to study in addition to the standard menu of Shakespeare, the Renaissance poets,

Victorian fiction and Indo-Anglian writing (works written in English by Indians). But I had studied almost nothing about Canada and had certainly never heard of Canlit.

I had once seen a picture in a geography book of vast, flat prairie with a grain elevator rising from its heart. Another time, in an ancient issue of *Reader's Digest*, I had read about a forest fire in the Rockies. The article was accompanied by a lurid picture of dark stands of pines licked by flames against a red, yellow and orange sky. These, and the photographs of the aurora borealis and of a grizzly bear, were the sum of my experience of Canada, a country that hitherto existed only in the outer edges of my imagination—until I found myself in the Calgary airport in March 1991, dressed in nothing warmer than a mohair sweater and a pair of canvas sneakers. My husband, who had already lived in the city for six months and had survived an extremely frigid winter, had buoyantly assured me that spring had come to Calgary. It was deliciously warm, there was joy in the air, all the trees were in bud, and I would love it. My four-year-old son and I emerged from the nearly empty airport to be hit by a blast of freezing air. I could see nothing for a few moments as my eyes and nose had started to water with the cold. My lungs had panicked and seized up. I was wheezing like an old pair of bellows. It was −15 Celsius, and we had just arrived from a city where the temperature had been hovering at 47 Celsius in the shade. In the week that followed, the desire to go back from whence I'd come became ever stronger. I missed the noise, the bustle of people, the smells and the circus-like atmosphere of Indian streets. What was I doing in this barren city where the sky covered everything like blue glass, where I could hear my own footsteps echoing on an empty street, and where I was frequently the only passenger on a bus? I wanted to go home.

Two months later, the lilacs were in bloom, filling the air with their scent. There were daffodils thrusting up from the earth, followed by tulips and irises and hundreds of other flowers. The trees had burst into bloom, and I was looking at a different world. I had spent all my life in a country where the seasons merge into one another. This drama of death and regeneration was something I had never witnessed. I was instantly captivated. I would stay another year, I told myself, if for nothing other than to see the seasons change. Four years slipped by and I was still in Canada. By now I had worked in a variety of places, including a china store, a book shop and a library. A few months after I'd arrived, I had signed up for a creative writing course at the University of Calgary and then began a master's degree in English literature. I'd had several stories published, and I'd begun to love the crisp winter mornings, the sudden excitement of a chinook, which seems to melt the snow in minutes and peel veils of cloud away from the distant snowcapped mountains. Now, every time I stepped out of my house, I bumped into a friend or someone I knew. It was a wonderful feeling to know so many people in the city. All my fears about leaving my writing career in India, about forgetting how to write, seemed ridiculous. I had also found my metier in fiction writing and had finished the first draft of a novel.

In 1995, my first novel was accepted for publication, and we moved to Vancouver. Once again I was filled with that feeling of being torn from all that was familiar and beloved, of leaving home, except this time, home was Calgary, and what I yearned for was long silent streets and canola fields shimmering yellow under an endless blue sky.

In the years since I arrived here I have travelled the length and breadth of this land and collected many different images of it. Now if somebody asks me what I think or feel about Canada, I tell of all the people and places, sights and events that have woven a pattern in my heart. I tell stories about Shinya and Mayo, who had come here from Japan and shared with us a passion for spicy eggplant curry and Charlie Chaplin. And Carole, who arrived like a Santa in the middle of our first spring with a bag full of toys for our son, just, she explained cheerfully, to make him feel at home. I talk about Serena and Mike, our neighbours, with whom we watched dozens of late-night movies after shared dinners and delicious fruit flans created by Mike. Or about Grant, who took us on a trip to Waterton Lakes National Park in southwestern Alberta, rowed us out to the middle of one of the many lakes and handed the paddles to my husband and me. "If you want to be Canadian," he declared, grinning, "you will have to learn to row a boat." And who, after watching us quarrel for 20 minutes, during which time we managed to describe tighter and tighter circles in the centre of the lake, decided that there were safer ways of becoming Canadian.

There were all those evenings with Suni and Ravi and Mayura and Ratna, celebrating Indian festivals just as winter was beginning to take hold, nudging away those last warm fall days, and the many times that they took care of me while I tried to juggle work and school and home.

My Canada, I tell anyone who asks, is the driver who made sure that I was on the last bus out of Calgary's North Hill Centre when I was working the late shift there, even if it meant delaying the bus an extra 10 minutes. And the members of my creative writing group, who gave me their undiluted comments and prepared me for a career as a novelist. "When your first book is out there being trashed by the reviewers," they told me, "you'll thank us for your thick skin." My Canada includes all those people who made me feel like I belonged.

To my album of memories I will add an enchanted night spent lying on a sloping field in Calgary with a group of friends to watch a meteor shower streaking silver lines across the midnight sky. I will tell all who ask about the time I stood on Alberta's Athabasca Glacier surrounded by mountains eternally capped by snow, and drank crystalline water from a deep spring so ancient that time itself had no measure for it; of the moon full and golden, floating up over the mountains surrounding Lake Louise, and a lynx's eyes flaring green at us before the creature snarled and vanished into the darkness; of the flood of people on Main Street, Vancouver, celebrating the Sikh festival Baisakhi; of Chinatown, where a beautiful woman in a small, dark shop sold me exquisite paper and a stamp with a character that, she told me, meant "good luck;" of writers' festivals all over the country, where a medley of voices from many cultures was heard; and of a café in a remote Yukon town where I met a man who believed that he was the reincarnation of Elvis Presley.

I visited India recently, the second time that I had gone back since 1991. When it was time to leave, I realized with a small jolt that I felt none of the regret that I had experienced on the previous trip. The needle of my emotional compass had swung around and set itself in a different direction. While I still cherished the brilliant colours of India, I was also beginning to recognize and appreciate the subtle tints and textures of the Canadian fabric. And I knew that even though a part of me would always look with love towards the land of my birth, and deep inside I would for ever straddle two continents, two realities (the East and the West), my home was now here, in Canada.

ᒣ Anita Rau Badami was born in India, the daughter of an Indian railway executive. Before immigrating to Canada in 1991, she worked as a journalist for the Indian national television network. She is a regular contributor to magazines and newspapers in Canada and has written a number of short stories. Her first novel, *Tamarind Mem*, was published in 1996 and a second novel, *Hero's Walk*, was published in 2000. She lives in Vancouver, British Columbia.

RESPONDING

Meaning

1. Search Anita Rau Badami's essay for one sentence that identifies her theme or controlling idea. Justify your answer.

2. After Anita Rau Badami finished writing her essay, she gave it a title: "My Canada." Summarize in 25 words or less what Canada means to Badami.

Form and Style

3. Badami's narrative essay is divided into four main sections. These are indicated by the extra wide spaces between certain paragraphs. The individual sections begin with the following phrases: "Early one morning," "Looking for the Canada," "We came to Canada from India," and "In the years since I arrived." What does Badami accomplish by dividing her essay into sections this way?

4. Using an organizer, identify two examples each of metaphor, simile, and personification in this essay. Explain the purpose and effects of each one. Why does the author use these kinds of devices?

Creative Extension

5. In this essay, Badami says of Canada: "I find her at unexpected moments: in the sudden kindness of a stranger's smile; in the graceful flight of a hundred snow geese; or in the cascading, iridescent shimmer of the aurora borealis lighting up the midnight sky." What events, experiences, people, sights, sounds, and smells reflect what Canada means to you? Write a narrative essay or create a photo essay answering this question.

6. Badami knew almost nothing about Canada when she arrived in this country. By referring to an atlas, choose a country you know nothing about and then research it, using the Internet, print resources, and travel offices. Design a travel brochure for Canadians who are thinking of moving to that country permanently.

Mother Tongue

❧ Amy Tan

Learning Goals

- examine meaning through a close reading
- recognize an author's personal opinions and credibility
- examine use of conjunctions
- use colloquial speech effectively in writing
- hold a panel discussion

I am not a scholar of English or literature. I cannot give you much more than personal opinions on the English language and its variations in this country or others.

I am a writer. And by that definition, I am someone who has always loved language. I am fascinated by language in daily life. I spend a great deal of my time thinking about the power of language—the way it can evoke an emotion, a visual image, a complex idea, or a simple truth. Language is the tool of my trade. And I use them all—all the Englishes I grew up with.

Recently, I was made keenly aware of the different Englishes I do use. I was giving a talk to a large group of people, the same talk I had already given to half a dozen other groups. The nature of the talk was about my writing, my life, and my book, *The Joy Luck Club.* The talk was going along well enough, until I remembered one major difference that made the whole talk sound wrong. My mother was in the room. And it was perhaps the first time she had heard me give a lengthy speech, using the kind of English I have never used with her. I was saying things like, "The intersection of memory upon imagination" and "There is an aspect of my fiction that relates to thus-and-thus"—a speech filled with carefully wrought grammatical phrases, burdened, it suddenly seemed to me, with nominalized forms, past perfect tenses, conditional phrases, all the forms of standard English that I had learned in school and through books, the forms of English I did not use at home with my mother.

Just last week, I was walking down the street with my mother, and I again found myself conscious of the English I was using, the English I do use with her. We were talking about the price of new and used furniture and I heard myself saying this: "Not waste money that way." My husband was with us as well, and he didn't notice any switch in my English. And then I realized why. It's because over the twenty years we've been together I've often used that same kind of English with him, and sometimes he even uses it with me. It has become our language of intimacy, a different sort of English that relates to family talk, the language I grew up with.

So you'll have some idea of what this family talk I heard sounds like, I'll quote what my mother said during a recent conversation which I video-taped and then transcribed. During this conversation, my mother was talk-ing about a political gangster in Shanghai who had the same last name as her family's, Du, and how the gangster in his early years wanted to be adopted by her family, which was rich by comparison. Later, the gangster became more powerful, far richer than my mother's family, and one day showed up at my mother's wedding to pay his respects. Here's what she said in part:

"Du Yusong having business like fruit stand. Like off the street kind. He is Du like Du Zong—but not Tsung-ming Island people. The local people call putong, the river east side, he belong to that side local people. That man want to ask Du Zong father take him in like become own family. Du Zong father wasn't look down on him, but didn't take seriously, until that man big like become a mafia. Now important person, very hard to inviting him. Chinese way, came only to show respect, don't stay for dinner. Respect for making big celebration, he shows up. Mean gives lots of respect. Chinese custom. Chinese social life that way. If too important won't have to stay too long. He come to my wedding. I didn't see, I heard it. I gone to boy's side, they have YMCA dinner. Chinese age I was nineteen."

You should know that my mother's expressive command of English belies how much she actually understands. She reads the *Forbes* report, listens to *Wall Street Week*, converses daily with her stockbroker, reads all of Shirley MacLaine's books with ease—all kinds of things I can't begin to understand. Yet some of my friends tell me they understand 50 percent of what my mother says. Some say they understand 80 to 90 percent. Some say they understand none of it, as if she were speaking pure Chinese. But to me, my mother's English is perfectly clear, perfectly natural. It's my mother tongue. Her language, as I hear it, is vivid, direct, full of observa-tion and imagery. That was the language that helped shape the way I saw things, expressed things, made sense of the world.

Lately, I've been giving more thought to the kind of English my mother speaks. Like others, I have described it to people as "broken" or "fractured" English. But I wince when I say that. It has always bothered me that I can think of no way to describe it other than "broken," as if it were damaged and needed to be fixed, as if it lacked a certain wholeness and soundness. I've heard other terms used, "limited English," for example. But they seem just as bad, as if everything is limited, including people's perceptions of the limited English speaker.

I know this for a fact, because when I was growing up, my mother's "limited" English limited my perception of her. I was ashamed of her English. I believed that her English reflected the quality of what she had to say. That is, because she expressed them imperfectly her thoughts were imperfect. And I had plenty of empirical evidence to support me: the fact that people in department stores, at banks, and at restaurants did not take her seriously, did not give her good service, pretended not to understand her, or even acted as if they did not hear her.

My mother has long realized the limitations of her English as well. When I was fifteen, she used to have me call people on the phone to pretend I was she. In this guise, I was forced to ask for information or even to complain and yell at people who had been rude to her. One time it was a call to her stockbroker in New York. She had cashed out her small portfolio and it just so happened we were going to go to New York the next week, our very first trip outside California. I had to get on the phone and say in an adolescent voice that was not very convincing, "This is Mrs. Tan."

And my mother was standing in the back whispering loudly, "Why he don't send me check, already two weeks late. So mad he lie to me, losing me money."

And then I said in perfect English, "Yes, I'm getting rather concerned. You had agreed to send the check two weeks ago, but it hasn't arrived."

Then she began to talk more loudly. "What he want, I come to New York tell him front of his boss, you cheating me?" And I was trying to calm her down, make her quiet, while telling the stockbroker, "I can't tolerate any more excuses. If I don't receive the check immediately, I am going to have to speak to your manager when I'm in New York next week. And sure enough, the following week there we were in front of this astonished stockbroker, and I was sitting there red-faced and quiet, and my mother, the real Mrs. Tan, was shouting at his boss in her impeccable broken English.

We used a similar routine just five days ago, for a situation that was far less humorous. My mother had gone to the hospital for an appointment, to find out about a benign brain tumour a CAT scan had revealed a month ago. She said she had spoken very good English, her best English, no mistakes. Still, she said, the hospital did not apologize when they said they had lost the CAT scan and she had come for nothing. She said they did not seem to have any sympathy when she told them she was anxious to know the exact diagnosis, since her husband and son had both died of brain tumours. She said they would not give her any more information until the next time and she would have to make another appointment for that. So she said she would not leave until the doctor called her daughter. She wouldn't budge. And when the doctor finally called her daughter, me, who spoke in perfect English—lo and behold—we had assurances the CAT scan would be found, promises that a conference call on Monday would be held, and apologies for any suffering my mother had gone through for a most regrettable mistake.

I think my mother's English almost had an effect on limiting my possibilities in life as well. Sociologists and linguists probably will tell you that a person's developing language skills are more influenced by peers. But I do think that the language spoken in the family, especially in immigrant families which are more insular, plays a large role in shaping the language of the child. And I believe that it affected my results on achievement tests, IQ tests, and the SAT. While my English skills were never judged as poor, compared to math, English could not be considered my strong suit. In grade school I did moderately well, getting perhaps B's, sometimes B-pluses, in English and scoring perhaps in the sixtieth or seventieth percentile on achievement tests. But those scores were not good enough to override the opinion that my true abilities lay in math and science, because in those areas I achieved A's and scored in the ninetieth percentile or higher.

This was understandable. Math is precise; there is only one correct answer. Whereas, for me at least, the answers on English tests were always a judgement call, a matter of opinion and personal experience. Those tests were constructed around items like fill-in-the-blank sentence completion, such as, "Even though Tom was_____, Mary thought he was_____." And the correct answer always seemed to be the most bland combinations of thoughts, for example, "Even though Tom was shy, Mary thought he was charming," with the grammatical structure "even though" limiting the correct answer to some sort of semantic opposites, so you wouldn't get answers like, "Even though Tom was foolish, Mary thought he was ridiculous."

Well, according to my mother, there were very few limitations as to what Tom could have been and what Mary might have thought of him. So I never did well on tests like that.

The same was true with word analogies, pairs of words in which you were supposed to find some sort of logical, semantic relationship—for example, "*Sunset* is to *nightfall* as _____ is to _____." And here you would be presented with a list of four possible pairs, one of which showed the same kind of relationship: *red* is to *stoplight*, *bus* is to *arrival*, *chills* is to *fever*, *yawn* is to *boring*. Well, I could never think that way. I knew what the tests were asking, but I could not block out of my mind the images already created by the first pair, "*sunset* is to *nightfall*"—and I would see a burst of colours against a darkening sky, the moon rising, the lowering of a curtain of stars. And all the other pairs of words—red, bus, stoplight, boring—just threw up a mass of confusing images, making it impossible for me to sort out something as logical as saying: "A sunset precedes night-fall" is the same as "a chill precedes a fever." The only way I would have gotten that answer right would have been to imagine an associative situation, for example, my being disobedient and staying out past sunset, catching a chill at night, which turns into feverish pneumonia as punishment, which indeed did happen to me.

I have been thinking about all this lately, about my mother's English, about achievement tests. Because lately I've been asked, as a writer, why there are not more Asian Americans represented in American literature. Why are there few Asian Americans enrolled in creative writing programs? Why do so many Chinese students go into engineering? Well, these are broad sociological questions I can't begin to answer. But I have noticed in surveys—in fact, just last week—that Asian students, as a whole, always do significantly better on math achievement tests than in English. And this makes me think that there are other Asian-American students whose English spoken in the home might also be described as "broken" or "limited." And perhaps they also have teachers who are steering them away from writing and into math and science, which is what happened to me.

Fortunately, I happen to be rebellious in nature and enjoy the challenge of disproving assumptions made about me. I became an English major my first year in college, after being enrolled as pre-med. I started writing non-fiction as a freelancer the week after I was told by my former boss that writing was my worst skill and I should hone my talents toward account management.

But it wasn't until 1985 that I finally began to write fiction. And at first I wrote using what I thought to be wittily crafted sentences, sentences that would finally prove I had mastery over the English language. Here's an example from the first draft of a story that later made its way into *The Joy Luck Club*, but without this line: "That was my mental quandary in its nascent state." A terrible line, which I can barely pronounce.

Fortunately, for reasons I won't go into today, I later decided I should envision a reader for the stories I would write. And the reader I decided upon was my mother, because these were stories about mothers. So with this reader in mind—and in fact she did read my early drafts—I began to write stories using all the Englishes I grew up with: the English I spoke to my mother, which for lack of a better term might be described as "simple"; the English she used with me, which for lack of a better term might be described as "broken"; my translation of her Chinese, which could certainly be described as "watered down"; and what I imagine to be her translation of her Chinese if she could speak in perfect English, her internal language, and for that I sought to preserve the essence, but neither an English nor a Chinese structure. I wanted to capture what language ability tests can never reveal: her intent, her passion, her imagery, the rhythms of her speech, and the nature of her thoughts.

Apart from what any critic had to say about my writing, I knew I had succeeded where it counted when my mother finished reading my book and gave me her verdict: "So easy to read."

Amy Tan's parents left China in 1949 to settle in the United States. Their daughter grew up in San Francisco. Before she began writing novels, she worked as a reporter, editor, and consultant to programs for children with disabilities. Her first novel, *The Joy Luck Club* (1989), was a finalist for the prestigious National Book Critics Circle Award and was made into a major motion picture, for which Amy Tan co-wrote the screenplay. *(Born Oakland, California 1952)*

RESPONDING

Meaning

1. Discuss the significance of the following statements from this essay:
   a) "And I use them all—all the Englishes I grew up with."
   b) "It has always bothered me that I can think of no way to describe it other than 'broken,' as if it were damaged and needed to be fixed, as if it lacked a certain wholeness and soundness."
   c) "I've heard other terms used, 'limited English,' for example. But they seem just as bad, as if everything is limited, including people's perceptions of the limited English speaker."
   d) "Fortunately, I happen to be rebellious in nature and enjoy the challenge of disproving assumptions made about me."

2. How does Amy Tan view her "mother tongue"? Support your response with evidence from the text.

Form and Style

3. a) How does Amy Tan signal to her reader that this is a personal narrative essay?
   b) At the same time, how does she let her reader know that her opinions have credibility?

4. A number of sentences and paragraphs in this essay begin with conjunctions. Identify one or two paragraphs where this is the case, note the conjunctions, and explain why you think the author uses them and their effects.

Creative Extension

5. Incorporating the language of everyday speech can add authenticity and vividness to a piece of writing. In what forms of writing would it be most appropriate? When would it not be appropriate?

   Over the course of one day, listen carefully to the colloquial conversations people have around you and the situations in which they take place. Choose one situation and write a short piece, in a genre of your choice, that incorporates colloquial speech. Share your piece with a partner or small group, by reading or performing it. Ask for their reactions to its authenticity. Use their suggestions to revise your work.

6. Hold a panel discussion in your class on the topic of whether standardized achievement tests or IQ tests are really an accurate measure of intelligence and abilities.

Non-Fiction

Gabriel Garcia Marquez on non-fiction:

In [non-fiction] just one fact that is false prejudices the entire work. In contrast, in fiction, one single fact that is true gives legitimacy to the entire work. That's the only difference and it lies in the commitment of the writer.

A Walk in the Woods

⌇ Bill Bryson

Learning Goals

• examine appropriateness of titles

• analyze the purpose of specific elements and references in a text

• interpret tone and humour

• apply effective research techniques

• compare stylistic elements in two literary works

In 1993, travel writer Bill Bryson decided to hike the famous Appalachian trail, which runs 2900 km north-south in the eastern United States. He had never undertaken such a long and, as he discovered, perilous walk before. In the following excerpt from his book, he recounts some of the reading he did before his trip and the unsettling effects it had on him.

Chapter 2

On the afternoon of July 5, 1983, three adult supervisors and a group of youngsters set up camp at a popular spot beside Lake Canimina in the fragrant pine forests of western Quebec, about eighty miles[1] north of Ottawa, in a park called La Vérendrye Provincial Reserve. They cooked dinner and, afterwards, in the correct fashion, secured their food in a bag and carried it a hundred or so feet into the woods, where they suspended it above the ground between two trees, out of reach of bears.

About midnight, a black bear came prowling around the margins of the camp, spied the bag, and brought it down by climbing one of the trees and breaking a branch. He plundered the food and departed, but an hour later he was back, this time entering the camp itself, drawn by the lingering smell of cooked meat in the campers' clothes and hair, in their sleeping bags and tent fabric. It was a long night for the Canimina party. Three times between midnight and 3:30 a.m. the bear came to the camp.

Imagine, if you will, lying in the dark alone in a little tent, nothing but a few microns of trembling nylon between you and the chill night air, listening to a 400-pound[2] bear moving around your campsite. Imagine its quiet grunts and mysterious snufflings, the clatter of upended cookware and sounds of moist gnawings, the pad of its feet and the heaviness of its breath, the singing brush of its haunch along your tent side. Imagine the hot flood of adrenaline, that unwelcome tingling in the back of your arms, at the sudden rough bump of its snout against the foot of your tent, the alarming wild wobble of your frail shell as it roots through the backpack

[1] 129 km; [2] 181 kg

that you left casually propped by the entrance—with, you suddenly recall, a Snickers in the pouch. Bears adore Snickers, you've heard.

And then the dull thought—oh, God—that perhaps you brought the Snickers in here with you, that it's somewhere in here, down by your feet or underneath you or—here it is. Another bump of grunting head against the tent, this time near your shoulders. More crazy wobble. Then silence, a very long silence, and—wait, *shhhh* . . . yes!—the unutterable relief of realizing that the bear has withdrawn to the other side of the camp or shambled back into the woods. I tell you right now, I couldn't stand it.

So imagine then what it must have been like for poor little David Anderson, aged twelve, when at 3:30 a.m., on the third foray, his tent was abruptly rent with a swipe of claw and the bear, driven to distraction by the rich, unfixable, everywhere aroma of hamburger, bit hard into a flinching limb and dragged him shouting and flailing through the camp and into the woods. In the few moments it took the boy's fellow campers to unzip themselves from their accoutrements—and imagine, if you will, trying to swim out of suddenly voluminous sleeping bags, take up flashlights and makeshift cudgels, undo tent zips with helplessly fumbling fingers, and give chase—in those few moments, poor little David Anderson was dead.

Now imagine reading a non-fiction book packed with stories such as this—true tales soberly related—just before setting off alone on a camping trip of your own into the North American wilderness. The book to which I refer is *Bear Attacks: Their Causes and Avoidance*, by a Canadian academic named Stephen Herrero. If it is not the last word on the subject, then I really, really, really do not wish to hear the last word. Through long winter nights in New Hampshire, while snow piled up outdoors and my wife slumbered peacefully beside me, I lay saucer-eyed in bed reading clinically precise accounts of people gnawed pulpy in their sleeping bags, plucked whimpering from trees, even noiselessly stalked (I didn't know this happened!) as they sauntered unawares down leafy paths or cooled their feet in mountain streams. People whose one fatal mistake was to smooth their hair with a dab of aromatic gel, or eat juicy meat, or tuck a Snickers in their shirt pocket for later, or in some small, inadvertent way pique the olfactory properties of the hungry bear. Or, come to that, whose fatal failing was simply being very, very unfortunate—to round a bend and find a moody male blocking the path, head rocking appraisingly, or wander unwittingly into the territory of a bear too slowed by age or idleness to chase down fleeter prey.

Now it is important to establish right away that the possibility of a serious bear attack on the Appalachian Trail is remote. To begin with, the really terrifying American bear, the grizzly—*Ursus horribilis*, as it is so vividly and correctly labelled—doesn't range east of the Mississippi, which is good news because grizzlies are large, powerful, and ferociously bad-tempered. . . .

Herrero recounts an incident that nicely conveys the near indestructibility of the grizzly. It concerns a professional hunter in Alaska named Alexei Pitka, who stalked a large male through snow and finally felled it with a well-aimed shot to the heart from a large-bore rifle. Pitka should probably have carried a card with him that said: "First make sure bear is dead. Then put gun down." He advanced cautiously and spent a minute or two watching the bear for movement, but when there was none he set the gun against a tree (big mistake!) and strode forward to claim his prize. Just as he reached around it, the bear sprang up, clapped its expansive jaws around the front of Pitka's head, as if giving him a big kiss, and with a single jerk tore off his face.

Miraculously, Pitka survived. . . .

If I were to be pawed and chewed—and this seemed to me entirely possible, the more I read—it would be by a black bear, *Ursus americanus*. There are at least 500 000 black bears in North America, possibly as many as 700 000. They are notably common in the hills along the Appalachian Trail (indeed, they often use the trail, for convenience), and their numbers are growing. Grizzlies, by contrast, number no more than 35 000 in the whole of North America, and just 1000 in the mainland United States, principally in and around Yellowstone National Park. Of the two species, black bears are generally smaller (though this is a decidedly relative condition; a male black bear can still weigh up to 650 pounds[3]) and unquestionably more retiring.

Black bears rarely attack. But here's the thing. Sometimes they do. All bears are agile, cunning, and immensely strong, and they are always hungry. If they want to kill you and eat you, they can, and pretty much whenever

---

[3] 272 kg

they want. That doesn't happen often, but—and here is the absolutely salient point—once would be enough. Herrero is at pains to stress that black bear attacks are infrequent, relative to their numbers. From 1900 to 1980, he found just twenty-three confirmed black bear killings of humans (about half the number of killings by grizzlies), and most of these were out west or in Canada. In New Hampshire there has not been an unprovoked fatal attack on a human by a bear since 1784. In Vermont, there has never been one.

I wanted very much to be calmed by these assurances but could never quite manage the necessary leap of faith. After noting that just 500 people were attacked and hurt by black bears between 1960 and 1980—twenty-five attacks a year from a resident population of at least half a million bears—Herrero adds that most of these injuries were not severe. "The typical black bear-inflicted injury," he writes blandly, "is minor and usually involves only a few scratches or light bites." Pardon me, but what exactly is a light bite? Are we talking a playful wrestle and gummy nips? I think not. And is 500 certified attacks really such a modest number, considering how few people go into the North American woods? And how foolish must one be to be reassured by the information that no bear has killed a human in Vermont or New Hampshire in 200 years? That's not because the bears have signed a treaty, you know. There's nothing to say that they won't start a modest rampage tomorrow.

So let us imagine that a bear does follow us out in the wilds. What are we to do? Interestingly, the advised stratagems are exactly opposite for grizzly and black bear. With grizzly, you should make for a tall tree, since grizzlies aren't much for climbing. If a tree is not available, then you should back off slowly, avoiding direct eye contact. All the books tell you that, if the grizzly comes for you, on no account should you run. This is the sort of advice you get from someone who is sitting at a keyboard when he gives it. Take it from me, if you are in an open space with no weapons and a grizzly comes for you, run. You may as well. If nothing else, it will give you something to do with the last seconds of your life. However, when the grizzly overtakes you, as it most assuredly will, you should fall to the ground and play dead. A grizzly may chew on a limp form for a minute or two but generally will lose interest and shuffle off. With black bears, however, playing dead is futile, since they will continue chewing on you until you are considerably past caring. It is also foolish to climb a tree because black bears are adroit climbers and, as Herrero dryly notes, you will simply end up fighting the bear in a tree.

To ward off an aggressive black bear, Herrero suggests making a lot of noise, banging pots and pans together, throwing sticks and rocks, and "running at the bear." (Yeah, right. You first, Professor.) On the other hand, he then adds judiciously, these tactics could "merely provoke the bear." Well, thanks. Elsewhere he suggests that hikers should consider making noises from time to time—singing a song, say—to alert bears of their presence, since a startled bear is more likely to be an angry bear, but then a few pages later he cautions that "there may be danger in making noise," since that can attract a hungry bear that might otherwise overlook you.

The fact is, no one can tell you what to do. Bears are unpredictable, and what works in one circumstance may not work in another. In 1973, two teenagers, Mark Seeley and Michael Whitten, were out for a hike in Yellowstone when they inadvertently crossed between a mother and her cubs. Nothing worries and antagonizes a female bear more than to have people between her and her brood. Furious, she turned and gave chase—despite the bear's lolloping gait, it can move at up to thirty-five miles[4] an hour—and the two boys scrambled up trees. The bear followed Whitten up his tree, clamped her mouth round his right foot, and slowly and patiently tugged him from his perch. (Is it me, or can you feel your fingernails scraping through the bark?) On the ground, she began mauling him extensively. In an attempt to distract the bear from his friend, Seeley shouted at it, whereupon the bear came and pulled him out of his tree, too. Both young men played dead—precisely the wrong thing to do, according to all the instruction manuals—and the bear left.

I won't say I became obsessed by all this, but it did occupy my thoughts a great deal in the months while I waited for spring to come. My particular dread—the vivid possibility that left me staring at tree shadows on the bedroom ceiling night after night—was having to lie in a small tent, alone in an inky wilderness, listening to a foraging bear outside and wondering what its intentions were. I was especially riveted by an amateur photograph in Herrero's book, taken late at night by a camper with a flash at a campground out West. The photograph caught four black bears as they

---

[4] 56 km

puzzled over a suspended food bag. The bears were clearly startled but not remotely alarmed by the flash. It was not the size or demeanour of the bears that troubled me—they looked almost comically unaggressive, like four guys who had gotten a Frisbee caught up in a tree—but their numbers. Up to that moment it had not occurred to me that bears might prowl in parties. What on earth would I do if four bears came into my camp? Why, I would die, of course.

Herrero's book was written in 1985. Since that time, according to an article in the *New York Times*, bear attacks in North America have increased by 25 percent. The *Times* article also noted that bears are far more likely to attack humans in the spring following a bad berry year. The previous year had been a very bad berry year. I didn't like any of this.

American travel writer Bill Bryson lived in England for almost two decades and then returned to the United States just before he made his walk on the Appalachian Trail. He has written many humorous travel books that have appeared on best-seller lists including *In a Sunburned Country* (2000) and *I'm a Stranger Here Myself* (1999). *A Walk in the Woods* was published in 1998. (Born Des Moines, Iowa 1951)

RESPONDING

Meaning

1. a) A good title should summarize the main idea of a piece of writing and reflect its overall tone or mood. Bill Bryson called his book *A Walk in the Woods*. Based on the excerpt you have read, do you think this title is an appropriate one? Explain.

   b) Bryson did not give his individual chapters a title. Compose a title for this chapter excerpt. Justify your choice using persuasive arguments and specific references to the text.

2. In small groups, discuss the purpose of the
   a) story about the Lake Canimina campers
   b) three references to Snickers bars
   c) David Anderson account
   d) several references to Stephen Herrero
   e) paragraph about Alexei Pitka

   Ask yourselves why the author incorporated these specifics, what they add to the narrative quality of the excerpt, and how each of you reacted.

Form and Style

3. In this travelogue, Bryson uses an interesting literary style—the choice and arrangement of words that convey his attitudes, personality, and view of the world. What impression or *tone* does this literary style convey? Support your answer by choosing two paragraphs from the excerpt that you believe best illustrate this tone.

4. Quickly reread or scan the reading again, focusing on the wit and humour. Which paragraphs did you find most humorous? On what does the humour rely? Is this your usual travelogue? Why or why not?

Creative Extension

5. Locate a map of the Appalachian Trail and plan a hike on a section of it. With a partner, determine how long the journey would take, when would be the best time of year to make the trip, and what supplies you would need. Using the Internet, research articles by people who have made the trek and contact agencies such as the US National Park Services and The Appalachian Trail Conference for further information. Present your itinerary and detailed plans to the class.

    If you prefer, investigate a hiking trail closer to home. Contact groups such as Parks Canada and Canadian hiking groups for information.

6. Research the different types of humour used as stylistic tools in writing. Some authors go beyond simple humour and delve into irony and satire. One of those most famous for his satire is Jonathan Swift. Read his essay, "A Modest Proposal," and summarize the effect Swift hoped to achieve. What is the basic difference between the two types of humour found in the work of Swift and Bryson?

The Urban Indian

ᘓ Drew Hayden Taylor

Learning Goals

- interpret meaning and summarize a main idea
- analyze tone
- analyze an author's argument
- write a journal entry and compare two opinion pieces

I was visiting my mother on the Reserve when it hit me.

I had been out for a country walk in the quiet evening air when I noticed something I hadn't seen since last year: a single, tiny mosquito. And as is the mosquito mentality, within an incredibly short period of time, they were everywhere. And I do mean everywhere! Feeling like I was Pearl Harbour and the mosquitoes were Japanese Zeros, I fled.

As I scooted in through the door [of my mother's house], barricaded behind the window screening, I noticed my mother and aunts laughing quietly. Their one statement revealed a sad but true reality: "You've been in the city too long."

I have spent years denying it, ignoring the evidence, but I just can't do it anymore. I have reached a point of personal awareness in my life where I must face certain unavoidable realities, no matter how painful. After 16 years of living in Canada's largest city I have finally admitted to myself the painful truth: I . . . am . . . an . . . urban Indian.

Not that I have anything against urban Indians. Some of my best friends are urban Indians. In fact, most of my friends are urban Indians.

I just never thought I would ever be one. In just two more years I'll have spent exactly half my life in Toronto, drinking café au laits, eating in Thai restaurants (it's hard to find good lemongrass soup on the reserve), riding the subways (also notoriously difficult to locate on a reserve), and having pizza delivered to my door. I've grown soft.

A long time ago I heard an elder wisely say to a group of young people, "we must go from being hunters in the forest to being hunters in the city." I now hunt for a good dry-cleaners.

By trade I am a writer (though some might argue). I write plays, scripts, and short stories—all, oddly enough, taking place on an Indian reserve. In the past I used this simple fact to tell myself that although my body lived in an apartment near Bathurst and St. Clair, my spirit was somehow fishing in an unspoiled, unpolluted lake, nestled in the bosom of Mother Earth, somewhere up near Peterborough, Ontario.

Work and education were the reasons I originally came to Toronto those many years and fewer pounds ago. I sought to explore the world outside the reserve boundaries and taste what the world had to offer. As with all things in life, there is a give and take involved in exploration. Instead of the easy "I'll-get-there-when-I-get-there" saunter so many of my "rez" brothers and sisters have, I now have my own "I have to get there in the next five minutes or life as I know it will end" hustle.

I've traded roving the back roads in pick-up trucks for weaving in and out of traffic on my bicycle. Where once I camped on deserted islands, I now get a thrill out of ordering room service in a hotel.

Somehow, it loses something in translation.

Unfortunately, there are many people who live on these reserves who feel you aren't a proper Native person unless you are born, live and die on that little piece of land put aside by the government to contain Indians. How quickly they forget most aboriginal nations were nomadic in nature. When I tell these people "take a hike," I mean it in the most aboriginal of contexts.

I don't have to explain to my critics that I've spent 18 years growing up in that rural community. It shaped who I am and what I am, and if

psychologists are correct, barring any serious religious conversion, I should remain roughly the same. The reserve is still deep within me. Given a few seconds of preparation, I can still remember the lyrics to most of Charley Pride's greatest hits. I can remember who the original six hockey teams were. And I know that contrary to popular belief, fried foods are actually good for you.

There is always the opinion, of course, that someday, if the Gods permit, I could return to the community that spawned me. As my mother says, I know home will always be there. So will the mosquitoes and the gossip and relatives who still treat you like you were twelve years old—and those who walk in my moccasins know the rest.

Until then, if there is a then, I shall be content to acknowledge my current civic status. To celebrate, I think I shall go out this morning unto the urban landscape, partake of some brunch and perhaps peruse a newspaper or two.

I may be an urban Indian, but I am also an urbane Indian.

Drew Hayden Taylor grew up on the Curve Lake Reserve near Peterborough, Ontario. He has established a reputation as an award-winning playwright. His first play, *Toronto at Dreamer's Rock*, won a Chalmers Award in 1992. He is also well known for his humorous commentaries that appear regularly in the *Globe and Mail* and *Toronto Star*. (Born Ontario 1962)

RESPONDING

Meaning

1. In the fourth paragraph, the author clearly states, "I have spent years denying it, ignoring the evidence, but I just can't do it anymore. I have reached a point of personal awareness in my life where I must face certain unavoidable realities..." What are these "unavoidable realities" in his life? Provide specific examples.

2. a) Is the author comfortable with these "unavoidable realities?" How does he define his identity?
   b) What is the main point Drew Hayden Taylor is making in this opinion piece? Summarize it in a few sentences.

Form and Style

3. a) *Tone* is the overall mood or attitude in a piece of writing. What is the tone in this opinion piece? When is this tone set?
   b) How does the author maintain this tone throughout the article? Scan the text for specific techniques and stylistic devices he uses.

4. Drew Hayden Taylor has a strong point to make in this article, but he also tries to present a balanced view of his situation. Provide evidence that he considers both sides of his nature in this article. Discuss the effect of this technique on you as the reader of this piece.

Creative Extension

5. Imagine that you have moved from your hometown to find a job or get an education in a different place. Write a journal entry exploring how the move might affect your sense of identity. How do you think you would adjust? How would you deal with the critical opinions of other people?

6. Find another short opinion piece in a newspaper or magazine. Compare the tone, language, and presentation of the argument in that piece with those in Drew Hayden Taylor's article. Suggest reasons for similarities and differences.

Cyberschool

Clifford Stoll

Learning Goals

- determine points an author is addressing
- analyze use of stylistic and rhetorical devices
- hold a debate
- write an effective opinion piece

Welcome to the classroom of the future! Complete with electronic links to the world, it'll revolutionize education. Students will interact with information infrastructures and knowledge processors to learn group work and tele-work, whatever that means. You'll be enriched, empowered, and enabled by the digital classroom: immersed in an optimal learning environment. Yee-ha!

Worried that things rarely turn out as promised? Well, let me present a pessimal view of the schoolroom of the future.

Suppose you're a harried school board member. Voters complain about high taxes. Teachers' unions strike for higher wages and smaller classes. Parents worry about plummeting scores on standardized tests. Newspapers criticize backward teaching methods, outdated textbooks, and security problems. Unruly students cut classes and rarely pay attention or, worse, inject their own opinions into subject matter.

Sounds like a tough call? Naw—it's easy to solve all these problems, placate the taxpayers, and get re-elected. High technology!

First, the school district buys a computer for every student. Sure this'll set back the budget—maybe a few hundred dollars per student. Quantity discounts and corporate support should keep the price down, and class-room savings will more than offset the cost of the equipment.

Next buy a pile of CD ROMs for the students, each pre-programmed with fun edutainment programs. The educational games will exactly cover the curriculum . . . for every paragraph in the syllabus, the game will have an interactive aspect. As students climb to more advanced levels, the game naturally becomes more challenging and rewarding. But always fun.

Every student will work at her own pace. The youngest will watch happy cartoon characters and exciting animations. The kid that likes horses will listen to messages from a chatty pony; the child that dreams of fire engines will hear from Fred the Firefighter. High schoolers get multimedia images of film stars and rock and roll celebrities. With access to interactive video sessions, chat rooms, and e-mail, students can collaborate with each other. It's the ultimate in individualized, child-centred instruction.

Naturally, the edu-games will be programmed so that students become adept at standardized tests. No reason to teach anything that's not on the ACT, PSAL, or SAT exams. And the students will have fun because all this information will be built into games like Myst, Dungeon, or Doom. They'll master the games, and automatically learn the material.

Meanwhile, the computers will keep score, like pinball machines. They'll send e-mail to parents and administrators . . . scores that will become part of each kid's permanent record. No more subjectivity in grading. The principal will know instantly how each child's doing. And if a student gets confused or falls behind, automated help will be just a mouse click away.

We'll update crowded classrooms, too. Replace desks with individual cubicles, comfortable chairs, and multimedia monitors. With no outside interruptions, kids' attention will be directed into the approved creative learning experiences, built into the software. Well compartmentalized, students will hardly ever see each other . . . neatly ending classroom discipline problems.

Naturally, teachers are an unnecessary appendix at this cyberschool. No need for 'em when there's a fun, multimedia system at each student's fingertips. Should a student have a question, she can turn to the latest on-line encyclopedia, enter an electronic chat room, or send e-mail to a professional educator. Those laid-off teachers can be retrained as data entry clerks.

As librarians and teachers become irrelevant, they'll be replaced by a cadre of instructional specialists, consultants, and professional hall monitors. Any discipline problems could be handled by trained security guards, who'd monitor the cubicles via remote video links.

Effect? With no more wasted time on student teacher interactions or off-topic discussions, education will become more efficient. Since the computers' content would be directed at maximizing test performance, standardized test scores will zoom.

Eliminating teachers and luxuries such as art lessons and field trips will save enough to recoup the cost of those fancy computers. With a little effort, this electronic education could even become a profit centre. Merely sell advertising space in the edutainment programs. Corporate sponsors, eager to market their messages to impressionable minds, would pay school systems to plug their products within the coursework.

Concerned that such a system might be dehumanizing? Not to worry. Interactive chat sessions will encourage a sense of community and enhance kids' social skills. Should a student have questions, the Internet will put her in instant touch with a trained support mentor. When necessary, real-time instructors will appear on the distance learning displays, available to interact via two way video.

The Cyberschool will showcase technology and train students for the upcoming electronic workplace. As local employment prospects change, the school board will issue updates to the curriculum over its interactive Web site. And the school board will monitor what each student learns—without idiosyncratic teachers to raise unpopular topics or challenge accepted beliefs.

Advanced students can sign up for on-line extracurricular activities—perhaps joining the Virtual Compassion Corps. There, students will be paired up across racial, gender, and class lines. Our children would offer foreigners advice and even arrange interviews with prospective employers. In this way, students will perform community service and mentor others, while displaying their cultural awareness over the network. All without ever having to shake hands with a real person, travel to a distant country, or (gasp!) face the real problems of another culture.[1] Simple, safe, and sterile.

Should parents worry about Johnny's progress, they need only log in over the Internet to see their son's latest test scores. In addition, they'll receive e-mailed reports summarizing their child's work. And at any time, they can click on an icon to see live images of their young scholar, automatically uploaded by a school video camera.

Yep, just sign up for the future: the parent-pleasin', tax-savin', inter-active-educatin', child-centrin' Cyberschool. No stuffy classrooms. No more teacher strikes. No outdated textbooks. No expensive clarinet lessons. No boring homework. No learning. Coming soon to a school district near you!

An astronomer and writer, Clifford Stoll teaches astrophysics at Berkeley in California and publishes books on Internet culture. His first internationally acclaimed book, *The Cuckoo's Egg* (1989), was followed by *Silicon Snake Oil* in 1995. (Born Buffalo, New York 1950)

---

[1] An actual proposal from the director of MIT's Laboratory for Computer Science, Michael Dertouzos.

RESPONDING

Meaning

1. Reread the first five paragraphs. The author suggests that many people are hailing high technology and an increased number of computers in schools as the answer to many problems. What are these problems?

2. Stoll presents a number of other innovations that may "solve problems" in the classroom of the future. Outline these innovations and their effects.

Form and Style

3. This opinion piece is a *satire*; it combines a critical attitude with humour and wit. The purpose of satire is to point out a weakness in the hope of contributing to its reform. What two phrases in paragraph one signal the reader that this piece is a satire? What is the weakness Stoll directs us to consider?

4. Stoll uses a number of stylistic techniques and rhetorical devices to make his point. Identify at least one example of each of the following and comment on its effect.
   a) irony
   b) interjections
   c) colloquial language
   d) sentence fragments
   e) questions directed at the reader
   f) parallelism

   Then choose one paragraph from the piece and rewrite it in a non-satirical tone to clarify Stoll's point. Compare the two paragraphs. Which do you find most effective? Why?

Creative Extension

5. Hold a debate on the statement: "Computer systems that provide fully interactive, multimedia programs to cover all aspects of the curriculum are the answer to the current problems in the education system." Divide into teams to develop arguments for the pro and con sides. Do research to find facts and opinions that will support your arguments. Finally, work on presenting your arguments clearly and persuasively.

6. Satire can be used as a tool for reform. Focus on a reform you would like to see in your school or community (increased funding for athletes, a voice for student government in school administration, changes in exam procedures, etc.). Write an opinion piece for your school or community newspaper on your topic. Research your topic well to guarantee you have all the pertinent information that will add validity to your piece. Also choose your tone and your words carefully. The key is to state your opinion persuasively without offending. Readers who are offended will not likely continue reading and your point will be lost.

The Search for the Perfect Body

✑ Mary Walters Riskin

Learning Goals

- assess validity of information and opinions
- evaluate an author's choice of form and style
- create a series of public service advertisements
- prepare a research report or essay

How do the media, particularly television, movies, and magazines, affect our view of the perfect body image?

Too tall!   Too short!   Too fat!   Too thin!   Too clumsy!   Too weak!

Who do we say these negative things about? Not our friends. Not people we respect. Sometimes, maybe, we think or say them about people we don't like. But mostly they're said about ourselves. No matter how good you feel about your abilities and accomplishments, it's pretty difficult to be confident if you don't feel good about the way you look.

I hate the way I look.—Darlene, 15, a typical teenager

The present epidemic of self-dislike is related to the whole idea of "body image." Body image is really two images. One stares back at us when we look in the mirror: that's our Actual Body Image. The other is a mental picture of what we think we ought to look like: our Idealized Body Image.

Sometimes the Idealized Body Image is so firmly planted in our minds that it affects our judgement of the actual image in the mirror. We don't see our legs the way they really are—instead we see them compared to "how they ought to look." Instead of saying, "Those are my legs, not bad!" we say, "Those are my legs and they're too fat!" or "That's my nose and it's too big."

Walking away from the mirror, we feel inadequate and miserable. Unhappy with our perceived appearance, we can't relax or feel secure with other people. If you tell yourself over and over, "I'm ugly," you start to believe it and act like it's true. Self-confidence goes right out the window.

I learned the truth at seventeen / that love was meant for beauty queens / and high-school girls with clear-skinned smiles . . .
—Janis Ian, "At Seventeen"

Deep down, we know that there are things much more important than looks. When other people ask us what's important, we say, "Being kind,"

"Being friendly," or "Being loyal." But when we look in the mirror, we say to ourselves, "What's important is the way I look, and I don't look good enough."

Like our ideas about what's right or what's wrong, or about what's in or out, our ideas about ideal body image come from a number of places . . . starting with our parents and our friends. Even when we're very young, we see adults going on diets, working out, and worrying about the desserts they want to eat. People often apologize before eating, as if they were about to do something immoral. Have you ever made an excuse like, "I didn't eat all day," or "My blood sugar is low" before pigging out?

Kids who are overweight get teased and learn from the experience that bodies are supposed to be thin and muscular, and that there is one perfect body that everyone, especially us, must have.

The image of what that perfect body looks like hits us over and over in the media, particularly in television, movies, and magazines. TV programs and advertisements tell us that women should be thin and tall, with a small waist, slender thighs, and no hips; while height, large biceps, and strong thighs and quads are desirable in men.

Styles change over the years and this affects what people imagine the ideal body to look like. In the forties and fifties, the pudgy, (by today's standards) Marilyn Monroe look was the style. In the early sixties, everyone wanted to be blond and tanned; the "Beach Boys" look was in. Today, blondes are unhappy because people make jokes about them, and tans are associated with over-age movie stars and with over-exposure to the sun, so the look has changed again.

One glance around the school or the shopping mall makes it clear that in the real world people come in every shape, size, age, and colour. But after looking at models and actors all day long, the fact that we don't look the way they do makes us feel inadequate.

> **When I was 18-years-old, and did look perfect, I was so insecure that I would face the wall in elevators because I knew the lighting was bad.**
> —*Cybill Shepherd, actor*

We're "too fat" compared to whom? "Too short" compared to whom? Sometimes the perfect body we're looking for doesn't even belong to the person we think it does.

But we continue to diet, exercise, and contemplate the cost of plastic surgery, trying to turn ourselves into people we can't be. Some people make themselves exhausted and even sick with starvation diets to lose weight or with drugs to improve their strength, only to discover that no matter what they do, they're still not happy with the way they look.

She ain't pretty; she just looks that way.—The Northern Pikes

With so many unhappy people lacking self-esteem and a positive self-image, sales of hair-dyes, make-up, exercise equipment, and diet plans are booming. People want to buy things because they think they'll make them perfect. And perfect is happy. Well, at least the advertisers are happy!

There's some evidence that things are changing. Magazines such as *Sports Illustrated* are actually telling their models to gain a few pounds. Suddenly, the anorexic look is out. Not every character on television has to be perfect anymore, and some TV shows . . . have made a genuine effort to portray people the way they really are. But there's still a lot of room for improvement.

If I spent my life worrying about what I didn't like about myself, I'd never have fun.—Susan, 15

While we're waiting for the media to change, we can change ourselves. Not our bodies, but our attitudes. We can stop playing the Ideal Body Image game in our heads. We can accept that the way we are right now is okay. We look like us, and each one of us is different. When we start to focus on ourselves as individuals, we begin to develop the self-confidence behind the most attractive look of all.

I look like this because I want to. I like looking like this.
—Sinead O'Connor

Canadian writer Mary Walters Riskin is the author of books such as *The Woman Upstairs* (1987), for which she received an Alberta Literary Award in 1987. "The Search for the Perfect Body" first appeared in *Zoot Capri* magazine. (Born 1949)

RESPONDING

Meaning

1. According to Mary Walters Riskin, "body image" is really two images. What does she mean? What are the effects of this dual image?

2. Walters Riskin suggests that today the media is attempting to right a wrong, or at least present some realism. List current TV shows that you feel do not present "idealized" people as co-stars or stars. In a journal entry, analyze the type of characters these stars represent. Do we aspire to be just like them, do we envy them, do we laugh with them, or are we encouraged to laugh at them? Assess whether or not TV is indeed doing as Walters Riskin suggests.

Form and Style

3. What stylistic devices make this opinion piece effective? Support your answers with specific references from the text.

4. What does this piece most closely resemble: an essay, a script, an interview, or the basis of a 15-minute media clip? Why? Why do you think the author chose this form? Provide evidence for your view.

Creative Extension

5. In groups, create a series of public service advertisements to promote a positive body image. You may wish to refer to the Kellogg's ad on page 485 and investigate other ads in that successful campaign. Choose a medium (print, television, Internet, etc.), clearly define your target audience, and outline your strategy. Assign specific roles to members of your creative team. Brainstorm powerful images and slogans. Include a short analysis explaining how you made your decisions.

6. Images of beauty have changed over time. Choose a particular period (a decade in the twentieth century, for example, or the Victorian Age) and research the beauty ideal of that era. Check books of quotations, look for visuals (fashions, advertisements, art), research song lyrics, and consider passages in novels, stories, or poems from that time period. Prepare a report on your findings or write an essay comparing the beauty ideal of that era with the beauty ideal today.

Proclamation of the Canadian Constitution, 1982

ℰ Pierre Elliott Trudeau

Learning Goals

- demonstrate understanding by examining context
- summarize and assess key ideas
- analyze appeals to intellect or emotion
- analyze and report on effects of nonverbal cues
- write and record an effective speech

Your Majesty, Your Royal Highness, Excellencies, Fellow Canadians.

Today, at long last, Canada is acquiring full and complete national sovereignty. The Constitution of Canada has come home. The most fundamental law of the land will now be capable of being amended in Canada, without any further recourse to the Parliament of the United Kingdom.

In the name of all Canadians, may I say how pleased and honoured we are that Your Majesty and your Royal Highness have journeyed to Canada to share with us this day of historic achievement.

For more than half a century, Canadians have resembled young adults who leave home to build a life of their own, but are not quite confident enough to take along all their belongings. We became an independent country for all practical purposes in 1931, with the passage of the Statute of Westminster. But by our own choice, because of our inability to agree upon an amending formula at that time, we told the British Parliament that we were not ready to break this last colonial link.

After fifty years of discussion, we have finally decided to retrieve what is properly ours. It is with happy hearts, and with gratitude for the patience displayed by Great Britain, that we are preparing to acquire today our complete national sovereignty. It is my deepest hope that Canada will match its new legal maturity with that degree of political maturity which will allow us all to make a total commitment to the Canadian ideal.

I speak of a Canada where men and women of Aboriginal ancestry, of French and British heritage, of the diverse cultures of the world, demonstrate the will to share this land in peace, in justice, and with mutual respect.

I speak of a Canada which is proud of, and strengthened by, its essential bilingual destiny, a Canada whose people believe in sharing and in mutual support, and not in building regional barriers.

I speak of a country where every person is free to fulfill himself or herself to the utmost, unhindered by the arbitrary actions of governments.

The Canadian ideal which we have tried to live, with varying degrees of success and failure for a hundred years, is really an act of defiance against the history of mankind. Had this country been founded upon a less noble vision, or had our forefathers surrendered to the difficulties of building this nation, Canada would have been torn apart long ago. It should not surprise us, therefore, that even now we sometimes feel the pull of those old reflexes of mutual fear and distrust—fear of becoming vulnerable by opening one's arms to other Canadians who speak a different language or live in a different culture, fear of becoming poorer by agreeing to share one's resources and wealth with fellow citizens living in regions less favoured by nature.

The Canada we are building lies beyond the horizon of such fears. Yet it is not, for all that, an unreal country, forgetful of the hearts of men and women. We know that justice and generosity can flourish only in an atmosphere of trust.

For if individuals and minorities do not feel protected against the possibility of the tyranny of the majority, if French-speaking Canadians or native peoples or new Canadians do not feel they will be treated with justice, it is useless to ask them to open their hearts and minds to their fellow Canadians.

Similarly, if provinces feel that their sovereign rights are not secure in those fields in which they have full constitutional jurisdiction, it is useless to preach to them about co-operation and sharing.

The Constitution which is being proclaimed today goes a long way toward removing the reasons for the fears of which I have spoken.

We now have a Charter which defines the kind of country in which we wish to live, and guarantees the basic rights and freedoms which each of us shall enjoy as a citizen of Canada. It reinforces the protection offered to French-speaking Canadians outside Quebec, and to English-speaking Canadians in Quebec. It recognizes our multicultural character. It upholds the equality of women, and the rights of disabled persons.

The Constitution confirms the longstanding division of powers among governments in Canada, and even strengthens provincial jurisdiction over natural resources and property rights. It entrenches the principle of equalization, thus helping less wealthy provinces to discharge their obligations without excessive taxation. It offers a way to meet the legitimate demands of our native peoples. And, of course, by its amending formula, it now permits us to complete the task of constitutional renewal in Canada.

The government of Quebec decided that it wasn't enough. It decided not to participate in this ceremony, celebrating Canada's full independence. I know that many Quebecers feel themselves pulled in two directions by that decision. But one need look only at the results of the referendum in May, 1980, to realize how strong is the attachment to Canada among the people of Quebec. By definition, the silent majority does not make a lot of noise; it is content to make history.

History will show, however, that in the guarantees written into the Charter of Rights and Freedoms, and in the amending formula—which allows Quebec to opt out of any constitutional arrangement which touches upon language and culture, with full financial compensation—nothing essential to the originality of Quebec has been sacrificed.

Moreover, the process of constitutional reform has not come to an end. The two orders of government have made a formal pledge to define more precisely the rights of native peoples. At the same time, they must work together to strengthen the Charter of Rights, including language rights in the various provinces. Finally, they must try to work out a better division of powers among governments.

It must however be recognized that no Constitution, no Charter of Rights and Freedoms, no sharing of powers can be a substitute for the willingness to share the risks and grandeur of the Canadian adventure. Without that collective act of the will, our Constitution would be a dead letter, and our country would wither away.

It is true that our will to live together has sometimes appeared to be in deep hibernation; but it is there nevertheless, alive and tenacious, in the hearts of Canadians of every province and territory. I wish simply that the bringing home of our Constitution marks the end of a long winter, the breaking up of the ice-jams and the beginning of a new spring.

For what we are celebrating today is not so much the completion of our task, but the renewal of our hope—not so much an ending, but a fresh beginning.

Let us celebrate the renewal and patriation of our Constitution; but let us put our faith, first and foremost, in the people of Canada who will breathe life into it.

It is in that spirit of faith, and of confidence, that I join with Canadians everywhere in sharing this day of national achievement. It is in their name, Your Majesty, that I now invite you, the Queen of Canada, to give solemn proclamation to our new Constitution.

Pierre Elliott Trudeau served as prime minister of Canada from 1968–1979 and again from 1980 to 1984. As prime minister, he pushed strongly for changes to the Canadian Constitution. He achieved his goals with the proclamation of the Constitution Act on April 17, 1982. The proclamation added the Canadian Charter of Rights and Freedoms to the Constitution. (*Born Montreal, Quebec 1919; died 2000*)

RESPONDING

Meaning

1. a) From the context of paragraphs 14 and 15, explain what the terms "Charter" and "Constitution" mean as they exist in Canada.
    b) Discuss the meaning of the following statements:
    - After fifty years, we have finally decided to retrieve what is properly ours.
    - The Canadian ideal . . . is really an act of defiance against the history of mankind.
    - . . . fear of becoming poorer by agreeing to share one's own resources and wealth with fellow citizens living in regions less favoured by nature.

2. a) The recurring theme of Canada as a "just society" is a large part of this proclamation speech. Summarize Trudeau's vision of the just society by outlining the conditions he sees as necessary to create it.
    b) Has Canada come closer to realizing Trudeau's vision? If so, how? If not, why not? Support your views.

Form and Style

3. Does this speech follow a logical order? Or, does it seem to flow more from emotion than reason? Support your view with specific references from the text.

4. Trudeau uses a number of techniques common to effective speechwriting (powerful metaphors, repetition, parallelism, direct appeals to the audience, etc.). Choose one very effective passage. What appealed to you about that passage? How did the writer convey his point? Share your findings with other students and develop a complete list of the techniques used in this speech.

Creative Extension

5. View videos of famous speeches, films available in your school, or 15 to 30 minutes of a television series. Choose one speech or video clip. View the video several times, paying particular attention to the *nonverbal cues* of a key speaker. Make notes on these cues, their purpose, and their effects. Play your video clip for the class while explaining your findings.

6. Choose another selection in this anthology that expressed ideas you felt strongly about. Adapt and expand this selection into a short speech. Keep in mind the techniques of effective speech writing. Practise and record your speech on videotape. Pay particular attention to volume, pace, pitch, stress, and juncture (pauses or breaks between words or word groups) in your delivery. When you feel you have a polished presentation, record a final version of your speech.

The Fire of the Human Spirit

When faced with major community or
world issues, can the individual really
make a difference?

Often when things in life aren't right, we wait for them to change. Can we
always depend on someone else to take a stand and begin the process that
will set things right or make our lives better? What inspires some individuals
to be bold, to sacrifice, to risk their safety and comfort to make important
changes? In this Echo section, a speech, interview, essay, song, and poster
provide various perspectives on these questions.

Learning Goals

- analyze theme in a variety of genres
- recognize and reflect on differences in form and style
- explore the diverse ways in which texts reveal and produce ideologies,
  identities, and positions
- create original texts in response to specific texts

Inauguration Speech

♂ Nelson Mandela

*This inaugural speech, delivered in 1994 by Nelson Mandela, the newly elected President of South
Africa, officially celebrated the end of apartheid (the South African policy of segregation and
discrimination against non-whites). The speech calls for the country's factions to forgive the past
and with a "spiritual and physical oneness" unite and build a new, glorious South Africa.*

Your Majesties, Your Highnesses, Distinguished Guests, Comrades and
Friends.

Today, all of us do, by our presence here, and by our celebrations in other parts of our country and the world, confer glory and hope to new-born liberty.

Out of the experience of an extraordinary human disaster that lasted too long, must be born a society of which all humanity will be proud.

Our daily deeds as ordinary South Africans must produce an actual South African reality that will reinforce humanity's belief in justice, strengthen its confidence in the nobility of the human soul and sustain all our hopes for a glorious life for all.

All this we owe both to ourselves and to the peoples of the world who are so well represented here today.

To my compatriots, I have no hesitation in saying that each one of us is as intimately attached to the soil of this beautiful country as are the famous jacaranda trees of Pretoria and the mimosa trees of the bushveld.

Each time one of us touches the soil of this land, we feel a sense of personal renewal. The national mood changes as the seasons change.

We are moved by a sense of joy and exhilaration when the grass turns green and the flowers bloom.

That spiritual and physical oneness we all share with this common homeland explains the depth of the pain we all carried in our hearts as we saw our country tear itself apart in a terrible conflict, and as we saw it spurned, outlawed and isolated by the peoples of the world, precisely because it has become the universal base of the pernicious ideology and practice of racism and racial oppression.

We, the people of South Africa, feel fulfilled that humanity has taken us back into its bosom, that we, who were outlaws not so long ago, have today been given the rare privilege to be host to the nations of the world on our own soil.

We thank all our distinguished international guests for having come to take possession with the people of our country of what is, after all, a common victory for justice, for peace, for human dignity.

We trust that you will continue to stand by us as we tackle the challenges of building peace, prosperity, non-sexism, non-racialism and democracy.

We deeply appreciate the role that the masses of our people and their political mass-democratic, religious, women, youth, business, traditional and other leaders have played to bring about this conclusion. Not least among them is my Second Deputy President, the Honourable F. W. de Klerk.

We would also like to pay tribute to our security forces, in all their ranks, for the distinguished role they have played in securing our first democratic elections and the transition to democracy, from blood-thirsty forces which still refuse to see the light.

The time for the healing of the wounds has come.

The moment to bridge the chasms that divide us has come.

The time to build is upon us.

We have, at last, achieved our political emancipation. We pledge ourselves to liberate all our people from the continuing bondage of poverty, deprivation, suffering, gender and other discrimination.

We succeeded to take our last steps to freedom in conditions of relative peace. We commit ourselves to the construction of a complete, just and lasting peace.

We have triumphed in the effort to implant hope in the breasts of the millions of our people. We enter into a covenant that we shall build the society in which all South Africans, both black and white, will be able to walk tall, without any fear in their hearts, assured of their inalienable right to human dignity—a rainbow nation at peace with itself and the world.

As a token of its commitment to the renewal of our country, the new Interim Government of National Unity will, as a matter of urgency, address the issue of amnesty for various categories of our people who are currently serving terms of imprisonment.

We dedicate this day to all the heroes and heroines in this country and the rest of the world who sacrificed in many ways and surrendered their lives so that we could be free.

Their dreams have become reality. Freedom is their reward.

We are both humbled and elevated by the honour and privilege that you, the people of South Africa, have bestowed on us, as the first President of a united, democratic, non-racial and non-sexist South Africa, to lead our country out of the valley of darkness.

We understand it still that there is no easy road to freedom.

We know it well that none of us acting alone can achieve success.

We must therefore act together as a united people, for national reconciliation, for nation building, for the birth of a new world.

Let there be justice for all.

Let there be peace for all.

Let there be work, bread, water and salt for all.

Let each know that for each the body, the mind and the soul have been freed to fulfill themselves.

Never, never and never again shall it be that this beautiful land will again experience the oppression of one by another and suffer the indignity of being the skunk of the world.

Let freedom reign.

The sun shall never set on so glorious a human achievement!

God bless Africa!

Thank you.

Nelson Mandela was a South African politician before he became president in 1994. As a result of organizing a political party against apartheid, Mandela was imprisoned in 1964 for 27 years. During this time, he became a symbol of the struggle against South African apartheid. After his release, he reentered politics; he received the Nobel Peace Prize in 1993 for his reforms to the government. (*Born South Africa 1918*)

RESPONDING

Meaning

1. The title of a written piece distinguishes it from all others. It is a descriptive name and should give the reader the main idea of the content. Recalling the tone and essence of Nelson Mandela's inaugural speech, develop a number of appropriate titles. Choose one and write a one-sentence descriptor.

2. According to Peggy Noonan, author of *On Speaking Well*, speeches are ". . . great because (the speaker) says big important things in a beautiful way." Find three strong examples in Mandela's inaugural speech where he does just that. Support your answers.

Form and Style

3. Many speechwriters and linguists agree that one of the strongest signal systems in the English language is *intonation*. Intonation includes *pitch* (the degree of highness or lowness of vocal tones), *stress* (the amount of emphasis given to syllables or words), and *juncture* (the pauses or breaks between words and word groups). With a partner, try using intonation techniques when reading paragraphs 6, 9, and 32 of Mandela's speech. As a class, listen to two or three students read a paragraph from the speech. Who seemed to capture the essence of the paragraph? Why?

4. a) Skim Mandela's speech in its entirety counting the number of paragraphs that begin with the same word. What effect does the speaker hope to achieve?

    b) In your view, is Mandela appealing primarily to emotion, reason, or both? Provide evidence for your interpretation.

Creative Extension

5. Look in the newspaper for a strongly worded editorial or letter to the editor. Rewrite it to create repetition, and add an image or an analogy. Using the intonation techniques outlined in question 3, prepare to read the piece aloud as a speech. Explain why you chose to use each technique when you did.

6. Do further research into the career of Nelson Mandela. How is he an example of an individual who made a difference? Write an editorial in which you present your view on what Nelson Mandela means to you as an individual, and what he can mean for Canada.

O Siem

🎵 *Susan Aglukark*

Songs often encapsulate messages in a powerful way. This lyric, by contemporary Inuit artist Susan Aglukark, presents her view on the importance of building a strong sense of community, of joining in spirit to initiate positive change.

> *Chorus:*
> O Siem[1]
> We are all family
> *O Siem*
> We're all the same
> *O Siem*
> The fires of freedom
> Dance in the burning flame
>
> *Siem o siyeya*[2]
> All people rich and poor
> *Siem o siyeya*
> Those who do and do not know
> *Siem o siyeya*
> Take the hand of one close by

---

[1] O Siem—an exclamation of joy at seeing family and friends

[2] Siem o siyeya—all people, all cultures, all races

Siem o siyeya
Of those who know because they try
And watch the walls come tumbling down

(Chorus)

Siem o siyeya
All people of the world
Siem o siyeya
It's time to make the turn
Siem o siyeya
A chance to share your heart
Siem o siyeya
To make a brand new start
And watch the walls come tumbling down

(Chorus)

Fires burn inside us
Hearts in anger leave
The wheel of change is turning
For the ones who truly need
To see the walls come tumbling down

(Chorus till fade)

Inuit singer and songwriter Susan Aglukark often combines traditional Inuit chants and themes with contemporary pop melodies. While reviving and celebrating traditional rituals and values, she also sings about the social realities of life in today's North. Susan Aglukark worked for the Department of Indian and Northern Affairs and the Inuit Tapirisat before launching her music career. She has gained international recognition and received an Aboriginal Achievement Award in 1995. "O Siem" is from her album *This Child. (Born Churchill, Manitoba 1967)*

Connecting

1. State the theme of this song in your own words. How do the images in the song support this theme?

2. In groups, brainstorm an image or icon that would best represent this song. Do the same for the Nelson Mandela speech. Explain your decisions.

3. Which verses in this song best capture the theme of Nelson Mandela's inaugural speech? Identify specific paragraphs from the speech with which you would pair these verses. Support your decisions. How are the two calls for change similar and different?

Making a Difference

⚮ June Callwood

In this excerpted essay, Canadian writer and social activist June Callwood argues that individuals can make a difference and she focuses on concrete, practical ways that people can effect change. Apathy, in her view, is the worst evil.

About a year ago, newspapers were full of a story about a woman new to Canada who had been beaten by her husband. Many people who read about it felt sympathy for the stranger hiding in a women's shelter, facing an uncertain future.

A widow of small means, a woman with grown children, called some friends. "We should do something about this," she said.

"You're right," one of her friends replied. "You should."

"Oh dear," she replied. "Me?"

"Why not?" the friend said.

The next day, news stories about the case included a few lines about a new fund that had been established. The public was informed that donations to help the battered woman could be sent to a bank, and an address was given. The widow had done three things: after consulting her bank manager, she opened an account in the woman's name with a donation of her own; then she called the media to tell of the existence of the fund; and then she contacted the police officer in charge of the case and asked him to give the woman her name and telephone number.

The assaulted woman gratefully called and they met for coffee. Over the next few weeks her benefactor raised enough money to help the woman get resettled and became the woman's companion, assisting her to find her way around the city.

"I feel very good about this," she told everyone. "I've learned a lot."

What she meant by this was her visits to a women's shelter where she talked to women fleeing from violence, and her indignant discoveries about how the welfare system works. Her experiences had changed her comfortable view of society and she was telling her friends about it, her opinions given weight because she was the only one among them with first-hand knowledge. She didn't seem to notice that she had changed greatly. She had been a warm, sympathetic woman who believed herself to be hopelessly ineffective; she had discovered instead that she was a warm, sympathetic woman who was capable and resourceful. The difference in her was pronounced; there was a new firmness in her voice and bounce in her walk.

Hannah Arendt, philosopher and writer, was absorbed much of her life with an effort to understand the nature of good and evil. In her book, *Eichmann in Jerusalem*, a study of the trial of Adolf Eichmann, the Nazi who bore a major responsibility in the Holocaust, she directed her considerable intellect to an analysis of evil. Her conclusion was that evil thrives on apathy and cannot exist without it; hence, apathy *is* evil.

When injustice encounters inertia, it uses that passivity exactly as if it were approval. In the absence of protest, evil is nourished and can flourish. The nature of goodness, therefore, bears a keen relationship to intervention. Individuals who seek to save their souls, or serve their consciences, or find meaning in their lives, or who wish to attain the quiet splendour of moral growth, are obliged to participate in their society. . . .

Nietzsche said that people wait all their lives for an opportunity to do good in their own way. Such patience is rarely rewarded. Moments when a useful contribution can be made by taking action almost never wear a name tag. Instead, they always look like "someone else's responsibility— not my business."

In moments when they are dissatisfied with themselves, most people yearn for a chance to do a redemptive good deed. They fantasize about taking leadership to get a much-needed crosswalk for the neighbourhood, or throwing themselves into good works. The problem is: how to start.

First, no one should shrink from the healthy element of selfishness that nourishes selflessness. While seeking to better their society, it is reasonable for people also, and not incidentally, to hope to improve their self-worth. It is a motive not to be derided or denied. Elevating self-esteem by behaving admirably has an ancient and honourable tradition. . . .

Altruism is the expression of the individual's best self, the god in the machinery. Instead of waiting shyly to be asked, some people simply seize an opportunity. One woman who visited a geriatric facility seven years ago noted that some of the aged were too weak to lift a spoon. Since then, twice a day she feeds a meal and chats to lonely people. Another woman read about children on ventilators who live in a hospital. She enrolled as a volunteer and goes twice a week to see a little girl she takes for walks in the corridor, reads to, and for whom she entertainingly describes the caprices of her cat. Another woman dropped in at Nellie's, a Toronto hostel for women, and asked what she could do. The staff person was dealing with an emergency at the time and asked her to get herself a cup of coffee and wait. Later, when she went in search of the volunteer, she found her scrubbing the stairs.

Another woman, a welfare recipient, was incensed that a developer had his eye on some green space where children played. She went to City Hall and persevered through polite evasions and pointed snubs until she found a civil servant and a councillor who listened. What she began snowballed into a noisy community meeting that resulted in saving the playground.

Making a difference starts with having a spunky attitude. The first thing to get out of the way is expectation that virtue always triumphs; in truth, most attempts to confront and defeat misdeeds are only partially successful or else seem to be outright failures. It doesn't matter; nothing is wasted in the universe. Even an effort that apparently goes nowhere will influence the future. Though the system looks untouched, it has a fatal crack in it. The next assault, or the one after that, will bring it down. At the very least, someone, somewhere, has learned a lesson and will be more thoughtful.

Victory, though highly desirable, is the second-best outcome of wading into a controversy on behalf of others. The real triumph is the act of making a stand and taking on the battle. It matters when someone makes an attempt to improve the quality of life for the neighbourhood, the society, the world. Even if contaminated soil continues to be dumped in the nearby lake, or better street lighting is denied, something has been achieved; someone cared enough to fight.

Real defeat isn't failure to attain the objective: it's not trying. Most people, as theatre critic Walter Kerr once put it, live half-lives halfheartedly. They cast themselves in the role of spectator, whatever the provocation to take action. The excuses are that no effort of theirs would succeed, or that in any case they don't know what to do, or they might look foolish, or what they do might make matters worse. "Innocent bystander" is an oxymoron. People who do not intervene when something is amiss give tacit permission for injustice to continue.

Becoming an activist takes practice, which can start on a small scale—like a beginner's slope for skiers-to-be. People can rehearse by responding to minor acts of tyranny: a racial insult, for instance; a clerk being high-handed with someone too intimidated to protest. The very young are powerless to challenge wrongdoing and therefore must tolerate it, but futile hand-wringing is unsuitable and unbecoming in an adult.

In recent years, so many people have taken up slingshots against corporate and government Goliaths that the paths are blazed for newcomers. Expertise abounds in where and how to apply pressure. Umbrella groups have been established in such fields as environment and disarmament; libraries list them in catalogues. Many communities have information centres that provide the location of such specialized services as daycare advocacy specialists or ratepayers groups. The National Action Committee on the Status of Women knows the field of women's issues and Tools for Peace or Oxfam in Canada can give the latest information about what's happening in Nicaragua.

A critical step, in short, is information-gathering. It makes no sense to waste enthusiasm and indignation by plunging blindly into a fight. Do as the 19th-century Prussian military strategist Carl von Clausewitz always advised: secure your base, gather informed cohorts, study the terrain: knowledge is power. . . .

Success is no fluke. When the government changes its mind about allowing a logging road through a park, when officials do an about-face concerning schooling for learning-disabled children, those desirable outcomes are the consequence of a hundred meetings, most of them tiring and frustrating, where people with good information plan strategy and put together briefs. Often the catalytic force is one event or one person whose life has been touched by loss, but the movement that results depends for its power on attracting the most creditable expertise the community can provide.

A well-informed team, making thought-out moves, is invincible. Often the opposition is frayed and fragmented in comparison. It whines, obfuscates, denies. Positive-minded, fair-speaking citizenry, equipped with clear, well-researched proposals, has a distinct advantage. . . .

People fear being ridiculous more than they fear disaster. It takes courage to go against the stream. Never mind. If the path has heart in it, it's the right one and you're right to be on it. Moreover, you'll enjoy yourself.

In the 1950s, June Callwood began publishing her writings in established Canadian magazines. Her books, including *Love, Fear, Hate and Anger* (1964) and *Portrait of Canada* (1981), explore a variety of subjects. Many of her works address social activism. She was appointed an Officer of the Order of Canada in 1986. *(Born Chatham, Ontario 1924)*

Connecting

1. a)   Who are the individuals creating change in Callwood's essay? What kinds of changes are they making?
   b)   Are the obstacles they face more or less intimidating than Mandela's? Explain your views.
2. What qualities does Callwood state individuals must have to effect change? How does change happen? Do you agree? Why or why not?
3. Much of Mandela's speech has an emotional tone, while most of Callwood's essay has a logical one. Which do you find most effective? Why?
4. Mandela dedicates his inaugural day to "... the heroes and heroines ... who sacrificed and ... surrendered their lives ..." to the good of others. Would Callwood be comfortable with such a statement? What would her reaction be? Cite a section from her essay to support your view.

Icon of Hope

5 *John Pilger*

After years of living and raising a family in England, Aung San Suu Kyi returned to her native Burma (now called Myanmar) in 1988 to look after her dying mother. There she quickly emerged as an effective political leader and founded the National League for Democracy. In 1990 she won a colossal victory and was elected president. But the military regime refused to transfer power and Aung was placed under house arrest. This excerpt is taken from an interview shortly after she was released.

JP: Three years ago an official of the regime said: 'You can forget about Suu Kyi. She's finished.' Here you are, hardly finished. How do you explain that?

SK: I think it's because democracy is not finished in Burma. Until we finish this course for democracy, none of us who are involved in it will be finished.

JP: How can you reclaim the democracy that you won at the ballot box ...?

SK: We are not the first people to have had to face an uncompromising, brutal power in the quest for freedom and basic human rights. I think we have to depend chiefly on the will of our own people for democracy. In Buddhism we are taught the four basic ingredients for success: first you must have the will to want it; then you must have the right kind of attitude; then you must have perseverance; and then you must have wisdom. So we hope to combine these four. The will of the people for democracy is there and many of us have the right kind of spirit or attitude. A number of our people have shown tremendous perseverance; and I hope we'll acquire wisdom as we go along the way. . .

JP: But it still comes down to the fact that on one side there is a power that has all the guns . . .

SK: I think it is getting more difficult in this world to resolve things through military means. The fact that the authorities are so keen on attacking us in their newspapers indicates that they themselves are not depending on guns alone. . .

JP: Well, they are clearly frightened of you. . .

SK: (Laughs) I think the age has passed when the gun can solve problems and even the military authorities know that. Why are they using the pen if they think the gun can solve all problems?

JP: Burma—with 40 per cent of its population consisting of ethnic minorities—seems like an Asian Yugoslavia. How will the country be united in the democracy that you plan?

SK: We have been disunited in Burma because there's a tremendous lack of trust between the Burmans and the other ethnic groups and among the ethnic groups themselves. In order to build up trust there has to be openness and that is why democracy is necessary. Yugoslavia is a very good example of a country where there was no sufficient openness to resolve the problems between the Serbs and the Croats. They were not provided with a framework within which they could discuss their differences and so they ended up shooting each other. In Burma we badly need the kind of framework that will allow us to 'talk about' our grievances without killing each other. I do not think there will ever be true unity, without democracy—as

Yugoslavia has proved. For more than 40 years nobody knew what was going on there: under the surface. Because there was a strong government keeping everyone in order we thought there was unity. But unity comes from within, and unless we create a framework for all of us to talk very openly and to generate trust we'll never get unity. It's not a question of 'how will democracy ever achieve unity?', but 'how will we ever achieve unity *without* democracy?'

JP: You've become quite an extraordinary icon of hope. Is that a burden?

SK: Yes and no. Yes, because if people base their hopes on you, then of course it's a responsibility. No, because I've always said that I can't do it alone and neither can the National League for Democracy. We need the help of the people and we need the rest of the world. I have always said I would do my best. I have never promised that will get the people democracy.

JP: No, but it's what people expect of you. The people I've spoken to clearly regard you as something of a saint—almost a miracle worker.

SK: I am not a saint and I think you'd better tell the world . . . I would not like to be thought of as a saint . . .

JP: What are your sinful qualities then?

SK: I've got a short temper. I'd rather sit down and read than really be engaged in public meetings and things like that . . .

JP: Your husband Michael Aris has written movingly of his early commitment to you. Could you tell me something about that?

SK: It's not all that complicated. I just said, 'I am Burmese and there may come a time when I have to go back to Burma and when that time comes I would expect you to be understanding and sympathetic' and he said, 'yes.' It was very simple—not a big negotiation process at all . . .

JP: But you couldn't—either of you—have foreseen the events that were coming. Or could you?

SK: No. But I always had every intention of coming back to do what I could do for Burma because that's where my roots are. When I got the phone call about my mother's illness it was a matter of coming home and making all the practical arrangements necessary. I had no time to think of it as a 'day of reckoning.' I knew my mother's life was probably coming to a close, but I did not know how long I would be in Burma . . .

JP: During all those years when you were under house arrest, did you ever waver in your resolve not to accept exile?

SK: No, of course I didn't. I had promised the people I would do everything I could do to get democracy. . . So there was no question of going into exile . . .

JP: What was the most difficult time for you personally during your house arrest?

SK: There isn't any particular time that stands out . . . I was worried for my colleagues, about our people out there when there was a lot of repression . . . And of course, I missed my family and I worried about my sons very much . . . My youngest was only 12 and had to be put in boarding school. But I would remind myself that the families of my colleagues were much worse off, some were in prison, whereas I knew my family was safe . . .

JP: You hadn't been able to speak to your husband or sons for two whole years. That must have produced an aloneness that in itself is frightening, surely?

SK: Yes, well I didn't feel really alone because I had the radio, you know. I listened to the radio five or six hours a day and that kept me in touch with the rest of the world and of course I had my books. And I think loneliness comes from inside. People who are free and live in big cities often suffer from terrible loneliness . . .

JP: Is Burma going to be free in your lifetime?

SK: I can't tell what my lifetime is going to be, so I can't answer that question.

JP: All right, then. Will Burma be free within the forseeable future, let's say within the next ten years?

SK: I think so, yes.

JP: What can people around the world do to help?

SK: First, think about the situation in Burma. Then I would ask them to study the UN General Assembly Resolution on Burma and to help implement it. It's a good resolution: it calls for the early and full restoration of democracy, for the acknowledgement of the will of the people in the 1990 elections and for the full participation of the people in the political life of Burma. And, of course, it calls for the release of political prisoners and observation of basic human rights.

John Pilger has worked as a war correspondent, filmmaker, and playwright. Based in London, he twice won British journalism's highest award—Journalist of the Year—for his work in Vietnam and Cambodia. He is an award-winning broadcaster and creator of documentaries. He published a collection of his writings entitled *Hidden Agendas* (1998). *(Born Sydney, Australia)*

Connecting

1. In the interview, Aung refers to the four tenets for success according to the Buddhist faith. Explain these in your own words. Why, in your view, are all four important?

2. Pilger notes that Aung is being called both an icon and a saint. How does she respond to those titles? What can you infer about her character from her responses? Support your inference.

3. In an article in *The Humanist*, journalist Penny Sanger writes about Aung, "... As she nursed her mother and heard the concerns and fears of the people ... she must have found the challenge of her own involvement unavoidable. Not to act was to collude with the oppression." Does the interview with Aung support this view? How does this quotation compare with the views in Mandela's speech and Callwood's essay? How is it reflected in Susan Aglukark's song?

A Call to Volunteer

Daily Bread Food Bank

This poster combines words and visuals to convey a powerful message about making a difference.

Connecting

1. View this poster with two other students. Share responses to the following:
   a) the focal point of the poster—what does it suggest or represent?
   b) the dominant feeling you have when you look at the image
   c) the use of colour (or lack of it) and its impact
   d) the use of words and the size and style of type

2. Summarize the main idea conveyed in this visual. How does it connect to the theme of this Echo section? Scan the other selections in this Echo and choose a paragraph or phrase that could be used as a caption to this visual. Explain your choice.

REFLECTING ON THE ECHO

1. This Echo section presented a number of different styles and genres. Which do you think most effectively presented the author's perspective on the power of people, and individuals in particular, to create change? Why? Which most engaged you? Write a short analysis explaining your view. Consider aspects of form, style, and appeal to the reader in your analysis.

2. Research another visual or audio selection that could be included in this Echo section. Consider posters, art, photographs or photo essays, songs, speeches, etc. Present your selection to a small group clearly explaining the reasons for your choice.

3. Write or create an original work that could be included in this Echo section. Choose a form, style, and medium you feel is most appropriate. Display your work and include an explanation for your decisions. You may have work that you have already done which could be included.

Fantastic Voyager

With Lord of Emperors, Toronto's Guy Gavriel Kay is confirmed as king of the imaginary world

⸱ Katherine Govier

Learning Goals

- pair-share reading and comprehension
- analyze organization and common features of reviews
- model an author's style
- develop a publicity campaign and write a review

His three-barrelled name does not come up in conventional lists of Canada's top-selling writers. He has never won a major literary prize. Yet Toronto's Guy Gavriel Kay is a global phenomenon who sells in the millions of copies in 14 languages and is consistently placed near the top of the heap in his fantasy genre. His eighth novel, *Lord of Emperors* (Viking Penguin Canada; $32) has been released to legions of passionate adherents—mostly post-adolescent boys, some boomers and seniors interested in history. His publishers hope that this book will break Kay out into the mainstream and bring him to literary respectability, the way *The Skull Beneath the Skin* did for mystery writer P. D. James. Kay deserves it, but the manoeuvre is tricky.

Compulsively readable and five years in the making, *Lord of Emperors* is set in 6th century Byzantium[1] during the reign of Justinian I and Theodora. Like its prequel, *Sailing to Sarantium*, this is a costume drama on the page, with a cast of hundreds. In *Sailing*, Crispin, a dedicated young mosaicist,[2] was called to Sarantium to build a great dome, as artists from all over the world were in fact summoned by Justinian to similar purpose. In *Lord of Emperors*, Rustem, a Bassanid physician, also makes his way to the glittering city, his powers as healer giving him access to every stratum of society. He witnesses the mounting tension in the imperial city, where every person is engaged in a struggle to leave his mark—be it in the form of an heir, a monument or an empire. As the character Strumosis . . . muses, "The past does not leave us until we die . . . and then we become someone else's memories, until they die. For most men it is all that endures."

---

[1] Byzantium—an ancient Greek city founded in the seventh century and located on the south end of the Bosporus Sea in southern Europe. Today it is the site of the modern city of Istanbul, Turkey.

[2] mosaicist—a creator of mosaics

Kay is a storyteller on the grandest scale, his Sarantine empire peopled by charioteers, senators, and slaves, all drawn in fine detail. Yet despite the distance of time and place, his historical characters breathe and bleed; we feel they are our intimates. . . . Kay has complete control of all he creates. There is genuine excitement in his evocations of the mass entertainment of chariot racing—the team building, the horse trading and the deadly race itself. He is particularly good with women characters, investing them with a cunning and licentiousness most often reserved for males in genre fiction. (The corrupt and glamorous Styliane contends for the throne to avenge her father, who was burned alive with "Sarantine fire.")

Kay's prose is surefooted and poetic, filled with references to William Butler Yeats' Byzantium poems—images of golden birds, the dancer who cannot be distinguished from the dance, and the widening gyre. But the leitmotif of the book is the glittering mosaic dome in the centre of Sarantium, which was built to last forever but was destroyed by the Christian iconoclasts,[3] whom Kay has teleported from the 8th century to the 6th for his dramatic purposes. Kay's real subject is the power of art to survive and give posterity its version of the world, even of the Emperor: only the artist is "Lord of Emperors," at least for a time.

Mosaic serves as both subject and style: Kay's method is to juxtapose chunks of contrasting tales, breaking and building suspense, inviting parallels between individuals high and low in society. It is fascinating, in a mathematical way, to see how the fractured stories connect. For fantasy readers this intellectual game, combined with high action and headlong narrative, is the basis of Kay's appeal. But for mainstream readers, it's unfashionably complex.

The shy, fiercely intelligent Kay calls his categorization as a fantasy writer both a blessing and a curse. But it seems mostly a blessing, and an accidental one at that. Kay was inspired to write fantasy after he met Christopher Tolkien, son of perhaps the greatest fantasist of all, J. R. R. Tolkien, while studying philosophy at the University of Manitoba in 1974. The two hit it off, and Kay went to Britain to work on the deceased Tolkien's final manuscript. After returning to Toronto to get a law degree, Kay began

---

[3] iconoclasts—breakers of images, especially those who were part of a movement in the eighth to ninth centuries against the use of images in religious worship in churches of the Eastern Roman Empire

publishing high fantasy in 1984 with the first volume of the trilogy The *Finovar Tapestry*. But he soon dropped wizards to develop his own brand of speculative historical fiction. In 1990 he created a huge best seller with *Tigana*, set in the Italian city-states of the Renaissance, and again in 1995 with *The Lions of Al-Rassan*, set in Moorish Spain.

Obviously, Kay is not complaining. "I've managed to break most of the rules of a genre while hanging on to most of the respect," he says. But now he wants to win broader recognition, which means that the reclusive author may have to change the pace of his life, as well as that of his narrative, and emerge from his quiet home in Toronto's Casa Loma district into the lime-light of best-seller-dom. That won't be easy. "The notion of being private is vanishing," Kay says, hinting at why he may be happiest in far-off times.

Award-winning author Katherine Govier has lived in Toronto much of her life. She publishes short stories in both Canadian and British magazines, as well as in books such as *Before and After* (1989). Two of her novels are *Random Descent* (1979) and *Angel Walk* (1996). "Fantastic Voyager" appeared in *Time* magazine on March 13, 2000. *(Born Edmonton, Alberta 1948)*

RESPONDING

Meaning

1. Pair-share this reading. Then choose a different partner to answer the following.
   a) What is a mosaic?
   b) Who is Lord of the Emperors?
   c) Who reads Kay's novels?
   d) Why does Kay say that being categorized as a fantasy writer is both a bless-ing and a curse?
   e) How does Kay differ from most writers in his dealing with female characters and their roles?
   f) Of the seven paragraphs in this review, which did you find most interesting? Why?

2. This book review also includes a character sketch of the author. In a 200-word paragraph, encapsulate his persona.

Form and Style

3. a) Outline the structure of this review by briefly describing the purpose of each paragraph. Develop a diagram that you feel best represents the review's organization.

b) Gather examples of other book and movie reviews. Consider their organization and style. In what ways is this review typical of most book or movie reviews? In what ways is it different? What common features of reviews can you identify?

4. Chose three strong sentences from this review. Using the same sentence structure, model Govier's style by writing three sentences about a book you are currently reading. If you are reading shorter fiction or non-fiction, rewrite sentences from those texts using Govier's sentence patterns.

Creative Extension

5. In small groups, do further research into the background, career, and accomplishments of Guy Gavriel Kay. Look for recent interviews, profiles, and other reviews of his books. Use a variety of print and electronic sources in your research. Then plan a publicity campaign to promote this author. Consider his major audience and decide:
   - where you would book public appearances (readings, book signings, interviews)
   - in what media (print, radio, etc.) you would place advertisements
   - what kind of advertisements they should be
   - what other promotional items to develop such as posters, bookmarks, etc.

   Include an analysis of your campaign explaining what challenges you faced, how you met them, and why you made the decisions you did.

6. Keeping in mind the major features of reviews that you have identified, write a critical review of a book, story, or non-fiction piece you have recently read. Include an appraisal of the author's style and techniques and present a clear opinion of the work.

THE AMAZING VIKINGS

They earned their brutal reputation—but the Norse were also craftsmen, explorers and believers in democracy

By **MICHAEL D. LEMONICK** and **ANDREA DORFMAN**

Learning Goals

- consider cues to learning and memory
- write a summary
- analyze purpose of visuals, design, and layout
- examine use of direct quotations
- compare design and layout in various magazines and create an original article

Ravagers, despoilers, pagans, heathens —such epithets pretty well summed up the Vikings for those who lived in the British Isles during medieval times. For hundreds of years after their bloody appearance at the end of the 8th century A.D., these ruthless raiders would periodically sweep in from the sea to kill, plunder and destroy, essentially at will. "From the fury of the Northmen, deliver us, O Lord" was a prayer uttered frequently and fervently at the close of the first millennium. Small wonder that the ancient Anglo-Saxons—and their cultural descendants in England, the U.S. and Canada—think of these sea-faring Scandinavians as little more than violent brutes.

Mythic View. This romantic depiction of the Vikings has errors galore—a winged helmet, a female warrior— but captures their adventurous spirit.

But that view is widely skewed. The Vikings were indeed raiders, but they were also traders whose economic network stretched from today's Iraq all the way to the Canadian Arctic. They were democrats who founded the world's oldest surviving parliament while Britain was still mired in feudalism. They were master metalworkers, fashioning exquisite jewellery from silver, gold and bronze. Above all, they were intrepid explorers whose restless hearts brought them to North America some 500 years before Columbus.

The broad outlines of Viking culture and achievement have been known to experts for decades, but a spate of new scholarship, based largely on archaeological excavation in Europe, Iceland, Greenland and Canada, has begun to fill in the elusive details.

The term Viking (possibly from the Old Norse *vik*, meaning bay) refers properly only to men who went on raids. All Vikings were Norse, but not all Norse were Vikings—and those who were did their viking only part time. Vikings didn't wear horned helmets (a fiction probably created for 19th century opera). And while rape and pillage were part of the agenda, they were a small part of Norse life.

In fact, this mostly blue-eyed, blond or reddish-haired people who originated in what is now Scandinavia were primarily farmers and herdsmen. They grew grains and vegetables during the short summer but depended mostly on livestock—cattle, goats, sheep and pigs. They weren't Christian until the late 10th century, yet they were not irreligious. Like the ancient Greeks and Romans, they worshipped a pantheon of deities, three of whom—Odin, Thor and Freya—we recall every week, as Wednesday, Thursday and Friday were named after them. (Other Norse words that endure in modern English: berserk and starboard.)

Nor were the Norse any less sophisticated than other Europeans. Their oral literature—epic poems known as *Eddas* as well as their sagas—was Homeric in drama and scope. During the evenings and throughout the long, dark winters, the Norse amused themselves with such challenging board games as backgammon and chess (though they didn't invent them). By day the women cooked, cleaned, sewed and ironed, using whalebone plaques as boards and running a heavy stone or glass smoother over the seams of garments.

The men supplemented their farm work by smelting iron ore and smithing it into tools and cookware; by shaping soapstone into lamps, bowls and pots; by crafting jewellery; and by carving stone tablets with floral motifs, scenes depicting Norse myths and runic inscriptions (usually to commemorate a notable deed or personage).

Most important, though, they made the finest ships of the age. Thanks to several Viking boats disinterred from burial mounds in Norway, archaeologists know beyond a doubt that the wooden craft were "unbelievable—the best in Europe by far," according to William Fitzhugh, director of the National Museum's Arctic Studies Center. Sleek and streamlined, powered by both sails and oars, quick and highly manoeuvrable, the boats could operate equally well in shallow waterways and on the open seas.

The Norse were skilled blacksmiths, using hammers like this to beat hot iron into weapons and other implements.

With these magnificent craft, the Norse searched far and wide for goods they couldn't get at home: silk, glass, sword-quality steel, raw silver and silver coins that they could melt down and rework. In return they offered furs, grindstones, Baltic amber, walrus ivory, walrus hides and iron.

At first, the Norse traded locally around the Baltic Sea. But from there, says Fitzhugh, "their network expanded to Europe and Britain, and then up the Russian rivers. They reached Rome, Baghdad, the Caspian Sea, probably Africa too. Buddhist artifacts from northern India have been found in a Swedish Viking grave, as has a charcoal brazier from the Middle East." The Hagia Sophia basilica in Istanbul has a Viking inscription in its floor. A Mycenaean lion in Venice is covered with runes of the Norse alphabet.

Sometime in the late 8th century, however, the Vikings realized there was a much easier way to acquire luxury goods. The monasteries they dealt with in Britain, Ireland and mainland Europe were not only extremely wealthy but also situated on isolated coastlines and poorly defended—sitting ducks for men with agile ships. With the raid on England's Lindisfarne monastery in 793, the rein of Viking terror officially began. Says archaeologist Colleen Batey of the Glasgow Museums: "They had a preference for anything that looked pretty," such as bejewelled books or gold, silver and other precious metals that could be recrafted into jewellery for wives and sweethearts. Many monasteries and trading centres were attacked repeatedly, even annually. In some cases the Vikings extorted protection money, known as danegeld, as the price of peace.

The Vikings didn't just pillage and run; sometimes they came to stay. Dublin became a Viking town; so did Lincoln and York, along with much of the surrounding territory in northern and eastern England. In Scotland, Vikings maintained their language and political links to their homeland well into the 15th century. Says Batey: "The northern regions of Scotland, especially, were essentially a

Scandinavian colony up until then." Vikings also created the duchy of Normandy, in what later became France, as well as a dynasty that ruled Kiev, in Ukraine.

Given their hugely profitable forays into Europe, it's not entirely clear why the Vikings chose to strike out across the forbidding Atlantic. One reason might have been a growing population; another might have been political turmoil. The search for such exotic trade goods as furs and walrus ivory might have also been a factor. The timing, in any event, was perfect: during the 9th century,

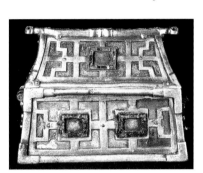

This ornate box, snatched from a Scottish monastery, ended up with a Norsewoman named Ranvaig, who put her name on it.

when the expansion began, the climate was unusually warm and stable. Pastures were productive, and the pack ice that often clogged the western North Atlantic was at a minimum.

So westward the Vikings went. Their first stop, in about 860, was the Faeroe Islands, northwest of Scotland. Then, about a decade later, the Norse reached Iceland. Experts believe as many as 12 000 Viking immigrants ultimately settled there, taking their farm animals with them. (Inadvertently, they also brought along mice, dung beetles, lice, human fleas and a host of animal parasites, whose remains, trapped in soil, are helping archaeologists form a detailed picture of early medieval climate and Viking life. Bugs, for example, show what sort of livestock the Norse kept.)

Agriculture was tough in Iceland; it was too cold, for instance, to grow barley for that all important beverage, beer. "They tried to grow barley all over Iceland, but it wasn't economical," says archaeologist Thomas McGovern of New York City's Hunter College.

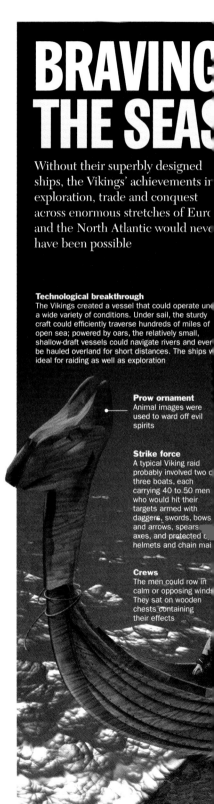

BRAVING THE SEAS

Without their superbly designed ships, the Vikings' achievements in exploration, trade and conquest across enormous stretches of Euro and the North Atlantic would neve have been possible

Technological breakthrough
The Vikings created a vessel that could operate und a wide variety of conditions. Under sail, the sturdy craft could efficiently traverse hundreds of miles of open sea; powered by oars, the relatively small, shallow-draft vessels could navigate rivers and ever be hauled overland for short distances. The ships w ideal for raiding as well as exploration

Prow ornament
Animal images were used to ward off evil spirits

Strike force
A typical Viking raid probably involved two o three boats, each carrying 40 to 50 men who would hit their targets armed with daggers, swords, bows and arrows, spears axes, and protected b helmets and chain mai

Crews
The men could row in calm or opposing winds They sat on wooden chests containing their effects

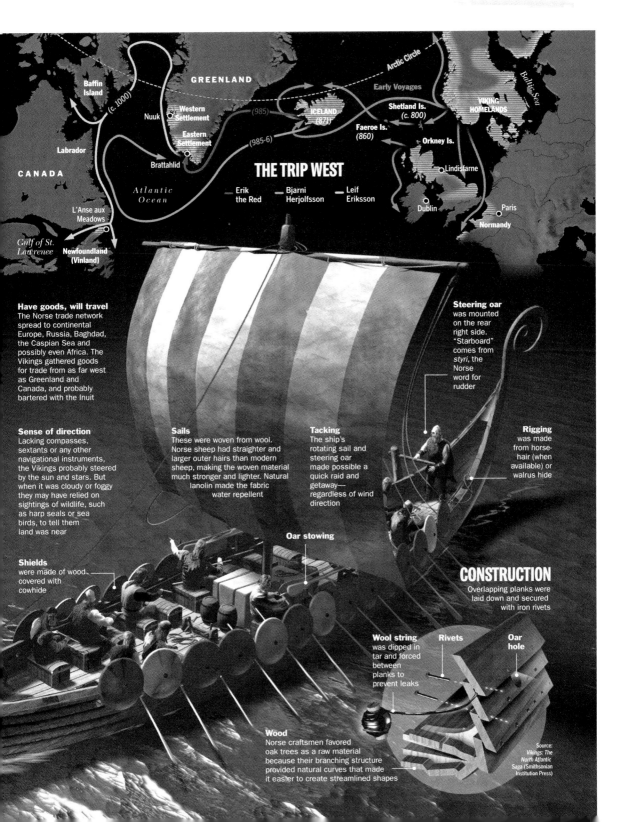

THE TRIP WEST

GREENLAND

Arctic Circle

Baltic Sea

Baffin Island

(c. 1000)

Early Voyages

Nuuk

Western Settlement

(985)

ICELAND (871)

Shetland Is. (c. 800)

VIKING HOMELANDS

Eastern Settlement

Faeroe Is. (860)

Labrador

(985-6)

Orkney Is.

CANADA

Brattahlid

Lindisfarne

Atlantic Ocean

— Erik the Red   — Bjarni Herjolfsson   — Leif Eriksson

L'Anse aux Meadows

Dublin

Paris

Gulf of St. Lawrence

Newfoundland (Vinland)

Normandy

Have goods, will travel
The Norse trade network spread to continental Europe, Russia, Baghdad, the Caspian Sea and possibly even Africa. The Vikings gathered goods for trade from as far west as Greenland and Canada, and probably bartered with the Inuit

Steering oar
was mounted on the rear right side. "Starboard" comes from *styri*, the Norse word for rudder

Sense of direction
Lacking compasses, sextants or any other navigational instruments, the Vikings probably steered by the sun and stars. But when it was cloudy or foggy they may have relied on sightings of wildlife, such as harp seals or sea birds, to tell them land was near

Sails
These were woven from wool. Norse sheep had straighter and larger outer hairs than modern sheep, making the woven material much stronger and lighter. Natural lanolin made the fabric water repellent

Tacking
The ship's rotating sail and steering oar made possible a quick raid and getaway—regardless of wind direction

Rigging
was made from horse-hair (when available) or walrus hide

Oar stowing

Shields
were made of wood covered with cowhide

CONSTRUCTION
Overlapping planks were laid down and secured with iron rivets

Wool string
was dipped in tar and forced between planks to prevent leaks

Rivets

Oar hole

Wood
Norse craftsmen favored oak trees as a raw material because their branching structure provided natural curves that made it easier to create streamlined shapes

Source: Vikings: The North Atlantic Saga (Smithsonian Institution Press)

Nevertheless, the colony held on, and in 930 Iceland's ruling families founded a general assembly, known as the Althing, at which representatives of the entire population met annually to discuss matters of importance and settle legal disputes. The institution is still in operation today, more than a thousand years later.

In 982 the Althing considered the case of an ill-tempered immigrant named Erik the Red. Erik, the saga says, had arrived in Iceland several years earlier after being expelled from Norway for murder. He settled down on a farm, married a Christian woman named Thjodhild (the Norse were by now starting to convert) and had three sons, Leif, Thorvald and Thorstein, and one daughter, Freydis. It wasn't long, though, before Erik began feuding with a neighbour—something about a cow and some wallboards—and ended up killing again.

The Althing decided to exile him for three years, so Erik sailed west to explore a land he had heard about from sailors who had been blown off course. Making his way around a desolate coast, he came upon magnificent fjords flanked by lush meadows and forests of dwarf willow and birch, with glacier-strewn mountain ranges towering in the distance. This "green land," he decided (in what might have been a clever bit of salesmanship), would be a perfect place to live. In 985 Erik returned triumphantly to Iceland and enlisted a group of followers to help him establish the first Norse outposts on Greenland. Claiming the best plot of land for himself, Erik established his base at Brattahlid, a verdant spot at the neck of the fjord on the island's southwestern tip, across from what is now the modern airport at Narsarsuaq. He carved out a farm and built his wife a tiny church, just 3 m wide by 4 m long. (According to one legend, she refused to sleep with him until it was completed.)

The remains of this stone-and-turf building were found in 1961. The most spectacular discovery from the Greenland colonies was made in 1990, however, when two Inuit hunters searching for caribou about 55 miles east of Nuuk (the modern capital) noticed several large pieces of wood sticking out of a bluff. Because trees never grew in the area, they reported their discovery to the national museum. The wood turned out to be part of an enormous Norse building, perfectly sealed in permafrost covered by 15 m

Helmet. The only complete example known, it was found at a cremation site.

of sand: "definitely one of the best-preserved Norse sites we have," says archaeologist Joel Berglund, vice director of the Greenland National Museum and Archives in Nuuk.

According to Berglund, a leader of the dig at the "Farm Beneath the Sand" from 1991 through 1996, the site was occupied for nearly 300 years, from the mid-11th century to the end of the 13th century. "It went from small to big and then from big to small again," he explains. "They started with a classic longhouse, which later burned down." The place was abandoned for a while and then rebuilt into what became a "centralized farm," a huge, multifunction building with more than 30 rooms housing perhaps 15 or 20 people, plus sheep, goats, cows and horses.

The likeliest reason for this inter-species togetherness was the harsh climate. Observes Berglund: "The temperature today gets as cold as −50°C." Bones recovered from trash middens in the house indicate that the occupants dined mostly on wild caribou and seals, which were plentiful along the coast. (The domesticated animals were apparently raised for their wool and milk, not meat.) Scientists recovered more than 3000 artifacts in the ruins, including a wooden loom, children's toys and

ID tag. Wood markers were used to identify property. This rune-covered example comes from Bergen.

combs. Along with hair, body lice and animal parasites, these items will be invaluable in determining what each room was used for. Researchers also found bones and other remnants from meals, and even a mummified goat. That means, says Berglund, "we'll even be able to tell whether there was enough food and whether the people and animals were healthy."

As Greenland's overlord, Erik the Red took a cut of virtually everyone's profits from the export of furs and ivory. Material success apparently did not keep Erik and his family content, though; they undoubtedly heard of a voyage by a captain named Bjarni Herjolfsson, who had been blown off course while en route to Greenland from Iceland. After drifting for many days, Bjarni spotted a forested land. But instead of investigating this unknown territory, he turned back and reached Greenland.

Intrigued by this tale, Erik's eldest son Leif, sometime between 997 and 1003, decided to sail westward to find the new land. First, say the sagas, the crew came to a forbidding land of rocks and glaciers. Then they sailed on to a wooded bay, where they dropped anchor for a while. Eventually they continued south to a place he called Vinland ("wineland," probably for the wild grapes that grew there). Leif and his party made camp for the winter, then sailed home. Members of his family returned in later years, but

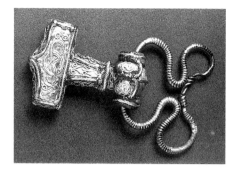

Kingly gifts. Norse rulers would bestow valuable jewellery, like this amulet, on local officials to ensure their allegiance.

VIKINGS AND HISTORY

Leif never did. Erik died shortly after his son returned, and Leif took over the Greenland colony. Though he retained ownership of the Norse base in North America and received a share of the riches that were brought back, he stopped exploring.

This much had long been known from the Icelandic sagas, but until 1960 there was no proof of Leif's American sojourns. In retrospect, it is astonishing that the evidence took so long to be found. That year Norwegian explorer Helge Ingstad and his wife, archaeologist Anne Stine Ingstad, went to Newfoundland to explore a place identified on an Icelandic map from the 1670s as "Promontorium Winlandiae," near the small fishing village of L'Anse aux Meadows, in the province's northern reaches. They were certain that it marked the location of an ancient Norse settlement.

Finding the settlement turned out to be absurdly easy. When the Ingstads asked the locals if there were any odd ruins in the area, they were taken to a place known as "the Indian camp." They immediately recognized the grass-covered ridges as Viking-era ruins like

those in Iceland and Greenland.

During the next seven years, the Ingstads and an international team of archaeologists exposed the foundations of eight separate buildings. Sitting on a narrow terrace between two bogs, the buildings had sod walls and peaked sod roofs laid over a (now decayed) wooden frame; they were evidently meant to be used year-round. The team also unearthed a Celtic-style bronze pin with a ring-shaped head similar to ones the Norse used to fasten their cloaks, a soapstone spindle whorl, a bit of bone needle, a small whetstone for sharpening scissors and needles, lumps of worked iron and iron boat nails. (All these items helped win over detractors, since the artifacts were clearly not native to America.)

Further excavation in the mid-1970s under the auspices of Parks Canada, the site's custodian, made it plain that this was most likely the place where Leif set up camp. Among the artifacts turned up: loom weights, another spindle whorl, a bone needle, jasper fire starters, pollen, seeds, butternuts and, most important, about 2000 scraps of worked wood that were subsequently radiocarbon dated to between 980 and 1020—just when Leif visited Vinland.

The configuration of the ruined buildings, the paucity of artifacts and garbage compared with those found at other sites, and the absence of a cemetery, stables and holding pens for animals have convinced Birgitta Linderoth

Wallace, the site's official archaeologist, that L'Anse aux Meadows wasn't a permanent settlement and was used for perhaps less than 10 years.

Instead, she believes, it served as a base camp for several exploratory expeditions up and down the coast, perhaps as far south as the Gulf of St. Lawrence. "We know this because of the butternuts," she says. "The closest places they grow are east of Quebec near the Gulf of St. Lawrence or in eastern New Brunswick. They are too heavy for birds to carry, and they can't float. And we know the Norse considered them a delicacy."

The National Museum's Fitzhugh notes that the location of the camp was advantageous for various reasons. "L'Anse aux Meadows is rocky and dangerous," he admits. "There are much better places just a few miles away—but there's a good view. They could watch out for danger, and they could bring their boats in and keep an eye on them." What's more, Fitzhugh says, "they would have built where they could easily be found by other people. That's why they chose the tip of the peninsula. All they had to tell people was, 'Cross the Big Water, turn left and keep the land on your right.'" With fair winds, the voyage would have taken about two weeks; a group of men who tried it in the replica Viking ship Snorri (named after the first European born in America) in 1998 were stuck at sea for three months.

Despite all the natural resources, the Norse never secured a foothold in the New World. Within a decade or so after Leif's landing at L'Anse aux Meadows, they were gone. Wallace, for one, believes that there were simply too few people to keep the camp going and that those stationed there got homesick: "You had a very small community that could barely sustain itself. Recent research has shown it had only 500 people, and we know you need that many at a minimum to start a colony in an uninhabited area. They had barely got started in Greenland when they decided to go to North America. It wasn't practical, and I think they missed their family and friends."

Fitzhugh offers another theory. "I think they recognized that they had found wonderful resources but decided they couldn't defend themselves and were unable to risk their families to stay there," he says. "Imagine 30 Norsemen in a boat on the St. Lawrence meeting a band of Iroquois. They would have been totally freaked out."

As for discovering additional Norse outposts in North America, most experts think the chances are very slim. "These areas were heavily occupied by Native Americans," says archaeologist Patricia Sutherland of the Canadian Museum of Civilization in Hull, "so while there may have been some trade, relations would have been hostile. Maybe someone will find an isolated Norse farm on the coast of Labrador or Baffin Island, but not an outpost."

Michael D. Lemonick studied economics and journalism at university, but became a science writer for *Time* in 1986 and, later, an Associate Editor. He contributes articles to other magazines and has written *The Light at the Edge of the Universe* and *Other Worlds* (Born Princeton, New Jersey 1953). Andrea Dorfman is the New York-based science correspondent for *Time*. Since joining *Time* in 1985, she has reported dozens of cover stories on topics as diverse as dinosaurs, undersea exploration, genetics, the Shroud of Turin, human evolution, and the Vikings. "The Amazing Vikings" appeared in the May 8, 2000 issue of *Time*. (Born New York City, New York)

RESPONDING

Meaning

1. In small groups, record information you learned about the Vikings from this article, information that you did not know before. Do this from memory, without rereading the article. As you make your lists, discuss why you remember certain pieces of information. What cues prompt you to think and remember?

2. In an organizer, compare the commonly accepted negative information about the Vikings with the various positive contributions that are outlined in this article. Use this information to write a concise summary of this article, stating the main idea and examples of key supporting details.

Form and Style

3. a) What purposes do the visuals serve in this article? Note the different ways they contribute to the article and enhance understanding.

   b) How does the design and layout of this article contribute to its impact? Refer specifically to elements such as the following in your response:
   - size and style of type for headings
   - size and placement of visuals
   - use and effectiveness of photo captions and labels in illustrations
   - use of sidebar or marginal elements
   - use of colour

4. List the direct quotations used in this article. Why have the authors included them? What effects do they have on you as the reader?

Creative Extension

5. Gather other examples of feature articles from different magazines. Choose two and compare the design, layout, and use of visuals with those elements in this article. How do the design and layout of the articles reflect the purpose of the article and the magazine? What overall tone or impression is the design aiming to create? What specific impact do the various elements have on you as the reader?

6. In small groups, research the archaeological site at L'Anse aux Meadows, Newfoundland. Work together to prepare an article for a magazine such as *Canadian Geographic*. Include visuals with captions, diagrams, maps, and any other features you feel are important. Decide how you will lay out the article and consider the size and style of type to use. If possible, design your article on computer.

A Whack on the Side of the Head

How You Can Be More Creative

Learning Goals

- examine meaning and relate it to personal experience
- analyze organization and relate it to purpose
- apply knowledge in a new context
- develop a commercial and multimedia presentation

The Right Answer

Exercise: Five figures are shown below. Select the one that is different from the others.

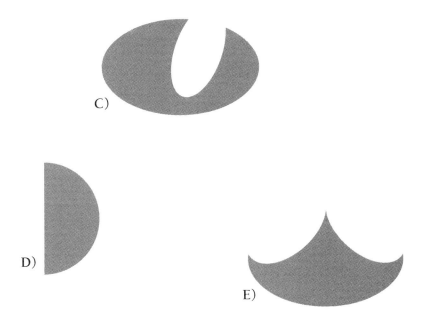

Learning How to Think

Children enter school as question marks and leave as periods.
—Neil Postman, Educator

Life can be like a big noisy party with people talking, music playing, and glasses clinking. But even with all this noise, it's possible for you to understand the person across from you. Or the one thirty feet [9 m] away. That's because our attention is selective—we can tune in certain things and tune out others.

See for yourself. Take a look around where you're sitting and find four things that have "red" in them. Go ahead and do it. With a "red" mindset, you'll find that red jumps right out at you: a red telephone book, red in the blister on your index finger, red in the wallpaper, and so on. Similarly, whenever you learn a new word, you hear it eight times in the next three days. In like fashion, you've probably noticed that after you get a new car, you see that make everywhere. That's because people find what they are looking for. If you look for beauty, you'll find beauty. If you look for conspiracies, you'll find conspiracies. It's all a matter of setting your mental channel.

Where do you learn how to set your mental channel? One important source is your formal education. There you learn what is appropriate and what is not. You learn many of the questions you use to probe your surroundings. You learn where to search for information, which ideas to pay attention to, and how to think about these ideas. Your educational training gives you many of the concepts you use to order and understand the world.

Speaking of education, how did you do on the five-figure exercise on the previous page? If you chose figure B, congratulations! You've picked the right answer. Figure B is the only one that has all straight lines. Give yourself a pat on the back!

Some of you, however, may have chosen figure C, thinking that C is unique because it's the only one that is asymmetrical. And you are also right! C is the right answer. A case can also be made for figure A: it's the only one with no points. Therefore, A is the right answer. What about D? It is the only one that has both a straight line and a curved line. So, D is the right answer too. And E? Among other things, E is the only one that looks like a projection of a non-Euclidean triangle into Euclidean space. It is also the right answer. In other words, they are all right depending on your point of view.

But you won't find this exercise in school. Much of our educational system is geared toward teaching people to find "the right answer." By the time the average person finishes college, he or she will have taken over 2600 tests, quizzes, and exams—many similar to the one you just took. The "right answer" approach becomes deeply ingrained in our thinking. This may be fine for some mathematical problems where there is in fact only one right answer. The difficulty is that most of life isn't this way. Life is ambiguous; there are many right answers—all depending on what you are looking for. But if you think there is only one right answer, then you'll stop looking as soon as you find one.

When I was a sophomore in high school, my English teacher put a small chalk dot like the one below on the blackboard.

She asked the class what it was. A few seconds passed and then some-one said, "A chalk dot on the blackboard." The rest of the class seemed relieved that the obvious had been stated, and no one else had anything more to say. "I'm surprised at you," the teacher told the class. "I did the same exercise yesterday with a group of kindergartners, and they thought of fifty different things it could be: an owl's eye, a cigar butt, the top of a telephone pole, a star, a pebble, a squashed bug, a rotten egg, and so on. They had their imaginations in high gear.

In the ten-year period between kindergarten and high school, not only had we learned how to find the right answer, we had also lost the ability to look for more than one right answer. We had learned how to be specific, but we had lost much of our imaginative power.

Consequences

"I'm not returning until you fix it," bandleader Count Basie told a nightclub owner whose piano was always out of tune. A month later Basie got a call that everything was fine. When he returned, the piano was still out of tune. "You said you fixed it!" an irate Basie exclaimed. "I did," came the reply. "I had it painted."

The practice of looking for the "one right answer" can have serious conse-quences in the way we think about and deal with problems. Most people don't like problems, and when they encounter them, they usually react by taking the first way out they can find—even if they solve the wrong prob-lem as did the nightclub owner in the above story. I can't overstate the danger in this. If you have only one idea, you have only one course of action open to you, and this is quite risky in a world where flexibility is a requirement for survival.

An idea is like a musical note. In the same way that a musical note can only be understood in relation to other notes (either as a part of a melody or a chord), an idea is best understood in the context of other ideas. If you have only one idea, you don't have anything to compare it to. You don't know its strengths and weaknesses. I believe that the French philosopher Emilé Chartier hit the nail squarely on the head when he said:

**Nothing is more dangerous than an
idea when it's the only one you have.**

For more effective thinking, we need different points of view. Otherwise, we'll get stuck looking at the same things and miss seeing things outside our focus.

The Second Right Answer

A leading business school did a study that showed that its graduates performed well at first, but in ten years, they were overtaken by a more streetwise, pragmatic group. The reason according to the professor who ran the study: "We taught them how to solve problems, not recognize opportunities. When opportunity knocked, they put out their 'Do Not Disturb' signs."

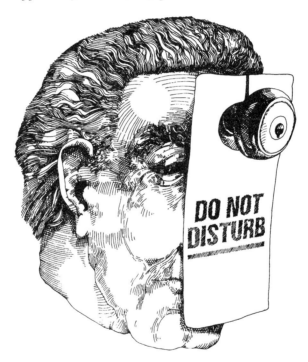

Not long ago I did a series of creative thinking workshops for the executive staff of a large computer company. The president had called me in because he was concerned about the stagnant thinking environment at the top. It seemed that whenever his subordinates would make a proposal, that's all they'd make—just one. They wouldn't offer any alternative ideas. Since they had been trained to look for the right answer, they usually didn't go beyond the first one they found. The president knew that it was easier to make good decisions if he had a variety of ideas from which to choose. He was also concerned with how conservative this "one-idea" tendency had made his people's thinking. If a person were presenting only one idea, he would generally propose the "sure thing" rather than take a chance on a less likely offbeat idea. This state of affairs created a less than ideal climate for generating innovative ideas. I told them that one way to be more creative is to:

Look for the second right answer.

Often, it is the second right answer which, although offbeat or unusual, is exactly what you need to solve a problem in an innovative way.

One technique for finding the second right answer is to change the questions you use to probe a problem. For example, how many times have you heard someone say, "What is the answer?" or "What is the meaning of this?" or "What is the result?" These people are looking for *the* answer, and *the* meaning, and *the* result. And that's all they'll find—just one. If you train yourself to ask questions that solicit plural answers like "What are the answers?" or "What are the meanings?" or "What are the results?" you will find that people will think a little more deeply and offer more than one idea. As the Nobel Prize winning chemist Linus Pauling put it:

The best way to get a good
idea is to get a lot of ideas.

You may not be able to use all of them, but out of the number you generate you may find a few that are worthwhile. This is why professional photographers take so many pictures when shooting an important subject. They may take twenty, sixty, or a hundred shots. They'll change the exposure, the lighting, the filters, and so on. That's because they know that out of all the pictures they take, there may be only a few that capture what they're looking for. It's the same thing with creative thinking: you need to generate a lot of ideas to get some good ones.

Inventor Ray Dolby (the man who took "hiss" out of recorded music) has a similar philosophy. He says:

> Inventing is a skill that some people have and some people don't.
> But you can learn how to invent. You have to have the will not to
> jump at the first solution, because the really elegant solution might

be right around the corner. An inventor is someone who says, "Yes, that's one way to do it, but it doesn't seem to be an optimum solution." Then he keeps on thinking.

When you look for more than one right answer, you allow your imagination to open up. How do you keep a fish from smelling? Cook it as soon as you catch it. Freeze it. Wrap it in paper. Leave it in the water. Switch to chicken. Keep a cat around. Burn incense. Cut its nose off.

Change Your Question

*The second assault on the same problem should come
from a totally different direction.*
—Tom Hirshfield, Physicist

Another technique for finding more answers is to change the wording in your questions. If an architect looks at an opening between two rooms and thinks, "What type of *door* should I use to connect these rooms?" that's what she'll design—a door. But if she thinks "What sort of *passageway* should I put here?" she may design something different like a "hallway," an "air curtain," a "tunnel," or perhaps a "courtyard." Different words bring in different assumptions and lead your thinking in different directions.

Here's an example of how such a strategy can work. Several centuries ago, a curious but deadly plague appeared in a small village in Lithuania. What was curious about this disease was its grip on its victim; as soon as a person contracted it, he'd go into a deep almost death-like coma. Most died within a day, but occasionally a hardy soul would make it back to the full bloom of health. The problem was that since eighteenth century medical technology wasn't very advanced, the unafflicted had quite a difficult time telling whether a victim was dead or alive.

Then one day it was discovered that someone had been buried alive. This alarmed the townspeople, so they called a town meeting to decide what should be done to prevent such a situation from happening again. After much discussion, most people agreed on the following solution. They decided to put food and water in every casket next to the body. They would even put an air hole from the casket up to the earth's surface. These procedures would be expensive, but they would be more than worthwhile if they would save people's lives.

Another group came up with a second, less expensive, right answer. They proposed implanting a twelve-inch long stake in every coffin lid directly over where the victim's heart would be. Then whatever doubts there were about whether the person was dead or alive would be eliminated as soon as the coffin lid was closed.

What differentiated the two solutions were the questions used to find them. Whereas the first group asked, "What should we do if we bury somebody *alive*?" the second group wondered, "How can we make sure everyone we bury is *dead*?"

I'd like to conclude this "right answer" chapter with one of my favourite Sufi stories.

> Two men had an argument. To settle the matter, they went to a Sufi judge for arbitration. The plaintiff made his case. He was very eloquent and persuasive in his reasoning. When he finished, the judge nodded in approval and said, "That's right, that's right."
>
> On hearing this, the defendant jumped up and said, "Wait a second, judge, you haven't even heard my side of the case yet." So the judge told the defendant to state his case. He, too, was very persuasive and eloquent. When he finished, the judge said, "That's right, that's right." When the clerk of court heard this, he jumped up and said, "Judge, they both can't be right." The judge looked at the clerk and said, "That's right, that's right."

Moral: Truth is all around you; what matters is where you place your focus.

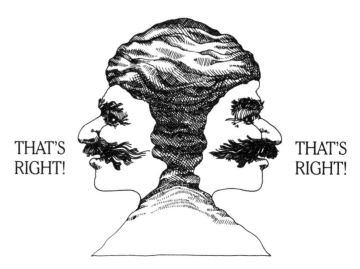

THAT'S RIGHT!   THAT'S RIGHT!

Summary

Much of our educational system has taught us to look for the one right answer. This approach is fine for some situations, but many of us have a tendency to stop looking for alternative right answers after the first right answer has been found. This is unfortunate because often it's the second, or third, or tenth right answer which is what we need to solve a problem in an innovative way.

There are many ways to find the second right answer—asking "what if," playing the fool, reversing the problem, breaking the rules, etc. Indeed, that's what much of this book is about. The important thing, however, is to look for the second right answer, because unless you do, you won't find it.

Tip: The answers you get depend on the questions you ask. Play with your wording to get different answers. One technique is to solicit plural answers. Another is to ask questions that whack people's thinking. One woman told me that she had a manager who would keep her mind on its toes by asking questions such as: "What are three things you feel totally neutral about?" and "What parts of your problem do you associate with tax returns and what parts with poetry?"

Roger von Oech runs lectures, seminars, and workshops aimed to stimulate creativity and innovation in business. He is president and founder of the consulting company Creative Think. "The Right Answer" was published in his book *A Whack on the Side of the Head: How You Can Be More Creative*. He has also written *A Kick in the Seat of the Pants*.

RESPONDING

Meaning

1. In small groups, discuss what the following phrases from the reading mean. Remember to consider the context of each one.
    a) our attention is selective
    b) it's all a matter of setting your mental channel
    c) formal education gives you the training and concepts you use to order and understand the world
    d) right depends on your own point of view
    e) flexibility is a requirement for survival
    f) different words bring in different assumptions and lead your thinking in different directions

2. For any two of the phrases in question 1, create an example (this need not be in written form) or write a personal anecdote to illustrate. Share your work with others in a small group. Gather examples from the class into a collection of personal reflections on "The Right Answer."

Form and Style

3. Outline the organization of this excerpt. List the title, headings, and main point of each section. Identify the different elements von Oech uses to clarify and highlight his main points. Consider visual layout including the use of different sizes and styles of type as well. Conclude with a comment on how well you think the organization of this excerpt suits its purpose.

4. Reread the summary at the end of the article. How well does it explain the author's thesis? Would you remember von Oech's message as well without this summary? Why or why not? Why do you think he added the "Tip" at the end?

Creative Extension

5. Von Oech discusses how important creative thinking is in the business world. The creators of television commercials, for example, have to brainstorm to find their "right way" to advertise a product by selecting a channel and tuning into a consumer type and market. Analyze two television commercials to determine their advertising strategy. Then with two other students, create a commercial to sell or promote a product or cause of your choice. Apply von Oech's ideas on creative thinking.

6. In groups, prepare a multimedia presentation entitled "How You Can Be More Creative" for a group of business people or students. Base your presentation on the ideas presented in von Oech's excerpt. Incorporate visual aids effectively and use pace, pitch, volume, and eye contact with your audience to emphasize key ideas. If you have the equipment, develop a PowerPoint presentation.

It's All About Approach

⌐ Alice M. Patterson

Venturing into unfamiliar territory without a map is a sure-fire way to get lost. Another sure-fire path to getting lost is making an informative instructional video without picking the proper approach.

Learning Goals

- define technical terms
- examine tone in a "how-to" article
- create an outline
- adapt an article to a storyboard for a video
- write an original "how-to" article

In this article, we'll explore a variety of approaches you can use in your videos, and uncover several production elements you can use to make your instructional videos top-notch. We can't cover every approach within this short article, but we will explore the basics needed to get you on the road to producing a quality video. Read on as we explore the possibilities with help from *Videomaker's* own experts: Staff Videographer Perry Jenkins and Associate Editor Keith Lander, who explain some of the approaches *Videomaker* currently uses in making our own tapes.

Approach With Caution

Making an instructional video without some type of plan will likely lead you in a direction other than the one you intended. Think of the approach you use in making your video as a roadmap allowing you to reach your final destination: the finished videotape. Before you begin, though, you'll want to consider the following questions.

• How long should your video be? Before choosing your approach, decide how long you want your completed production to be. The instructional videotapes produced at *Videomaker* are generally 30 minutes in length and are broken down into six, four-minute segments separated by 10-second "bumpers" or lead-ins to the next segment. In addition, each tape begins with an animated opening, followed by a 30-second introduction, and ends with a 30-second wrap-up followed by the closing credits.

"We use three different approaches in each of our 30-minute videos," said Lander, the video editor. "It breaks up the video, and gives it a better feel."

• How much time do you have? As you'll see later in this article, some approaches are more time-consuming than others. It's important to evaluate how much time you have—and how much time you're willing to put into your project—to choose the proper approach. If you're on a tight schedule, for example, you won't want to choose an approach involving grandiose, time-consuming shots or extra time in the editing room.

• Who are you trying to reach? Identifying your target audience is key to picking an appropriate approach. Is your audience a group of teens? Business associates? Pre-schoolers?

Know who you're trying to reach and plan your approach before you develop your script to avoid producing a video that's out-of-touch with your intended audience.

• What type of equipment and budget do you have? You don't have to have any fancy bells or whistles to

to use, the experts advise heeding these basic concepts during the production process.

"Think of keeping continuity throughout your production, and always keep the theme of your videotape in mind," Lander advises.

One way to keep continuity throughout your video, Lander said, is to use the same colour background in each segment. Lander said the *Videomaker* crew often uses this technique, but adds variety to each segment through the use of different camera angles or lighting techniques.

Another important consideration, no matter which approach you decide

Know who you're trying to reach and plan your approach before you develop your script to avoid producing a video that's out-of-touch with your intended audience.

produce a winning informative video, but taking stock of your equipment—and your budget—is essential when deciding on which approach to use. As you'll see in this article, some approaches lend themselves to higher-end lighting equipment, or depend on hiring professional talent. Unless you have endless monetary resources, be realistic about what you can achieve with the equipment, money and personnel you already have.

Approaching It Like the Pros
No matter which approach you decide

to use, is the way you frame your shot.

"When you frame a shot, always think of the rule of thirds," said videographer Perry Jenkins.

The rule of thirds uses the notion that a scene is most appealing to the eye if its main elements appear at certain points on the screen. To use it, divide the screen into thirds—vertically and horizontally—similar to a tic-tac-toe game, and place the important elements along the imaginary lines and wherever they intersect.

Now that we've covered some of the basics, let's look at some real approaches you can use today, straight from the *Videomaker* pros.

The Expert Interview

The "Expert Interview" approach is one often used by the pros at *Videomaker*. The approach involves using an expert on a particular subject to relay information to your audience (for example, you might recruit a local historian who can accurately describe your town's history for the documentary you're producing).

This approach, according to Lander and Jenkins, lends credibility to your topic and can be modified to suit just about any shooting situation. The expert can appear as the lone narrator of your videotape, or can appear on-screen with talent, who poses questions for the expert to answer.

the building process step-by-step. Camera close-ups of the repair person's "work in progress" can serve to illustrate the main points.

Person on the Street

This approach, in which a person-on-the-street poses a question, which the narrator or expert answers, is ideal if you're short on time. "It's quick to shoot, and fast to edit," Lander said. This approach is also a good choice for a beginner who might not have the budget to hire acting talent, because you can ask a friend or two to be your talent at no charge.

Both Lander and Jenkins agreed that the "Person on the Street" approach adds realism to a video, and is a great approach to use in connecting with an audience.

Think of the approach you use in making your video as a roadmap allowing you to reach your final destination: the finished videotape.

Another variation of the "Expert Interview" is using two experts on location. Say you are shooting a videotape showing how to build your own greenhouse. By choosing two experts—a gardener and a handyperson—you can creatively show your audience how to take the project from start to finish using a hands-on approach. You might have your gardening expert serve as the narrator, while your handyperson expert leads your audience through

"It really lets you get to the viewer on a personal level," Lander said.

Lander said when using this approach, however, it is important to make sure that your person on the street is someone the intended audience can relate to. If, for example, you are shooting a training video for a corporation, you'd likely want your talent to be dressed in business attire.

"Appealing to the audience is essential," Lander said.

News Magazine

Another favourite of the *Videomaker* team is the "News Magazine" approach. In this approach, the narrator of the video takes on the role of the reporter, and leads the audience from scene to scene. This approach is similar to segments on the hour—long news programs you see on television, like *Dateline NBC* or *60 Minutes*.

Say you want to document your hometown's fascinating history. Using this approach, you might start at your local museum, and lead your audience through a video tour of the facility, followed by an on-location report in your town's old downtown district. The approach puts you (or your talent) in the role of roving reporter, while giving the audience an up-close-and-personal view of your topic.

Narrator

Narrators guide your viewers through your video, but don't necessarily have to be experts on your subject. The "Narrator approach" is ideal for getting across a lot of information in a short amount of time.

There are two basic variations of the "Narrator approach;" in one approach, the narrator is off-screen and is heard via a voice-over with B-roll footage (the *Videomaker* pros call this the "Invisible Narrator Approach"). A second variation puts the narrator on-screen, reading from a script (also known as the "Visible Scripted Narrator Approach"). It is important to

note that all the narrator approaches, whether they are visible or invisible, are fully-scripted and read, not improvised.

It's Elementary, My Dear

Now that you've chosen the approach (es) you'll be using, it's time to determine which production elements to include. This is where it gets really fun. By choosing the right elements, you can turn a so-so production into something extraordinary. Let's look at some of the elements used by the production crew at *Videomaker*.

•   IDs & Pull Quotes—The use of talent IDs, subject IDs and pull quotes in your production is a simple way to add variety to your video. Talent and subject IDs are simply two-to-four word descriptions that identify who or what the viewer is seeing on screen. The talent ID could be the name and title of your talent, while the subject ID could be the name of the city where you are shooting. Pull quotes highlight what the talent is saying by taking a key word or phrase and showing it on-screen as a graphic. The pull quote doesn't necessarily have to be a verbatim account, but should capture the essence of what the subject says.

"Pull quotes are a perfect way to emphasize an important point," Jenkins said.

•   Lander uses Adobe After Effects for producing pull quotes, talent IDs and subject IDs for *Videomaker* tapes, but said a simpler titler or nonlinear editor can also produce the effects. "After Effects allows me to control every possible parameter of motion and transparency with keyframe animation-type controls."

• Bulleted lists—A good example of a bulleted list is seen when watching a cooking show on television. Often, a list of ingredients or instructions pop onto your screen.

• Chromakey allows you to generate virtual backgrounds around a

way to smooth out jarring jump cuts (a jump cut is an instantaneous video transition between two scenes that have identical subjects in slightly different screen locations).

Other elements might include the use of black and white (to add variety, or to bridge segments), varying camera angles and lighting, or using dolly or crane moves during the production process. Making use of special sound effects, or creating foley sound effects (the homemade variety) are other ways to spice up your video.

By choosing the right elements, you can turn a so-so production into something extraordinary.

subject shot against a blue (or green) screen. Chromakeying is usually done during post-production, but it is possible to do it straight to tape during a production using a switcher.

• Music is one of the easiest ways to spice up your video. You'll want to be sure to choose music that's appropriate to your subject matter. You might consider purchasing a buyout music library.

• Behind The Scenes—Shots that bring the viewer behind the scenes of your video production are the perfect

What Next?
You've picked your topic, narrowed down your approaches, and decided which production elements to use. Now, it's time to get to work! By using the simple approaches and production elements outlined in this article, you're on your way to a winning production. Remember, the approaches and elements we've covered here are just the tip of the iceberg. Using your imagination, with a little foresight and planning, you're destined to end up with a top-notch video.

Alice Patterson is a freelance journalist and frequent contributor to *Videomaker*. This article appeared in the February 2000 issue of the magazine.

RESPONDING

Meaning

1. Record the meaning of the following words using the context.
    a) bumpers
    b) rule of thirds (use a diagram)
    c) pull quotes
    d) Chromakey
    e) virtual backgrounds
    f) buyout music

2. Before a person begins actually making a video, what are the questions Patterson says must be answered?

Form and Style

3. This is an instructional "how-to" article, yet the author uses several techniques to make the tone informal and "user-friendly." Identify specific sentences and phrases that make this technical article accessible.

4. In point form, create the outline of this article. To do this accurately, look carefully at headings, subheadings, bulleted points, spacing, and punctuation.

Creative Extension

5. Use this article to create a video on "How to Make an Information Video." Reread the article several times and follow the outline you created in question 3. Create storyboards for your video to clearly indicate visuals, sound effects, and music.

6. Choose a skill you have recently learned. Write a process (how-to) article for a magazine clearly explaining this skill. Include comments on why certain approaches and strategies are important.

Media

Marshall McLuhan on media:

No medium has its meaning or existence alone, but only in constant inter-play with other media . . . More and more we turn from the content of messages to study total effect. Concern with effect rather than meaning is a basic change in our electric time . . . .

Subliminal and docile acceptance of media impact has made [these media] prisons without walls for their human users.

Persuasion in Advertising

Learning Goals

- identify clear and hidden messages in ads
- analyze persuasive techniques and their effects
- examine and create parodies
- write a persuasive essay

DARREN RATCLIFFE IS A SMOKIN' FOOL.

BUT HE WON'T TOUCH A CIGARETTE.

17-year-old Olympic hopeful, Darren Ratcliffe, has smoked opponents from California to Vermont. But he doesn't smoke cigarettes. In his own words, "I'm not smokin' anything that's gonna stop me from smokin'."

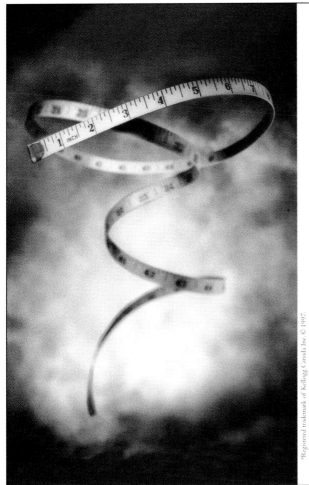

DON'T LET IT MEASURE YOUR SELF-ESTEEM.

It's unfortunate that something as insignificant as a tape measure can have such an impact on how we feel about ourselves. Don't let it. It can't measure who you are. Exercise. Refuse to skip meals. Start with a balanced breakfast every morning and go from there. Kellogg's Special K* cereal is fat free and a source of nine essential nutrients so it's a light, sensible way to start your day. After all, looking your best is about being strong and healthy. And the standards you measure yourself by should be your own.*

*Registered trademark of Kellogg Canada Inc. © 1997.

Kellogg's Special K
www.specialk.ca

Look good on your own terms.

This is a COMPACT DISC COVER. This writing is the DESIGN upon the cover.
The DESIGN is to help SELL the compact disc. We hope to draw your
attention to it and encourage you to pick it up. When you have done
that maybe you'll be persuaded to listen to the music - in this case XTC'
Go 2 album. Then we want you to BUY it. The idea being that the more of
you that buy this compact disc the more money Geffen Records, the manager
Ian Reid and XTC themselves will make. To the aforementioned this is know
as a PLEASURE. A good cover DESIGN is one that attracts more buyers and
gives more pleasure. This writing is trying to pull you in much like an
eye-catching picture. It is designed to get you to READ IT. This is
called luring the VICTIM, and you are the VICTIM. But if you have a free
mind you should STOP READING NOW! because all we are attempting to do is
to get you to read on. Yet this is a DOUBLE BIND because if you indeed
stop you'll be doing what we tell you, and if you read on you'll be doing
what we've wanted all along. And the more you read on the more you're
falling for this simple device of telling you exactly how a good commercia
design works. They're TRICKS and this is the worst TRICK of all since it'
describing the TRICK whilst trying to TRICK YOU, and if you've read this
far then you're TRICKED but you wouldn't have known this unless you'd
read this far. At least we're telling you directly instead of seducing
you with a beautiful or haunting visual that may never tell you. We're
letting you know that you ought to buy this compact disc because in
essence it's a PRODUCT and PRODUCTS are to be consumed and you are a
consumer and this is a good PRODUCT. We could have written the band's
name in special lettering so that it stood out and you'd see it before
you'd read any of this writing and possibly have bought it anyway. What
we are really suggesting is that you are FOOLISH to buy or not buy a
compact disc merely as a consequence of the design on its cover. This
is a con because if you agree then you'll probably like this writing -
which is the cover design - and hence the disc inside. But we've just
warned you against that. The con is a con. A good cover design could be
considered as one that gets you to buy the record, but that never actuall
happens to YOU because YOU know it's just a design for the cover. And thi
is the COMPACT DISC COVER.

his is the back of a COMPACT DISC. Catalogue No.GEFD-24375. This writing
s the DESIGN on the back of the cover. This design is not like that on
he FRONT. Its aim is to impart information about the COMPACT DISC and
he BOOKLET within rather than trying to sell it by being impactful or
lever or any of those things. We have kept it in the same style so that
he entire package has a sense of IDENTITY whichever way you see it. The
OMPACT DISC is by XTC. This is taken from their second album. We won't
ttempt to describe their music because all you have to do is play it and
ou can describe it for yourself. XTC is made up of Andy Partridge, Barry
ndrews, Colin Moulding and Terry Chambers. We have shown photos of them
elow because this is regarded as commercially sensible and helpful in
reating their image. And if you're curious at all you might find it
nteresting to see what the musicians actually look like. And there are
ore pictures and words in the very colourful booklet which you can only
ee if you buy the whole thing.

Many people think it helpful and useful to know
songs on the compact disc inside, so here they are:
1. Meccanic Dancing (Oh We Go!) 2. Battery Brides
3. Buzzcity Talking 4. Crowded Room 5. The Rhythm 6.
Are you Receiving Me? 7. Red 8. Beatown 9. Life is
Good in the Greenhouse 10. Jumping in Gomorrah 11. My
Weapon 12. Super-Tuff 13. I Am the Audience. You may
also be interested to know that this CD was produced
and engineered by John Lackie with assistance from
Pete James at Abbey Road, also, Andy Llewellewyn from
Matrix and that Barry's Roots photos were by catalogue
number in the booklet for bureaucratic reasons.

astly we would like to make it clear that this is a product of Geffen
ecords, partly because they wanted us to and partly because it is a legal
ecessity. Geffen Records' head office is located at 9130 Sunset Blvd., Los
ngeles, CA 90069-6197. Manufactured and Distributed in the United States by
ni Distribution Corp. ©℗ 1978 Virgin Records Ltd. Made in U.S.A. All
ights Reserved. Unauthorized duplication is a violation of applicable laws.

RESPONDING

Meaning

1. a) Examine the Kellogg's Special K ad and the ad featuring Darren Ratcliffe. In your own words, briefly summarize the message of each ad. Who is the target audience? Justify your answers.

    b) In small groups, identify the techniques (types of people and images, placement of logos, size and style of print text, etc.) each ad uses to get across its message. How effective are these techniques? Which ad did you find most persuasive? Why? Share your findings with other groups.

2. The "Nature . . . It'll Grow Back" ad and CD cover are both examples of parodies. A *parody* is a humorous, exaggerated imitation or copy designed to ridicule or satirize. Effective parodies include some elements of the originals that they parody, but there is always a "twist."

    a) What aspects of the sport-utility vehicle (SUV) ad are similar to other SUV ads? What is different? What is the message in this ad?

    b) How is the XTC CD cover different from most CD covers? What does it reveal about the design and advertising of most CD covers?

Form and Style

3. Examine the Special K ad, the Darren Ratcliffe ad, and the parody of an SUV ad. Compare the amount of written text with the space given to visuals in each ad. What is the relationship between the pictures and the text? Why does the Special K ad have so much more text?

4. The tone of the XTC CD cover is *ironic*. Provide specific examples of the irony. What effect does this tone have on you? Would you buy this CD? Why or why not? Explain the reasons for your decision.

Creative Extension

5. The Special K ad shows a picture of a tape measure and states: "Don't let it measure your self-esteem." Does much of the advertising we see imply that our weight and physical looks are the measure of our self-esteem? Write a persuasive essay of 500 words in which you argue one or the other side of this question. Use examples from advertising to support your position.

6. Create your own parody of a print advertisement. To examine more examples of parodies before you create your own, visit these Web sites:
    www.adbusters.org/home/- (*Adbusters* magazine) or
    www.dnai.com/~sharrow/parody/html (Gallery of Advertising Parody).
    Try designing your ad parody on computer.

Shampoo Planet

❦ Douglas Coupland

This excerpt from the novel Shampoo Planet *by Canadian writer Douglas Coupland serves as an interesting parody of persuasive techniques in advertising.*

Learning Goals

- interpret an author's implicit message
- understand the goals and techniques of parody
- identify specific advertising techniques
- create original ads and parodies

Chapter 2

Hair is important.

Which shampoo will I use today? Maybe PsycoPath®, the sports shampoo with salon-grade microprotein packed in a manly black injection-molded plastic motor-oil canister. Afterward? A bracing energizer splash of Monk-On-Fire®, containing placenta, nectarine-pit extract, and B vitamins. And to hold it all together? First-Strike® sculpting mousse manufactured by the *plu*TONium™ hair-care institute of Sherman Oaks, California. It's self-adjusting, with aloe, chamomile, and resins taken from quail eggs. Gloss, hold, *and* confidence. What a deal.

Figuring out your daily hair is like figuring out whether to use legal- or letter-size paper in a copy machine. Your hair is you—your tribe—it's your badge of clean. Hair is your document. What's on top of your head says what's inside your head. Wash every day? Use ComPulsion®, with marigold and beer. Hormone-hair changing texture every five minutes? Use MOODSwing®, the revitalizing power toner from Sweden with walnut leaf for self-damaging hair. It's hot—nuclear—bust the needle on my scorch meter.

❦ Douglas Coupland is from Vancouver, British Columbia. His first novel was *Generation X*, published in 1991. Since then, he has published several novels including *Shampoo Planet* (1992). Coupland also regularly contributes to magazines such as *Wired*. (Born Baden-Sollingen, Germany 1961)

RESPONDING

Meaning

1. The narrator begins the excerpt by saying, "Hair is important." Is he right? What message do you think he is trying to convey? Do you agree?

2. Although none of the hair products described in the excerpt really exist, the type of advertising language that Douglas Coupland uses is very familiar to us. Gather or recall as many shampoo advertisements as you can. Make a list of all the advertising claims they make. In what ways does Coupland make fun of these claims?

Form and Style

3. *Hyperbole* is defined as extravagant exaggeration. Find and list at least four examples of hyperbole from the excerpt. What effect do you think the author is trying to create?

4. Advertisers often use puns (wordplay), jargon, glittering generalities, symbols, and pseudo-scientific claims to persuade people to buy products. Which of these techniques is Douglas Coupland parodying in this excerpt? Provide specific examples.

Creative Extension

5. Using this short excerpt as a model, write a parody of some other aspect of modern life, using the language of advertising and hyperbole to make your point. Begin your piece: _____ is important.

6. Design a bottle and a print advertisement for one of the hair products described in this excerpt. Use a computer program to design your ad if possible. Include an explanation of the language and techniques you used.

Fido Cellphone Advertising Report

In 1999, the Fido cellphone advertising campaign won the Gold for Best Launch of a New Product or Service and the Gold for Services from the Canadian Advertising Success Stories (CASSIES) Awards. The following report summarizes the campaign and provides insight into the real-life world of advertising.

Learning Goals

- analyze an advertising campaign
- explain how ads in different media get across their message
- assess how advertising targets an audience

Executive summary

Microcell and Bos live by the tenet: "If you build it, they will come." By challenging the rules of the market, and by creating a fresh, meaningful brand, well supported by advertising, we have made Fido a top contender, right on the heels of the big players: Bell Mobility and Cantel/AT&T.

In its first year of operation, Fido built a base of 66 000 subscribers, over-achieving budget by 10%. This grew to 217 000 subscribers in 1998—46% above budget. In 1999, Fido will break the 500 000 mark; and it will have done this faster than any player in the market. This was not without facing tremendous challenges:

- being a newcomer without pedigree in a well-established market
- being functional in limited geographical areas
- starting with very limited distribution

Nonetheless, with an advertising campaign rolled out market by market, starting late fall '96 in Montreal and spring '97 in Toronto, unaided brand awareness had reached 55% by the end of 1998. Perceived advertising noise was at the 30% level, way ahead of every other competitor. And Fido's ads were the best liked and remembered in the category. In fact, research revealed that Fido scores were twice as high as the nearest competitor's.

Situation analysis

From the mid 1980s until 1996, there were really only two players in the mobile phone market: Bell Mobility (& Telcos) and Cantel/AT&T. They split the market of 3 million users almost 50/50. Both played by rules they had established. Phones were offered free with a 24, 36 or 48 month contract—including a fixed monthly connection charge plus a cost per minute of use. Both companies had equivalent pricing and consumer offers.

Nokia 5190 PCS

$75

- Small, light and user-friendly
- Long-lasting, high-performance battery
- One-touch *Navi-Key* providing access to all features
- Crystal clear voice transmission
- Fido smart card only $25

Talk about a great gift!

Get double your airtime for one full month!
Plus a blue or red faceplate free of charge.

On activation of Fido' Service between November 12 and December 31, 1998, Fido will double the minutes of your PCS airtime package for one month, for the billing period starting in January 1999. This promotion does not apply to Fidomatic™ Service. While supplies last.

Call him by name:
1 888 481-FIDO
www.fido.ca

YOU ARE THE MASTER.

Fido and Fidomatic are trademarks of Microcell Solutions Inc.

fido STORES

- 2279 Yonge Street (formerly Frao's), Toronto
- Yorkdale Shopping Centre, Toronto
- Toronto Eaton Centre, Toronto
- Dufferin Mall, Toronto
- Upper Canada Mall, Newmarket
- Oakville Place, Oakville
- Mapleview Shopping Centre, Burlington
- Square One Shopping Centre, Mississauga
- Erin Mills Town Centre, Mississauga

- Dixie Value Mall, Mississauga
- Scarborough Town Centre, Scarborough
- Woodbine Centre, Etobicoke
- Cloverdale Mall, Etobicoke
- Lime Ridge Mall, Hamilton
- Pickering Town Centre, Pickering
- Fairview Mall, Willowdale
- Oshawa Centre, Oshawa
- Georgian Mall, Barrie

- Bramalea City Centre, Brampton
- Shoppers World, Brampton
- Fairview Park, Kitchener
- Stone Road Mall, Guelph
- Pen Centre, St. Catharines
- Niagara Square, Niagara Falls
- Westmount Shopping Centre, London
- Masonville Place, London
- 497 Wellington RD .S London

- Markville Shopping Centre, Markham
- Hillcrest Shopping Centre, Richmond Hill
- Eastgate Square, Stoney Creek
- The Promenade, Vaughan
- Conestoga Mall, Waterloo
- Don Mills Shopping Centre, Don Mills

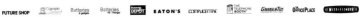

Neither had managed to create an advantage from advertising; no campaign stood out. Moreover, campaign styles kept changing every year or two. Consumers chose the "entrepreneurial" company, Cantel, or the "corporate" one, Bell Mobility.

But late in 1996 the federal government awarded Personal Communication Service (PCS) licences for digital mobile phones to two new players, Microcell and Clearnet. The landscape was bound to change. But how could a newcomer with a name like Microcell carve out its own territory?

Strategy & execution

Microcell understood that success meant differentiating its offering, and making it relevant to as wide an audience as possible. The marketing strategy included three elements:

1. Address the weaknesses of the existing mobile phone business:
    - eliminate the long-term contract
    - bill by the second, not the minute
    - deal with the cost, making it affordable to use a mobile phone
2. Simplify the proposition:
    - do away with complicated plans & price structures
    - establish fixed cost to use, both local and long distance
    - whatever the time of day
3. Use advertising as the weapon to build the business

Although 1 and 2 played a crucial role, we will focus on element 3, and show how it contributed more than its fair share in propelling Microcell to where it is today.

Advertising strategy

Fighting head-to-head with the two heavyweights would have been a terrible mistake. Both had entrenched credibility. And like two super fighters in the ring, they were going at each other blow for blow, using contractual packages to lure consumers.

This situation gave us an opening. They were so focused on promotional offerings that they had neglected to build strong brand personalities and connections with their user base and prospects. If Microcell couldn't be big, corporate and credible, then it could be unique, playing on personal human appeal.

This led to the first decision: we would get close to the consumer. To capture the benefits of our service—friendly, simple, loyal, confidential, follows you everywhere—we developed the brand name Fido, and the logo. This would be the symbol of all communication. It connected strongly with consumers, and would be a source of continuity over the years.

The second decision—in sharp contrast to the practices of Bell Mobility and Cantel/AT&T—was that in every ad Fido branding would dominate over specific messages and offers. The third decision was to overspend our real market position, to deliver accelerated growth, and to be seen as important as the big guys.

Advertising execution

Fido was introduced in major markets beginning with Montreal in November 1996, Toronto in 1997, and others at different times throughout 1997–98. The launches all followed a 3-phase pattern:

Phase 1 Create a "buzz" around the new brand name:

Step 1 – use Blimp advertising to create the first stir in the marketplace.
Step 2 – introduce teaser TV commercials to increase awareness and interest in the upcoming brand.

Phase 2 Introduce the Fido concept to consumers:

Associate trustworthiness and solidity by using a 90-second format and double-page spreads to give all relevant information (transparent, nothing hidden) in a friendly, approachable way.

Phase 3 Develop the Fido brand:

Use multimedia to communicate that with Fido you are the master. He follows you everywhere. All you have to do is call him by name.

Use this as the platform for specific messages, either core or promotional, over time.

To keep the campaign focused and consistent, we used exceptional elements that would become part of the Fido look and feel—dogs as icons in every ad; a black and white texture; and original music.

Results

Microcell's business performance for 1997 and 1998 is as follows:

	Total Net Acquisitions	Objectives	Overachievement
1997	66 000	60 000	10%
1998	217 000	149 000	46%
Cumulative	283 000	209 000	35%

There's just one tiny little thing that might finally convince you

to pick up your own Fido.

And that'd be the price of our Nokia handset: just $50, until March 31st.

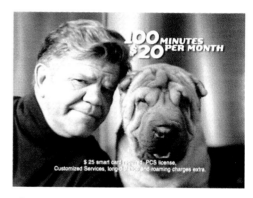

Although it could be the extremely low price of our monthly airtime package: $20 for 100 minutes, any time of day.

Either way, we know you're going to love your Fido.

It's written all over your face. Fido. You are the master.

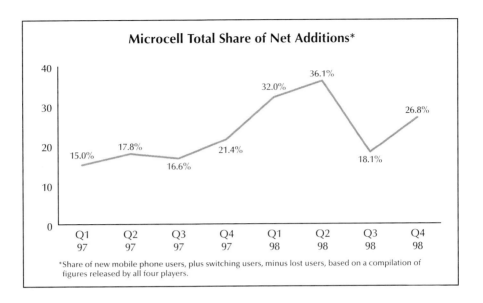

Microcell Total Share of Net Additions*

*Share of new mobile phone users, plus switching users, minus lost users, based on a compilation of figures released by all four players.

Note that the dip in the share in Q3 1998 is directly linked to seriously reduced spending effort. Significant investment resumed in Q4, delivering the 26.8% share. That may be one of the best supports to prove the importance of advertising in Fido's success story.

Isolating advertising as the variable

The success of something as complex as Fido, in such a competitive market, obviously traces to more than one element, as noted by André Tremblay, CEO of Microcell:

> "The excellent quality of Microcell's services, its effective advertising, competitive pricing, leading-edge handsets, and quality network have all contributed to the impressive increase in the company's subscriber base."

However, it is clear from tracking (and the rebound in acquisitions already noted for 4th quarter '98) that advertising was a significant driving force.

By the end of 1998, total unaided awareness for Fido was 55% in Montreal and 54% in Toronto, just on the heels of the big players, and well ahead of Clearnet.

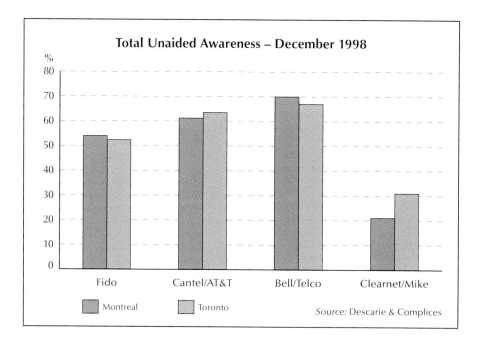

This was achieved with advertising noise (i.e., the perceived level of effort) well ahead of actual—very gratifying given our objective of being seen as as important as the big guys. Actual share of advertising dollars was in the 10%–25% range, with Cantel/AT&T and Bell (+ other Telcos) outspending us, and Clearnet lagging behind.

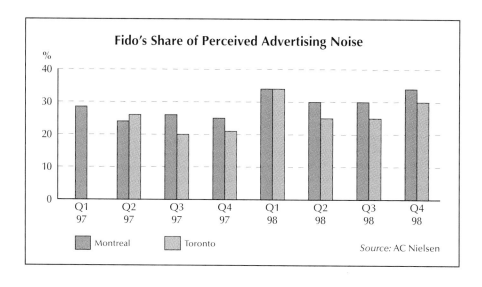

However, through 1998, Fido was the clear leader in impact:

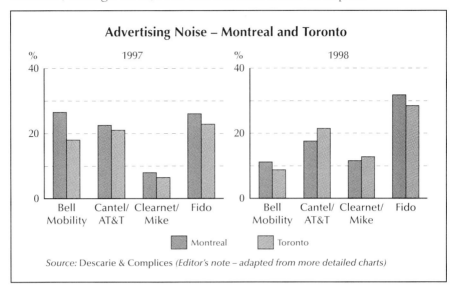

Advertising Noise – Montreal and Toronto

Source: Descarie & Complices (Editor's note – adapted from more detailed charts)

Moreover, through 1998, Descarie & Complices analyzed the performance of the commercials from the four players, based on multiplying four indices:

Recall of the advertising message
(multiply)
Likeability of the message
(multiply)
Identification of the announcer
(multiply)
Understanding of the message

The chart shows Fido's domination in the advertising battleground.

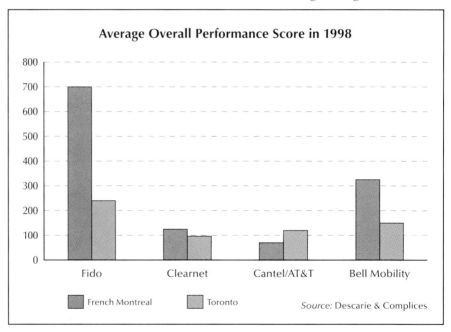

Average Overall Performance Score in 1998

Source: Descarie & Complices

Summary

With an innovative approach to the market, relying heavily on the advertising campaign that has focused on building the brand, Fido has managed to outperform its competitors and capture more than its fair share of market. And thanks to its advertising, it is the only mobile phone service provider that has people call it by name:

"Call me on my Fido!"

ᔓ This advertising campaign report appeared in *Canadian Advertising Success Stories—CASSIES 1999* published by the Canadian Congress of Advertising. Awards are given each year for advertising campaigns in a number of categories. Entries come from across the country from a number of different advertisers and agencies.

RESPONDING

Meaning

1. a) In your own words, describe the challenges Microcell faced when it launched its new product—Fido cellphones.
    b) What three specific decisions did Microcell make when it developed its advertising strategy for Fido? In what ways did these decisions differ from what the competitors were doing?

2. The campaign had three phases. What were they? What steps were taken to carry out each one?

Form and Style

3. This report begins with an executive summary. Based on your reading, discuss the purpose of this summary. Why would a business writer include it in a report?

4. Work in small groups. Choose one of the ads presented in this report—the print, TV, or billboard ad. Make notes on how the ad:
    a) uses images
    b) uses words (in print or audio)
    c) gets across specific information about the product
    d) presents the Fido brand name and logo
    e) meets the goal of making the product "friendly, simple, loyal, confidential, follows you everywhere"

    Share your findings. Discuss similarities and differences in the ways that each type of ad (print, TV, billboard) gets across the message.

Creative Extension

5. Gather and make notes on as many examples of cellular phone advertisements as you can. Look for these ads in different media (magazines, newspapers, television, etc.). How are these ads different from those that launched Fido? How are they similar? Do different ads emphasize different features (price, convenience, reliability, fashion, etc.)? Prepare a report on your findings.

6. In class, identify two or three television programs that many students watch. View one episode of a program and note the products advertised during the show. For one product, make notes on how the advertising targets its audience. What images and audio elements are used? What is the message of the ad? How effectively does it get its message across? If you were the target audience, would you be tempted to buy the product or service? Present an oral report on your findings.

Frankenstein: From Novel to Film

Frankenstein: The Novel

Mary Shelley

Learning Goals

- compare a novel excerpt and screenplay
- analyze visual and sound effects in a screenplay
- examine point of view
- create a shooting script

Chapter V

It was on a dreary night of November, that I beheld the accomplishment of my toils. With an anxiety that almost amounted to agony, I collected the instruments of life around me, that I might infuse a spark of being into the lifeless thing that lay at my feet. It was already one in the morning; the rain pattered dismally against the panes, and my candle was nearly burnt out, when, by the glimmer of the half-extinguished light, I saw the dull yellow eye of the creature open; it breathed hard, and a convulsive motion agitated its limbs.

How can I describe my emotions at this catastrophe, or how delineate the wretch whom with such infinite pains and care I had endeavoured to form? His limbs were in proportion, and I had selected his features as beautiful. Beautiful!—Great God! His yellow skin scarcely covered the work of muscles and arteries beneath; his hair was of a lustrous black, and flowing; his teeth of a pearly whiteness; but these luxuriances only formed a more horrid contrast with his watery eyes, that seemed almost of the same colour as the dun white sockets in which they were set, his shriveled complexion and straight black lips.

The different accidents of life are not so changeable as the feelings of human nature. I had worked hard for nearly two years, for the sole purpose of infusing life into an inanimate body. For this I had deprived myself of rest and health. I had desired it with an ardour that far exceeded moderation; but now that I had finished, the beauty of the dream vanished, and breathless horror and disgust filled my heart. Unable to endure the aspect of the being I had created, I rushed out of the room, and continued a long time traversing my bedchamber, unable to compose my mind to sleep. At length lassitude succeeded to the tumult I had before endured; and I threw myself on the bed in my clothes, endeavouring to seek a few moments of forgetfulness. But it was in vain; I slept, indeed, but I was disturbed by the wildest dreams. I thought I saw Elizabeth, in the bloom of health, walking in the streets of Ingolstadt. Delighted and surprised, I embraced her; but as I imprinted the first kiss on her lips, they became livid with the hue of death; her features appeared to change, and I thought that I held the corpse of my dead mother in my arms; a shroud enveloped her form, and I saw the graveworms crawling in the folds of the flannel. I started from my sleep with horror; a cold dew covered my forehead, my teeth chattered, and every limb became convulsed; when, by the dim and yellow light of the moon, as it forced its way through the window shutters, I beheld the wretch —the miserable monster whom I had created. He held up the curtain of the bed; and his eyes, if eyes they may be called, were fixed on me. His jaws opened, and he muttered some inarticulate sounds, while a grin wrinkled his cheeks. He might have spoken, but I did not hear; one hand was stretched out, seemingly to detain me, but I escaped, and rushed down stairs. I took refuge in the courtyard belonging to the house which I inhabited; where I remained during the rest of the night, walking up and down in the greatest agitation, listening attentively, catching and fearing each sound as if it were to announce the approach of the demoniacal corpse to which I had so miserably given life.

Oh! no mortal could support the horror of that countenance. A mummy again endued with animation could not be so hideous as that wretch. I had gazed on him while unfinished; he was ugly then; but when those muscles and joints were rendered capable of motion, it became a thing such as even Dante could not have conceived.

I passed the night wretchedly. Sometimes my pulse beat so quickly and hardly, that I felt the palpitation of every artery; at others, I nearly sank to the ground through languor and extreme weakness. Mingled with this horror, I felt the bitterness of disappointment; dreams that had been my food and pleasant rest for so long a space were now become a hell to me; and the change was so rapid, the overthrow so complete!

و   Mary Wollstonecraft Shelley was one of the few well-known female writers in the England of the early 1800s. In addition to *Frankenstein*, published in 1818, she wrote several other novels, short stories, and biographies. She also edited the poems, essays, and letters of her husband, the Romantic writer Percy Bysshe Shelley. *(Born England 1797; Died 1851)*

Mary Shelley's Frankenstein

❧ A film directed by Kenneth Branagh
❧ Screenplay by Steph Lady and Frank Darabont

Victor's Garret

Night

Back in the garret: Victor is sitting as he scribbles in his journal:

VICTOR

"Time running out. Rioting in town. Decay of flesh accelerating. Must strike now . . ."

Victor gets up and marches through his workshop like Merlin the Magician. He switches on the Wimshurst machine and sets the steam engine wheels revolving as he passes.

He rounds the corner and we crane up to reveal for the first time Victor's Creation, lying on a metal grill, covered in a sheet.

Victor pulls off his robe, discarding it onto the floor, and moves over to the wall where he unties a rope. He pulls on the rope and the creature on the grill begins to rise up towards the roof. Victor continues to pull

Kenneth Branagh as Victor Frankenstein in his laboratory, just as he is about to bring the creature to life.

and from below we see the body on the grill, arms out, not unlike the anatomical drawing.

The grill gets to the top. Victor moves over to another rope tied on the other side of his bedroom door. He unties it and then pulls hard on it and gives it a huge flick. This releases a wooden buffer hanging from the ceiling, which swings across to hit the grill and pushes it off onto the track running along the roof of the garret.

Victor runs after the body, and gets ahead, watching it as it goes, passing down the length of the lab. He climbs up to stand at the head end of the sarcophagus, looking down into the steaming liquid and then up to watch the body coming towards him.

Victor stares at the sarcophagus as he lowers the body on the grill down into the murky liquid. Once it is in position, he pulls off the shroud, which has covered it all this time.

Victor pulls the sarcophagus along its rail towards the fire as the lid comes down. He lines up the lid and the sarcophagus and slots them together. He tightens down the lid with the main lock on the lid. The bolts slide into place.

Victor guides a glass tube out of a huge container hanging from the ceiling, its contents thrashing madly. The glass tube fits onto the lid of the sarcophagus and Victor fastens the two together.

Close on the acupuncture needles hanging on a wooden rack as Victor takes them off one by one, fitting them through the holes in the sarcophagus and into the Creature's skin. One in its neck, one in its head, one in its knee.

The last needle is fitted into the foot and Victor moves off to the power terminals. He clips on the power connectors, and electricity races through the batteries and along the wires leading to the sarcophagus.

Victor races over to the glass tube of the sarcophagus and pulls a chain, which releases hundreds of eels down the tube and into the sarcophagus. The eels do whatever they do . . .

Victor, now standing on top of the sarcophagus, crawls forward on his stomach and looks through the portholes at the head end.

VICTOR
Live, live, live. *Live* . . . Yes!

Suddenly the Creature's eyes open.

Victor sits back in surprise. He leaps off the sarcophagus and races to the power supply, ripping off the clips. The power dies down, everything goes quiet and still.

The Creature goes limp inside the sarcophagus. Victor walks slowly over to his creation and looks in through the head porthole. Nothing is moving. Its eyes are closed.

VICTOR
No, no, no!

Slowly he turns and walks away, his experiment, all his work, a failure.

We move slowly in on the porthole by the Creature's hand. It taps on the glass. Inside the sarcophagus the Creature's eyes open—and register panic.

Victor, hearing the noise, turns. Is he imagining it?

The sarcophagus begins to convulse.

VICTOR
It's alive. It's alive . . .

He races towards the sarcophagus, which is now shaking madly, and reaches out to the main lock. But before he can get to the lead bolts, they snap from the power inside the sarcophagus.

Suddenly the lid flies off, sending Victor backwards into the spill tank as a wave of fluid lands on him.

The lid of the sarcophagus flies through the lab, sending shelves and equipment flying, finally ending up near the door, having knocked the shelf holding Victor's coat onto the ground.

Victor stares aghast at the sarcophagus. Slowly he gets to his feet and walks towards the now motionless vat. He walks up to the side of it, looking in, anticipating his creation is alive. But everything is still, no sign of life.

He looks down towards the feet—and suddenly the Creature flies up in front of him, grabbing for him. As he does this, the sarcophagus starts to topple off its rail and tips over onto its side, sending Victor and the Creature flying across the spill tank amongst the fluid and eels.

Slowly Victor looks up as the Creature crawls through the fluid.

VICTOR
I knew it could work. I knew it!

He moves over to his creation and tries to lift him to his feet. The Creature seems as helpless as the newly born.

VICTOR
Stand, please stand, come on.

The Creature, his vision hazy, manages to get to his feet.

VICTOR
(monologue during the following action)
Breathe, come on breathe.
Stand, you can stand, come on, come on, that's it.
What's wrong? What's wrong with you?
That's it, that's it.
You can do it, come on.
Stand, yes. Now walk. No, no.

With Victor still on his knees, they then slowly slide across the tank, the Creature managing to stand some of the time.

VICTOR
Let me help you. I'll help you to stand—the chains, the chains, over here.

Victor leads him over to some chains hanging from a bar and, in an attempt to help him to stand, he fits the Creature's arms into some ropes.

VICTOR
This must work, you're alive. What is wrong? What's wrong with you? Be careful of the rope—look out!

As Victor steps back, he loses his balance and, falling backwards, grabs a rope. A counterweight snaps, overloading the pulley, and the wooden bar of chains begins to rise up, carrying the Creature with it, moaning and twitching.
    A piece of wood comes down past him and hits him over the head. The bar of chains continues to rise and the Creature continues to struggle.
    Victor stands, dripping fluid and goo, chest heaving, staring up at the Creature. The full horror sinks in.

Now the Creature's death throes are complete. Silence. Softly:

VICTOR
It's dead, it's dead, I've killed it! (*pause*)
What have I done? I gave it life and then I killed it.

Victor moves away, picks up his journal and walks away from the lifeless Creature hanging in the chains.

VICTOR (*writing in journal*)
"Massive birth defects. Greatly enhanced physical strength but the resulting re-animant is malfunctional and pitiful, and dead."

He closes the journal and places it in the pocket of his greatcoat.

VICTOR (*continued*)
"Tomorrow this journal and this evil must be destroyed . . . forever."

He walks away.

Robert de Niro as the monster in Kenneth Branagh's film *Mary Shelley's Frankenstein.*

British director, actor, and filmmaker Kenneth Branagh has adapted a number of classic works of literature for the screen including Shakespeare's *Henry V* and *Much Ado About Nothing*. *Mary Shelley's Frankenstein* was produced by TriStar Pictures and starred Robert de Niro as the monster and Kenneth Branagh as Victor Frankenstein.

RESPONDING

Meaning

1. For almost two centuries, readers have been thrilled by the gothic terror of Mary Shelley's *Frankenstein*. Discuss the theme of the story. Why do you think Kenneth Branagh chose to make a film version for audiences today?

2. a) What challenges do you think filmmakers face when they adapt a novel for film? What aspects of the excerpt you have read from Mary Shelley's novel might make it especially challenging?

   b) After several close readings, compare the descriptions of the creature's "birth" in the screenplay and in the novel excerpt. Focus on elements such as characters, details of the setting, plot action, description, and speech/dialogue.

Form and Style

3. A *screenplay* provides a description of what the audience sees and hears in a film. Using specific examples, describe what visual and sound details the screenwriters added that were not described in the original novel by Mary Shelley. Why do you think the screenwriters added these details for the film? What effects do they create?

4. In this excerpt from the novel, Mary Shelley writes in the first-person point of view. This allows us to follow Victor Frankenstein's thoughts and feelings as the monster is born. Since the filmmaker had to shoot the scene from an objective (i.e., third-person) point of view, how did the screenwriter deal with the problem of helping us understand Victor's inner thoughts and feelings?

Creative Extension

5. Create a shooting script of the monster's birth scene. Use either the screenplay or novel excerpt as your source text. Refer to the following shooting script on pages 510–511 as a model.

6. Rewrite the novel excerpt from the point of view of either: a) the monster or b) a villager who has managed to see the events through the laboratory window. Include imagery to describe clearly the mood and emotions you are feeling.

Canadiana Shooting Script

Learning Goals

- examine how a shooting script integrates words, sounds, and visuals to convey ideas
- practise critical listening skills
- create an original shooting script

VISUAL	AUDIO
1. *Close up:* Flag of Canada	1. Piano accompanying group, singing: "O Canada, our home and native land" *Fade out*
2. Map of Canada	2. Voice: "Canada, Beautiful Canada Natural and peaceful Willpower to be free Home"
3. *Sequence:* Vancouver Island, Alberta highland, Prairies, Great Lakes, Ontario skyscrapers, Mount Royal chimes, Maritimes coastline, girl singing	3. Group singing with piano: "From Vancouver Island to the Alberta highland Cross the prairies, the lakes, to Ontario towers From the sound of Mount Royal's chimes, Out to the Maritimes, Something to sing about, This land of ours."
4. *Medium shot:* Boy on shore in red bathing suit and T-shirt, single footprint behind.	4. Voice: "The warm and mushy sand squeezes between my toes. The cold water freezes my feet."
5. *Medium shot:* Boy on shore, rocks in water, double footprints behind.	5. Voice: "When I walk in the water the sand rushes through my toes. And the waves crash against the rocks."
6. *Long shot:* Cliff, water crashing against shore	6. Voice: "Whoosh! The waves hit the rocks. You can hear the enormous noise. Whoosh! *Sound effects:* Waves crashing against the shore. Voice: "The waves are crashing on the shore The wild crescendo mounts The spray is landing everywhere In a very delicate mist."
7. *Close up:* Sand on shore in Newfoundland.	7. Solo singing with piano: "I have walked 'cross the sand on the Grand Banks of Newfoundland."

VISUAL	AUDIO
8. *Long shot:* Banks of Miramichi River.	8. "Lazed on the ridge of the Miramichi."
9. *Close up:* Rocks and waves.	9. "Seen the waves tear and roar on the stone coast of Labrador."
10. *Long shot:* Waves on coast	10. "Watched them roll back to the great northern sea."
11. Sun over horizon, colourful sky.	11. Voice: "The sun bursts over the horizon and lightens the golden fields of swaying wheat and grain." Voice: "The cool morning breeze whistles across the grain packed fields."
12. Eight mountain peaks.	12. Voice: "The sun climbs up into the horizon peeking over the mountains."
13. Three mountain peaks encircled in clouds.	13. Voice: "The snow-peaked mountains are hidden by the clouds as the yodeller drives out his sound." *Sound: Yodelling—fade in and fade out.*
14. *Close up:* Sun in wheat field.	14. Quartet singing with piano: "I have welcomed the dawn from the fields of Saskatchewan.
15. *Long shot:* Car following sun.	15. Followed the sun to the Vancouver shore,
16. *Long shot:* Snow-peaked mountain.	16. Watched it climb shiny new up the snow peaks of caribou,
17. *Long shot:* Sunrise over horizon.	17. Telling the promise of great things to come."
18. *Long shot:* Vancouver Island	18. Group singing with piano: "From Vancouver Island
19. *Long shot:* A group of small hills	19. to the Alberta highland,
20. *Long shot:* Prairies with grain elevators.	20. Cross the prairies, the lakes,
21. *Long shot:* Tall buildings.	22. to Ontario's towers, From the sound of Mount Royal's chimes,
22. *Med. shot:* Boats in a harbour.	23. Out to the Maritimes,
23. *Long shot:* Canadian flag flying on flag pole.	24. Something to sing about, this land of ours."

RESPONDING

Meaning

1. What images open and close this script? Why would the scriptwriter choose to open and close with these images? Why is the opening shot a close-up and the closing image a long shot?

2. This script includes some visual images that are very specific geographical locations and others that are more general landscape scenes. Make a list of the specific geographical places and the general locations mentioned. Why did the scriptwriter mix both kinds of images?

Form and Style

3. The script alternates between group singing, spoken words, music, individual singing, and other sound effects. Why do you think the scriptwriter does this? Why doesn't the scriptwriter ever present a visual image of any of the speakers or singers?

4. a)   What is the *mood* and *tone* in this script? How are they created?
    b)   What *symbols* are used? What theme do these symbols suggest?

Creative Extension

5. Work with a partner. Choose either the audio or visual portion of the script. If you have chosen the audio, cover up the visual portion and write a new set of visuals to accompany the audio material. If you have chosen the visual, cover up the audio portion of the script and write a new audio track.

6. Choose a poem or story from this anthology, or choose one of the excerpts from Canadian literature in "Landscape and Images" (pp. 522–540, the Echo section of this unit). Write a shooting script for your chosen selection including music, sound effects, and visuals.

Dot-com this!

The brave new world of cyberlanguage

↻ Stephanie Nolen

Learning Goals

• assess the impact
  of e-mail and
  the Internet on
  language

• examine
  characteristics of
  on-line writing

• identify and define
  new words and
  phrases

• create an article
  for an on-line
  magazine

• write a position
  paper or hold
  a debate

It was inevitable, Jamie Reid says, that his love letters and his dinner-table chats would show the effect. Reid, 23, is what you might call a paid hacker —a self-taught network security expert, hired by a desperate corporate world right out of his Toronto high school. He lives totally immersed in the Internet world—and he knows it shows.

"You begin to look at things in a very logical and inductive way after working with machines for a long time," he says. "You rely less on intuition. The problems that computers solve have few variables; things add up. And you apply those same ways of doing things to your everyday life. It only makes sense that people who spend their days dealing with those sorts of questions would attempt to quantize everything from their shopping lists to their politics."

In truth, Reid didn't say that, he wrote it. As if to illustrate his own point, he offered that observation via e-mail a couple of hours after I put the question to him in a conversation. His reply, articulate and eloquent, was also a textbook example of many of the other ways in which the Internet is changing the way we use language. He wrote in one-sentence paragraphs. He listed points. He used mathematical jargon ("quantize") in an everyday context. About the only thing he *didn't* do was toy with capitaLetters.

It's all dot.com and network and I-this and e-that, these days, and so ubiquitous are these words and symbols that we don't tend to give them much thought. But in many subtle ways the Internet is dramatically altering the way we use language: How we write, how we speak, how we use words when we think.

"It was inevitable that our language would be affected because the Internet is not simply a technical phenomenon, it's a cultural phenomenon, and it doesn't even matter if you're on it or not, you are nonetheless affected by its presence in the culture. So says Liss Jeffrey, adjunct professor at the

McLuhan Program in Culture and Technology at the University of Toronto, and director of the byDesign eLab, an electronic lab engaged in the design of public space on-line. "New horizons open up and we, as human beings, have to find ways to describe those places. We create new things, we dream them up, and then we find ways to talk about them."

Take cyberspace. It's now a universally accepted idea that most of us spend part of each day there. We all know what it means. The term was coined by William Gibson in 1984; it is, Jeffrey says, something people have experiences of, an interactive participatory reality, and thus something for which we needed words.

There have been lots of other new words in the six years most of us have been visiting cyberspace. The Internet was invented in 1969, but didn't have public use until the early 1990s. The explosion came in early 1995, as service providers switched to flat-rate billing, instead of charging for volume of mail received. The 1994 edition of the *Canadian Internet Handbook* included two pages on the World Wide Web, predicting it might one day come into widespread use. A Nielsen survey found that in 1996, 23 per cent of Canadians used the Internet; a year later, it was 31 per cent. Angus Reid found 55 per cent of us using it in 1999 and says this year, the number is up to 70 per cent.

But while much of the cultural analysis of the Internet is about the Web, Clive Thompson, editor-at-large at *Shift* magazine in New York, says the most significant factor has been e-mail, however pedestrian it may seem. "It's had by far the most immediate effects and more visceral effect," he says. "When people get to work, do they look at a groovy new site, or watch some streaming video, or something with generation-enhanced Flash content? Of course not. They check their e-mail." And the often-overlooked result of our addiction to e-mail is that we write more. Much more.

"Before e-mail, the vast majority of people never wrote anything," Thompson says. "Their jobs didn't require it, their pastimes didn't require it, and it wasn't easy to do—before computers we didn't write a lot of text." Now people have a motive: "It's not that people want to write, but they want to talk to other people, and they have to write to do that."

But how are they writing? Well, in English, for one thing. There has been an explosion in the number of people for whom English is a second language, even as the number of native speakers of English has steadily declined over the last 10 years." English is changing its function in the world," says Eric McLuhan, author of *Electric Language*, adding that English, as the language with the greatest flexibility and largest vocabulary, was the only language prepared for this shift.

But McLuhan, who is the son of the legendary communications theorist Marshall McLuhan, says the 15 years of the computing era have had drastic effects on the building blocks of writing. Attention spans have declined sharply, and with them, sentence length. Twenty years ago, the average sentence length in a novel was 20 words; today it is 12 to 14 words. In mass-market books such as Harlequin Romance novels, the average sentence is only seven or eight words.

Paragraphs, too, have changed. Most prominently, one-sentence paragraphs have become ubiquitous. That means, McLuhan says, that the traditional one-sentence paragraph has lost its role of transition or dramatic impact. In addition, he says, ideas are no longer developed in paragraphs. And all objective distance is lost. "It's all up front and in your face. That makes for high [reader] involvement and low detachment."

And the style of bullet-point writing, also a function of Internet communication, results in a compressed, discontinued presentation of information, heavy with parallelism—qualities once reserved for poetry, McLuhan observes. "We are reinventing poetics from the bottom up."

Robert Logan says all this should come as no surprise. A physicist at the University of Toronto and the author of *The Sixth Language*, he uses chaos theory to argue that each time human society needs to deal with an information overload, a new language emerges. "Speech, writing, math, science, computing and the Internet form an evolutionary chain of languages," he says. Writing and math emerged in 3300 BC in Sumer to keep track of tributes; then came science because of the need to teach how to organize that knowledge, and then, when everyone wanted to communicate with computers, the Internet emerged. "To communicate, to operate in the 21st century, you must be fluent in all six languages," says Logan, adding, "You can speak some with an accent."

Each language has its own grammar and syntax, evolving with the vestigial structures of its predecessors. When writing emerged, it took the vocabulary of speech but added new words. Plato's Greek has many more words and grammatical structures than Homer's. With math came the grammar of logic; with science, the grammar of the scientific method; with the Internet, the grammar of hypertext and search engines.

This is, in Logan's mind, the key contribution of the Internet era: We write, speak and think in hypertext—the code in which text is written on the web—the links. It is tangential, not sequential.

"I am much more hypertext in my talking now," says Logan. "I jump off into something else, then return to where I was, to what I was talking about." It is the verbal equivalent of clicking on a blue-underlined link.

Reid hears something else, when his "geek" friends and colleagues are talking. "Knowledge is what's valued in this industry, and that's how people speak," he says. "There's a rapid-fire passing back and forth of facts . . . . But it's just exchanging knowledge. There's no wisdom or value attached."

Jargon, of course, be it mathematical, scientific, computer-specific, has crept into everyday speech. Jeffrey calls it the democratizing of expert knowledge. . . . Thompson also argues that the style of discourse has also fundamentally changed.

"E-mail created an entirely new style of argument and discussion," he says, referring to the cut-and-paste back-and-forth. He compares it to the passing back and forth of illuminated manuscripts between medieval monks, who left wide margins for each other's comments—only that process took years. "This is: Here's what you said right back at you. You can't get away from your words."

Stephanie Nolen has written for several journals, magazines, and newspapers during her career, including the *New Internationalist*, *Newsweek*, and currently *The Globe and Mail*. She covers mainly international news and lived in Ramallah on the West Bank for several years, starting in 1994.

RESPONDING

Meaning

1. List the specific characteristics of e-mail and on-line writing that this article describes. Do you agree with these points? Which characteristics can you identify in your own on-line writing or in examples of Internet writing that you have seen?

2. Explain the meaning of the following statement: "We write, speak and think in hypertext—the code in which text is written on the web—the links. It is tangential, not sequential." Do you agree with this statement? Support your opinion with examples.

Form and Style

3. Many new words have come into the language since the invention of the Internet. Other words and phrases have taken on new meanings. Find and list a number of these words and phrases from this article. With a partner, discuss what they mean and write a definition. Add other words and phrases you know of related to the Internet.

4. Using the Internet, find examples of writing for on-line magazines. Choose one example. On a printout, make marginal notes highlighting the features of on-line writing that are included. Do you notice any other interesting characteristics of style or content in the article? Summarize your findings.

Creative Extension

5. Write in on-line style! Choose a topic that interests you and write a story for an on-line magazine. Apply some of the characteristics of on-line writing described in this reading. If you have design software, experiment with different styles of type, graphics, and layout for your article.

6. Media critic Jon Katz has said that on-line writing has created "a whole new fractured language—definitely not as elegant or polished as English used to be, but in a way, much more vital." Do you agree? Has the Internet made English more vital or just sloppier? Write a short position paper on this question or hold a debate.

Editorial: What is a Magazine?

Robert Chodos

Learning Goals

- identify the purpose and target audience of magazines
- examine layout and design
- create a magazine cover
- compare coverage of news in different media

What is a magazine? In the company of my colleagues on the Canadian Magazine Publishers Association membership committee, I struggle with this question regularly. Can something be a magazine if it's tabloid size and printed on newsprint? (It can be, depending on the content.) Can something be a magazine if it's distributed only to members of a particular association? (No, that's a house organ.) Can something be a magazine if it's only available electronically? (We're not sure.)

While there are lots of grey areas (between magazines and newspapers, magazines and books, magazines and catalogues, magazines and websites), I also carry around with me a core notion of what constitutes a magazine—let's call it a Magazine, with a capital M. And for me, this notion is a matter not only of format but of content as well. A Magazine, in this sense, is an intelligent observer of its society. It reports and reflects on matters of common interest: public affairs, culture, ideas. And yet as I look through the 300 or so entries in the latest edition of the CMPA's member directory, I see only a handful that fit this description.

There are magazines for people who live in particular parts of Canada (*Alberta Views*, *Toronto Life*), have particular hobbies (*Antique Showcase*, *Canadian Sportscard Collector*) or political interests (*Peace Magazine*, *Monetary Reform*), or belong to particular ethnic groups (*Rungh: A South Asian Quarterly*, *Swedish Press*). Many of these publications are excellent and some appeal to people beyond their niche—among the Canadian magazines I read regularly are *Catholic News Times*, the feminist spirituality journal *Vox Feminarum* and northern Ontario's feisty *High Grader*, even though I am a male Jew who has never lived farther north in Ontario than Ottawa. But they serve a different purpose from the classical general-interest Magazines.

The marginalization of the Magazine is related to wider trends. All-encompassing television networks such as the CBC in Canada or CBS, NBC and ABC in the United States have been losing market share to specialty cable channels. Internet chat groups and websites bring people with particular interests together while dividing them from others with different interests. The general phenomenon of a declining public space has been widely noted.

In late January 2000, Conrad Black's publishing empire announced that it was folding its general-interest monthly magazine, *Saturday Night*, into the *National Post*. Instead of being available to subscribers and newsstand buyers, *Saturday Night* is a weekly supplement in the Saturday edition of the *Post*.

The *Saturday Night* announcement was a fruitful source of gossip and speculation—about what the new publication would look like, who would be in charge . . . To my mind, it won't replace the old one. The new *Saturday Night* is a section of a newspaper. The old one was a Magazine. While its political sympathies and range of interests were quite different from the *Forum*'s, there was something important that the two publications held in common. They have both been places where a conversation took place that could, at least in theory, involve all Canadians. This is a concept that more and more publishers and editors seem to think is obsolete. We are not among them.

ᔥ Robert Chodos is the editor of *The Canadian Forum* magazine. In recent years, he has written *Quebec and the American Dream* and *Canada and the Global Economy*.

RESPONDING

Meaning

1. Robert Chodos notes that all-encompassing television networks like CBC are losing large numbers of viewers to cable specialty channels. He feels the same is happening to general interest magazines. They are losing readers and market share to the large number of specialty magazines. In your opinion, is this a positive or negative trend? Why or why not?

2. Chodos argues that to him a magazine is "an intelligent observer of its society." Do you agree? Which magazine covers on the next page support this view? How? Describe the purpose and target audience of each magazine based on its cover. Support your answers.

Form and Style

3. Compare the layout and visual effects of two magazine covers from page 521.
   a) What feature immediately catches your eye and what is its effect?
   b) What other visuals are included and how are they presented? (in the background? foreground? out of focus? etc.)
   c) How is colour used?
   d) How is text type used?

   How do these features reflect the purpose of the magazine? How effective are they in attracting a reader?

4. Find a copy of one of the magazines you chose. What types of advertising does the magazine contain? What key features do you note about the interior layout? How do the advertising and interior layout suit the purpose and audience of the magazine?

Creative Extension

5. Using the examples provided as a guide, design a magazine cover. Decide on your purpose and target audience. Use visual design elements that will appeal to your readers. If possible, design your cover on computer.

6. With your teacher, choose an issue or event currently in the news. Compare a newspaper report, television news spot, newsmagazine article, and Internet news report on the same issue or event. Consider aspects such as importance given to the story (front page, top story of the day, etc.), length, amount of detail, depth of analysis, and use of visuals. Report your findings. Which medium provided the most indepth coverage? Which was easiest to understand? Why?

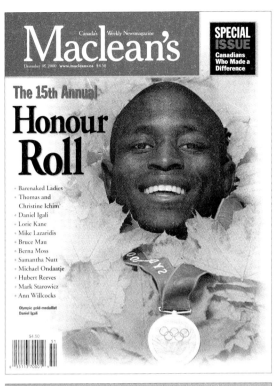

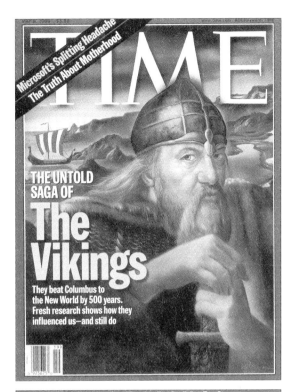

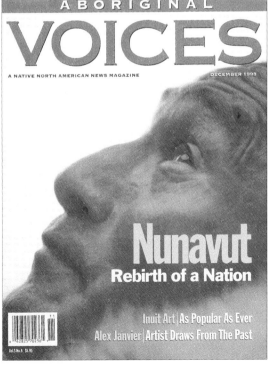

Landscapes and Images

How do the landscapes around us help to shape who we are?

Canada's Group of Seven artists in the 1920s and 1930s were among the most famous artists to explore the relationship between the landscape and the Canadian identity. Since then, many other artists and writers have expressed how the landscape around us can help to shape who we are. In this Echo section, photographers, writers, a painter, and a radio broadcaster consider how our inner and outer landscapes are connected.

Learning Goals

- examine a theme from different perspectives
- explore how artists use different media to create meaning
- examine how different forms, techniques, language, and styles affect meaning
- create original media works based on a theme

W.O. Mitchell Country

Courtney Milne

In the following excerpt, Canadian landscape photographer Courtney Milne describes how the writings of prairie author W.O. Mitchell inspired him. Milne created photographs of scenes from Mitchell's novels. Where W.O. Mitchell used words, Milne used photographs and the techniques of light, colour, camera angles, and focus to express ideas and emotions.

In 1926, when W.O. was twelve, he developed bovine tuberculosis in his wrist, which prevented him from attending school on a regular basis. From 9:00 to 4:00, when all his friends were in school, he would go out onto the prairie and it felt, he said, as if "some great blackboard eraser had wiped all the children off all the streets—but missed me." He soon developed an introspectiveness beyond his years:

I would walk to the end of the street and out over the prairie with the clickety grasshoppers bunging in arcs ahead of me and I could hear the hum and twang of the wind in the great prairie harp of telephone wires. I remember looking down at the dried husk of a dead gopher crawling with ants and flies and undertaker beetles. Standing there with the total thrust of prairie sun on my vulnerable head, I guess I learned—at a very young age—that I was mortal.

(An Evening with W.O. Mitchell)

W.O. believed, as this passage indicates, that one's childhood landscape did more than imprint its physical geography; it also fixed an "inner perspective." He learned to see drama and poetry in small things, and he became acutely aware of his own separateness and his own mortality. Another prairie writer, Wallace Stegner, noted in *Wolf Willow* how prairie landscape affects you: "It is a country to breed mystical people, egocentric people, perhaps poetic people. But not humble ones. At noon the total sun pours on your single head: at sunrise or sunset you throw a shadow a hundred yards long. . . . Puny you may feel there, and vulnerable, but not unnoticed."

• • •

Sometimes when I am out photographing I do a simple exercise in order to see things a fresh way. I shut my eyes, swivel around with the camera to my face, then open my eyes and peer through the viewfinder. The resulting de-composed scene can shock the senses. The focus might be off—the lines softened—perhaps the subject matter can't even be identified. No matter. What can happen is that the mix of tones, hues, and quality of light takes on a new identity, as though you are seeing it for the first time.

Impressionistic technique is not something new to me. I have been experimenting with camera movement, multiple exposures, and water reflections for most of my career. But in this book for the first time I found myself linked with a writer who invites, endorses, and applauds this way of seeing, not just with the camera but in living life creatively. I believe W.O. saw landscapes in much the same way I attempt to portray them on film. I am inspired by his textured descriptions of the land; sometimes it seems as though he has subtly layered his words on the page with a palette knife. With my photography, I am not so much interested in what objects represent, as I am in the play of light and how the subtleties of line, tone, form, and colour combine to nourish our inner landscapes.

ECHO

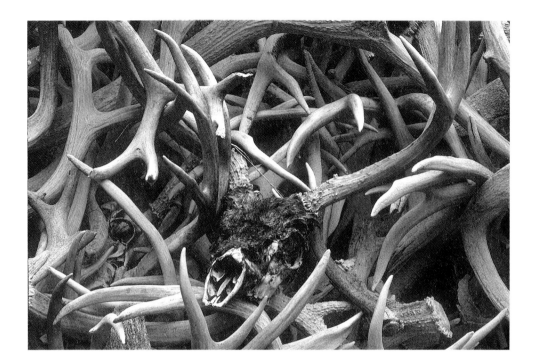

The tailless gopher lay upon an ant pile, strangely still with the black bits of ants active over it. A cloud of flies lifted from it, dispersed, then came together again as at one command. Brian stared down at the two rodent teeth, the blood that had run down the nose and crusted there; he saw a short stump of tail skeleton with a ragged tab of skin that had stayed with the body. . . . It was difficult to believe that this thing had once been a gopher that ran and squeaked over the prairie. It was difficult to believe that this was anything but dirt. . . .

The feeling was in Brian now, fierce—uncontrollably so with wild and unbidden power, with a new frightening quality. . . .

Prairie's awful, thought Brian, and in his mind there loomed vaguely fearful images of a still and brooding spirit, a quiescent power unsmiling from everlasting to everlasting to which the coming and passing of the prairie's creatures was but incidental. He looked out over the spreading land under intensely blue sky.

Text from *Who Has Seen the Wind* by W.O. Mitchell
Photograph by Courtney Milne

Once more he was looking down on water mirror, reflecting wolf willow silver along its edge. Over there the spear green of bull rushes. The pond's mud margin held deep hoof pocks where Hutterian cattle had come down to drink.

He was startled by a frog plop. The water surface was creased with the lilliputian wake of a water bug moving. . . . Stopped. Held still. Twitched on again over pure surface.

He knelt and began to unlace his shoes. Perhaps the pond could wash sorrow away. With mild chill it embraced him; he pulled himself down and through the cool under-water murk, then arching broke the surface to expel pent breath and spray. He lay floating with the sting of pond water in his nostrils, the flat earth taste of it at the back of his mouth and throat. As though not part of him his hands fluttered at his sides; his knees moved lazily and unbidden as he stared up to the sky and still cloud.

Text from *For Art's Sake* by W.O. Mitchell
Photograph by Courtney Milne

ECHO

Their descent took them within sight of the river. It was no longer the wide and smooth flowing river they had known to the East. They caught glimpses of its narrow ribbon—the glacial green of all mountain streams, deep between the chasm of hundred foot cut banks of grey rock and shale. Whole tortured stretches of it were milky below them. . . .

They walked over the open field, came to the cliff edge of the river; before they had reached it the roar of the falls had begun to hush their ears. They looked down to a tarn-like pool below; just above, the river flowed over a shelf, to drop in an anguished web of mist and spray.

Text from *The Alien* by W.O. Mitchell
Photograph by Courtney Milne

W.O. Mitchell is one of Canada's best-known prairie writers. *Who Has Seen the Wind* was his first novel, published in 1947. In addition to novels, he wrote several short stories, radio scripts, and plays. He was also a popular speaker and performer. *(Born Weyburn, Saskatchewan 1914; died 1998)* Courtney Milne is a freelance photographer who focuses on landscape and nature. He has published several books and magazine articles, and has travelled extensively giving workshops, lectures, and multimedia shows. *(Born Saskatoon, Saskatchewan 1943)*

RESPONDING

Meaning

1. Courtney Milne says that W.O. Mitchell "developed an introspectiveness beyond his years." What do you think he meant by this? What is introspection? Why would this be an advantage to a writer?

2. Milne suggests that the landscapes we grow up in can create "an inner perspective." In his photographs, he aims to nourish these "inner landscapes." What do you think he means? Do you think the landscape you have grown up in has affected you? Has it given you a different character from people who have grown up in other parts of the country or the world?

Form and Style

3. W.O. Mitchell provided a starting point for Courtney Milne's photographs with the strong visual techniques he used in his writing. Using specific examples from the excerpts, identify these techniques. How does W.O. Mitchell help us to see, hear, smell, touch, and feel the world he describes in each excerpt? What is the mood he creates? What central idea does he want to convey in each passage?

4. Choose one of the photographs. Describe the photographic images and techniques (e.g., lighting, camera angle, point of view, focus, colour) Courtney Milne used to convey the central idea of W.O. Mitchell's written words.

Creative Extension

5. In a short piece of writing or in an audio recording, describe one of the photographs as if you were trying to describe it over the telephone to someone far away who has never been to Canada. Include details that will allow the person to visualize the scene clearly.

6. Select a passage from a novel or short story you have read. Find a photograph or piece of artwork from a magazine, newspaper, or other source that reflects the central idea in the passage. Alternatively, you could take a photograph of your own. Mount the visual and text passage on a background. Explain your choices and interpretations.

Eulogy for W.O. Mitchell

Rex Murphy

This eulogy for W.O. Mitchell was broadcast on CBC Radio's Cross Country Checkup, March 1, 1998 during a break in a program about Finance Minister Paul Martin's budget. In this speech, Rex Murphy presents his views on how W.O. Mitchell's interpretation of the landscape has helped to shape our Canadian identity. The text below was written to be read.

It is not for everyone that we would dare an intermission, during a program with a Finance Minister who may claim the credit for the first deficit-less budget in almost three decades.

But then W.O. Mitchell—is NOT just everyone, or anyone for that matter—and it would be unjust if a program that calls itself *Cross Country Checkup*, did not—at the very least—take a 'time out' to salute the passing of one of this country's most respected, most enduring, and most affecting writers: W.O. Mitchell.

The practice of W.O. Mitchell offers an interesting variation on one of Shakespeare's most compact observations. It's a familiar one. As Shakespeare had it, the "imagination of a poet" gave to "airy nothings" . . . "a local habitation and a name." In my judgement W.O. Mitchell worked that famous transaction in reverse.

He gave to "local habitations and names"—a residence in the minds and imaginations of thousands. It was the province of his distinct genius to take the local and the particular—places, landscapes and people—a boy, a family, the prairies—immensely familiar to him, and fashion that 'material' so that it awakened recognition across the entire wide territory— from Alberta to Zanzibar—of human response.

This is not easy stuff to do—to set out characters, detail a setting, render an account of how things were in a different time—with its Biblical overtones, prairie evocation, and mix of bitter and sweet nostalgia—that it's as if it were one of those pieces of phrasecraft or melody that sweep into us from the air, and have always been with us. It is startlingly right, so pitch-perfectly eloquent.

That is one other thing about W.O. Mitchell—and his masterwork. This quality of being so startlingly, so beautifully (for *Who Has Seen the Wind* is a beautiful book) right.

There is in the very best writing (I am speaking here of extended prose, short story or novel, essay or article) a signal from the very beginning of the work, that everything here is in tune, that everything is working in perfect co-operation, in symmetry of sound and sense. This intimation pulsates from the very first word, and radiates the entire work. There is, almost 'behind' the words, a presence of integrity and fitness—a background tracing of the sureness of touch of the writer's perfected instinct.

Who Has Seen the Wind is aglow with that instinct, with the enchanted harmony of a story perfectly told. It sings the melody of language—when language, as it so rarely does—reaches perfect design and execution.

It is truly amazing what Mitchell's career, so extended and fertile, managed to accomplish so early.

Now Mitchell was a writer—everyone will give him that—but he was more. He—I was going to say worked, but I'll change that—he lived a variety of public guises (extra-authorial incarnations let us call them): lecturer, performer, stage raconteur, friend of a legion of fledgling writers, and not least, broadcast familiar, that even outside his writing—he made himself a "presence" in the life and minds of Canadians. I do not know if there is such a thing in Nature as a one-man ambience—but W.O. Mitchell unarguably was a felt and vital constituent in the distinctly Canadian way of seeing things.

Which is really what all the very best writers ever do—they do not 'teach' us; so much as guide us to way of seeing and feeling. And the absolute best—the handful of consummate artists—not only expand the repertoire of OUR seeing and feeling—As well they add—these words are Johnson's—to the "common stock of harmless pleasures."

W.O. Mitchell: he multiplied our delights; he gave comfort and strength to the Canadian imagination; he lent his full playful authority to the trade and craft of writer storyteller. The life and example of W.O. Mitchell are a sweet Canadian greatness.

Rex Murphy is a popular Canadian radio broadcaster and commentator from Newfoundland. As well as hosting *Cross Country Checkup*, he contributes essays to various other CBC shows and writes book reviews. He has won several provincial broadcasting awards.

Connecting

1. This text is a *eulogy*, a speech written to honour someone who has died. How is this speech different from a straight written biography or critical account of W.O. Mitchell's life? How does the speaker convey his emotions?

2. Murphy says that Mitchell reversed the process of giving "airy nothings"..."a local habitation and a name." Explain what this means using evidence from the excerpts of W.O. Mitchell's writings.

3. Murphy claims that the best writers do not *teach* us, but guide us to ways of seeing and feeling. He adds that W.O. Mitchell is an important part of a distinctly Canadian way of seeing things. Do you agree? Is there a distinctly Canadian way of seeing things? Is it influenced by our landscape? Support your answer by referring to selections in this Echo section.

Lens

✑ *Anne Wilkinson*

In the following poem, Anne Wilkinson considers how a poet sees and interprets the world. She offers another interpretation on how we connect our inner and outer landscapes.

I

The poet's daily chore
Is my long duty;
To keep and cherish my good lens
For love and war
And wasps about the lilies
And mutiny within.

My woman's eye is weak
And veiled with milk;
My working eye is muscled
With a curious tension,
Stretched and open
As the eyes of children;
Trusting in its vision
Even should it see
The holy holy spirit gambol
Counterheadwise,
Lithe and warm as any animal.

My woman's iris circles
A blind pupil;
The poet's eye is crystal,
Polished to accept the negative,
The contradictions in a proof
And the accidental
Candour of the shadows;
The shutter, oiled and smooth
Clicks on the grace of heroes
Or on some bestial act
When lit with radiance
The afterwords the actors speak
Give depths to violence,

Or if the bull is great
And the matador
And the sword
Itself the metaphor.

II
In my dark room the years
Lie in solution,
Develop film by film.
Slow at first and dim
Their shadows bite
On the fine white pulp of paper.

An early snap of fire
Licking the arms of air
I hold against the light, compare
The details with a prehistoric view
Of land and sea
And cradles of mud that rocked
The wet and sloth of infancy.

A stripe of tiger, curled
And sleeping on the ribs of reason
Prints as clear
As Eve and Adam, staring at an apple core;
And death, in the black and white
Or politic in green and Easter film,
Lands on steely points, a dancer
Disciplined to the foolscap stage,
The property of poets
Who command his robes, expose
His moving likeness on the page.

Anne Wilkinson is a Canadian poet known for her wit and for the vivid details in her poems, often presented as contrasts. She was the founding editor of the literary magazine *The Tamarack Review*. (Born Toronto, Ontario 1910; died 1961)

Connecting

1. What is the "Lens" that Wilkinson is referring to in the title?
2. How is the way the speaker sees things through the lens different from what she sees through her eyes?
3. Like W.O. Mitchell and Courtney Milne, Anne Wilkinson is describing an inner landscape in this poem. What are some features of this inner landscape? Support your answer by referring to specific lines in the poem.

Imaginary Landscapes

The magazine Canadian Geographic *includes a feature section called "Imaginary Landscapes" in which photographers interpret scenes from Canadian literature. The following examples show how two writers and photographers from different regions of Canada have interpreted the landscape around them.*

Some had still not got used to the place. I'd heard them talking about this in my tea room, sometimes up at the Store. I suppose they'd grown accustomed to their homes— stumps and half-cleared fields and donkey —piles of burning roots out every window. But coming down to the beach reminded them of how different everything was from where they'd lived before—Alberta or New Brunswick or the Ottawa Valley. The trees were bigger than they'd ever dreamed, too broad and tall, draped with heavy limbs so green they hurt your eyes. The Island mountains were a high jagged wall all down one side of the world, with nothing beyond them but ocean and Japan. You thought you might know the name of something you saw—flower or bush, twice the size you were used to—and discovered that you didn't. And the sea—just looking out at the Strait put some of them into a trance. They'd go cold from their toes right up to their necks, they said, sensing how deep and cold and wide it was, moving like something alive.

Text from *Broken Ground* by Jack Hodgins
Photograph by Bob Herger

Mary presses her face to the window and the sunshine feels like the palm of a hand against her cheek. Everything outdoors seems fresh and new. Even Father's old fishflake, rickety and splayed atop a thicket of knotted posts, from this angle looks like a living crab. She half expects to see the frame pick itself up and scrabble across the landwash. Not a strain of weather inhabits the sky—only the bright moon and the clear blue, the very thing. The lighthouse down on the point stands stark and bleached, a pillar gleaming. A red punt far outside, off the ledge, drifts underneath the belly of the sun and slides into the bolt of flame on the sea—maybe it is the same boat she heard last night, in the dark. The water is just as calm as it was then.

Text from *Gaff Topsails* by Patrick
Kavanagh
Photograph by Ned Pratt

Jack Hodgins is a well-known short-story and novel writer. Many of his works are set on Vancouver Island where he was born. Bob Herger is a freelance photographer whose work has appeared in several magazines. Patrick Kavanagh is a Newfoundland writer known for his short stories, features, and reviews. *Gaff Topsails*, published in 1996, was his first novel. Ned Pratt is a Newfoundland photographer.

Connecting

1. In the passage from Jack Hodgins's *Broken Ground*, the writer talks of a place where "the trees were bigger than they'd ever dreamed." What techniques did photographer Bob Herger use to portray this visually in his photograph?

2. The passage from Patrick Kavanagh's *Gaff Topsails* is told as if it is seen through Mary's eyes. How did photographer Ned Pratt recreate the details of what Mary sees? How did he reflect the mood in the passage?

3. In each of the photographs, a different geographical area of Canada is featured. What thoughts and feelings does the landscape evoke in each case? How do these excerpts reflect the idea that the landscapes around us can shape who we are?

Against the Grain

Tish Holland

Like writers and photographers, artists have also expressed our relationship with the landscape through their art. In this painting, contemporary artist Tish Holland presents her vision of the sea.

Tish Holland is known for the energy and vibrancy of her art. She often focuses on the landscape and her work shows a strong concern for the environment. In addition to painting, she also specializes in printmaking and her work has been featured in several exhibitions. *(Born St. John's Newfoundland 1959)*

Connecting

1. In your notebook, describe the following elements in this artwork:
   a) the dominant image
   b) the colours
   c) the sense of movement
   d) the overall shape and composition.

2. Imagine you are standing *in* this painting. Free write the thoughts and feelings that come to your mind. What "inner landscape" does this painting create for you?

3. Why do you think Tish Holland called this painting "Against the Grain"? Compare the image of water and the sea in this painting with that in one other selection in this Echo section and suggest reasons for the differences.

REFLECTING ON THE ECHO

1. This Echo section has explored how novelists, photographers, an artist and a poet interpret the landscapes around them. Research a landscape painting by a Canadian artist or an artist from another country or culture of your choice. Describe the techniques this artist used to convey the details of the landscape and the mood of the scene.

2. W.O. Mitchell was a prairie writer. Choose a writer from another area of Canada and a short passage in which this writer focuses on his or her local landscape. Write a compare-and-contrast essay in which you examine the different ways in which this writer and W.O. Mitchell portray the landscape.

3. How do you think the landscape of your childhood helped to shape who you are? Create a photo essay, collage, painting, poem, or other work to show how your landscape left an impression on you. What experiences or images do you most remember? Why? Include a journal entry explaining your choices.

Text Credits

2-3 Pablo Neruda, 'Poetry' from *Selected Poems*, translated by Alastair Reid, edited by Nathaniel Tarn (London: Jonathan Cape). Reprinted by permission of The Random House Group Ltd.; **4-5** Tom Wayman, 'Did I Miss Anything?' from *Did I Miss Anything?: Selected Poems 1973-1993* (Madeira Park, BC: Harbour Publishing, 1993). Reprinted by permission of Harbour Publishing; **6-7** Gwendolyn MacEwen, '1958' from *Afterworlds* by Gwendolyn MacEwen (Toronto: McClelland & Stewart, 1987). Permission granted by the author's family; **8-9** Marilyn Dumont, 'Letter to Sir John A. Macdonald' from *A Really Good Brown Girl* by Marilyn Dumont (London, ON: Brick Books, 1996). Reprinted by permission of Brick Books; **10** Maxine Tynes, 'Reach Out and Touch' from *Borrowed Beauty* (Porters Lake, NS: Pottersfield Press, 1987). Reprinted by permission of the author; **11** Dorothy Livesay, 'Experience' from *Collected Poems: The Two Seasons of Dorothy Livesay* (Toronto: McGraw-Hill Ryerson, 1972). Reprinted by permission of Jay Stewart, literary executrix of the Estate of Dorothy Livesay; **12-13** 'Common Magic' by Bronwen Wallace is reprinted from *Common Magic* by permission of Oberon Press; **20-21** Afua Cooper: 'Memories Have Tongue' from *Memories Have Tongue*. Toronto: Sister Vision Press. 1992; **22-23** Ben Okri, 'An African Elegy' from *An African Elegy* by Ben Okri published by Jonathan Cape. Used by permission of The Random House Group Limited; **24-25** Milton Acorn, 'Callum' from *Poetic Voice from the Maritimes*; **26-27** Lenore Keeshig-Tobias, 'I Grew Up' from *Canadian Women's Studies*, 1983. Reprinted by permission of the author; **28-29** 'Siren Song' from *Selected Poems 1966-1984* by Margaret Atwood. Copyright © 1990 by Margaret Atwood. Reprinted by permission of Oxford University Press Canada; **30** 'Go to the Ant' from *For My Brother Jesus* by Irving Layton. Used by permission, McClelland & Stewart, Ltd. *The Canadian Publishers*; **31** Alden Nowlan, 'Weakness' from *An Exchange of Gifts* by Alden Nowlan (Toronto: Irwin Publishing, 1985). Reprinted by permission of the Estate of Alden Nowlan; **37-39** 'January Morning/Downtown Vancouver' from *The Collected Poems of Earle Birney*. Used by permission, McClelland & Stewart, Ltd. *The Canadian Publishers*; **40-41** Ogden Nash, 'Kindly Unhitch that Star, Buddy', copyright © 1935 by Ogden Nash, renewed. Reprinted by permission of Curtis Brown, Ltd; **42** Rita Joe, 'I Lost My Talk' from *Song of Eskasoni: More Poems of Rita Joe* (Charlottetown, PEI: Ragweed Press, 1988). Reprinted by permission of the author; **43** 'A Speech at the Lost and Found' from *Poems, New and Collected: 1957-1997* by Wislawa Szymborska, English translation by Stanislaw Baranczak and Clare Cavanagh copyright © 1998 by Harcourt, Inc., reprinted by permission of the publisher; **44-45** Barbara Kingsolver, 'In Exile' from *Another America/Otra America* (Seattle, WA: Seal Press, 1992). Reprinted by permission of the author. Barbara Kingsolver is the author of nine books including the novels *Poisonwood Bible* and *Prodigal Summer*; **46** Tom Dawe, 'A Consecration' from *Island Spell: Poems by Tom Dawe*, (St. John's, NF: Harry Cuff Publications, 1981); **47-48** Seamus Heaney, 'Digging' from *Death of a Naturalist* by Seamus Heaney (London: Faber and Faber, 1966). Reprinted by permission of Faber and Faber; **55-56** 'In Goya's Greatest Scenes' by Lawrence Ferlinghetti, from *A Coney Island of the Mind*, copyright © 1958 by Lawrence Ferlinghetti. Reprinted by permission of New Directions Publishing Corp.; **59** Heather Cadsby, 'The Baker' from *Traditions* (Fredericton, NB: Fiddlehead Poetry Books, 1981). Reprinted by permission of the author; **60-61** Joy Kogawa, 'Hiroshima Exit' from *A Choice of Dreams* by Joy Kogawa (Toronto: McClelland & Stewart, 1974). Reprinted by permission of the author; **61-64** Excerpt from 'B.C. Times' produced by Paperny Films. Reprinted by permission; **64-65** Chris de Burgh: 'The Sound of a Gun' from *Man on the Line*, Universal Music Publishing (Rondor Music International, 1984); **90-96** Excerpts from 'The Titanic' from *E.J. Pratt: Complete Poems*, ed. Sandra Djwa and R.G. Moyles (Toronto: University of Toronto Press, 1989). Reprinted by permission of University of Toronto Press Inc.; **97-98** Vikram Seth: 'Doctor's Journal Entry 1945' from *All You Who Sleep Tonight*, (London: Faber and Faber, 1990) Sheil Land Associates Ltd.; **99-100** Thomas King, 'Coyote Goes to Toronto' copyright © Thomas King, 1990. Originally published in *Canadian Literature*, Vol. 124-125, Spring/Summer 1990. Reprinted with permission; **108-109** Extracted from *Forbidden City* by William Bell. Copyright © 1990. Reprinted by permission of Doubleday Canada, a division of Random House of Canada Limited; **111-112** Eric Clapton and Martin Sharp: 'Tales of Brave Ulysses' (lyrics only) from *Disraeli Gears*, 1967 Warner Bros. Publications US Inc.; **114** Yannis Ritsos, trans. Nikos Stangos,

'Penelope's Despair' from *The Times Literary Supplement*, 21 August 1970. Reprinted by permission; **116** The Random House Group no longer control rights and have no contact information for the copyright holder; **117** 'Sunset' reprinted from *Sounds of a Cowhide Drum* by Oswald Mbuyiseni Mtshali copyright © The Third Press, Joseph Okpaku Publishing Co. Inc. by permission of Okpaku Communications Corporation; **118** Ted Hughes, 'Thistles' from *Selected Poems by Ted Hughes* (London: Faber and Faber, 1972). Reprinted by permission of Faber and Faber Limited; **119-122** 'Hands' from *Angels of Flesh, Angels of Silence* by Lorna Crozier. Used by permission, McClelland & Stewart, Ltd. *The Canadian Publishers*; **123** Robert Gibbs, 'Knister's Plowman in Winter' from *Earth Charms Heard So Early* (Fiddlehead Poetry, 1970). Reprinted by permission of the author; **128-151** Excerpt from *Salt-Water Moon* by David French (Vancouver: Talonbooks, 1988). Reprinted by permission; **153-155** Sandra Shamas 'Pie-in-the Sky Guy' from *National Post*, 31 January 2000, reprinted by permission of the author; **156-158** 'Separations' by Leona Gom from *Private Properties*, © 1986. Reprinted by permission of Sono Nis Press, Victoria, BC; **159-160** Changing Concepts of Marriage and Family from *Culture and Customs of Japan*, Noriko Kamachi, (Westport, CT: Greenwood Press, 1999), p. 133; **161-177** Beth McMaster, *Once Upon a Greek Stage* is reprinted by permission of Beth McMaster. For performance rights contact Playwrights Union of Canada, 54 Wolseley Street, Toronto, ON M5T 1A5, telephone 416-703-0201; **178-180** Excerpt from *The Confession of Many Strangers* by Lavonne Mueller. Copyright © 1998 by Lavonne Mueller. First printed in *The Best American Short Plays 1997-98* (New York: Applause Books). Reprinted by permission; **182-187** One Ocean by Betty Quan. Originally broadcast on radio by CBC-Morningside. Copyright © 1994 by Betty Quan. Reprinted by permission; **190-196** Louise Erdrich, 'The Leap' copyright © 1990 by *Harper's Magazine*. All rights reserved. Reproduced from the March 1990 issue by special permission; **198-202** Anton Chekhov: 'The Lottery Ticket'; **204-211** Mavis Gallant, 'Wing's Chips' from *The Other Parts: Stories by Mavis Gallant*. Copyright © 1956 by Mavis Gallant. Reprinted by permission of Georges Borchardt, Inc., for the author; **213-217** Eric Wright, 'Twins' from *A Suit of Diamonds*. Copyright © Eric Wright 1990; reprinted by arrangement with Bella Pomer Agency Inc.; **219-234** Sinclair Ross, 'Cornet at Night' from *The Lamp at Noon and Other Stories* by Sinclair Ross. Used by permission, McClelland & Stewart, Ltd. *The Canadian Publishers*; **236-244** Isabel Allende, 'Two Words' reprinted with the permission of Scribner, a Division of Simon & Schuster from *The Stories of Eva Luna* by Isabel Allende, translated from the Spanish by Margaret Sayers Peden. Copyright © 1989 Isabel Allende. English translation copyright © 1991 Macmillan Publishing Company; **245** Lake Sagaris: 'Translations' from *Medusa's Children: A Journey from Newfoundland to Chiloé*, (Regina: Coteau Books, 1993); **247-249** Roger Rosenblatt, 'I Am Writing Blindly' © 2000 Time Inc. Reprinted by permission; **251-255** Hanan Shaykh: 'The Persian Carpet' from *Arabic Short Stories*, trans. Denys Johnson-Davies, (London: Quartet Books, 1983); **257-259** Suzanne Jacob: 'Rich for One Day' from *Life, After All*, trans. Susanna Finnell, (Vancouver: Press Gang, 1989) Raincoast Books; **261-277** 'The Boat' from *Island: The Collected Short Stories of Alistair MacLeod*. Used by permission, McClelland & Stewart, Ltd. *The Canadian Publishers*; **279-282** Amita Handa, 'For Mataji' from *Fireweed*, February 1990. Reprinted by permission of the author; **284** Jerome Washington: 'The Blues Merchant' from *Iron House: Stories from the Yard* (Fort Bragg, CA: QED Press) 1994; **286-287** Alootook Ipellie, 'Nanuq, The White Ghost, Repents' from *Arctic Dreams and Nightmares* (Penticton, BC : Theytus Books, 1993). Reprinted by permission; **290-294** Excerpts from *Hockey Dreams: Memories of a Man Who Couldn't Play* by David Adams Richards. Copyright © 1996. Reprinted by permission of Doubleday Canada, a division of Random House of Canada Limited; **296-299** Excerpt from *The Concubine's Children* (Penguin Books, 1994) © 1994 Denise Chong. Reprinted with the permission of the author; **301-302** Alice Major: 'Phone Calls' from *Time Travels Light*, (Edmonton: Rowan Books, 1992); **303-304** 'Afro-American Fragment' from *The Collected Poems of Langston Hughes* by Langston Hughes, copyright © 1994 by The Estate of Langston Hughes. Used by permission of Alfred A. Knopf, a division of Random House, Inc.; **304** Cecil Foster "Caribana Dreams" from *A Place Called Heaven: The Meaning of Being Black in Canada* (Toronto: HarperCollins, 1996); **309-316** Excerpts from *Within Reach: My Everest Story* by Mark Pfetzer and Jack Galvin, copyright © 1998 by Mark Pfetzer and Jack Galvin. Used by permission of Dutton Children's Books, an imprint of Penguin Putnam Books for Young Readers, a division of Penguin Putnam Inc.; **318-322** Excerpts from *A Month and a Day: A Detention Diary* by Ken

Saro-Wiwa (Penguin Books, 1995) copyright © Ken Saro-Wiwa, 1995. Reproduced by permission of Penguin Books Ltd.; **325-326** Letter by Vic Daradick from *The Morningside Years* by Peter Gzowski (Toronto: McClelland & Stewart, 1997). Reprinted by permission; **327-329** George Saunders, 'I Can Speak!', originally published in *The New Yorker*, was reprinted by permission of the author who teaches in the Creative Writing Program at Syracuse University and is the author of *CivilWarLand in Bad Decline, Pastoralia*, and an illustrated fable for children, *The Very Persistent Gappers of Frip*; **332-335** Barbara Ehrenreich, 'Where the Wild Things Are' from *Civilization*, June/July 2000. Reprinted by permission of International Creative Management, Inc. Copyright © 2000 by Barbara Ehrenreich; **336-337** 'The Sprinters' from *The Sidewalk Racers and Other Poems of Sports and Motion* by Lillian Morrison. Copyright © 1977 Lillian Morrison. Used by permission of Marian Reiner for the author; **338** Norman Cousins: 'Who Killed Benny Paret?' from *The Saturday Review*, 1979. © General Media International; **340-341** 'Flying' copyright © 1984 Stan Rogers. Used by permission of Fogarty's Cove Music and Ariel Rogers; **342-344** Margaret A. Whitney, 'Playing to Win' copyright © 1988 by the New York Times Co. Reprinted by permission; **352-355** Bronwen Wallace, 'Humans and Other Animals' from *Arguments with the World: Essays by Bronwen Wallace*, Joanne Page ed. (Kingston: Quarry Press, 1992). Reprinted by permission; **357-358** David Suzuki, 'Young People' from *Time to Change: Essays* copyright © 1994 by David Suzuki. Reprinted by permission of Stoddart Publishing Company Ltd.; **360-361** 'Loose Ends' excerpted from 'A Handful of Inwardness', in *The Poet's World* (Washington, DC: The Library of Congress), © 1995 by Rita Dove. Reprinted by permission of the author; **363-366** 'When was the murder of Duncan first plotted?' from *Shakespearean Tragedy: Lectures on Hamlet, Othello, King Lear, Macbeth* by A.C. Bradley (Macmillan Press, 1992); **368-372** 'The Truth About Lying' copyright © 1981 by Judith Viorst. Originally appeared in *Redbook*. This usage granted by permission of Lescher & Lescher, Ltd.; **374-376** Adam Goodheart, 'How to Paint a Fresco' originally appeared in *Civilization* magazine. Copyright © 1995, 2001 by Adam Goodheart. Reprinted with permission; **379-385** Lewis Thomas: 'Seven Wonders'; **387-389** John Ralston Saul: excerpt from *The Next Best Thing*, (Toronto: Vintage, 1997), pp. 154-156 © Random House of Canada Ltd.; **397-402** 'My Canada' by Anita Rau Badami, originally published in the Summer 2000 issue of *Imperial Oil Review*, Vol. 84, no. 437, copyright © 2000 by Anita Rau Badami; **404-409** Copyright © 1990 by Amy Tan. First appeared in *The Threepenny Review*. Reprinted by permission of the author and the Sandra Dijkstra Literary Agency; **412-417** Excerpts from *A Walk in the Woods* by Bill Bryson. Copyright © 1998. Reprinted by permission of Doubleday Canada, a division of Random House of Canada Limited; **419-420** Drew Hayden Taylor, 'The Urban Indian' from *This*, July/August 1996. Reprinted by permission of the author. Drew Hayden Taylor is an award winning playwright, journalist, and filmmaker. He was born on the Curve Lake (Ojibway) Reserve; **422-424** 'Cyberschool' from *High Tech Heretic* by Clifford Stoll, copyright © 1999 by Clifford Stoll. Used by permission of Doubleday, a division of Random House, Inc.; **426-428** Reprinted from *Zoot Capri*, the Magazine, Fall 1991 issue copyright The Alberta Alcohol and Drug Abuse Commission; **439-440** Susan Aglukark: 'O Siem' (lyrics only) from *This Child*, (Aglukark Entertainment Ltd.) Bumstead Productions Ltd.; **441-444** Excerpts from 'Making a Difference' by June Callwood reprinted by permission of the author; **445-449** John Pilger, 'Icon of Hope' from *New Internationalist*, June 1996. Reprinted with permission of New Internationalist Publications; **452-454** Katherine Govier, 'Fantastic Voyager: With Lord of Emperor's, Toronto's Guy Gavriel Kay is confirmed as king of the imaginary world' from *Time*, 13 March 2000. © 2000 Time Inc. Reprinted by permission; **456-465** Michael D. Lemonick and Andrea Dorfman, 'The Amazing Vikings' from *Time*, 8 May 2000. © 2000 Time Inc. Reprinted by permission; **467-475** 'The Right Answer' from *A Whack on the Side of the Head* by Roger von Oech. Copyright © 1983, 1990, 1998 by Roger von Oech. By permission of Warner Books, Inc.; **477-481** Alice M. Patterson, 'It's All About Approach' reprinted with permission from *Videomaker Magazine*, Chico, CA, Videomaker, Inc. (www.Videomaker.com). All rights reserved; **490** Douglas Coupland: excerpt from *Shampoo Planet*, (New York: Simon & Schuster, 1992), pp. 7-8; **492-500** Reprinted by permission of Microcell Solutions Inc and Bos Advertising; **504-508** Excerpts from *Mary Shelley's Frankenstein: The Classic Tale of Terror Reborn on Film*, Kenneth Branagh, screenplay by Steph Lady and Frank Darabont. Reprinted by permission of Newmarket Press, New York, NY; **513-516** Stephanie Nolen, 'Dot.com this!' from *The Globe and Mail*, 28 August 2000. Reprinted with permission from *The Globe and Mail*. **518-519** Robert Chodos, 'What is a magazine?' from *The Canadian Forum*, March 2000. Reprinted by permission of Canadian Forum Limited; **522-527** text and photographs, 'Mortality' OR 'Inscapes' from *W.O. Mitchell Country*, portrayed by Courtney Milne, (Toronto: McClelland & Stewart, 1999); **529-530** Rex Murphy on Cross Country Checkup, CBC Radio, 1 March 1998. Reprinted by permission; **534-535** Excerpt from *Broken Ground* by Jack Hodgins. Used by permission, McClelland & Stewart, Ltd. *The Canadian Publishers*; **536** From the novel *Gaff Topsails* by Patrick Kavanagh by permission of Cormorant Books.

Visuals Credits

57 *Colossus and Panic* by Francisco de Goya, Museo del Prado, Madrid, Spain/Scala/Art Resource, NY; **87** Mary Evans Picture Library; **94** The Toronto Star; **113** J.W. Waterhouse (1849-1917) *Ulysses and the Sirens*, 1891, oil on canvas, National Gallery of Victoria, Melbourne, Australia; **131**, **140** Rising Tide Theatre, Newfoundland; **162** Turner Fenton Secondary School; **246** Philippe Béha/i2i Art (www.i2iart.com); **307** *Esprit 2000* by Jane Ash Poitras, 1999. Reproduced with permission of the artist and Galerie d'Art Vincent; **310**, **314** Mark Pfetzer; **345** First Light; **346** Reuters New Media Inc./CORBIS; **347** Ryan Remiorz/CP Photo; **348** Kevin Frayer/CP Photo; **349** Scott Wachter/CORBIS; **350** Hans Deryk/CP Photo; **376** Michelangelo (1475-1564) *Creation of the Stars and Planets* (detail), Sistine Chapel, Vatican Palace/Art Resource, NY; **377** Musée des Asiatiques-Gui, Paris, France/Art Resource, NY; **391** Historical Picture Archive/CORBIS; **392** The Granger Collection; **393** Brian Vikander/CORBIS; **394** K. Straiton/First Light; **395** First Light; **456** From *Time* Magazine, May 8, 2000, © Timepix; **460** Kit Weiss/Danish National Museum/Smithsonian; **461** Lon Tweeten/Timepix; **459**, **462**, **463** University Museum of Cultural Heritage, Oslo/Smithsonian; **464** The Granger Collection; **484** Live Big public service announcement; **485** Courtesy of Kellogg Canada, © 1997; **486** Courtesy of Virgin Records; **488** Courtesy of *Abrupt*; **493** Courtesy of Microcell Solutions Inc. and Bos Advertising; **504**, **508** Tri Star/Courtesy KOBAL; **521 TL** Photo by John Lehmann/Maclean's Magazine; **521 TR** Timepix; **521 BL** *The Canadian Forum* (Canadian Forum Limited); **521 BR** Reprinted by permission of *Aboriginal Voices* magazine; **524**, **525**, **526** Courtney Milne; **534** Bob Herger; **536** Ned Pratt; **539** Tish Holland, Against the Grain, 1987, acrylic on wood, Memorial University Permanent Collection, Art Gallery of Newfoundland & Labrador/MUN Photographic Services. Reproduced with permission of the artist.

Every reasonable effort has been made to trace the original source of text material and visuals contained in this book. Where the attempt has been unsuccessful, the publisher would be pleased to hear from copyright holders to recify any omissions.